Written by James Farvour

Microsoft BASIC
Decoded & Other Mysteries

Foreword by Harvard Pennington

Edited by Jim Perry

Graphics by John Teal
Cover by Harvard Pennington

TRS-80 Information Series Volume 2

Contents

Foreword 4
Chapter 1: Introduction 5
Overview 6
Memory Utilization 6
Communications Region 8
Level II Operation 8
Input Phase 8
Interpretation & Execution 9
Verb Action 11
Arithmetic & Math 11
I/O Drivers 12
System Utilities 13
IPL 13
Reset Processing (non disk) 13
Reset Processing (disk) 14
Disk BASIC 14

Chapter 2: Subroutines 15
I/O Calling Sequences 15
Keyboard Input 15
Scan Keyboard 15
Wait For Keyboard 16
Wait For Line 16
Video Output 16
Video Display 16
Clear Screen 17
Blink Asterisk 17
Printer Output 17
Print Character 17
Get Printer Status 17
Cassette I/O 18
Select & Turn On Motor 18
Write Leader 18
Read Leader 18
Read One Byte 18
Write One Byte 18
Conversion Routines 19
Data Type Conversions 19
FP To Integer 19
Integer To SP 19
Integer TO DP 19
ASCII To Numeric 19
ASCII To Integer 19
ASCII To Binary 19
ASCII To DP 20
Binary To ASCII 20
HL To ASCII & Display 20
Integer To ASCII 20
FP To ASCII 20
Arithmetic Routines 21
Integer Routines 21
Integer Addition 21
Integer Subtraction 21
Integer Multiplication 21
Integer Division 21
Integer Comparison 21

Single Precision Routines 21
SP Addition 22
SP Subtraction 22
SP Multiply 22
SP Divide 22
SP Comparison 22
Double Precision Routines 22
DP Addition 22
DP Subtraction 23
DP Multiply 23
DP Division 23
DP Comparison 23
Math Routines 23
Absolute Value 23
Return Integer 23
Arctangent 24
Cosine 24
Raise Natural Base 24
Raise X To Power Of Y 24
Natural Log 25
FP To Integer 25
Reseed Random Seed 25
Random Number 25
Sine 25
Square Root 25
Tangent 26
Function Derivation 26
System Functions 27
Compare Symbol 27
Examine Next Symbol 27
Compare DE:HL 27
Test Data Mode 27
DOS Function CALL 28
Load DEBUG 28
Interrupt Entry Point 28
SP In BC:DE To WRA1 28
SP Pointed To By HL To WRA1 28
SP Into BC:DE 29
SP From WRA1 Into BC:DE 29
WRA1 To Stack 29
General Purpose Move 29
Variable Move 29
String Move 30
BASIC Functions 30
Search For Line Number 30
Find Address Of Variable 30
GOSUB 31
TRON 31
TROFF 31
RETURN 31
Write Message 31
Amount Of Free Memory 31
Print Message 32
Number Representation 32

Chapter 3: Cassette & Disk 33

Cassette I/O	33
Cassette Format	34
SYSTEM Format	34
Disk I/O	35
Disk Controller Commands	35
Disk Programming Details	37
DOS Exits	37
Disk BASIC Exits	38
Disk Tables	38
Disk Track Format	39
Granule Allocation Table	39
Hash Index Table	39
Disk DCB	40
Disk Directory	41
Chapter 4: Addresses & Tables	42
System Memory Map	42
Internal Tables	42
Reserved Word List	42
Precedence Operator Values	43
Arithmetic Routines	43
Data Conversion Routines	43
Verb Action Routines	43
Error Code Table	44
External Tables	44
Mode Table	44
Program Statement Table	44
Variable List Table	45
Literal String Pool Table	46
Communications Region	46
DCB Descriptions	48
Video DCB	48
Keyboard DCB	48
Printer DCB	48
Interrupt Vectors	48
Memory Mapped I/O	49
Stack Frame Configurations	49
FOR Stack	49
GOSUB Stack	50
Expression Evaluation	50
DOS Request Codes	51
Chapter 5: Example 1	52
A BASIC SORT Verb	52
Chapter 6: Example 2	55
BASIC Overlay Program	55
Chapter 7: BASIC Decoded	58
The New ROMs	58
Chapter 8: BASIC Decoded	61
Comments Disassembled ROMs	63

Microsoft BASIC Decoded
& Other Mysteries

Acknowledgments

This book has been a long time in its creation, without the help, advice and support of many people it would not have been possible. In particular thanks are due to Rosemary Montoya for her days of keyboarding, David Moore for hours of example testing, Jerry De Diemar, Mary and MG at Helens place for turning the Electric Pencil files into type and Al Krug for his 24 hour message service.

This book was produced with the aid of several TRS-80 computer systems, an NEC Spinterm printer, the Electric Pencil word processor with a special communications package to interface to an Itek Quadritek typesetter, plus lots of coffee and cigarettes.

Copyright 1981 James Farvour
Microsoft BASIC Decoded & Other Mysteries
ISBN 0 - 936200 - 01 - 4

The small print

First Edition
First Printing

January 1981

Published by

IJG Computer Services

1260 W Foothill Blvd,
Upland, CA 91786, USA

Foreword

A little over a year ago, I said to Jim Farvour, 'Jim, why don't you write a book about Microsoft BASIC and the TRS-80? You have the talent and the expertise and thousands of TRS-80 owners need help, especially me!'. Needless to say, he agreed. Now it's one thing to SAY you are going to write a book and quite another thing to actually do it.

Writing a book requires fantastic disipline, thorough knowledge of the subject matter, talent and the ability to communicate with the reader. Jim Farvour has all of the above.

This is no ordinary book. It is the most complete, clear, detailed explanation and documentation you will see on this or any similar subject.

There have been other books and pamphlets purporting to explain the TRS-80 BASIC interperter and operating system. They have had some value, but only to experienced machine language programers - and even then these books had many short-comings.

This book will delight both professional and beginner. Besides walking you through power-up and reset (with and without disk) there are detailed explanations of every single area of the software system's operation. Examples, tables, and flow-charts complement the most extensively commented listing you have ever seen. There are over 7000 comments to Microsoft's BASIC interperter and operating system.

These are not the usual machine language programmer's comments whose cryptic and obscure meanings leave more questions than answers. These are english comments that anyone can understand. Not only that, but when a comment needs more explanation, you will find it on the next page.

This book even has something for anyone running Microsoft BASIC on a Z-80 based computer. Microsoft, in its great wisdom, has a system that generates similar code for similar machines. Although you may find that the code is organized differently in your Heath or Sorceror the routines are, for the most part, identical!

Is this a great book? It's an incredible book! It may well be the most useful book you will ever own.

H.C. Pennington

November 1980

Chapter 1 ═══════════

Introduction

Level II consists of a rudimentary operating system and a BASIC language intrepreter. Taken together, they are called the Level II ROM System. There is a extension to the Level II system called the Disk Operating System DOS, and also an extension to the BASIC portion of Level II called Disk BASIC.

Both Level II and DOS are considered independent operating systems. How the two systems co-exist and co-operate is a partial subject of this book. The real purpose is to describe the fundamental operations of a Level II ROM so that assembly language programmers can make effective use of the system.

A computer without an operating system is of little use. The reason we need an operating system is to provide a means of communication between the computer and the user. This means getting it to 'listen' to the keyboard so that it will know what we want, and having it tell us what's going on by putting messages on the video. When we write programs, which tell the computer what to do, there has to be a program inside the machine that's listening to us. This program is called an operating system.

It is impossible to give an exact definition of an operating system. There are thousands of them, and each has slight variations that distinguish it from others. These variations are the result of providing specific user features or making use of hardware features unique to the machine that the operating system is designed for. In spite of the differences between operating systems, the fundamental internal routines on most are very similar - at least from a functional point of view.

The common components in a general purpose, single user system, such as Level II would consist of:

1. Drivers (programs) for all peripheral devices such as the keyboard, video, printer, and cassette.

2. A language processor capability (such as BASIC, COBOL, or FORTRAN) of some kind.

3. Supporting object time routines for any language provided. This would include math and arithmetic routines, which are implied by the presence of a language.

4. Ancillary support routines used by the language processor and its implied routines. These are usually invisible to the user. They manage resources such as memory and tables, and control access to peripheral devices.

5. A simple monitoring program that continually monitors the keyboard, or other system input device, looking for user input.

6. System utility commands. These vary considerably from system to system. Examples from Level II would be: EDIT, LIST, CLOAD, etc.

Remember that these definitions are very general. The exact definition of any individual component is specific to each operating system. In the case of the Level II ROMs we'll be exploring each of the components in more detail later on. First we will discuss how the operating system gets into the machine to begin with.

Generally, there are two ways an operating system can be loaded. The operating system can be permanently recorded in a special type of memory called Read Only Memory (ROM) supplied with the system. In this case the operating system is always present and needs only to be entered at its starting point, to initialize the system and begin accepting commands.

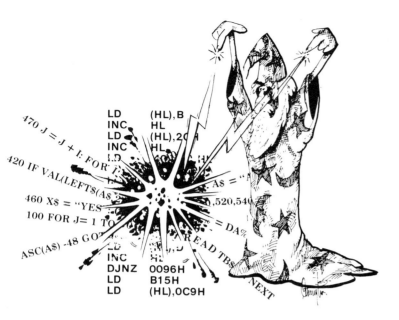

Level II And DOS Overview

Level II is a stand alone operating system that can run by itself. It is always present, and contains the BASIC interpreter plus support routines necessary to execute BASIC programs. It also has the facility to load programs from cassette, or save them onto a cassette.

A Disk Operating System, (such as TRSDOS or NEWDOS) is an extension to Level II that is loaded from disk during the IPL sequence. It differs from Level II in several ways. First, it has no BASIC interpreter, in order to key-in BASIC statements control must be passed from DOS to Level II. This is done by typing the DOS command BASIC. As well as transfering control from DOS to Level II this command also performs important initialization operations which will be discussed later. Second, the commands recognized by DOS are usually disk utility programs not embedded routines - such as those in Level II. This means they must be loaded from disk before they can be used. In turn this means that there must be an area of RAM reserved for the loading and execution of these utilities.

Memory Utilization

From the description of DOS and Level II we can see that portions of RAM will be used differently depending on which operating system is being used. Immediately after IPL the memory is setup for each of the operating systems as shown in figure 1.1 below. Notice the position of the Central Processing Unit (CPU) in each part of the figure.

Another way of getting the operating system into the machine is to read it in from some external storage medium such as a disk or cassette. In this case however, we need a program to read the operating system into the machine. This program is called an Initial Program Loader (or IPL), and must be entered by hand or exist in ROM somewhere in the system. For the sake of simplicity, we'll assume that all machines have at least an IPL ROM or ROM based operating system.

In the TRS-80 Model I we have a combination of both ROM and disk based operating systems. A Level II machine has a ROM system which occupies the first 12K of addressable memory. When the Power On or Reset button is pressed control is unconditionally passed to location 0 or 66 respectively. Stored at these locations are JUMPS to another region of ROM which initializes the system and then prints the user prompt 'MEMORY SIZE?'.

In a Level II system with disks, the same ROM program still occupies the first 12K of memory, however during Power On or Reset processing another operating system is read from disk and loaded into memory. This Disk Operating System (DOS) occupies 5K of RAM starting at 16K. After being loaded control is then transferred to DOS which initializes itself and displays the prompt 'DOS READY'. So, even though a ROM operating system is always present, if the machine has disks another operating system is loaded also. In this case, the Level II ROM acts as an IPL ROM.

It should be emphasized that the DOS and ROM operating systems are complementary and co-operative. Each provides specific features that the other lacks. Elementary functions required by DOS are found in ROM, and DOS contains extensions to the ROM, as well as unique capabilities of its own.

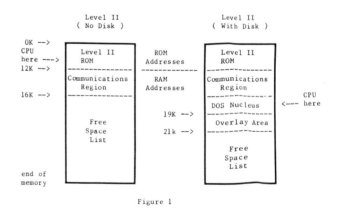

Figure 1.1: Memory organization after the Initial Program Load.

A Level II system with disks that has had a BASIC command executed would appear as in figure 1.2.

The first 16K of memory is dedicated to Level II and the Communications Region regardless of the operating system being used.

Starting at the end of the Communications Region or the Disk BASIC area, depending on the system being used, is the part of memory that will be used by Level II for storing a BASIC program and its variables. This part of memory can also be used by the programmer for keeping assembly language programs. A detailed description of this area for a Level II system without disks follows.

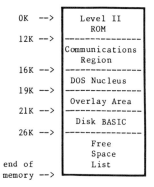

Figure 1.2: Memory allocation for a system with disks, after a BASIC command.

Although figure 1.3 shows the sub-divisions of RAM as fixed they are not! All of the areas may be moved up or down depending on what actions you perform. Inserting or deleting a line from a program, for example, causes the BASIC Program Table (called the Program Statement Table or PST) to increase or decrease in size. Likewise defining a new variable would increase the length of the variables list. Since the orgin of these tables may shift, their addresses are kept in fixed locations in the Communications Region. This allows the tables to be moved about as required, and provides a mechanism for letting other users know where they are.

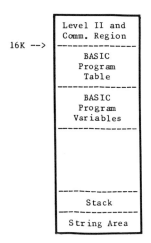

Figure 1.3: Allocation of memory in a Level II system without disks.

The Program Statement Table (PST) contains source statements for a BASIC program in a compressed format (reserved words have been replaced with tokens representing their meaning). The starting address for this table is fixed, but its ending address varies with the size of the program. As program statements are added or deleted, the end of the PST moves accordingly. A complete description of this table can be found in chapter 4 (page 44).

Following the PST is the Variable List Table (or VLT). This contains the names and values for all of the variables used in a BASIC program. It is partitioned into four sub-tables according to the following variable types: simple variables (non dimensioned); single dimensioned lists; doubley dimensioned lists and triple dimensioned lists. Variable names and their values are stored as they are encountered during the execution of a program. The variable table will change in size as new variables are added to a program, and removing variables will cause the table to shrink. After a variable is defined it remains in the table, until the system is reinitialized. For a full description of this table see chapter 4 (page 45).

Not shown in figure 1.3 is the Free Space List or FSL. It is a section of memory that initially extends from the end of the Communications Region to the lower boundery of the String Area. There are two parts to this list, the first is used to assign space for the PST and VLT. For these areas space is assigned from low to high memory. The second part of the FSL is used as the Stack area. This space is assigned in the opposite direction - beginning at the top of the String Area and working down towards Level II.

The stack area shown is a dynamic (changable) table. It is used by the Level II and DOS systems as a temporary storage area for subroutine return addresses and the hardware registers. Any CALL or RST instruction will unconditionally cause the address of the following instruction to be saved (PUSH'd) onto the stack, and the stack pointer is automatically decremented to the next lower sequential address. Execution of a RET instruction (used when exiting from a subroutine) removes two bytes from the stack (the equivalent of a POP instruction) and reduces the stack pointer by two.

Storage space in the stack area can be allocated by a program, but it requires carefull planning. Some BASIC subroutines such as the FOR-NEXT routine, save all values related to their operation on the stack. In the FOR-NEXT case an eighteen byte block (called a frame) is PUSH'd onto the stack and left there until the FOR-NEXT loop is completed.

Before space is assigned in either part of the FSL (except for Stack instructions such as CALL or PUSH) a test is made (via a ROM call) to insure there is enough room. If there is insufficient space an Out of Memory error is given (OM). See chapter 2 (page 31) for a description of the ROM calls used to return the amount of space available in the FSL.

The last area shown in the memory profile is the string

area. This is a fixed length table that starts at the end of memory and works toward low memory. The size of this area may be specified by the CLEAR command. Its default size is 50 bytes. String variables are stored in this area, however strings made equal to strings, String$ and quoted strings are stored in the PST.

Earlier it was mentioned that there are six general components that form an operating system. Because of the way Level II was put together the individual pieces for some components are scattered around in ROM, instead of being collected together in a single area. Figure 1.4 is an approximate memory map of addresses in Level II. For exact addresses and description of these regions see chapter 4.

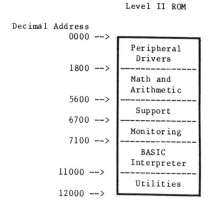

Figure 1.4: Approximate memory map of Level II addresses.

The Communications Region

The Communications Region is a scratch pad memory for the Level II ROMs. An example of addresses stored here are those for the PST and the variables list. Also BASIC supports variable types that require more space than the working registers can provide, and as a result certain arithmetic operations require temporary storage in this region.

Another important use of the Communications Region is to provide a link between Level II and DOS - for passing addresses, and data, back and forth. The DOS Exit addresses and Disk BASIC addresses are kept in this area. As mentioned earlier a Level II system, with disks, begins execution in the DOS system. Control is passed from DOS to Level II only after the command BASIC has been executed (which also updates the Communications Region by storing the DOS Exits and Disk BASIC addresses).

Because Level II is in ROM it is impractical to try and modify it. Yet, changes to an operating system are a practical necessity that must be considered. In order to solve this problem the Level II system was written with jumps to an area in RAM, so that future changes could be incorporated into the ROM system. Those jumps are called DOS Exits, and on a system without a DOS they simply return to Level II. When a DOS is present, the

jump addresses are changed to addresses within Disk BASIC which allows changes to be made to the way Level II operates.

The Disk BASIC addresses are used by Level II when a Disk BASIC command such as GET or PUT is encountered. They are needed because the code that supports those operations is not present in Level II. It is a part of Disk BASIC that is loaded into RAM, and since it could be loaded anywhere Level II needs some way of locating it. The Disk BASIC exits are a group of fixed addresses, known to both Level II and Disk BASIC, which allows Level II to pass control to Disk BASIC for certain verb action routines.

Another interesting aspect of the Communications Region is that it contains a section of code called the Divide Support Routine. This code is called by the division subroutines, to perform subtraction and test operations. It is copied from Level II to the RAM Communications Region during the IPL sequence. When a DOS is present it is moved from ROM to RAM by the DOS utility program BASIC.

An assembly language program using the Level II division routine on a disk system which has not had the BASIC command executed will not work because the Divide Support Routine is not in memory. Either execute the BASIC utility or copy the support routine to RAM, when executing assembly language routines that make division calls.

Level II Operation

Earlier in this chapter there was a brief description of six components which are generally found in all operating systems. Using those components as a guideline, Level II can be divided into the following six parts:

Part 1 ... Input or scanner routine.
Part 2 ... Interpretation and execution routine.
Part 3 ... Verb action routines.
Part 4 ... Arithmetic and math routines.
Part 5 ... I/O driver routines.
Part 6 ... System function routines.

There is another part common to all systems which is not included in the above list. This part deals with system initialization (IPL or Reset processing), and it will be discussed separately. Continuing with the six parts of Level II, we will begin at the point where the system is ready to accept the first statement or command. This is called the Input Phase.

Part 1 - Input Phase

The Input Phase is a common part of all operating systems. Its function is to accept keyboard input and respond to the commands received. In the case of a Level II system it serves a dual purpose - both system commands and BASIC program statements are processed by this code.

Entry to the Input Scan routine is at. This is an initial entry point that is usually only called once. The message 'READY' is printed, and a DOS Exit (41AC) is taken before the main loop is entered. Systems without disks jump to this point automatically, at the end of IPL processing. For systems with disks, this code is entered by the DOS utility program BASIC at the end of its processing. The Input or Scanner phase is summarized below.

1. Get next line of input from keyboard.
2. Replace reserved words with tokens.
3. Test for a system command such as RUN, CLOAD, etc. or a DIRECT STATEMENT (BASIC statement without a line number) and branch to 6 if true.
4. Store tokenized statement in program statement table.
5. Return to step 1.
6. Begin interpretation and execution

The Input Phase loop begins at 1A33. After printing the prompt >, or a line number if in the Auto Mode a CALL to 03612 is made to read the next line. Then the line number is converted from ASCII to binary with a CALL to 1E5A. The statement is scanned and reserved words are replaced by tokens (CALL 1BC0). Immediately after tokenization a DOS Exit to 41B2 is taken. Upon return a test for a line number is made. If none is found a System Command or Direct Statement is assumed, and control is passed to the Execution Driver at 1D5A. On systems without disks this test is made at 1AA4. On a disk system the test, and branch, is made at the DOS Exit 41B2 called from 1AA1.

If a line number is present the incoming line is added to the PST, the pointers linking each line are updated by the subroutine at 1AFC to 1B0E. If the line replaces an existing line, the subroutine at 2BE4 is called to move all of the following lines down over the line being replaced.

When in the Auto Mode the current line number is kept in 40E2 and 40E3 the increment between lines is stored at 40E4. The code from 1A3F to 1A73 prints and maintains the automatic line number value. Null lines (statements consisting of a line number only) are discarded. They are detected by a test at 1ABF.

Part 2   - Interpretation & Execution

Statement and command execution in a Level II system is by interpretation. This means that a routine dedicated to the statement type, or command, is called to interpret each line and perform the necessary operations. This is a common method for system command execution. With DOS, for example, seperate modules are loaded for commands such as FORMAT and COPY. In some systems, commands which are related may be combined into a single module, after the module has been loaded it decides which sub-function to execute by examining (interpreting) the name which called it.

Program execution by interpretation is not common except on microcomputers, and even then only for selected languages such as BASIC and APL. The alternative to an interpreter is program compilation and execution, with the use of a compiler.

Compilers translate source statements into directly executable machine language code (called object code). The object code is then loaded into RAM as a seperate step using a utility program called a Loader. After loading the object code into RAM, control is passed to it and it executes almost independently of the operating system.

Not all source code is converted to object code by a compiler. Some statements such as READ and WRITE or functions such as SINE or COSINE may be recognized by the compiler, and rather than generate code for them, subroutine calls for the specific routines will be produced.

These routines are in object code form in a library file. When the loader loads the object code, for the compiled program, any subroutine calls are satisfied (the subroutines are loaded) from the library file. A loader that will take modules from a library is called a linking loader.

An interpreter operation is much simpler by comparison. Each source statement is scanned for reserved words such as FOR, IF, GOTO, etc.. Every reserved word is replaced by a unique numeric value called a token then the tokenized source statement is saved. In Level II it is saved in the Program Statement Table. When the program is run control goes to an execution driver which scans each statement looking for a token. When one is found control is given to a routine associated with that token. These token routines (also called verb action routines) perform syntax checks such as testing for valid data types, commas in the correct place, and closing parenthesis. In a compiler entered action routine there is no syntax checking because that would have been done by the compiler - and the routine would only be called if all of the parameters were correct.

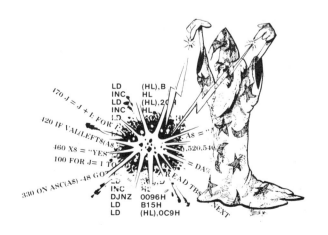

In Level II the execution phase is entered when a statement without a line number has been accepted, or when a RUN command is given. This may be a system command or a single BASIC statement that is to be executed. When a RUN command is received an entire BASIC program is to be executed. The Execution driver loop starts at 1D5A and ends at 1DE1. These addresses are deceptive though, because portions of this code are shared with other routines.

The steps in this phase are summerized as follows. For more details see figure 1.5.

1. Get the first character from the current line in the PST. If the end of the PST has been reached then return to the Input Phase.
2. If the character is not a token, go to step 6.
3. If the token is greater than BC it must be exactly FA (MID$), otherwise a sytnax error is given.
4. If the token is less than BC, use it as an index into the verb action table.
5. Go to action routine and return to step 1.
6. Assignment section. Locate variable name, if it's not defined, then create it.
7. Call expression evaluation.
8. Return to step 1.

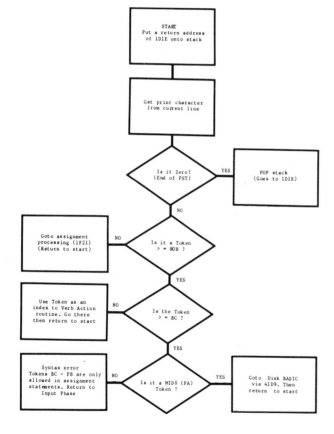

Figure 1.5: Flowchart of the execution driver routine.

The Execution driver begins by loading the first character from the current line in the PST. This character is tested to see if it is a token (80-FA) if not, the current line is assumed to be an assignment statement such as:

A = 1.

The assignment statement routine begins at 1F21. It is similiar to the other action routines, except that it is

entered directly rather than through a table look-up process. Before it is entered a return address of 1D1E in the execution driver is PUSH'd onto the stack, so it can exit as any other action routine.

The assignment routine assumes that the pointer for the current line is immediately to the left of the variable name to be assigned. It locates, or creates an entry for the variable name, tests for an equals () after the name - and then CALLs 2337. The routine at this location evaluates the expression. The result is converted to the correct mode, and stored at the variable address.

Assuming that a good token was found as the first character, a second test is made to see if it is valid as the first token in a line. Valid tokens which can occur at the start of a line are 80 - BB. The tokens BC - F9 can only occur as part of an assignment statement or in a particular sequence such as 8F (IF) 'Expression' CA (then) XXXX. The MID$ token FA is the only exception to this rule. There is a test for it at 2AE7 where a direct jump to its Disk BASIC vector (41D9) is taken. If the token is between 80 and BB it is used as an index into a verb action routine table and the address of the the action routine, for that token is located. Control is then passed to that action routine which will do all syntax checking and perform the required function.

Parameters for the verb routines are the symbols in the statement following the token. Each routine knows what legitimate characters to expect, and scans the input string from left to right (starting just after the token) until the end of the parameters are reached. The end of the parameters must coincide with the end of the statement, or a syntax error is produced.

Symbols which terminate a parameter list vary for each action routine. Left parentheses ')' terminate all math and string functions. A byte of machine zeros (00) stops assignment statements, other routines may return to the execution phase after verifying the presence of the required value.

As each verb routine is completed control is returned to the Execution driver, where a test for end of statement (EOS) or a compound statement (:) is made. The EOS is one byte of machine zeros. If EOS is detected the next line from the Program Statement Table is fetched, and it becomes the current input line to the Execution driver.

When a System Command or a Direct Statement has been executed there is no pointer to the next statement, because they would have been executed from the Input Phase's input buffer. This is in a different area than the PST where BASIC program statements are stored. When the RUN command is executed, it makes the Execution driver get its input from the PST.

When the end of a BASIC program, or a system command, is reached, control is unconditionally passed to the END verb which will eventually return to the Input Phase. Any errors detected during the Execution and Interpretion phase cause control to be returned to the Input Phase after printing an appropriate error code. An exception is the syntax error, which exits directly to the edit mode.

Part 3 - Verb Action

The verb action routines are where the real work gets done. There are action routines for all of the system commands such as CLOAD, SYSTEM, CLEAR, AUTO as well as the BASIC verbs such as FOR, IF, THEN, GOTO, etc. In addition there are action routines for all the math functions and the Editor sub-commands.

Verb action routines continue analyzing the input string beginning at the point where the Execution phase found the verb token. Like the Execution phase, they examine the string in a left to right order looking for special characters such as (,), or commas and tokens unique to the verb being executed. If a required character is missing, or if an illogical condition arises, a syntax error is generated.

The verb routines use a number of internal subroutines to assist them while executing program statements. These internal routines may be thought of as part of the verb action routines, even though they are used by many other parts of the Level II system.

A good example of an internal routine is the expression evaluation routine, which starts at 2337. Any verb routine that will allow, and has detected, an expression as one of its arguements may CALL this routine. Examples of verb action routines that allow expressions in their arguements are IF, FOR, and PRINT. In turn the expression evaluation routine will CALL other internal routines (such as 260D to find the addresses of variables in expressions being evaluated). Since subscripted variables can have expressions as their subscript, the find address routine may in turn CALL back to the expression evaluation routine!

This type of processing is called recursion, and may be forced by the following expression:

c0 = c(1a/bc(2d)/c(1*c0))

Other internal routines used by the verb action routines are : skip to end of statement 1F05; search Stack for a FOR frame 1936 and build a literal string pool entry 2865.

Any intermediate results, which may need to be carried forward, are stored Work Register Area 1 (WRA1) in the Communications Region. Some verbs such as FOR build a stack frame which can be searched for and recognized by another verb such as NEXT. All of the action routines except MID$ are entered with the registers set as shown in figure 1.6. A full list of verb action routines, and their entry points is given in chapter 4 (page 43).

Register	Contents
AF -	Next element from code string following token. CARRY - if numeric No CARRY - if alpha
BC -	Address of the action routine
DE -	Address of action token in code string
HL -	Address of next element in code string

Figure 1.6: Register settings for verb action routine entry.

Part 4 - Arithmetic & Math

Before going into the Arithmetic and Math routines we should review the arithmetic capabilities of the Z-80 CPU and the BASIC interpreter.

The Z-80 supports 8 bit and 16 bit integer addition and subtraction. It does not support multiplication or division, nor does it support floating point operations. Its register set consists of seven pairs of 16 bit registers. All arithmetic operations must take place between these registers. Memory to register operations are not permitted. Also operations between registers are extremely restricted, especially with 16 bit quantities.

The BASIC interpreter supports all operations e.g., addition, subtraction, multiplication, and division for three types (Modes) of variables which are: integer, single precision and double precision. This support is provided by internal subroutines which do the equivalent of a hardware operation. Because of the complexity of the software, mixed mode operations, such as integer and single precision are not supported. Any attempt to mix variable types will give unpredictable results.

The sizes for the variable types supported by BASIC are as follows:

Integer .... 16 bits (15 bits 1 sign bit)
Single Precision ..... 32 bits (8 bit biased exponent plus 24 bit signed mantissa)
Double Precision ..... 56 bits (8 bit biased exponent plus 48 bit signed mantissa)

From this it is clear that the registers are not large enough to hold two single or double precison values, even if floating point operations were supported by the hardware. Because the numbers may be too big for the registers, and because of the sub-steps the software must go through an area of RAM must be used to support these operations.

Within the Communications Region two areas have been set aside to support these operations. These areas are labeled: Working Register Area 1 (WRA1) and Working Register Area 2 (WRA2). They occupy locations 411D to 4124 and 4127 to 412E respectively. They are used to hold one or two of the operands, depending on their type, and the final results for all single and double precision operations. A description of the Working Register Area follows.

AddresS	Integer	Single Precision	Double Precision
411D			LSB
411E			NMSB
411F			NMSB
4120			NMSB
4121	LSB	LSB	NMSB
4122	MSB	NMSB	NMSB
4123		MSB	MSB
4124		Exponent	Exponent

Where:
```
    LSB = Least significant byte
   NMSB = Next most significant byte
    MSB = Most significant byte
```

WRA2 has an identical format.

Figure 1.7: Working Register Area layout.

Integer

Destination Register	Operation	Source Registers
HL	Addition	HL + DE
HL	Subtraction	HL - DE
HL	Multiplication	HL * DE
WRA1	Division	DE / HL

Single Precision

Destination Register	Operation	Source Registers
WRA1	Addition	WRA1 + (BCDE)
WRA1	Subtraction	WRA1 - (BCDE)
WRA1	Multiplication	WRA1 * (BCDE)
WRA1	Division	WRA1 / (BCDE)

Double Precision

Destination Register	Operation	Source Registers
WRA1	Addition	WRA1 + WRA2
WRA1	Subtraction	WRA1 - WRA2
WRA1	Multiplication	WRA1 * WRA2
WRA1	Division	WRA1 / WRA2

Figure 1.8: Register arrangements usesd by arithmetic routines.

Because mixed mode operations are not supported integer operations can only take place between integers, the same being true for single and double precision values. Since there are four arithmetic operations (, -, *, and /), and three types of values, there must be twelve arithmetic routines. Each of these routines knows what type of values it can operate on, and expects those values to be loaded into the appropriate hardware or working registers before being called. Figure 1.8 shows the register assignments used by the arithmetic routines. These assignments are not valid for the Math routines because they operate on a single value, which is always assumed to be in WRA1.

The math routines have a problem in that they must perform arithmetic operations, but they do not know the data type of the argument they were given. To overcome this another byte in the Communications Region has been reserved to indicate the data type (Mode) of the variable in WRA1. This location is called the Type flag. Its address is 40AF and contains a code indicating the data type of the current contents of WRA1. Its codes are:

```
CODE            DATA TYPE (MODE)
02 ........... Integer
03 ........... String
04 ........... Single precision
08 ........... Double precision
```

The math routines do not usually require that an argument be a particular data type, but there are some exceptions (see chapter 2, page xx, for details).

Part 5 - I/O Drivers

Drivers provide the elementary functional capabilities necessary to operate a specific device. Level II ROM contains Input/Output (I/O) drivers for the keyboard, video, parallel printer, and the cassette. The disk drivers are part of the DOS system and consequently will not be discussed.

All devices supported by Level II, with the exception of the cassette, require a Device Control Block (DCB). The drivers use the DCB's to keep track of perishable information, such as the cursor position on the video and the line count on the printer. The DCB's for the video, keyboard, and printer are part of the Level II ROM. Since information must be stored into them, they are moved from ROM to fixed addresses in RAM (within the Communications Region) during IPL.

The Level II drivers must be called for each character that is to be transmitted. The drivers cannot cope with the concept of records or files, all record blocking and de-blocking is left to the user. Level II has no general purpose record management utilities. For BASIC programs you must use routines such as PRINT and INPUT to block off each record.

When writting to a cassette, for example, the PRINT routine produces a header of 256 zeroes, followed by an A5. After the header has been written each individual variable is written as an ASCII string, with a blank space between each variable, finally terminating with a carriage return. Non string variables are coonverted to their ASCII equivalent.

INPUT operation begins with a search for the 256 byte header. Then the A5 is skipped and all variables are read into the line buffer until the carriage return is detected. When the INPUT is completed all variables are converted to their correct form and moved to the VLT.

The keyboard, video and line printer drivers can be entered directly or through a general purpose driver entry point at 03C2. Specific calling sequences for each of these drivers are given in chapter 2

The cassette driver is different from the other drivers in several respects. It does its I/O in a serial bit mode whereas all of the other drivers work in a byte (or character) mode. This means that the cassette driver must transmit data on a bit-by-bit basis. The transmission of each bit is quite complex and involves many steps. Because of the timing involved, cassette I/O in a disk based system, must be done with the clock off (interrupts inhibited). For more details on cassette I/O see chapter 4

Part 6 - System Utilities

System utilities in Level II ROM are the Direct Commands:
AUTO, CLEAR, CSAVE, CLOAD, CLEAR, CONT, DELETE, EDIT, LIST, NEW, RUN, SYSTEM, TROFF and TRON. These commands may be intermixed with BASIC program statements. However, they are executed immediately rather than being stored in the program statement table (PST). After executing a Direct Command, control returns to the Input Phase.

After an entire BASIC program has been entered (either through the keyboard or via CLOAD or LOAD, on a disk system), it must be executed by using the RUN command. This command is no different from the other system commands except that it causes the BASIC program in the PST to be executed (the Execution Phase is entered). As with other system commands, when the BASIC program terminates, control is returned to the Input Phase.

System Flow During IPL

The IPL sequence has already been discussed in general terms. A complete description of the procedure follows. The description is divided into seperate sections for disk and non-disk systems.

Reset Processing (non-disk)

Operations for this state begin at absolute location zero when the Reset button is pressed. From there control is passed to 0674 where the following takes place.
00UFC
A) Ports FF (255 decimal) to 80 (128 decimal) are initialized to zero. This clears the cassette and selects 64 characters per line on the video.

B) The code from 06D2 to 0707 is moved to 4000 - 4035 .This initializes addresses for the restart vectors at 8, 10, 18 and 20 (hex) to jump to their normal locations in Level II. Locations 400C and 400F are initialized to RETURNs.

If a disk system is being IPL'd 400C and 400F will be modified to JUMP instructions with appropriate addresses by SYS0 during the disk part of IPL. The keyboard, video, and line printer DCB's are moved from ROM to RAM beginning at address' 4015 to 402C after moving the DCB's locations 402D, 4030, 4032 and 4033 are initialized for non-disk usage. They will be updated by SYS0 if a disk system is being IPL'd.

C) Memory from 4036 to 4062 is set to machine zeros.(00)

After memory is zeroed, control is passed to location 0075 where the following takes place:
00UFC
A) The division support routine is moved from @FT218F7-191B to 4080-40A6 .This range also includes address pointers for the program statement table. Location 41E5 is initialized to:

$$LD \ A, (2C00)$$

B) The input buffer address for the scanner routine is set to 41E8 .This will be the buffer area used to store each line received during the Input Phase.

C) The Disk BASIC entry vectors 4152-41A5 are initialized to a JMP to 012D .This will cause an L3 ERROR if any Disk BASIC features are used by the program. Next, locations 41A6-41E2 (DOS exits) are set to returns (RETs). 41E8 is set to zero and the current stack pointer (CSP) is set to 41F8 .(We need a stack at this point because CALL statements will be executed during the rest of the IPL sequence and they require a stack to save the return address).

D) A subroutine at 1B8F is called. It resets the stack to 434C and initializes 40E8 to 404A . It then initializes the literal string pool table as empty, sets the current output device to the video, flushes the print buffer and turns off the cassette. The FOR statement flag is set to zero, a zero is stored as the first value on the stack and control is returned to 00B2

E) The screen is cleared, and the message 'MEMORY SIZE' is printed. Following that, the response is accepted and tested, then stored in **40B1** .Fifty words of memory are alloted for the string area and its lower boundry address is stored in **40A0**.

F) Another subroutine at **1B4D** is called to turn Trace off, initialize the starting address of the simple variables (**40F9**), and the program statement table (**40A4**). The variable type table **411A** is set to single precision for all variables, and a RESTORE is done. Eventually control is returned to **00FC** .

G) At **00FC** the message 'RADIO SHACK Level II BASIC' is printed and control is passed to the Input Phase.

Reset Processing (disk systems)

Operations for this state begin at location **0000** and jump immediately to **0674** . The code described in paragraphs A, B, and C for RESET processing (non-disk systems on page xx) is common to both IPL sequences. After the procedure described in paragraph C has taken place a test is made to determine if there are disks in the system. If there are no disk drives attached, control goes to **0075**, otherwise. . .
00UFC

A) Disk drive zero is selected and positioned to track 0 sector 0. From this position the sector loader (BOOT/SYS) is read into RAM locations **4200 - 4455**. Because the sector loader is written in absolute form it can be executed as soon as the READ is finished.

After the READ finishes, control is passed to the sector loader which positions the disk to track 11 sector 4. This sector is then read into an internal buffer at **4D00**. The sector read contains the directory entry for SYS0 in the first 32 bytes. Using this data the sector loader computes the track and sector address for SYS0 and reads the first sector of it into **4D00**.

B) Following the READ, the binary data is unpacked and moved to its specified address in RAM. Note that SYS0 is not written in absolute format so it cannot be read directly into memory and executed. It must be decoded and moved by the sector loader. Once this is done control is passed to SYS0 beginning
at address **4200**.

C) The following description for SYS0 applies to NEWDOS systems only. It begins by determining the amount of RAM memory and storing its own keyboard driver address in the keyboard DCB at **4015**. The clock interrupt vector address (**4012**) is initialized to a CALL **4518**. Next, more addresses are initialized and the NEWDOS header message is written.

D) After writing the header, a test for a carriage return on the keyboard is made. If one is found, the test for an AUTO procedure is skipped and control passes immediately to **4400** were the DOS Input SCANNER phase is initiated.

Assuming a carriage return was not detected the Granule Allocation Table (GAT) sector (track 11 sector 0) is read and the E0 byte is tested for a carriage return value. Again, if one is found (the default case) control goes to **4400**, otherwise a 20 byte message starting at byte E0 of the GAT sector is printed. Then control is passed to **4405** where the AUTO procedure is started. Following execution of the AUTO procedure control will be passed to the DOS Input Phase which starts at **4400**.

Disk BASIC

One of the DOS commands is a utility program called BASIC. In addition to providing a means of transfering control from DOS to Level II, it contains the interpretation and execution code for the following Disk BASIC statements:

```
TRSDOS and NEWDOS
CVI     CVS     CVD     MKI$    MKS$    MKD$    DEFFN   DEFUSR
TIME$   CLOSE   FIELD   GET     PUT     AS      LOAD    SAVE
KILL    MERGE   NAME    LSET    RSET    INSTR   LINE    &H
&O      CMD"S"  CMD"T"  CMD"R"  CMD"D"  CMD"A"  USR0-USR9
MID$ (left side of equation)            OPEN"R" OPEN"O" OPEN"I"

NEWDOS only
OPEN"E" RENUM   REF     CMD"E"  CMD"DOS command"

An additional command peculiar to TRSDOS only is:
              CMD"X", <ENTER>  - Version 2.1
              CMD"#", <ENTER>  - Version 2.2 & 2.3
```

These hidden, and undocumented commands display a 'secret' copyright notice by Microsoft. Also undocumented is CMD'A' which performs the same function as CMD'S'.

Disk BASIC runs as an extension to Level II. After being loaded, it initializes the following section of the Communications Region:
00UFC
1. DOS exits at **41A6 - 41E2** are changed from RETURN's to jumps to locations within the Disk BASIC utility.
2. The Disk BASIC exits at **4152 - 41A3** are changed from **JP 12D** L3 syntax error jumps to addresses of verb action routines within Disk BASIC.

Following the initialization of the Communications Region, DCBs and sector buffers for three disk files are allocated at the end of Disk BASIC's code. Control is then given to the Input Scanner in Level II (**1A19**).

Disk BASIC will be re-entered to execute any Disk BASIC statement, or whenever a DOS Exit is taken from Level II. The Disk BASIC entry points are entered as though they are verb action routines. When finished control returns to the execution driver.

Note: Disk BASIC occupies locations **5200 - 5BAD** (NEWDOS system). Each file reserved will require an additional (32 256 decimal) bytes of storage. Assembly programs should take care not to disturb this region when running in conjunction with a BASIC program.

Microsoft BASIC Decoded & Other Mysteries

Chapter 2

Subroutines

Level II has many useful subroutines which can be used by assembly language programs. This chapter describes a good number of the entry points to these subroutines. However there are many more routines than those described here. Using the addresses provided as a guide, all of the Level II routines dealing with a particular function may be easily located.

Before using the math or arithmetic calls study the working register concept and the mode flag (see chapter 1 page 14). Also, remember that the Division Support Routine (see chapter 1 page 10) is loaded automatically only when IPL'ing a non-disk system. On disk systems it is loaded by the Disk BASIC utility. If you are using a disk system and executing an assembly language program, which uses the any of the math or arithmetic routines that require division, you must enter BASIC first or load the Division Support Routine from within your program.

The I/O calling sequences described are for Level II only. The TRSDOS and Disk BASIC Reference Manual contains the DOS calling sequences for disk I/O.

The SYSTEM calls and BASIC functions are somewhat specialized, consequently they may not always be useful for an application written entirely in assembly language. However if you want to combine assembly and BASIC you will find these routines very useful.

I/O Calling Sequences

Input and Output (I/O) operations on a Model I machine are straight forward, being either memory mapped or port addressable. There are no DMA (direct memory access) commands and interrupt processing is not used for I/O operations.

The selection of entry points presented here is not exhaustive. It covers the more general ones and will point the reader in the right direction to find more specialized entry points, if needed.

In memory mapped operations, storing or fetching a byte from a memory location, causes the data to be transferred between the CPU register and the target device. Examples of memory mapped devices are the video, the keyboard, and the disk. Programmed I/O (via ports) is a direct transfer of data between a register and a device. The only device using port I/O is the cassette.

Keyboard Input

The keyboard is memory mapped into addresses 3800 - 3BFF. It is mapped as follows:

BIT	<————————— Keyboard Addresses ————————————>							
	3801	3802	3804	3808	3810	3820	3840	3880
0	@	H	P	X	0	8	ENTER	SHIFT
1	A	I	Q	Y	1	9	CLEAR	
2	B	J	R	Z	2	:	BREAK	
3	C	K	S		3	:	UP ARW	
4	D	L	T		4	,	DN ARW	
5	E	M	U		5	-	LT ARW	
6	F	N	V		6	.	RT ARW	
7	G	O	W		7	/	SP BAR	

When a key is depressed, a bit in the corresponding position in the appropriate byte, is set, also bits set by a previous key are cleared. You will notice that only eight bytes (3801 - 3880) are shown in the table as having any signifigance. This might lead one to believe that the bytes in between could be used. Unfortunately this is not the case as the byte for any active row is repeated in all of the unused bytes. Thus all bytes are used.

CALL 002B   Scan Keyboard

Performs an instantaneous scan of the keyboard. If no key is depressed control is returned to the caller with the A-register and status register set to zero. If any key (except the BREAK key) is active the ASCII value for that character is returned in the A-register. If the BREAK key is active, a RST 28 with a system request code of 01 is executed. The RST instruction results in a JUMP to the

DOS Exit **400C**. On non-disk systems the Exit returns, on disk systems control is passed to SYS0 where the request code will be inspected and ignored, because system request codes must have bit 8 on. After inspection of the code, control is returned to the caller of **002B**. Characters detected at **002B** are not displayed. Uses DE, status, and A register

```
;
;   SCAN KEYBOARD AND TEST FOR BREAK OR ASTERISK
;
      PUSH    DE              ; SAVE DE
      PUSH    IY              ; SAVE IY
      CALL    2BH             ; TEST FOR ANY KEY ACTIVE
      DEC     A               ; KEY ACTIVE, WAS IT A BREAK
      JR      M,NO            ; GO IF NO KEY HIT
      JR      Z,BRK           ; ZERO IF BREAK KEY ACTIVE
      INC     A               ; <A> BACK TO ORIGINAL VALUE
      CP      2AH             ; NO, TEST FOR * KEY ACTIVE
      JR      Z,AST           ; ZERO IF *
         .
         .
         .
```

CALL 0049   Wait For Keyboard Input

Returns as soon as any key on keyboard is pressed. ASCII value for character entered is returned in A-register. Uses A, status, and DE registers.

```
;
;   WAIT FOR NEXT CHAR FROM KEYBOARD AND TEST FOR ALPHA
;
      PUSH    DE              ; SAVE DE
      PUSH    IY              ; AND IY
      CALL    49H             ; WAIT TILL NEXT CHAR. ENTERED
      CP      41H             ; TEST FOR LOWER THAN "A"
      JR      NC,ALPHA        ; JMP IF HIGHER THAN NUMERIC
         .
         .
```

CALL 05D9   Wait For Next Line

Accepts keyboard input and stores each character in a buffer supplied by caller. Input continues until either a carriage return or a BREAK is typed, or until the buffer is full. All edit control codes are recognized, e.g. TAB, BACKSPACE, etc. The calling sequence is:
On exit the registers contain:

```
;
;   GET NEXT LINE FROM KEYBOARD. EXIT IF BREAK STRUCK.
;   LINE CANNOT EXCEED 25 CHARACTERS
;
SIZE  EQU     25              ; MAX LINE SIZE ALLOWED
      LD      HL,BUFF         ; BUFFER ADDRESS
      LD      B,SIZE          ; BUFFER SIZE
      CALL    5D9H            ; READ NEXT LINE FROM KEYBOARD
      JR      C,BREAK         ; JMP IF BREAK TYPED
         .
         .
BUFF  DEFS    SIZE            ; LINE BUFFER
         .
         .
```

HL   Buffer address
B   Number of characters transmitted excluding last.
C   Orginal buffer size
A   Last character received if a carriage return or BREAK is typed.
Carry   Set if break key was terminator, reset otherwise.

If the buffer is full, the A register will contain the buffer size.

Video Output

Video I/O is another example of memory mapped I/O. It uses addresses **3C00** thru **3FFF** where **3C00** represents the upper left hand corner of the video screen and **3FFF** represents the lower right hand corner of the screen.

Screen control codes such as TAB, CURSON ON/OFF, BACKSPACE and such are processed by the video driver routine. The video device itself does not recognize any control codes. Codes recognized by the driver and their respective actions are:

Code (hex.)	Action
08	backspace and erase character.
0E	turn on cursor.
0F	turn off cursor.
17	select line size of 32 char/line.
18	backspace one character (left arrow)
19	skip forward one character (right arrow)
1A	skip down one line (down arrow).
1B	skip up one line (up arrow).
1C	home cursor. select 64 char/line.
1D	position cursor to start of current line
1E	erase from cursor to end of line
1F	erase from cursor to end of frame

Character and line size (32/64 characters per line) is selected by addressing the video controller on port FF, and sending it a function byte specifying character size. The format of that byte is:

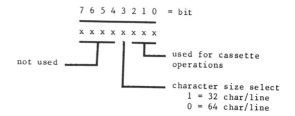

CALL 0033   Video Display

Displays the character in the A-register on the video. Control codes are permitted. All registers are used.

```
;
;   DISPLAY MESSAGE ON VIDEO
;
         LD     HL,LIST       ; MESSAGE ADDRESS
LOOP     LD     A,(HL)        ; GET NEXT CHARACTER
         OR     A             ; TEST FOR END OF MESSAGE
         JR     Z,DONE        ; JMP IF END OF MESSAGE (DONE)
         PUSH   HL            ; NT END, PRESERVE HL
         CALL   33H           ; AND PRINT CHARACTER
         POP    HL            ; RESTORE HL
         INC    HL            ; BUMP TO NEXT CHARACTER
         JR     LOOP          ; LOOP TILL ALL PRINTED
DONE
         .
         .
LIST     DEFM   ´THIS IS A TEST´
         DEFB   0DH           ; CARRIAGE RETURN
         DEFB   0             ; END OF MESSAGE INDICATOR
```

CALL 01C9   Clear Screen

Clears the screen, selects 64 characters and homes the cursor. All registers are used.

```
;
; CLEAR SCREEN, HOME CURSOR, SELECT 32 CHAR/LINE
; SKIP 4 LINES
;
       CALL   01C9H        ; CLEAR SCREEN
       LD     A,17H         ; SELECT 32 CHAR/LINE
       CALL   0033H         ; SEND CHAR SIZE TO VIDEO
       LD     B,4           ; NO. OF LINES TO SKIP
       LD     A,1AH         ; CODE TO SKIP ONE LINE
LOOP   PUSH   BC            ; SAVE BC
       CALL   33H           ; SKIP 1 LINE
       POP    BC            ; GET COUNT
       DJNZ   LOOP          ; LOOP TILL FOUR LINES DONE
```

CALL 022C   Blink Asterisk

Alternately displays and clears an asterisk in the upper right hand corner. Uses all registers.

```
;
; BLINK ASTERISK THREE TIMES
;       LD   B,3      ; NO. OF TIMES TO BLINK
LOOP   PUSH BC        ; SAVE COUNT
       CALL 022CH     ; BLINK ASTERISK ONCE
       POP  BC        ; GET COUNT
       DJNZ LOOP      ; COUNT 1 BLINK
DONE    .
        .
```

Printer Output

The printer is another example of a memory mapped device. Its address is 37E8H. Storing an ASCII character at that address sends it to the printer. Loading from that address returns the printer status. The status is returned as a zero status if the printer is available and a non-zero status if the printer is busy.

CALL 003B   Print Character

The character contained in the C-register is sent to the printer. A line count is maintained by the driver in the DCB. When a full page has been printed (66 lines), the line count is reset and the status register returned to the caller is set to zero. Control codes recognized by the printer driver are:

CODE	ACTION
00	Returns the printer status in the upper two bits of the A-register and sets the status as zero if not busy, and non-zero if busy.
0B	Unconditionally skips to the top of the next page.
0C	Resets the line count (DCB 4) and compares its previous value to the lines per page (DCB 3) value. If the line count was zero, no action is taken. If the line count was non-zero then a skip to the top form is performed.
0D	Line terminator. Causes line count to be incremented and tested for full page. Usually causes the printer to begin printing.

```
;
; WRITE MESSAGE ON PRINTER. IF NOT READY WITHIN 1.5 SECONDS
;
; DISPLAY ERROR MESSAGE ON VIDEO
;
        LD    HL,LIST      ; ADDR OF LINE TO PRINT
START   LD    B,5          ; PREPARE TO TEST FOR PRINTER
                            ; READY
LOAD    LD    DE,10H       ; LOAD DELAY COUNTERS
TST     CALL  05D1H        ; GET PRINTER STATUS
        JR    Z,RDY        ; JP IF PRINTER READY
        DEC   DE           ; NOT READY, DECREMENT
                           ; COUNTERS AND
        LD    A,D          ; TEST IF 1.5 SEC HAS ELAPSED

        OR    E            ; FIRST DE MUST = 0
        JR    NZ,TST       ; JMP IF DE NOT 0
        DJNZ  LOAD         ; LOOP TILL 1.5 SEC PASSED
        JP    NTRDY        ; GO DISPLAY ´PRINTER NOT
                           ; READY
RDY     POP   HL           ; RESTORE ADDR OF PRINT LINE

        LD    A,(HL)       ; GET NEXT CHAR TO PRINT
        OR    A            ; TEST FOR END OF LINE
        JR    Z,DONE       ; JMP IF END OF LINE
        LD    C,A          ; PUT CHAR IN PROPER REGISTER

        CALL  58DH         ; PRINT CHARACTER
        INC   HL           ; BUMP TO NEXT CHAR
        JR    START        ; LOOP TILL ALL CHARS PRINTED

NTRDY   LD    HL,NTRDM     ; HL = ADDR OF NOT READY MSG

        CALL  VIDEO*       ; PRINT MSG
DONE    .                  ; LINE PRINTED ON PRINTER
        .
        .
LIST    DEFM  ´THIS IS A TST´
        DEFB  0DH          ; CR MAY BE REQUIRED TO START
                           ; PRINTER
        DEFB  0            ; END OF MSG FLAR
NTRDM   DEFM  ´PRINTER NOT READY´
        DEFB  0            ; TERMINATE PRINTED MSG
```

CALL 05D1   Get Printer Status

Returns the status of the line printer in the status register as zero if the printer is ready, and non-zero if not ready.

Other status bits returned are as shown:

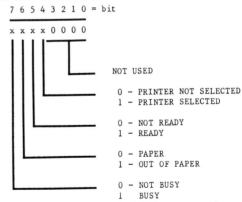

The out of paper and busy bits are optional on some printers.

```
;
; MONITOR PRINTER STATUS ACCORDING TO STATUS BITS ABOVE
; AND PRINT APPROPRIATE ERROR MESSAGE.
;
        LD    BC,10        ; TIMER COUNT FOR PRINTER
START   CALL  05D1H        ; GET PRINTER STATUS
        JR    Z,OK         ; JUMP IF READY
        BIT   7,A          ; IS IT STILL PRINTING?
        JR    Z,TIME       ; YES IF NZ. GO TIME IT
        BIT   4,A          ; NOT PRINTING, IS IT SELECTED
        JR    Z,NS         ; ZERO IF NOT SELECTED
                           ; WE HAVE   HARDWARE PROBLEM
        BIT   5,A          ; UNIT IS SELECTED AND NOT BUSY
        JR    Z,NR         ; ZERO IF NOT READY
```

```
;
; UNIT IS SELECTED, READY, AND NOT BUSY. ASSUME OUT OF PAPER
;
      OP    LD    HL,OPM      ; DISPLAY OUT OF PAPER MSG
                  .
                  .
            JP    WAIT        ; GO WAIT FOR OPERATOR REPLY
                              ; AND RETRY OR ABORT
      NR    BIT   6,A         ; UNIT IS NOT READY, TEST FOR OUT
            JR    NZ,OP       ; OF PAPER ALSO. JMP IF OUT OF PAPER
                  .
            LD    HL,NRM      ; DISPLAY NOT READY MRG
                  .
                  .
            JP    WAIT        ; GO WAIT FOR OPERATOR REPLY
                              ; AND RETRY OR ABORT
                  .
      NS    LD    HL,NSM      ; GET DISPLAY NOT SELECTED MSG
                  .
                  .
            JP    WAIT        ; GO WAIT FOR OPERATOR REPLY
                              ; AND RETRY OR ABORT
      TIME  POP   BC          ; GET TIME COUNTER
            DEC   BC          ; COUNT 1 LOOP
            PUSH  BC          ; SAVE NEW VALUE
            LD    A,B         ; IF ITS GONE TO ZERO
            OR    C           ; WE HAVE TIMED OUT
            JR    NZ,START    ; LOOP TILL OP FINISHED OR TIME-OUT
                  .
            LD    HL,TOM      ; DISPLAY TIMEOUT MSG
                  .
                  .
            JP    WAIT        ; GET OPERATOR REPLY AND RETRY
                              ; OR ABORT
                  .
                  .
```

Cassette I/O

Cassette I/O is not memory mapped. Cassettes are addressed via port **FF** after selecting the proper unit, and I/O is done a bit at a time whereas all other devices do I/O on a byte basis (except for the RS-232-C)

Because of the bit-by-bit transfer of data, timing is extremely critical. When any of the following calls are used, the interrupt system should be disabled to guarantee that no interruptions will occur and therefore disturb the critical timing of the output.

CALL 0212   Turn On Motor

Selects unit specified in A-register and starts motor. Units are numbered from one. All registers are used.

```
      LD    A,1         ; CODE TO SELECT CASSETTE 1
      CALL  0212H       ; SELECT UNIT 1, TURN ON MOTOR
            .
            .
            .
```

CALL 0284   Write Leader

Writes a Level II leader on currently selected unit. The leader consists of 256 (decimal) binary zeros followed by a hex **A5**. Uses the B and A registers.

```
      LD    A,1         ; CODE TO SELECT UNIT 1
      CALL  212H        ; SELECT UNIT, TURN ON MOTOR
      CALL  284H        ; WRITE HEADER
            .
            .
            .
```

CALL 0296   Read Leader

Reads the currently selected unit until an end of leader (A5) is found. An asterisk is displayed in the upper right hand corner of the video display when the end is found. Uses the A-register.

```
      LD    A,1         ; CODE FOR UNIT 1
      CALL  0212H       ; SELECT UNIT 1,TURN ON MOTOR
      CALL  0296H       ; READ HEADER. RTN WHEN A5 ENCOUNTERED
            .
            .
```

CALL 0235   Read One Byte

Reads one byte from the currently selected unit. The byte read is returned in the A-register. All other registers are preserved.

```
      LD    A,1         ; UNIT TO SELECT
      CALL  0212H       ; SELECT UNIT TURN ON MOTOR
      CALL  0296H       ; SKIP OVER HEADER
      CALL  0235H       ; READ FOLLOWING BYTE
      CP    41H         ; TEST FOR OUR FILE NAME (A)
      JR    Z,YES       ; JMP IF FILE A
            .
            .
            .
```

CALL 0264   Write One Byte

Writes the byte in the A-register to the currently selected unit. Preserves all register.

```
      LD    A,1         ; UNIT NO. MASK.
      CALL  0212H       ; SELECT UNIT, START MOTOR
      CALL  0284H       ; WRITE HEADER (256 ZEROS AND A5)
      LD    A,41H       ; WRITE FILE NAME (OURS IS A)
      CALL  0264H       ; WRITE A AFTER HEADER
            .
            .
            .
```

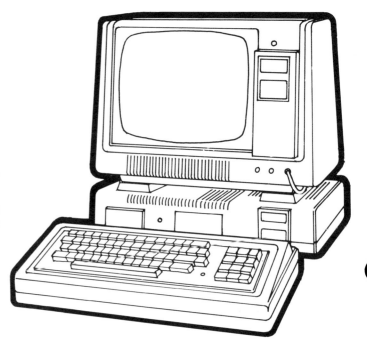

Conversion Routines

These entry points are used for converting binary values from one data type or mode to another, such as integer to floating point, and for conversions between ASCII and binary representation. These conversion routines assume the value to be converted is in WRA1 and that the mode flag (40AF) reflects the current data type. The result will be left in WRA1 and the mode flag will be updated.

Data Type Conversions

CALL 0A7F   Floating Point Integer

The contents of WRA1 are converted from single or double precision to integer. No rounding is performed. All registers are used.

```
;
; CONVERT SINGLE PRECISION VALUE TO INTEGER AND MOVE THE RESULT
; TO IVAL
;
        LD      HL,4121H      ; ADDR OF LSB IN WRA1
        LD      DE,VALUE      ; ADDR OF LSB OF SP NO.
        LD      BC,4          ; NO OF BYTES TO MOVE
        LDIR                  ; MOVE VALUE TO WRA1
        LD      A,4           ; TYPE CODE FOR SP
        LD      (40AFH),A     ; SET TYPE TO SP
        CALL    0A7FH         ; CONVERT SP VALUE TO INTEGER
        LD      A,(4121H)     ; LSB OF INTEGER EQUIVALENT
        LD      (IVAL),A      ; SAVE IN INTEGER LOCATION
        LD      A,(4122H)     ; MSB OF INTEGER EQUIVALENT
        LD      (IVAL+1),A    ; SAVE IN INTEGER LOCATION
        .
        .
VALUE   DEFB    0EH           ; LSB OF 502.778 (SP)
        DEFB    B6H           ; NLSB
        DEFB    00H           ; MSB
        DEFB    88H           ; EXPONENT
IVAL    DEFB    0             ; WILL HOLD INTEGER EQUIVALENT OF

        DEFB    0             ; SP 502.778
        .
        .
```

CALL 0AB1   Integer To Single

The contents of WRA1 are converted from integer or double precision to single precision. All registers are used.

```
;
; CONVER INTEGER VALUE TO SINGLE PRECISION AND MOVE TO
; LOCAL AREA
;
        LD      A,59H
        LD      (4121H),A     ; LSB OF INTEGER 26457 (10)
        LD      A,67H
        LD      (4122H),A     ; MSB OF INTEGER 26457 (10)
        LD      A,2           ; TYPE CODE FOR INTEGER
        LD      (40AFH),A     ; SET TYPE TO INTEGER
        CALL    0AB1H         ; CONVERR INTEGER TO SP
        LD      HL,VALUE      ; ADDR. OF AREA FOR SP EQUIVALENT
        CALL    09CBH         ; MOVE SP VALUE FROM WRA1 TO VALUE
        .
        .
VALUE   DEFS    4             ; WILL HOLD 26457 IN SP FORMAT
        .
        .
```

CALL 0ADB   Integer To Double

Contents of WRA1 are converted from integer or single precision to double presicion. All registers are used.

```
;
;
        LD      A,59H
        LD      (4121H),A     ; LSB OF 26457 (10)
        LD      A,67H
        LD      (4122H),A     ; MSB OF 26457 (10)
        LD      A,2           ; TYPE CODE FOR INTEGER
        LD      (40AFH),A     ; SET TYPE TO INTEGER
        CALL    0ADBH         ; CONVER INTEGER TO DP
        LD      DE,VALUE      ; NOW, MOVE DP VALUE
        LD      HL,411DH      ; FROM WRA1 TO LOCAL AREA
        LD      BC,8          ; NO. OF BYTES TO MOVE
        LDIR                  ; MOVE VALUE
        .
        .
VALUE   DEFS    8             ; HOLDS DP EQUIVALENT OF 26457
        .
```

ASCII To Numeric Representation

The following entry points are used to convert between binary and ASCII. When converting from ASCII to binary the HL register pair is assumed to contain the address of the ASCII string. The result will be left in WRA1 or the DE register pair and the mode flag will be updated accordingly.

CALL 1E5A   ASCII To Integer

Converts the ASCII string pointed to by HL to its integer equivalent. The result is left in the DE register pair. Conversion will cease when the first non-numeric character is found.

```
;
;
        LD      HL,AVAL       ; HL = ADDR. OF ASCII NUMBER
        CALL    1E5AH         ; CONVERT IT TO BINARY
        LD      (BVAL),DE     ; SAVE BINARY VALUE
        .
AVAL    DEFM    '26457'       ; ASCII VALUE 26457
        DEFB    0             ; NON-NUMERIC STOP BYTE
BVAL    DEFW    2             ; HOLDS BINARY VALUE 26457
        .
```

CALL 0E6C   ASCII To Binary

Converts the ASCII string pointed to by HL to binary. If the value is less than 2**16 and does not contain a decimal point or an E or D descriptor (exponent), the string will be converted to its integer equivalent. If the string contains a decimal point or an E, or D descriptor or if it exceeds 2**16 it will be converted to single or double precision. The binary value will be left in WRA1 and the mode flag will be to the proper value.

```
;
;
;
        LD      HL,AVAL         ; ASCII NUMBER
        CALL    0E6CH           ; CONVERT ASCII TO BINARY
                .
                .
                .
AVAL    DEFM    ´26457´         ; ASCII VALUE TO BE CONVERTED
        DEFB    0               ; NON-NUMERIC STOP BYTE
                .
                .
                .
```

CALL 0E65   ASCII To Double

Converts the ASCII string pointed to by HL to its double precision equivalent. All registers are used. The result is left in WRA1.

```
;
;
;
        LD      HL,AVAL         ; ADDR OF ASCII VALUE TO CONVERT
        CALL    0E65H           ; CONVERT VALUE TO DP
        LD      DE,BVAL         ; THEN MOVE VALUE FROM
        LD      HL,411DH        ; WRA1 TO A LOCAL AREA
        LD      BC,8            ; NO. OF BYTES TO MOVE
        LDIR                    ; MOVE DP VALUE TO LOCAL AREA
                .
                .
                .
AVAL    DEFM    ´26457´         ; ASCII VALUE TO BE CONVERTED
        DEFB    0               ; NONNUMERIC STOP BYTE
BVAL    DEFS    8               ; LOCAL AREA THAT HOLDS BINARY
                                    EQUIVALENT
                .
                .
                .
```

Binary To ASCII Representation

The next set of entry points are used to convert from binary to ASCII.

CALL 0FAF   HL To ASCII

Converts the value in the HL register pair (assumed to be an integer) to ASCII and displays it at the current cursor position on the video. All registers are used.

```
;
;
;
        LD      HL,64B8H        ; HL = 25784 (10)
        CALL    0FAFH           ; CONVERT TO ASCII AND DISPLAY
                .
                .
                .
```

CALL 132F   Integer To ASCII

Converts the integer in WRA1 to ASCII and stores the ASCII string in the buffer pointed to by the HL register pair. On entry, both the B and C registers should contain a 5 to avoid any commas or decimal points in the ASCII string. All registers are preserved.

```
;
;
;
        LD      HL,500
        LD      (4121H),HL      ; 500 (10) TO WRA1
        LD      BC,505H         ; SUPRESS COMMAS OR DEC. PTS.
        LD      HL,BUFF         ; BUFFER ADDR FOR ASCII STRING
        CALL    132FH           ; CONVERT VALUE IN WRA1 TO ASCII
                .               ; AND STORE IN BUFF.
                .
                .
BUFF    DEFS    5               ; BUFFER FOR ASCII VALUE
                .
                .
                .
```

CALL 0FBE   Floating to ASCII

Converts the single or double precision number in WRA1 to its ASCII equivalent. The ASCII value is stored at the buffer pointed to by the HL register pair. As the value is converted from binary to ASCII, it is formatted as it would be if a PRINT USING statement had been invoked. The format modes that can be specified are selected by loading the following values into the A, B, and C registers.

```
REGISTER  A = 0 ... Do not edit. Strictly binary to ASCII.
REGISTER  A = X ... Where X is interpreted as:

          7 6 5 4 3 2 1 0  = BIT
          x x x x x x x x

                              EXPONENTIAL NOTATION

                              RESERVED

                              SIGN FOLLOWS VALUE

                              INCLUDE SIGN

                              PRINT LEADING $ SIGN

                              INCLUDE LEADING ASTERISKS

                              PRINT COMMAS EVERY 3RD DIGIT

                              0 - DO NOT PERFORM EDIT FUNCTIONS
          :                   1 - EDIT VALUE ACCORDING TO OPTIO

REGISTER  B = The number of digits to the left of the
              decimal point.
REGISTER  C = The number of digits after the decimal point
;
;
;
        LD      HL,AVAL1        ; ASCII VALUE TO CONVERT
        CALL    0E6CH           ; CONVERT ASCII TO BINARY
        LD      HL,AVAL2        ; BUFFER ADDR. FOR CONVERTED VALUE
        LD      A,0             ; SIGNAL NO EDITING
        CALL    0FBEH           ; CONVERT SP VALUE BACK TO ASCII
                .
                .
                .
AVAL1   DEFM    ´1103.25´       ; ORGINAL ASCII VALUE
        DEFB    0               ; NON-NUMERIC STOP BYTE
AVAL2   DEFS    7               ; WILL HOLD RECONVERTED VALUE
                .
                .
                .
```

Arithmetic Routines

These subroutines perform arithmetic operations between two operands of the same type. They assume that the operands are loaded into the correct hardware or Working Register Area, and that the data type or mode is set to the correct value. Some of these routines may require the Divide Support Routine (See Chapter 1 for details.)

Integer Routines

The following routines perform arithmetic operations between integer values in the DE and HL register pairs. The orginal contents of DE is always preserved and the result of the operations is always left in the HL register pair.

CALL 0BD2 — Integer Add

Adds the integer value in DE to the integer in HL. The sum is left in HL and the orginal contents of DE are preserved. If overflow occurs (sum exceeds $2**15$), both values are converted to single precision and then added. The result would be left in WRA1 and the mode flag would be updated.

```
        LD      A,2             ; TYPE CODE FOR INTEGER
        LD      (40AFH),A       ; SET TYPE TO INTEGER
        LD      HL,(VAL1)       ; LOAD FIRST VALUE
        LD      DE,(VAL2)       ; LOAD SECOND VALUE
        CALL    0BD2H           ; ADD SO THAT HL = HL + DE
        LD      A,(40AFH)       ; TEST FOR OVERFLOW
        CP      2               ; IF TYPE IS NOT INTEGER
        JR      NZ,...          ; NZ IF SUM IS SINGLE PRECISION
          .                     ; ELSE SUM IS INTEGER
          .
          .
VAL1    DEFW    25
VAL2    DEFW    20
          .
          .
          .
```

CALL 0BC7 — Integer Subtraction

Subtracts the value in DE from the value in HL. The difference is left in the HL register pair. DE is preserved. In the event of underflow, both values are converted to single precision and the subtraction is repeated. The result is left in WRA1 and the mode flag is updated accordingly.

```
        LD      A,2             ; TYPE CODE FOR INTEGER
        LD      (40AFH),A       ; SET TYPE TO INTEGER
        LD      HL,(VAL1)       ; VALUE 1
        LD      DE,(VAL2)       ; VALUE 2
        CALL    0BC7H           ; SUBTRACT DE FROM HL
        LD      A,(40AFH)       ; GET MODE FLAG
        CP      2               ; TEST FOR UNDERFLOW
        JR      NZ,...          ; NZ IF UNDERFLOW
          .
          .
VAL1    DEFW    25
VAL2    DEFW    20
          .
          .
```

CALL 0BF2 — Integer Multiplication

Multiplies HL by DE. The product is left in HL and DE is preserved. If overflow occurs, both values are converted to single precision and the operation is restarted. The product would be left in WRA1.

```
        LD      A,2             ; TYPE CODE FOR INTEGER
        LD      (40AFH),A       ; SET TYPE TO INTEGER
        LD      HL,(VAL1)       ; LOAD FIRST VALUE
        LD      DE,(VAL2)       ; LOAD SECOND VALUE
        CALL    0BF2H           ; HL = HL * DE
        LD      A,(40AFH)       ; GET MODE FLAG
        CP      2               ; TEST FOR OVERFLOW
        JR      NZ,...          ; NO IF VALUE HAS OVERFLOWED
          .
          .
VAL1    DEFW    25
VAL2    DEFW    20
          .
```

CALL 2490 — Integer Division

Divides DE by HL. Both values are converted to single precision before the division is started. The quotient is left in WRA1; the mode flag is updated. The orginal contents of the DE and HL register sets are lost.

```
        LD      DE,(VAL1)       ; LOAD VALUE 1
        LD      HL,(VAL2)       ; LOAD VALUE 2
        CALL    2490H           ; DIVIDE DE BY HL. QUOTIENT TO WRA1
          .
          .
VAL1    DEFW    50
VAL2    DEFW    2
```

CALL 0A39 — Integer Comparison

Algebraically compares two integer values in DE and HL. The contents of DE and HL are left intact. The result of the comparison is left in the A register and status register as:

OPERATION	A REGISTER
DE > HL	A = -1
DE < HL	A = +1
DE = HL	A = 0

```
;
;
;
        LD      DE,(VAL1)       ; DE AND HL ARE VALUES
        LD      HL,(VAL2)       ; TO BE COMPARED
        CALL    0A39H           ; COMPARE DE TO HL
        JR      Z,...           ; Z IF DE = HL
        JP      P,...           ; POSITIVE IF DE < HL
          .
```

Single Precision Routines

The next set of entry points are used for single precision operations. These routines expect one argument in the BC/DE registers and the other argument in WRA1.

CALL 0716 Single Precision Add

Add the single precision value in (BC/DE) to the single precision value in WRA1. The sum is left in WRA1

```
        LD      HL,VAL1     ; ADDR. OF ONE SP VALUE
        CALL    9B1H        ; MOVE IT TO WRA1
        LD      HL,VAL2     ; ADDR. OF 2ND SP VALUE
        CALL    9C2H        ; LOAD IT INTO BC/DE REGISTER
        CALL    716H        ; ADD VALUE 1 TO VALUE 2
            .               ; SUM IN WRA1
            .
            .
VAL1    DEFS    4           ; HOLDS A SP VALUE
VAL2    DEFS    4           ; HOLDS A SP VALUE
            .
            .
```

CALL 0713 Single Precision Subtract

Subtracts the single precision value in (BC/DE) from the single precision value in WRA1. The difference is left in WRA1.

```
        LD      HL,VAL1     ; ADDR OF ONE SP. VALUE
        CALL    9B1H        ; MOVE IT TO WRA1
        LD      HL,VAL2     ; ADDR OF 2ND SP VALUE
        CALL    9C2H        ; LOAD IT INTO BC/DE
        CALL    713H        ; SUBTRACT DE FROM WRA1
            .               ; DIFFERENCE LEFT IN WRA1
            .
            .
VAL1    DEFS    4           ; HOLDS A SP VALUE
VAL2    DEFS    4           ; HOLDS A SP VALUE
            .
            .
```

CALL 0847 Single Precision Multiply

Multiplies the current value in WRA1 by the value in (BC/DE). the product is left in WRA1.

```
        LD      HL,VAL1     ; ADDR OF ONE SP VALUE
        CALL    9B1H        ; MOVE IT TO WRA1
        LD      HL,VAL2     ; ADDR OF 2ND SP VALUE
        CALL    9C2H        ; LOAD 2ND VALUE INTO BC/DE
        CALL    847H        ; MULTIPLY
            .               ; PRODUCT LEFT IN WRA1
            .
            .
VAL1    DEFS    4           ; HOLDS A SP VALUE
VAL2    DEFS    4           ; HOLDS A SP VALUE
            .
            .
```

CALL 2490 Single Precision Divide

Divides the single precision value in (BC/DE) by the single precision value in WRA1. The quotient is left in WRA1.

```
        LD      HL,VAL1     ; ADDR OF DIVISOR
        CALL    9B1H        ; MOVE IT TO WRA1
        LD      HL,VAL2     ; ADDR. OF DIVIDEND
        CALL    9C2H        ; LOAD BC/DE WITH DIVIDEND
        CALL    2490H       ; DIVIDE BC/DE BY WRA1
            .               ; QUOTIENT IN WRA1
            .
            .
VAL1    DEFS    4           ; HOLDS DIVISOR
VAL2    DEFS    4           ; HOLDS DIVIDEND
            .
            .
```

CALL 0A0C Single Precision Comparison

Algebraically compares the single precision value in (BC/DE) to the single precision value WRA1. The result of the comparison is returned in the A and status as:

OPERATION	A REGISTER
(BC/DE) > WRA1	A = -1
(BC/DE) < WRA1	A = +1
(BC/DE) = WRA1	A = 0

```
;
;
;
        LD      HL,VAL1     ; ADDR OF ONE VALUE TO BE COMPARED
        CALL    9B1H        ; MOVE IT TO WRA1
        LD      HL,VAL2     ; ADDR OF 2ND VALUE TO COMPARE
        CALL    9C2H        ; LOAD 2ND VALUE INTO BC/DE
        CALL    0A0CH       ; COMPARE BC/DE TO WRA1
        JR      Z,...       ; ZERO IF (BC/DE) = WRA1
        JP      P,...       ; POSITIVE IF (BC/DE) < WRA1
            .
            .
VAL1    DEFS    4           ; HOLDS A SP VALUE
VAL2    DEFS    4           ; HOLDS A SP VALUE
            .
            .
```

Double Precision Routines

The next set of routines perform operations between two double precision operands. One operand is assumed to be in WRA1 while the other is assumed to be in WRA2 (4127-412E). The result is always left in WRA1.

CALL 0C77 Double Precision Add

Adds the double precision value in WRA2 to the value in WRA1. Sum is left in WRA1.

```
        LD      A,8         ; TYPE CODE FOR DP
        LD      (40AFH),A   ; SET TYPE TO DP
        LD      DE,VAL1     ; ADDR OF 1ST DP VALUE
        LD      HL,411DH    ; ADDR OF WRA1
        CALL    9D3H        ; MOVE 1ST DP VALUE TO WRA1
        LD      DE,VAL2     ; ADDR OF 2ND DP VALUE
        LD      HL,4127H    ; ADDR OF WRA2
        CALL    9D3H        ; MOVE 2ND VALUE TO WRA2
        CALL    0C77H       ; ADD WRA2 TO WRA1. SUM IN WRA1
            .
            .
VAL1    DEFS    8           ; HOLDS A DP VALUE
VAL2    DEFS    8           ; HOLDS A DP VALUE
            .
            .
```

CALL 0C70 Double Precision Subtraction

Subtracts the double precision value in WRA2 from the value in WRA1. The difference is left in WRA1.

```
        LD      A,8             ; TYPE CODE FOR DP
        LD      (40AFH),A       ; SET TYPE TO DP
        LD      DE,VAL1         ; ADDR OF 1ST DP VALUE
        LD      HL,411DH        ; ADDR OF WRA1
        CALL    9D3H            ; MOVE 1ST DP VALUE TO WRA1
        LD      DE,VAL2         ; ADDR OF 2ND DP VALUE
        LD      HL,4127H        ; ADDR OF WRA2
        CALL    9D3H            ; MOVE 2ND VALUE TO WRA2
        CALL    0C70H           ; SUBTRACT WRA2 FROM WRA1
         .                      ; DIFFERENCE IN WRA1
         .
         .
VAL1    DEFS    8               ; HOLDS A DP VALUE
VAL2    DEFS    8               ; HOLDS A DP VALUE
         .
         .
```

CALL 0DA1   Double Precision Multiply

Multiplies the double precision value in WRA1 by the value in WRA2. The product is left in WRA1.

```
        LD      A,8             ; TYPE CODE FOR DP
        LD      (40AFH),A       ; SET TYPE TO DP
        LD      DE,VAL1         ; ADDR OF 1ST DP VALUE
        LD      HL,411DH        ; ADDR OF WRA1
        CALL    9D3H            ; MOVE 1ST DP VALUE TO WRA1
        LD      DE,VAL2         ; ADDR OF 2ND DP VALUE
        LD      HL,4127H        ; ADDR OF WRA2
        CALL    9D3H            ; MOVE 2ND VALUE TO WRA2
        CALL    0DA1H           ; MULTIPLY WRA1 BY WRA2
         .                      ; PRODUCT IN WRA1
         .
         .
VAL1    DEFS    8               ; HOLDS A DP VALUE
VAL2    DEFS    8               ; HOLDS A DP VALUE
         .
         .
```

CALL 0DE5   Double Precision Divide

Divides the double precision value in WRA1 by the value in WRA2. The quotient is left in WRA1.

```
        LD      A,8             ; TYPE CODE FOR DP
        LD      (40AFH),A       ; SET TYPE TO DP
        LD      DE,VAL1         ; ADDR OF 1ST DP VALUE
        LD      HL,411DH        ; ADDR OF WRA1
        CALL    9D3H            ; MOVE 1ST DP VALUE TO WRA1
        LD      DE,VAL2         ; ADDR OF 2ND DP VALUE
        LD      HL,4127H        ; ADDR OF WRA2
        CALL    9D3H            ; MOVE 2ND VALUE TO WRA2
        CALL    0DE5H           ; DIVIDE WRA1 BY WRA2
         .                      ; QUOTIENT LEFT IN WRA1
         .
         .
VAL1    DEFS    8               ; HOLDS A DP VALUE
VAL2    DEFS    8               ; HOLDS A DP VALUE
         .
         .
```

CALL 0A78   Double Precision Compare

Compares the double precision value in WRA1 to the value in WRA2. Both register areas are left intact. The result of the comparison is left in the A and status registers as:

OPERATION	A REGISTER
WRA1 > WRA2	A = −1
WRA1 < WRA2	A = +1
WRA1 = WRA2	A = 0

```
;
;
;
        LD      A,8             ; TYPE CODE FOR DP
        LD      (40AFH),A       ; SET TYPE FLAG TO DP
        LD      DE,VAL1         ; ADDR OF 1ST DP VALUE
        LD      HL,411DH        ; ADDR OF WRA1
        CALL    9D3H            ; MOVE 1ST VALUE TO WRA1
        LD      DE,VAL2         ; ADDR OF 2ND DP VALUE
        LD      HL,4127H        ; ADDR OF WRA2
        CALL    9D3H            ; MOVE 2ND VALUE TO WRA2
        CALL    0A78H           ; COMPARE WRA1 TO WRA2
        JR      Z,...           ; ZERO IF THEY ARE EQUAL
        JP      P,...           ; POSITIVE IF WRA1 < WRA2
         .
         .
```

Math Routines

All of the following subroutines assume that location 40AF contains a code indicating the data type or mode of the variable e.g., integer, single precision, or double precision, and that the variable itself is in Working Register Area 1 (WRA1). Also, the floating point Division Support Routine must be loaded at **4080**.

CALL 0977   Absolute Value
                                     ABS (N)

Converts the value in Working Register Area 1 (WRA1) to its positive equivalent. The result is left in WRA1. If a negative integer greater than $2**15$ is encountered, it is converted to a single precision value. The data type or mode flag (**40AF**) will be updated to reflect any change in mode.

```
        LD      A,4             ; TYPE CODE FOR SP
        LD      (40AFH),A       ; SET TYPE TO SP
        LD      HL,VAL1         ; ADDR OF SP VALUE TO ABS
        CALL    09B1H           ; MOVE SP VALUE TO WRA1
        CALL    0977H           ; FIND ABS VALUE
         .
         .
         .
VAL1    DEFB    58H             ; SP 81.6022(10)
        DEFB    34H
        DEFB    23H
        DEFB    87H
         .
         .
```

CALL 0B37   Return Integer
                                     INT (N)

Returns the integer portion of a floating point number. If the value is positive, the integer portion is returned. If the value is negative with a fractional part, it is rounded up before truncation. The integer portion is left in WRA1. The mode flag is updated.

23

```
        LD      A,4                 ; TYPE CODE FOR SP
        LD      (40AFH),A           ; SET TYPE TO SINGLE PREC.
        LD      HL,VAL1             ; ADDR OF SP VALUE
        CALL    09B1H               ; MOVE SP VALUE TO WRA1
        CALL    0B37H               ; ISOLATE INTEGER PART OF SP VALUE
        LD      DE,4121H            ; ADDR OF WRA1 (INTEGER PART OF SP
VALUE
        LD      HL,VAL2             ; LOCAL ADDR FOR INTEGERIZED VALUE
        CALL    09D3H               ; MOVE INTEGERIZED SP VALUE TO LOCAL
AREA
          .
          .
          .
VAL1    DEFB    0E0H                ; SP -41.3418
        DEFB    05DH
        DEFB    0A5H
        DEFB    086H
VAL2    DEFS    4                   ; HOLDS INTEGER PORTION OF
                                    ;       -41.3418
          .
          .
          .
```

CALL 15BD   Arctangent
                                               ATN (N)

Returns the angle in radians, for the floating point tangent
value in WRA1. The angle will be left as a single precision
value in WRA1.

```
        LD      A,4                 ; TYPE CODE FOR SP
        LD      (40AFH),           ; SET TYPE TO SP
        LD      HL,TAN              ; ADDR OF VALUE FOR TANGENT
        CALL    09B1H               ; MOVE TAN TO WRA1
        CALL    15BDH               ; FIND ANGLE IN RADS
        LD      HL,ANGL             ; ADDR OF LOCAL STORAGE FOR ANGLE
        LD      DE,4121H            ; ADDR OF WRA1
        CALL    09D3H               ; MOVE ANGLE FROM WRA1 TO LOCAL AREA
          .
          .
TAN     DEFB    9AH                 ; TANGENT OF 30 DEG.
        DEFB    0C4H
        DEFB    13H
        DEFB    80H                 ; EXPONENT
ANGL    DEFS    4                   ; WILL HOLD  30 DEG. IN RADS (.5235)
```

CALL 1541   Cosine
                                               COS (N)

Computes the cosine for an angle given in radians. The
angle must be a floating point value; the cosine will be
returned in WRA1 as a floating point value.

```
        LD      A,4                 ; TYPE CODE FOR SP
        LD      (40AFH),A           ; SET TYPE TO SP
        LD      HL,ANGL             ; ADDR OF ANGLE VALUE
        CALL    09B1H               ; MOVE ANGLE TO WRA1
        CALL    1541H               ; COMPUTE COSINE
        LD      HL,CANGL            ; LOCAL ADDR FOR COSINE
        LD      DE,4121H            ; ADDR OF WRA1
        CALL    09D3H               ; MOVE COSINE FROM WRA1 TO LOCAL AREA
          .
          .
ANGL    DEFB    18H                 ; 30 DEG. IN RADS. (.5235)
        DEFB    04H
        DEFB    06H
        DEFB    80H                 ; EXPONENT
CANGL   DEFS    4                   ; WILL HOLD COSINE OF 30 DEG.
          .
```

CALL 1439   Raise Natural Base
                                               EXP (N)

Raises E (natural base) to the value in WRA1 which must
be a single precision value. The result will be returned in
WRA1 as a single precision number.

```
        LD      A,4                 ; TYPE CODE FOR SP
        LD      (40AFH),A           ; SET TYPE TO SP
        LD      HL,EXP              ; ADDR OF EXPONENT
        CALL    09B1H               ; MOVE EXPONENT TO WRA1
        CALL    1439H               ; FIND E ** 1.5708
        LD      DE,4121H            ; ADDR OF WRA1
        LD      HL,POW              ; ADDR OF LOCAL STORAGE
        CALL    09D3H               ; MOVE POWER TO LOCAL AREA
          .
          .
EXP     DEFB    0DBH                ; SP  1.5708(10)
        DEFB    00FH
        DEFB    049H
        DEFB    081H
POW     DEFS    4                   ; HOLDS E**1.5708
          .
          .
```

CALL 13F2   Raise X to the Y Power
                                               X**Y

Raises the single precision value which has been saved on
the STACK to the power specified in WRA1. The result
will be returned in WRA1.

```
;
; COMPUTE 16**2
;
        LD      BC,RETADD           ; RTN ADDR FOLLOWING
        PUSH    BC                  ; RAISING X TO Y
        LD      A,4                 ; TYPE CODE FOR SP
        LD      (40AFH),A           ; SET TYPE TO SP FOR X
        LD      HL,X                ; ADDR OF VAL TO BE RAISED
        CALL    09B1H               ; MOVE VAL TO WRA1
        CALL    09A4H               ; WRA1 TO STACK
        LD      HL,Y                ; ADDR OF POWER
        CALL    09B1H               ; MOVE POWER TO WRA1
        JP      13F2H               ; WRA1 = COMPUTE X**Y
RA        .                         ; RTN TO RA WHEN DONE
          .
X       DEFW    0                   ; SP FOR 16 (10)
        DEFW    85H
Y       DEFW    0                   ; SP FOR 2 (10)
        DEFW    82H
          .
          .
```

CALL 0809   Natural Log
                                  LOG (N)

Computes the natural log (base E) of the single precision
value in WRA1. The result is returned as a single
precision value in WRA1.

```
        LD      A,4             ; TYPE CODE FOR SP
        LD      (40AFH),A       ; SET TYPE TO SP
        LD      HL,POW          ; ADDR OF POWER
        CALL    09B1H           ; MOVE POWER TO WRA1
        CALL    0809H           ; FIND NAT.LOG. OF POWER
        LD      DE,4121H        ; ADDR OF WRA1
        LD      HL,NLOG         ; ADDR OF LOCAL STORAGE AREA
        CALL    09D3H           ; MOVE LOG FROM WRA1 TO LOCAL AREA
                .
                .
POW     DEFB    00              ; FLOATING POINT 3 (LSB)
        DEFB    00
        DEFB    04H
        DEFB    82HH            ; EXPONENT FOR 3.0
NLOG    DEFS    4               ; WILL HOLD NAT. LOG OF 3
                .
                .
                .
```

CALL 0B26   Floating To Integer
                                  FIX (N)

Unconditionally truncates the fractional part of a floating
point number in WRA1. The result is stored in WRA1
and the type flag is set to integer.

```
        LD      A,4             ; TYPE CODE FOR SP
        LD      (40AFH),A       ; SET TYPE TO SP
        LD      HL,FLPT         ; ADDR OF FLOATING POINT VALUE
        CALL    09B1H           ; MOVE FLT.PT. VALUE TO WRA1
        CALL    0B26H           ; TRUNCATE AND CONVERT TO INTEGER
        LD      HL,(4121H)      ; LOAD INTEGER PORTION FROM WRA1
        LD      (INTG),HL       ; AND STORE IN LOCAL AREA
                .
                .
FLPT    DEFB    0BAH            ; SP 39.7107(10)
        DEFB    0D7H
        DEFB    01EH
        DEFB    086H
INTG    DEFS    2               ; HOLDS INTEGER PORTION OF
                                ;         39.7107
                .
                .
                .
```

CALL 01D3   Reseed Random Seed
                                  RANDOM

Reseeds the random number seed (location 40AB) with
the current contents of the refresh register.

```
        CALL    01D3H           ; RESEED RANDOM NUMBER SEED
                .
                .
                .
```

CALL 14C9   Random Number
                                  RND (N)

Generates a random number between 0 and 1, or 1 and n
depending on the parameter passed in WRA1. The
random value is returned in WRA1 as an integer with the
mode flag set. The parameter passed will determine the
range of the random number returned. A parameter of 0
will return an interger between 0 and 1. A parameter
greater than 0 will have any fraction portion truncated and
will cause a value between 1 and the integer portion of the
parameter to be returned.

```
        LD      A,2             ; TYPE CODE FOR INTEGER
        LD      (40AFH),A       ; SET TYPE TO INTEGER
        LD      A,50
        LD      (4121H),A       ; PUT AN INTEGER 50 INTO WRA1
        CALL    14C9H           ; GET A RANDOM NO. BETWEEN 1 AND 50
        LD      HL,(4121H)      ; LOAD RANDOM NO. INTO HL
        LD      (RVAL),HL       ; AND MOVE IT TO LOCAL AREA
                .
                .
RVAL    DEFW    0               ; HOLDS RANDOM NUMBER (INTEGER)
                .
                .
```

CALL 1547   Sine
                                  SIN (N)

Returns the sine as a single precision value in WRA1. The
sine must be given in radians in WRA1.

```
        LD      A,4             ; TYPE CODE FOR INTEGER
        LD      (40AFH),A       ; SET TYPE TO SP
        LD      HL,ANGL         ; ADDR. OF ANGLE IN RADIANS
        CALL    09B1H           ; MOVE ANGLE TO WRA1
        CALL    1547H           ; COMPUTE SINE OF ANGLE
        LD      DE,4121H        ; ADDR OF SINE IN WRA1
        LD      HL,SANGL        ; ADDR OF LOCAL AREA FOR SIN
        CALL    09D3H           ; MOVE SINE TO LOCAL AREA
                .
                .
                .
ANGL    DEFB    18H             ; 30 DEGS. IN RADS. (.5235)
        DEFB    04H
        DEFB    06H
        DEFB    80H             ; EXPONENT
SANGL   DEFS    4               ; WILL HOLD SINE OF 30 DEG.
                .
                .
```

CALL 13E7   Square Root
                                  SQR (N)

Computes the square root of any value in WRA1. The
root is left in WRA1 as a single precision value.

```
        LD      A,4             ; TYPE CODE FOR SP
        LD      (40AFH),A       ; SET TYPE TO SP
        LD      HL,VAL1         ; VALUE TO TAKE ROOT OF
        CALL    09B1H           ; MUST BE IN WRA1
        CALL    13E7H           ; TAKE ROOT OF VALUE
        LD      DE,4121H        ; ADDR OF ROOT IN WRA1
        LD      HL,ROOT         ; ADDR OF LOCAL AREA
        CALL    09D3H           ; MOVE ROOT TO LOCAL AREA
                .
                .
VAL1    DEFB    00H             ; SP 4
        DEFB    00H
        DEFB    00H
        DEFB    83H             ; EXPONENT OF FLOATING POINT 4
ROOT    DEFS    4               ; HOLDS ROOT OF 4
                .
                .
```

Tangent
TAN (N)

Computes the tangent of an angle in radians. The angle must be specified as a single precision value in WRA1. The tangent will be left in WRA1.

```
        LD      A,4                 ; TYPE CODE FOR SP
        LD      (40AFH),A           ; SET TYPE TO SP
        LD      HL,ANGL             ; ADDR OF ANGLE IN RADIANS
        CALL    09B1H               ; MOVE ANGLE TO WRA1
        CALL    15A8H               ; FIND TAN OF ANGLE
        LD      DE,4121H            ; ADDR OF WRA1
        LD      HL,TANGL            ; ADDR OF LOCAL STORAGE FOR TAN
        CALL    09D3H               ; MOVE TAN FROM WRA1 TO LOCAL AREA
        .
        .
        .
ANGL    DEFB    18H                 ; VALUE FOR 30 DEG IN RADS
        DEFB    04H                 ; (.5235)
        DEFB    06H
        DEFB    80H                 ; EXPONENT
TANGL   DEFS    4                   ; WILL HOLD TANGENT OF 30 DEG.
        .
        .
        .
```

Function Derivation

The LEVEL II system supports sixteen arithmetic functions. Seven of those may be called math functions. They are the sine, cosine, arctangent, tangent, square root, exponential (base e) and natural log. Three of these functions are computed from the identities:

$$\cos \theta = \sin \theta + \frac{\pi}{2}$$

$$\tan = \theta \frac{\sin \theta}{\cos \theta}$$

$$\sqrt{X} = e^{\frac{\ln x}{2}}$$

An implied math function exists which computes powers using the identity:

$$x^y = e^{y \ln x}$$

Embeded in LEVEL II are routines for the sine, exponential, natural log and arctangent. The other math functions derive their values using the aforementioned identities.

SINE

The sine routine is based on five terms of the approximation:

$$\sin \theta = \theta - \frac{\theta^3}{3!} + \frac{\theta^5}{5!} + \frac{\theta^7}{7!} + \frac{\theta^9}{9!}$$

Where θ is in radians. The actual approximation used is:

$$\sin\beta(2\pi) = 2\pi\beta - \frac{(2\pi)^3}{3!}\beta^3 + \frac{(2\pi)^5}{5!}\beta^5 - \frac{(2\pi)^7}{7!}\beta^7 + \frac{(2\pi)^9}{9!}\beta^9$$

Where β is a ratio which when multiplied by 2π gives the angle in radians. If x is the angle in degrees, then β is also used to determine the sign of the result according to the following rules:

$$\beta = \beta \frac{X}{360}° \quad \text{if} \quad 0° \leqslant X \leqslant 90°$$

$$\beta = \beta \frac{180°}{360}° - \frac{X}{360}° \quad \text{if} \quad 90° < X \leqslant 180°$$

$$\beta = \beta \frac{180°}{360}° - \frac{X}{360}° \quad \text{if} \quad 180° < X \leqslant 270°$$

$$\beta = \beta \frac{X}{360}° - \frac{360°}{360}° \quad \text{if} \quad 270° < X \leqslant 360°$$

The coefficients used with the sine series are correct to four decimal places, the maximum error for sine x is $\leqslant .000003$, thus all values for sine x would be correct to five places.

EXPONENTIATION

The exponentiation routine computes e^x for all values of x where:

$$-88 \leqslant x \leqslant 88$$

The approximation used for this function is derived from the followin

Since $e^x = 2^{x \log_2 e}$

Consider $2^{[\![x\log_2 e]\!]+1}$ where $[\![$ represents the greatest integer function.

Now $e^x = e^{-t}\left[2^{[\![x\log_2 e]\!]+1}\right]$

if $t = -x + [\![x\log_2 e]\!] \ln 2 + \ln 2$

Since $x = \ln e^x = \ln e^{-t}\left[2^{[\![x\log_2 e]\!]} + 1\right]$

$x = -t + \{[\![x\log_2 e]\!] + 1\}\ln 2$

Now $t = -x \{[\![x\log_2 e]\!] + 1\}\ln 2$

and so $0 < t < \ln 2$

and because

$$e^{-t} = 1 - t + \frac{t^2}{2!} - \frac{t^3}{3!} - \frac{t^4}{4!} - \frac{t^5}{5!} - \frac{t^6}{6!} - \frac{t^7}{7!}$$

The following series is used to approximate e^{-t}.

$$e^{-t} = 1 - t + .5t^2 - .166t^3 + .0416t^4 - .0083t^5 + .0013298t^6 - .0001413t^7$$

Then e^x is found by multiplying the approximate value of e^{-t} by $2^{[\![x\log_2 e]\!]+1}$ giving a result that is usually correct to at least five significant digits or five decimal places whichever is larger.

ARCTANGENT

The arctangent routine uses the approximation:

$$\arctan X = -\frac{X^3}{3} + \frac{X^5}{5} - \frac{X^7}{9} + \frac{X^9}{9} - \frac{X^{11}}{11} + \frac{X^{13}}{13} - \frac{X^{15}}{15} + \frac{X^{17}}{17}$$

If $x < 0$, the series is computed using the absolute value of x and the sign of the result is inverted. If $x > 1$ the series is computed using the value $1/x$ and the result is returned as $\pi/2 - \arctan 1/x$. For values where $0 < x < 1$, the series is computed using the orignal value of x. The coefficients used in the computer series are different from those in the approximating series starting with the seventh term, and the accuracy on the fifth and sixth coefficients is marginal as well. The actual series used is:

$$\arctan X = X - .33331X^3 + .199936X^5 - .142089X^7 + .106563X^9$$
$$- .0752896X^{11} + .0429096X^{13} - .01616157X^{15} + .00286623X^{17}$$

The maximum error using this approximation is .026.

NATURAL LOG

The natural log routine is based on three terms from the series:

$$\ln x = 2\left[\left(\frac{x-1}{x+1}\right) + \frac{1}{3}\left(\frac{x-1}{x+1}\right)^3 + \frac{1}{5}\left(\frac{x-1}{x+1}\right)^5 \cdots\right]$$

This series in convergent for values of $x < 1$ so x must be redefined as:

$$x = X2^n$$

Where n is an integer scaling factor and

$$1/2 \leqslant X < 1$$

Through algebra, not shown here, the x term can be replaced by $\frac{X}{\ln 2}$ giving:

$$\ln x = \frac{2}{\ln 2}\left[\left(\frac{\frac{X}{\ln 2}-1}{\frac{X}{\ln 2}+1}\right) + \frac{1}{3}\left(\frac{\frac{X}{\ln 2}-1}{\frac{X}{\ln 2}+1}\right)^3 + \frac{1}{5}\left(\frac{\frac{X}{\ln 2}-1}{\frac{X}{\ln 2}+1}\right)^5 + \cdots\right]$$

Since $\ln x = \ln X 2^n = \ln X + n \ln 2$ and since

$$\frac{\ln \frac{X}{\ln 2}}{\ln 2}$$

from the series it follows that

$$\ln x = \left(\frac{\ln \frac{X}{\ln 2}}{\ln 2} - .5 + n\right)\ln 2$$

In this function ln2 has been approximated as .707092 and

$$\frac{\ln(\ln 2)}{\ln 2} \quad \text{as} \quad -.5$$

If x is reasonable where $0 < x$ then $\ln x$ should be accurate to four significant digits. If x is extremely close to zero or very large, this will not be the case.

SYSTEM FUNCTIONS

System Functions are ROM entry points that can be entered at This means that on a disk based system, for example, an assembly language program which CALLS these entry points could be executed immediately after IPL before executing the BASIC utility program first. These entry points are different from the BASIC Functions because they do not require the Communica--tions Region (CR) to be initialized in order to operate correctly. A Level II system without disks always has an initialized CR because of its IPL processing.

Some of the routines mentioned here do use the Communications Region , but none of them require any particular locations to be initialized. The System Error routine however, which may be called in the event of an error detected by these routines, will assume some words contain meaningfull data, and will return control to the BASIC Interpreter Input Phase.

RST 08   Compare Symbol

Compares the symbol in the input string pointed to by HL register to the value in the location following the RST 08 call. If there is a match, control is returned to address of the RST 08 instruction 2 with the next symbol in the A-register and HL incremented by one. If the two characters do not match, a syntax error message is given and control returns to the Input Phase.

```
;
; TEST THE STRING POINTED TO BY HL TO SEE IF IT
; CONIAINS THE STRING ´A=B=C´.
;
        RST    08      ; TEST FOR A
        DEFB   41H     ; HEX VALUE FOR A
        RST    08      ; FOUND A, NOW TEST FOR =
        DEFB   3DH     ; HEX VALUE FOR =
        RST    08      ; FOUND =, NOW TEST FOR B
        DEFB   42B     ; HEX VALUE FOR B
        RST    08      ; FOUND B, TEST FOR =
        DEFB   3DH     ; HEX VALUE FOR =
        RST    08      ; FOUND =, TEST FOR C
        DEFB   43H     ; HEX VALUE FOR C
        .               ; FOUND STRING A=B=C
        .
        .
```

RST 10   Examine Next Symbol

Loads the next character from the string pointed to by the HL register set into the A-register and clears the CARRY flag if it is alphabetic, or sets it if is alphanumeric. Blanks and control codes **09** and **0B** are ignored causing the following character to be loaded and tested. The HL register will be incremented before loading any character therfore on the first call the HL register should contain the string address minus one. The string must be terminated by a byte of zeros.

```
;
; THE CURRENT STRING POINTED TO BY HL IS ASSUMED
; TO BE PART OF AN ASSIGNMENT STATEMENT CONTAINING
; AN OPTIONAL SIGN FOLLOWED BY A CONSTANT OR A
; VARIABLE NAME. MAKE THE NECESSARY TESTS TO DETERMINE
; IF A CONSTANT OR A VARIABLE IS USED.
;
        RST    08      ; TEST FOR ´=´
        DEFB   3DH     ; HEX VAUE FOR =
NEXT    RST    10H     ; GET SYMBOL FOLLOWING =
        JR     NC,VAR  ; NC IF VARIABLE NAME
        CALL   1E5AH   ; GET VALUE OF CONSTANT
        JR     SKIP    ; JOIN COMMON CODE
VAR     CP     2BH     ; NOT NUMERIC, TEST FOR +,-,
                       ; OR ALPHA
        JR     Z,NEXT  ; SKIP + SIGNS
        CP     2DH     ; NOT A +, TEST FOR A -
        JR     Z,NEXT  ; SKIP - SIGNS
        CALL   260DH   ; ASSUME IT´S A GOOD ALPHA AND
                       ; SEARCH FOR A VARIABLE NAME
                       ; (SEE SECTION 2.6 FOR A
        .              ; DESCRIPTION OF 260D)
        .
SKIP    .
        .
        .
```

RST 18   Compare DE:HL

Numerically compares DE and HL. Will not work for signed integers (except positive ones). Uses the A-register only. The result of the comparison is returned in the status register as:

```
CARRY SET    -  HL  <  DE
NO CARRY     -  HL  >  DE
NZ           -  UNEQUAL
Z            -  EQUAL
```

```
;
; THIS EXAMPLE TESTS THE MAGNITUDE OF THE VALUE
; FOLLOWING THE = IN THE STRING POINTED TO BY HL
; TO MAKE SURE IT FALLS BETWEEN 100 AND 500
;
        RST    08      ; TEST FOR =
        DC     3DH     ;  HEX VALUE FOR =
        RST    10H     ; FOUND =, TEST NEXT CHAR
        JR     NC,ERR  ; NC IF NOT NUMERIC
        CALL   1E5AH   ; GET BINARY VALUE
        LD     HL,500  ; UPPER LIMIT VALUE
        RST    18H     ; COMPARE VALUE TO UPPER LIMIT
        JR     C,ERR   ; CARRY IF VALUE > 500
        LD     HL,100  ; LOWER LIMIT VALUE
        RST    18H     ; COMPARE VALUE TO LOWER LIMIT
        JR     NC,ERR  ; NO CARRY IF VALUE < 100
        .
        .
        .
```

RST 20   Test Data Mode

Returns a combination of STATUS flags and unique numeric values in the A-register according to the data mode flag (**40AF**). This CALL is usually made to determine the type of the current value in WRA1. It should be used with caution, however since the mode flag and WRA1 can get out of phase particularly if some of the CALLS described here are used to load WRA1.

TYPE	STATUS	A-REGISTER
02 (INTEGER)	NZ/C/M/E	-1
03 (STRING)	Z/C/P/E	0
04 (SINGLE PREC.)	NZ/C/P/O	1
08 (DOUBLE PREC.)	NZ/NC/P/E	5

```
;
; TEST DATA TYPE AFTER INTEGER ADDITION TO
; DETERMINE IF OVERFLOW OCCURED (RESULT WOULD
; BE CONVERTED TO SINGLE PRECISION
;
        LD      A,2         ; TYPE CODE FOR INTEGER
        LD      (40AFH),02; SET TYPE TO INTEGER
        LD      BC,(VAL1)   ; FIRST QUANTITY
        LD      HL,(VAL2)   ; SECOND QUANTITY
        CALL    0B2DH       ; DO INTEGER ADDITION
        RST     20H         ; TEST FOR OVERFLOW
        JP      M,OK        ; RESULT IS INTEGER
        .                   ; RESULT IS  NOT INTEGER
        .                   ; TEST FOR OTHER TYPES
OK      LD      (SUM),HL    ; SAVE INTEGER RESULT
        .
        .

VAL1    DEFW    125         ; 16 BIT INTEGER VALUE
VAU2    DEFW    4235        ; 16 BIT INTEGER VALUE
SUM     DEFW    0           ; HOLDS 16 BIT VALUE
```

RST 28   DOS Function CALL

Passes request code in A-register to DOS for processing. Returns for non-disk system. For disk systems, the A-register must contain a legitimate DOS function code. If the code is positive, the CALL is ignored and control returns to the caller. Note that the DOS routine discards the return address stored on the stack by the RST instruction. After processing control will be returned to the previous address on the stack. The calling sequence is:

```
;
; LOAD AND EXECUTE DEBUG
;
        LD      A,87H   ; DOS CODE FOR LOADING DEBUG
        CALL    DOS
        .               RETURN HERE
        .
DOS     RST     28H     MAKE DOS CALL (WILL RET TO CALLER)
        .
        .
```

RST 30   Load DEBUG

This CALL loads the DEBUG program and transfers control to it. When DEBUG processing is complete, control is returned to the orginal caller. For non-disk systems control is returned immediately.

```
; IF ILLOGICAL CONDITION ARISES LOAD AND EXECUTE DEBUG.
                ; TEST FOR LEGITIMATE CONDITIONS
        .
        JR      Z,OK    ; JMP IF CONDITIONS ARE CORRECT
        RST     30H     ; ELSE LOAD AND EXECUTE DEBUG
OK      .               ; CONTINUE
        .
        .
```

RST 38   Interrupt Entry Point

This is the system entry point for all interrupts. It contains a jump to section of code in the Communications Region designed to field interrupts. That section of code consists of a DI (disables further interrupts) followed by a RET (returns to the point of interrupt) for non-disk systems, or a jump to an interrupt processor in SYS0 if it is a DOS system. For DOS systems the interrupt handler consists of a task scheduler, where the exact cause of the interrupt is determined (usually a clock interrupt) and the next task from the task control block is executed. After task completion, control returns to the point of interrupt.

```
;
; INTERCEPT ALL CLOCK INTERRUPTS AND TEST THE WIDGET
; ON PORT AB. IF THE READY LINE (BIT 8) IS TRUE
; (HIGH OR A 1) TURN ON THE COFFEE POT ON PORT DE.
; THEN JUMP TO THE NORMAL DOS INTERRUPT HANDLER
;
        ORG     4012H       ; REPLACE THE JUMP
        JP      HERE        ; TO THE DOS INTERRUPT
                            ; PROCESSOR WITH A JUMP
                            ; TO OUR OWN.
        ORG     0F000H      ; OUR INTERRUPT HANDLER
HERE    DI                  ; DISABLE FURTHER
                            ; INTERRUPTS
        PUSH    AF          ; WE'LL NEED AF REGS
        IN      A,(0ABH)    ; GET WIDGET STATUS
        OR      A           ; SET STATUS FOR BIT 8
        JP      M,TOCP      ; WIDGET ON IF MINUS
        POP     AF          ; WIDGET OFF, RST REGS
        JP      4518H       ; GO TO DOS INTERRUPT
                            ; HANDLER
TOCP    LD      A,21H       ; CODE TO TURN ON COFFEE
        POT
        OUT     (0DEH),A    ; SEND COMMAND TO POT
        POP     AF          ; THEN RST REGS
        JP      4518H       ; AND GO TO DOS INTERRUPT
                            ; HANDLER
        .
        .
```

CALL 09B4   Move SP Value In BC/DC Into WRA1

Moves the single precision value in BC/DE into WRA1. HL is destroyed BC/DE is left intact. Note - the mode flag is not updated !

```
        .
        LD      BC,(PART1)  ; GET FIRST ARGUMENT
        LD      DE,(PART2)  ; REMAINDER OF ARGUMENT
                            ; NOTE - WE HAVE ASSUMED THAT
                            ; WRA1 CURRENTLY CONTAINS A
                            ; SINGLE PRECISION VALUE !!!
        CALL    09B4H       ; MOVE PART1 TO WRA1
        LD      BC,(PART3)  ; GET VALUE TO BE ADDED
        LD      DE,(PART4)  ; REST OF VALUE
        CALL    0716H       ; MOVE RESULT (SUM) TO WRA1
        .
        .
PART2   DEFW    0000H       ; LSB OF SP 1.5
PART1   DEFW    8140H       ; EXPONENT AND MSB OF SP 1.5
PART4   DEFW    0000H       ; LSB OF SP XX
PART3   DEFW    0000H       ; EXPONENT/MSB OF SP XX
        .
        .
```

CALL 09B1   Moves A SP Value Pointed To By HL To WRA1

Loads a single precision value pointed to by HL into BC/DE and then moves it to WRA1. Destroys HL/BC/DE.

```
        .
        LD      HL,VAL  ; GET ADDR OF VALUE TO MOVE
        CALL    09B1H   ; MOVE VALUE TO WRA1
        .
        .
VAL     DEFW    8140H   ; SINGLE PREC 1.5
        DEFW    0000H   ; REMAINDER OF 1.5
        .
        .
```

CALL 09C2 — Load A SP Value Into BC/DE

Loads a single precision value pointed to by HL into BC/DE. Uses all registers.

```
;
; COMPUTE THE PRODUCT OF TWO SP NUMBERS AND MOVE THE
; PRODUCT TO BC/DE.
;
        LD    HL,VAL1      ; ADDR OF VALUE 1
        CALL  09B1H        ; MOVE IT TO WRA1
        LD    HL,VAL2      ; ADDR OF VALUE 2
        CALL  09C2H        ; LOAD IT INTO BC/DE
        LD    BC,(4121H)   ; LOAD EXPONENT/MSB
        LD    DE,(4123H)   ; LOAD LSB
        .
        .
        .
VAL1    DEFW  XXXX
        DEFW  XXXX
VAL2    DEFW  XXXX
        DEFW  XXXX
        .
        .
        .
```

CALL 09BF — Loads A SP Value From WRA1 Into BC/DE

Loads a single precision value from WRA1 into BC/DE. Note, the mode flag is not tested by the move routine. It is up to the caller to insure that WRA1 actually contains a single precision value.

```
        .
        .
        LD    HL,VAL1      ; ADDR OF VALUE TO MOVE TO WRA1
        CALL  09B1H        ; MOVE VAL1 TO WRA1
        LD    HL,VAL2      ; ADDR OF VALUE TO BE ADDED
        CALL  09C2H        ; LOAD VALUE TO BE ADDED TO BC/DE

        CALL  0716H        ; DO SINGLE PRECISION ADD
        CALL  09BFH        ; LOAD RESULT INTO BC/DE
        LD    (SUM1),DE    ; SAVE LSB
        LD    (SUM2),BC    ; SAVE EXPONENT/MSB
        .
        .
SUM1    DEFW  0            ; HOLDS LSB OF SINGLE PRECSION
SUM2    DEFW  0            ; HOLDS EXPONENT/MSB
VAL1    DEFW  0000H        ; LSB OF S.P. 2.0
        DEFW  8200H        ; EXPONENT/MSB OF S.P. 2.0
VAL2    DEFW  00000;       ; LSB OF S.P. 5.0
        DEFW  8320H        ; EXPONENT/MSB OF S.P. 5.0
        .
        .
        .
```

CALL 09A4 — Move WRA1 To Stack

Moves the single precision value in WRA1 to the stack. It is stored in LSB/MSB/Exponent order. All registers are left intact. Note, the mode flag is not tested by the move routine, it is simply assumed that WRA1 contains a single precision value.

```
;
; ADD TWO SINGLE PRECISION VALUES TOGETHER AND SAVE
; THE SUM ON THE STACK. CALL A SUBROUTINE WHICH
; WILL LOAD THE VALUE FROM THE STACK, PERFORM IT'S OWN
; OPERATION AND RETURN.
;
```

```
        LD    HL,VAL1      ; ADDR OF VALUE TO MOVE TO WRA1
        CALL  09B1H        ; MOVE VAL1 TO WRA1
        LD    HL,VAL2      ; ADDR OF VALUE TO BE ADDED
        CALL  09C2H        ; LOAD VALUE TO BE ADDED ITO BC/DE
        CALL  0716H        ; DO SINGLE PRECISION ADD
        CALL  09A4H        ; SAVE SUM ON STACK
        CALL  NSUB         ; CALL NEXT SUBROUTINE
        .
        .                  ; RETURN WITH NEW VALUE IN
        .                  ; IN WRA1.
NSUB    POP   HL           ; GET RETURN ADDR
        LD    (RET),HL     ; MOVE IT TO A SAFE PLACE
        LD    HL,VAL3      ; ADDR OF QUANTITY TO ADD
        CALL  09B1H        ; MOVE VAL3 TO WRA1
        POP   BC           ; GET EXPONENT/MSB
        POP   DE           ; GET LSB
        CALL  0716H        ; ADD TO VALUE PASSED
        LD    HL,(RET)     ; GET RETURN ADDR
        JP    (HL)         ; AND RET TO CALLER
VAL1    DEFW  0000H        ; LSB OF S.P 2.0
        DEFW  8200H        ; EXPONENT/MSB OF S.P 2.0
VAL2    DEFW  00000;       ; LSB OF S.P. 5.0
        DEFW  8320H        ; EXPONENT/MSB OF S.P. 5.0
VAL3    DEFW  0AA6CH       ; LSB OF S.P. -.333333
        DEFW  7FAAH        ; EXPONENT/MSB OF S.P. -.33333
        .
        .
```

CALL 09D7 — General Purpose Move

Moves contents of B-register bytes from the address in DE to the address given in HL. Uses all registers except C.

```
;
; BLANK FILL A DCB THEN MOVE A NAME INTO IT
;
        LD    A,20H        ; HEX VALUE FOR BLANK
        LD    B,32         ; NO. OF BYTES TO BLANK
        LD    DE,IDCB      ; DE = ADDR OF DCB
LOOP    LD    (DE),A       ; STORE A BLANK INTO DCB
        INC   DE           ; BUMP STORE ADDR
        DJNZ  LOOP         ; LOOP TILL DCB BLANKED
        LD    DE,NAME      ; NOW, MOVE FILE NAME TO IDCB
        LD    HL,IDCB      ; DE = NAME ADDR, HL = DCB ADDR
        LD    B,LNG        ; NO. OF CHARS IN NAME TO MOVE
        CALL  09D7H        ; MOVE NAME TO DCB
        .
        .
IDCB    DEFS  32           ; EMPTY DCB
LNG     EQU   ENDX-$       ; LET ASSEMBLER COMPUTE LNG OF
                           ; FILE NAME
NAME    DEFM  'FILE1/TXT'  ; NAME TO BE MOVED TO DCB
ENDX    EQU   $            ; SIGNAL END OF NAME
        .
```

CALL 0982 — Variable Move Routine

Moves the number of bytes specified in the type flag (40AF) from the address in DE to the address in HL, uses registers A, DE, HL.

```
;
; LOCATE THE ADDRESS OF A DOUBLE PRECISION VARIABLE
; THEN MOVE IT TO A LOCAL STORAGE AREA.
;
        LD    HL,NAME1     ; NAME OF VARIABLE TO LOCATE
        CALL  260DH        ; GET ADDR OF STRING X
        RST   20H          ; MAKE SURE IT'S DBL PREC.
        JR    NC,OK        ; JMP IF DBL PREC.
        JP    ERR          ; ELSE ERROR
OK      LD    HL,LOCAL     ; HL = LOCAL ADDR
                           ; DE = VARIABLE ADDR
        CALL  0982H        ; MOVE VALUE FROM VLT TO LOCAL
        AREA.
        .
        .
ERR     .
NAME1   DEFM  'X'          ; NAME OF VARIABLE TO LOCATE
        DEFB  0            ; MUST TERM WITH A ZERO
LOCAL   DEFS  8            ; ENOUGH ROOM FOR DBL PREC. VALUE
        .
        .
```

CALL 29C8 — String Move

On entry HL points to the string control block for the string to be moved, and DE contains the destination address. All registers are used. The string length and address are not moved. String control blocks have the format:

```
DEFB     X              STRING LENGTH
DEFW     ADDR           STRING ADDRESS
         ;
         ; LOCATE THE ADDRESS OF A STRING VARIABLE CALLED F$.
         ; MOVE THE STRING F$ TO A LOCAL STORAGE AREA CALLED
           DCB.
         ;
         LD    HL,NAME    ; NAME OF VARIABLE TO LOCATE
         CALL  260DH      ; FIND ADDR OF SSTRING F$
         RST   20H        ; MAKE SURE IT´S A STRING
         JR    Z,OK       ; JMP IF STRING
         JP    ERR        ; ELSE ERROR
   OK    LD    A,(DE)     ; GET LENGTH OF STRING
         CP    33         ; WHICH MUST BE < 33
         JP    P,ERR      ; ERR, STRING LNG > 32
         PUSH  DE         ; SHORTCUT FOR MOVING DE TO HL

         POP   HL         ; ADDR OF STRING TO HL
         LD    DE,LOCAL   ; DE = LOCAL ADDR
         CALL  29C8H      ; MOVE STRING VARIABLE TO
                          ; LOCAL AREA

   ERR   .

   NAME  DEFM  ´F$´       ; NAME OF VARIABLE TO FIND
         DEFB  0          ; REQUIRED TO TERM NAME
   LOCAL DEFS  32         ; LOCAL STORAGE AREA
```

Basic Functions

Basic Functions differ from System Functions because they deal mainly with tables in the Communications Region (CR). Because of this, these entry points assume that the CR has been initialized and properly maintained. This means that the BASIC Interpreter must have been entered prior to calling any of these routines, and the BASIC utility in RAM must be intact. The assembly program making the CALL must be running as a subroutine called by a BASIC program.

For a complete description of the tables and storage areas in the Communication Region see chapter 4.

CALL 1B2C — Search For Line Number

Searches the Program Statement Table (PST) for a BASIC statement with the line number specified in the DE register pair. All registers are used. The exit conditions are:

STATUS	CONDITION	REGISTERS
C/Z	LINE FOUND. BC = STARTING ADDRESS OF LINE IN PST.	
NC/Z	LINE DOES NOT EXIST. LINE NUMBER TOO LARGE HL/BC = ADDRESS OF NEXT AVAILABLE LOCATION IN	HL = ADDRESS OF FOLLOWING LINE IN PST.
NC/NZ	LINE DOES NOT EXIST. BC = ADDRESS OF FIRST LINE NUMBER GREATER THAN THE ONE SPECIFIED. HL = ADDRESS OF FOLLOWING LINE.	

```
; LOCATE THE ADDRESS OF BASIC STATEMENT NUMBER 750
; IN THE PST. IF THE LINE DOES NOT EXIST RETURN A
; STATUS OF -1 IF IT IS LARGER THAN ANY CURRENT LINE
; NUMBER, OR A -2 IF IT THERE ARE LINES GREATER THAN
; 750. IF THE LINE IS FOUND RETURN A STATUS OF ZERO.
;
         LD    DE,750     ; LINE NUMBER TO SEARCH FOR
         CALL  1B2CH      ; SEEK LINE IN PST
         JR    NC,NO      ; NC SET IF LINE NOT THERE
         LD    HL,3       ; INCREMENT TO STEP OVER
         ADD   HL,BC      ; POINTER TO NEXT LINE/LINE NO.

                          ; RST BELOW WILL INCREMENT
                          ; BEFORE  LOADING
         RST   10H        ; FETCH FIRST CHAR OF OF
                          ;   STATEMENT.

         LD    A,0        ; SIGNAL LINE FOUND
         RET              ; RETURN TO CALLER
   NO    JR    NC,M2      ; JMP IF LINE NO. TOO BIG
         LD    A,0FFH     ; SIGNAL LINE NOT THERE
         RET              ; RETURN TO CALLER
   M2    LD    A,0FEH     ; SIGNAL LINE NOT THERE
                          ;   TOO BIG
         RET              ; RETURN TO CALLER
```

CALL 260D — Find Address Of Variable

This entry point searches the Variable List Table (VLT) for a variable name which matches the name in the string pointed to by HL. If the variable exists, its address is returned in DE. If it is not defined, then it is created with an initial value of zero and its address is returned in DE. Dimensioned and non-dimensioned variables may be located, and suffixes for data mode may be included in the name string. A byte of machine zeros must terminate the name string. All registers are used.

```
;
; LOCATE THE ADDRESS OF THE VARIABLE A3
;
         LD    HL,STRNG   ; NAME OF VARIABLE TO LOCATE
         CALL  260DH      ; FIND IT´S ADDRESS IN VLT
         LD    (ADDR),DE  ; SAVE FOR FUTURE REFERENCE
         .
   STRNG DEFM  ´A3´       ; VARIABLE NAME IS A3
         DEFB  0
   STRNG DEFM  ´A(25)´    ; VARIABLE NAME IS A(25)
         DEFB  0
   STRNG DEFM  ´A%´       ; VARIABLE NAME IS A%
         DEFB  0
```

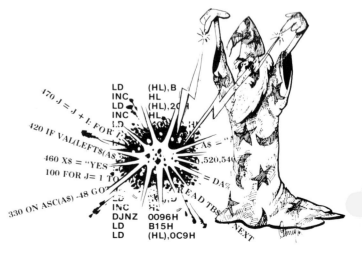

CALL 1EB1   GOSUB

Can be used to execute the equivalent of a GOSUB statement from an assembly program. It allows a BASIC subroutine to be called from an assembly subroutine. After the BASIC subroutine executes, control returns to the next statement in the assembly program. All registers are used. On entry, the HL must contain an ASCII string with the starting line number of the subroutine.

```
;
; SIMULATE A GOSUB STATEMENT FROM AN ASSEMBLY LANGUAGE PROGRAM
;
      LD    HL,STRNG  ; ADDRESS OF BASIC LINE NUMBER TO GOSUB TO
      CALL  1EB1H     ; EQUIVALENT OF A GOSUB 1020
      .
      .                ; WILL RETURN HERE WHEN BASIC PROGRAM
      .                ; EXECUTES A RETURN
STRNG DEFM  ´1020´    ; LINE NO. OF BASIC SUBROUTINE
      DEFB  0
```

CALL 1DF7   TRON

Turns TRON feature on. Causes line numbers for each BASIC statement executed to be displayed. Uses A-register.

```
;
; TURN TRACE ON THEN EXECUTE A BASIC SUBROUTINE
;
      CALL  1DF7H     ; TURN TRACE ON
      LD    HL,LN     ; LINE NO. TO GOSUB
      CALL  1EB1H     ; DO A GOSUB 1500
      .
      .
LN    DEFM  ´1500´    ; LINE NO. OF BASIC SUBROUTINE
      DEFB  0
```

CALL 1DF8   TROFF

Disables tracing feature. Uses A register.

```
;
; ENABLE TRACE. EXECUTE BASIC SUBROUTINE. UPON
; RETURN DISABLE TRACING.
;
      CALL  1DF7H     ; TURN TRACE ON
      LD    HL,LN     ; LINE NO. OF BASIC SUBROUTINE
      CALL  1EB1H     ; DO A GOSUB 2000
      CALL  1DF8H     ; TURN OFF TRACING
      RET             ; RETURN TO CALLER
LN    DEFM  ´2000´    ; LINE NO. OF BASIC SUBROUTINE
      DEFB  0
```

JP 1EDF   RETURN

Returns control to the BASIC statement following the last GOSUB call. An assembly program called by a BASIC subroutine may wish to return directly to the orginal caller without returning through the subroutine entry point. This exit can be used for that return. The return address on the stack for the call to the assembly program must be cleared before returning via 1EDF.

```
300 GOSUB 1500        CALL BASIC SUBROUTINE
310 GOSUB 1510        RETURN HERE FROM SUBROUTINE CALL
320   .

1500 Z=USR1(0)        CALL ASSEMBLY SUBROUTINE & RETURN

1510 Z=USR2(0)        CALL ANOTHER SUBROUTINE & RETURN

1530   .
       .
       .
; ENTRY POINT FOR USR1 SUBROUTINE
;
       .              ; DO WHATEVER PROCESSING IS
                      ;   REQUIRED
       .
      POP  AF         ; CLEAR RETURN  ADDR TO 1510
                      ; FROM STACK
      JP   1EDFH      ; RETURN DIRECTLY TO 310
; ENTRY POINT FOR USR2 SUBROUTINE
;
       .              ; PERFORM NECESSARY PROCESSING
                      ; FOR USR2 CALL
      POP  AF         ; CLEAR RETURN ADDR TO 1520
      JP   1EDFH      ; RETURN DIRECTLY TO 320
```

CALL 28A7   Write Message

Displays message pointed to by HL on current system output device (usually video). The string to be displayed must be terminated by a byte of machine zeros or a carriage return code 0D. If terminated with a carriage return, control is returned to the caller after taking the DOS exit at 41D0 (JP 5B99). This subroutine uses the literal string pool table and the string area. It should not be called if the communications region and the string area are not properly maintained.

```
;
; WRITE THE MESSAGE IN MLIST TO THE CURRENT SYSTEM
; OUTPUT DEVICE.
;
      .
      .
      LD   HL,MLIST   ; HL = ADDR OF MESSAGE
      CALL 28A7H      ; SEND TO SYSTEM OUTPUT DEVICE
      .
      .
MLIST DEFM ´ THIS IS A TEST´
      DEFB 0DH        ; THIS TERMINATOR REQUIRED
      .
      .
```

CALL 27C9   Return Amount Of Free Memory

Computes the amount of memory remaaining between the end of the variable list and the end of the stack. The result is returned as a single precision number in WRA1 (4121-4124).

```
;
; TAKE ALL AVAILABLE MEMORY BETWEEN THE STACK AND
; THE END OF THE VLT AND DIVIDE IT INTO REGIONS FOR
; USE IN A TOURNAMENT SORT
      .
      .
```

```
        DI                  ; MUST GO INHIBITED BECAUSE
                            ; THERE WILL BE NO STACK SPACE

                            ; FOR INTERRUPT PROCESSING
        CALL 27C9H          ; GET  AMT OF FREE SPACE
        CALL 0A7FH          ; CONVERT IT TO INTEGER
        LD   DE,(4121H)     ; GET IT INTO DE
        LD   HL,500         ; MAKE SURE IT'S AT
        RST  18H            ; LEAST 500  BYTES
        JR   C,ERR          ; ERR - INSUFFICIENT SPACE
        LD   HL,(40D1H)     ; START OF AREA
        LD   (EVLT),HL      ; SAVE FOR RESTORATION
        LD   HL,0           ; SO WE CAN LOAD CSP
        ADD  HL,SP          ; END OF AREA
        LD   (ECSP),HL      ; SAVE FOR RESTORATION
                    .
                    .
                    .
```

CALL 2B75   Print Message

Writes string pointed to by HL to the current output device. String must be terminated by a byte of zeros. This call is different from **28A7** because it does not use the literal string pool area, but it does use the same display routine and it takes the same DOS Exit at **41C1**. Uses all registers. This routine can be called without loading the BASIC utility, if a **C9** (RET) is stored in **41C1**.

```
;
; WRITE MESSAGE TO CURRENT OUTPUT DEVICE
;
                    .
                    .
        LD   HL,MLIST       ; ADDRESS OF MESSAGE
        CALL 2B75H          ; SEND MSG TO SYSTEM DEVICE

MLIST DEFM  'THIS IS A TEST'
      DEFB  0               ; REQUIRED TERMINATOR
                    .
                    .
                    .
```

Internal Number Representation

BASIC represents integers as signed 16 bit quantites. Bit 15 contains the sign bit while bits 0-14 hold the magnitude. The largest possible positive value that can be represented is 32767 (dec.) or 7FFF (hex). The smallest possible negative value that can be represented is -32768 (dec.) or 8000 (hex).

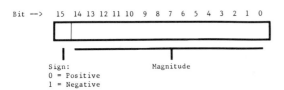

positive values 0000 - 7FFF (hex.) : 0 to 32767 (dec.)
Negative values   FFFF - 8000 (hex.) : -1 to -32768 (dec.)

Note - negative values are represented as the one's complement of the positive equivalent.

BASIC supports two forms of floating point numbers. One type is single precision and the other is double precision. Both types have a signed seven bit exponent. Single precision numbers have a signed 24 bit mantissa while double precision values have a signed 56 bit mantissa. Both types have the following format

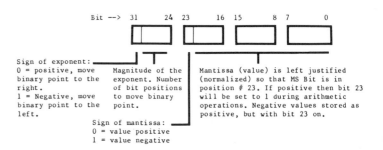

The only difference bettween single and double precision is in the number of bits in the mantissa. The maximum number of significant bits representable in a positive single precision value is $2^{**}24 -1$ or 8 388 607 decimal or 7F FF FF hex. Double precision numbers have an extended mantissa so positive values up to $2^{**}56-1$, or $3.578 \times 10^{**}16$ can be represented accurately.

These numbers 8 388 607 and $3.578 \times 10^{**}16$ are not the largest numbers that can be represented in a single or double precision number, but they are the largest that can be represented without some loss of accuracy. This is due to the fact that the exponent for either type of number ranges between $2^{**}-128$ and $2^{**}127$. This means that theoretically the binary point can be extended 127 places to the right for positive values and 128 to the left for negative values even though there are only 24 or 56 bits of significance in the mantissa. Depending of the type of data being used (the number of significant digits) this may be all right. For example Planck's constant which is $6.625 \times 10^{**}-34$ J-SEC could be represented as a single precision value without any loss of accuracy because it has only four significant digits. However if we were totalling a money value of the same magnitude it would have to be a double precision value because all digits would be significant

Chapter 3

Cassette & Disk

This chapter contains an introductory description of physical I/O operations for the cassette and disk. The sample programs are for purposes of illustration only and are not recommended for adaptation to general applications. There may be special situations, however when a simple READ/WRITE function is needed and for limited applications they will serve the purpose.

Cassette I/O

Cassette I/O is unusual from several aspects. First, each byte is tranmitted on a bit-by-bit basis under software control. This is radically different from all other forms of I/O where an entire byte is transfered at one time. For most I/O operations, referencing memory or executing an IN or OUT instruction, is all that is required to transfer an entrie byte between the CPU and an external device. However, If the device is a cassette, each bit (of a byte to be transferred) must be transfered individually by the software.

The second unusual aspect is the procedure used for transmitting these bits. Exact timing must be adhered to and the program must use different code depending on whether a binary zero or one is to be written. Each bit recorded consists of a clock pulse (CP) followed by a fixed amount of erased tape followed by either another CP if a binary one is represented, or a streach of erased tape if a binary zero is being represented. A binary one and zero would appear as:

The distance between points A, B, C, and D is measured in units of time. Because time can be measured in machine cycles the value given for distances will be in machine cycles where one instruction (any instruction regardless of how long it is) equals one cycle and one cycle equals one microsecond. This is crude but workable. The sum of A B is supposed to be 2 milliseconds for Level II.

Using the crudity described above and counting instructions used in the Level II software gives the following values.

A B 1.4 millisec per half bit 2.8 millisec per bit.
C .20 millisec * 2 per CP .40 millisec
D 1.0 millisec

Before discussing programming for cassette I/O in any detail we should review the fundementals. Drive selection is accomplished by storing either a 01 (drive 1) or 02 (drive 2) in 37E4. Motor start and loading or clearing the data latch is achieved by sending a command value to the cassette controller on port FF. The command value is shown below.

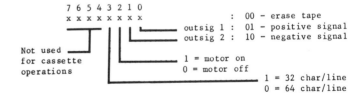

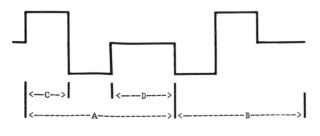

Binary one

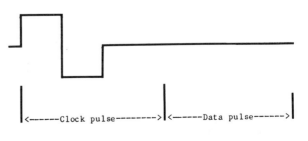

Binary zero

Be careful to preserve the current video character size when sending commands to the cassette. The system maintains a copy of the last command sent to the video controller in **403D**. Bit 3 of that word should be merged with any commans issued to the cassette.

A write operation of one bit (called a bit cell) can be divided into two steps. First a clock pulse (CP) is written to signal the start of a bit. It is followed by a strip of erased tape which is considered part of the CP. Next, another CP is written if the bit is a one, or more blank tape is written if the bit is a zero.

Read operations begin by searching for the clock pulse and skipping to the data pulse area. The data pulse area is then read returning a zero if blank tape was encountered or a one if non-blank tape was found. Below are examples of code that could be used for cassette operations. The code used by Level II can be found around the area **01D9 - 02A8** in the Level II listing.

Assembler Object Code Format

DOS loads disk object files with a utility program called LOAD. They can also be loaded under DOS by entering the name of a file that has an extension of CMD. The format of a disk object file is shown below. It is more complex than a cassette file because it has control codes embedded in the object code. The loader reads the file into a buffer before moving the object code to its designated address. The control codes are used to indicated to the loader where the code is to be loaded, how many bytes are to be loaded, and where execution is to begin.

```
Control Code:   01   (data to be loaded follows)
Count     :     XX   (count of bytes to load, 0 = 256)
Load Address:   XX   (load address in LSB/MSB order)
                XX
Load Data :     XX
                XX
                 .
Control Code:   02   (beginning execution address follows)
                XX   (this byte is to be discarded)
Address   :     XX   (execution address in
                XX   (LSB/MSB order)

Control Code:   03 - 05  (following data is to be skipped)
Count     :     XX   (count of bytes to skip)
Skip Data :     XX   (this data is to be skipped)
                XX
                 .
```

Cassette Recording Format

The recording format used by Level II is as follows:

1: BASIC Data Files

```
0 0 0 0 . . . 0 A5  X X X X . . . X
( 256 zeros )
```
Synch Bytes   Data Bytes

2: BASIC Programs

```
0 0 0 0 . . . 0 A5 D3 D3 D3 Y X X X X . . X 00 00 00
```
Synch Bytes
           File Header   BASIC   EOF
                 Name   Program   Marker

3: Absolute Assembler Programs

```
55 N N N N N N 3C Y ZZ X X X X . . . X C 78 TA
```
Synch   Start   Transfer address
             of   Program or Data   Transfer
File   binary   Checksum   address
Name   file   Load address   follows
                          Number of bytes to load

```
SELECT UNIT AND TURN ON MOTOR
        LD    A,01          ; CODE FOR UNIT 1
        LD    (37E4H),A     ; SELECT UNIT 1
        LD    A,04          ; COMMAND VALUE: TURN ON MOTOR
        OUT   (0FFH),A      ; START MOTOR, CLEAR DATA LATCH

WRITE BYTE CONTAINED IN THE A REGISTER
        PUSH  AF
        PUSH  BC
        PUSH  DE
        PUSH  HL            ; SAVE CALLERS REGISTERS
        LD    L,8           ; NUMBER OF BITS TO WRITE
        LD    H,A           ; H = DATA BYTE
LOOP    CALL  CP            ; WRITE CLOCK PULSE FIRST
        LD    A,H           ; GET DATA BYTE
        RLCA                ; HIGH ORDER BIT TO CARRY
        LD    H,A           ; SAVE REPOSITIONED BYTE
        JR    NC,WR         ; BIT WAS ZERO. WRITE BLANK TAPE
        CALL  CP            ; BIT WAS ONE. WRITE A ONE DATA PULSE
TEST    DEC   L             ; ALL BITS FROM DATA BYTES WRITTEN ?
        JR    NZ,LOOP       ; NO! JUMP TO LOOP
        POP   HL            ; YES! RESTORE CALLERS REGISTERS
        POP   DE
        POP   BC
        POP   AF
        RET                 ; RETURN TO CALLER
WR      LD    B,135         ; DELAY FOR 135 CYCLES (988 USEC) WHILE
WR1     DJNZ  WR1           ; BLANK TAPE IS BEING WRITTEN
        JR    TEST          ; GO TEST FOR MORE BITS TO WRITE
CP      LD    A,05          ; COMMAND VALUE MOTOR ONE, OUTSIG 1
        OUT   (0FFH),A      ; START OF CLOCK PULSE
        LD    B,57          ; DELAY FOR 57 (417 USEC) CYCLES
CP1     DJNZ  CP1           ; GIVES PART OF CP
        LD    A,06          ; COMMAND VALUE: MOTOR ON, OUTSIG 2
        OUT   (0FFH),A      ; 2ND PART OF CLOCK PULSE
        LD    B,57          ; DELAY FOR 57 CYCLES (417 USEC)
CP2     DJNZ  CP2           ; GIVES PART OF CP
        LD    A,4           ; COMMAND VALUE: MOTOR ON, NO OUTSIG
        OUT   (0FFH),A      ; START ERASING TAPE
        LD    B,136         ; DELAY FOR 136 CYCLES (995 USEC)
CP3     DJNZ  CP3           ; GIVES TAIL OF CLOCK PULSE
        RET                 ; RETURN TO CALLER

READ NEXT BYTE FROM CASSETTE INTO A REGISTER
        XOR   A             ; CLEAR DESGINATION REGISTER
        PUSH  BC
        PUSH  DE
        PUSH  HL            ; SAVE CALLERS REGISTERS
LOOP    LD    B,8           ; NUMBER OF BITSS TO READ
        CALL  RB            ; READ NEXT BIT. ASSEMBLE INTO
                            ; BYTE BUILT THUS FAR.
        POP   HL
        DJNZ  LOOP          ; LOOP UNTIL 8 BITS USED
        POP   DE
        POP   BC            ; RESTORE CALLERS REGISTERS
        RET                 ; RETURN TO CALLER

RB      PUSH  BC
        PUSH  AF
RB1     IN    (0FFH),A      ; READ DATA LATCH
        RLA                 ; TEST FOR BLANK/NON-BLANK TAPE
        JR    NC,RB1        ; BLANK, SCAN TILL NON-BLANK
                            ; IT WILL BE ASSUMED TO BE START
                            ; OF A CLOCK PULSE.
        LD    B,57          ; DELAY FOR 57 CYCLES WHILE
RB2     DJNZ  RB2           ; SKIPPING OVER FIRST PART OF CP
        LD    A,04          ; COMMAND VALUE: MOTOR ON, CLEAR
        OUT   (0FFH),A      ; DATA LATCHES
        LD    B,193         ; DELAY FOR 193 CYCLES WHILE
RB3     DJNZ  RB3           ; PASSING OVER END OF CP
        IN    A,(0FFH)      ; WE SHOULD BE POSITIONED INTO
                            ; THE DATA PULSE AREA. READ
                            ; THE DATA PULSE.
        LD    B,A           ; SAVE DATA PULSE
        POP   AF            ; ACCUMULATED BYTE THUS FAR
        RL    B             ; DATA PULSE TO CARRY WILL BE A
                            ; ZERO IF BLANK TAPE, 1 IF NON-BLANK
        RLA                 ; COMBINE NEW DATA PULSE (1 BIT)
        PUSH  AF            ; WITH REST OF BYTE AND SAVE
        LD    A,4           ; COMMAND VALUE: MOTOR ON, CLEAR OUTSIG
        OUT   (0FFH),A      ; CLEAR DATA LATCHES
        LD    B,240         ; DELAY LONG ENOUGH TO SKIP TO
RB4     DJNZ  RB4           ; END OF DATA PULSE
        POP   BC
        POP   AF            ; A = DATA BYTE
        RET

TURN OFF MOTOR
        LD    A,00          ; COMMAND VALUE: MOTOR OFF
        OUT   (0FFH),A      ; TURN MOTOR OFF
        RET
```

Disk I/O

The disk operations discussed in this section are elementary inasmuch as there is no consideration given to disk space management or other functions normally associated with disk I/O. What is presented are the fundamental steps necessary to position, read, and write any area of the disk without going through DOS. It will be assumed that the reader is familiar with the I/O facility provided by DOS and is aware of the pitfalls of writing a diskette without going through DOS.

Disks which normally come with a Model I system are single sided, 35 track 5 1/4' mini-drives. It is possible to substitute other drives with a higher track capacity such as 40, 77, or 80 tracks, but then a modified version of DOS must be used. Dual sided mini-drives are becoming available and eventually they should replace the single sided drives. Dual density drives are another type of mini-drive that are available, but like the dual sided drives they require a modified version of DOS.

The type of programming used in this example is called programmed I/O. It is called that because the program must constantly monitor the controller status in order to determine if it is ready to send or recieve the next data byte. Thus each byte is transfered individually under program control. An alternative to programmed I/O is DMA or Direct Memory Access. Using this method the controller is told the number of bytes to transfer and the starting transfer address and it controls the tranfer of data leaving the CPU free to perform other tasks. On the Model I systems there is no DMA facility so programmed I/O must be used.

This example will assume that a DOS formatted diskette is being used. New diskettes are magnetically erased. Before they can be used they must be formatted. That is each sector and track must be uniquely identified by recording its track and sector number in front of the data area of each sector. There is some variability in the coded information which preceeds each sector so it is not always possible to read any mini-diskette unless it orginated on the same type of machine.

Like most of the I/O devices on the Model I the disk is memory mapped. There are five memory locations dedicated to the disk. They are:

37E1	Unit Select Register
37EC	Command/Status Register
37ED	Track Update Register
37EE	Sector Register
37EF	Data Register

All disk commands except for unit selection are sent to **37EC**. If the command being issued will require additional information such as a track or sector number, then that data should be stored in the appropriate register before the command is issued. You may have noticed that the command and status register have the same address.

Because of that, a request for status (load **37EC**) cannot occur for 50 microseconds following the issuing a command (store **37EC**).

Unit selection is accomplished by storing a unit mask value into location **37E1**. That mask has the format:

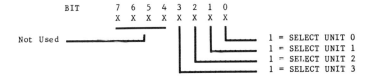

More than one unit can be selected at a time. For example a mask of 3 would select units 0 and 1. When any unit is selected the motor on all units are automatically turned on. This function is performed automatically by the expansion interface.

Controller Commands

The Model I uses a Western Digital FD1771B-01 floppy disk controller chip. It supports twelve 8-bit commands. They are:

Restore: Positions the head to track 0

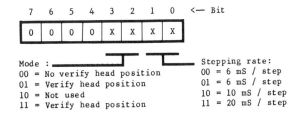

Seek: Positions the head to the track specified in the data register (37E). *37ED*

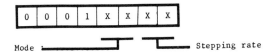

Step: Moves the head one step in the same direction as last head motion.

Step Head In: Moves the head in towards the innermost track one position.

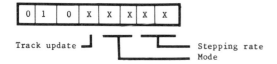

Track update ⌐ Stepping rate / Mode

Step Head Out: Moves the head out towards the outermost track one position.

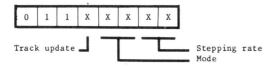

Track update ⌐ Stepping rate / Mode

Read Data: Transmits the next byte of data from the sector specified by the value in the sector register.

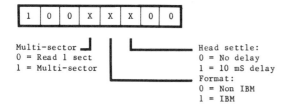

Multi-sector
0 = Read 1 sect
1 = Multi-sector

Head settle:
0 = No delay
1 = 10 mS delay
Format:
0 = Non IBM
1 = IBM

Write Data: Sends the byte of data in the data register to the next position in the sector specified by the value in the sector register.

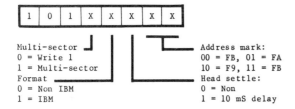

Multi-sector
0 = Write 1
1 = Multi-sector
Format
0 = Non IBM
1 = IBM

Address mark:
00 = FB, 01 = FA
10 = F9, 11 = FB
Head settle:
0 = Non
1 = 10 mS delay

Read Track: Reads an entire track beginning with the index mark.

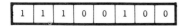

Read Address: Reads the address field from the next sector to pass under the head.

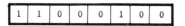

Write Track: Writes a full track starting at the index mark and continuing until the next index mark is encountered.

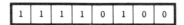

Force Interrupt: Terminates the current operation and / or generates an interrupt if one of the following four conditions is true:

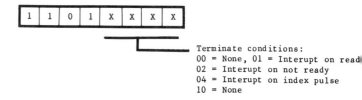

Terminate conditions:
00 = None, 01 = Interupt on read
02 = Interupt on not ready
04 = Interupt on index pulse
10 = None

Read Status: The status of the Floppy Controller is returned whenever location **37EC** is read. The status word has the following format:

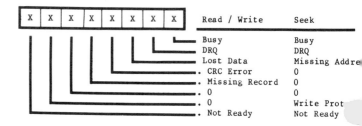

	Read / Write	Seek
Busy	Busy	Busy
DRQ	DRQ	DRQ
Lost Data	Lost Data	Missing Addre
. CRC Error	CRC Error	0
. Missing Record	Missing Record	0
. 0	0	0
. 0	0	Write Prot
. Not Ready	Not Ready	Not Ready

Disk Programming Details

Disk programming can be broken down into several easily managed steps. They are:

1. Select the unit and wait for ready.
2. Position the head over the desired track.
3. Isue the Read/Write command for the required sector
4. Transfer a sectors worth of data, on a byte at a time basis.

Each transfer must be preceeded by a test to see if the controller either has the next data byte, or is ready to accept the next data byte.

This program demonstrates a single sector read from track 25 (decimal), sector 3.

```
       ORG    7000H
       LD     BC,256        ; BYTE COUNT
       PUSH   BC            ; BC =1 C = 0
       LD     HL,BUFF       ; BUFFER ADDRESS
       LD     A,1           ; UNIT SELECT MASK (DRIVE 0)
       LD     (37E1H),A     ; SELECT DRIVE 0, START MOTOR
       LD     D,25          ; TRACK NUMBER
       LD     E,3           ; SECTOR NUMBER
       LD     (37EEH),DE    ; SPECIFY TRACK AND SECTOR
                            ; TRACK NO. TO DATA REGISTER
                            ; (37EFH)
                            ; SECTOR NO. TO SECTOR REGISTER.
       LD     A,1BH         ; SEEK OP CODE. NO VERIFY
                            ; (FOR VERIFY 17H)
       LD     (37ECH),A     ; SEEK REQ. TO COMMAND REGISTER.
       LD     B,6           ; GIVE CONTROLLER A CHANCE
                            ; TO DIGEST
DELAY  DJNZ   DELAY         ; COMMAND BEFORE ASKING STATUS
WAIT   LD     A,(37ECH)     ; GET STATUS OF SEEK OP
       BIT    0,A           ; TEST IF CONTROLLER BUSY
       JR     NZ,WAIT       ; IF YES, THEN SEEK NOT DONE
       LD     A,88H         ; SEEK FINISHED. LOAD READ
                            ; COMMAND
       LD     (37ECH),A     ; AND SEND TO CONTROLLER
       LD     B,6           ; GIVE CONTROLLER A CHANCE TO
DELAY1 DJNZ   DELAY1        ; DIGEST COMMAND BEFORE
                            ; REQUESTING
                            ; A STATUS
WAIT1  LD     A,(37ECH)     ; NOW, ASK FOR STATUS
       BIT    1,A           ; IS THERE A DATA BYTE PRESENT ?
       JR     Z,WAIT1       ; NO, WAIT TILL ONE COMES IN
       LD     A,(37EFH)     ; YES, LOAD DATA BYTE
       LD     (HL),A        ; STORE IN BUFFER
       INC    HL            ; BUMP TO NEXT BUFF ADDR
       DEC    BC            ; TEST FOR 256 BYTES TRANSFERED
       LD     A,B           ; COMBINE B AND C
       OR     C             ; TO TEST BOTH REGISTERS
       JR     NZ,WAIT       ; GO GET NEXT BYTE
       .
       .
       .
```

DOS Exits

DOS Exits were discussed in general terms in chapter 1. They are used as a means of passing control between Level II BASIC and Disk BASIC. The Exit itself is a CALL instruction in the ROM portion of the system to a fixed address in the Communications Region. Contained at that CALL'd address will be either a RETURN instruction or a JUMP to another address in Disk BASIC. On a Level II system without disks these CALL'd locations are set to RETURNS during IPL processing. On disk based systems they are not initialized until the BASIC command is executed. At that time JUMPS to specific addresses within Disk BASIC are stored at the CALL locations.

The term DOS Exit really has two different meanings. DOS Exits are calls from ROM BASIC to Disk BASIC while in the Input Phase, while executing a system level command, or while executing a verb action routine. These exits allow extensions to be made to the routines in ROM. The exits are not strategically located so that an entire ROM routine could be usurped, but they are conveniently placed for intercepting the majority of the ROM routine processing. Another type of DOS Exit is the Disk BASIC Exit. These exits are radically different from the other ones, they are only entered on demand when a Disk BASIC token is encountered during the Execution Phase. All of the processing associated with these tokens is contained in the Disk BASIC program. There is no code in ROM for executing these tokens.

The following descriptions are for DOS Exits as opposed to Disk BASIC Exits. The calling sequence for each of the DOS Exits vary. Before writing a program to replace any of these Exits study the code around the CALL, paying particular attention to register usage. What happens at the exits is not discussed here. If it is important, disassemble the Disk BASIC utility program and examine the code at the BASIC address assigned to the exit. An example of how both types of Exits can be intercepted can be found in chapter 6.

All these addresses are for NEWDOS 2.1, TRSDOS addresses will differ.

Level II ADDRESS	DESCRIPTION	DOS Exits ADDRESS	BASIC ADDRESS
19EC	Call to load DISK BASIC error processing. Error number must be in E-register.	41A6	
27FE	Start of USR processing	41A9	5679
1A1C	BASIC start up. Just before BASIC's 'READY' message.	41AC	5FFC
0368......	At start of keyboard input.	41AF	598E
1AA1	Input scanner after tokenizing ..... current statement.	41B2	6033
1AEC	Input scanner after udating .... program statement table.	41B5	5BD7
1AF2	Input scanner after reinitial- ..... izing BASIC.	41B8	5B8C
1B8C/1DB0	Initializing BASIC for .... new routine. During END processing.	41BB	60A1
2174	During initializing of system ...... output device.	41BE	577C
032C	During writing to system output .... device.	41C1	59CD
0358	When scanning keyboard. Called ..... from INKEY$, at end of execution of each BASIC statement.	41C4	59CD
1EA6	At start of RUN NNN .... processing.	41C7	5F78
206F	At beginning of PRINT .... processing.	41CA	5A15
20C6	During PRINT # or PRINT .... item processing.	41CD	5B9A
2103	When skipping to next line on .... video during a BASIC output operation.	41D0	5B99
2108/2141	At start of PRINT on cassette .... and during PRINT TAB processing.	41D3	5B65
219E	At beginning of INPUT processing. ...	41D6	5784
222D	During READ processing when a .... variable has been read.	41DC	5E63
2278/2278	At end of READ processing	41DF	579C
2B44/2B44	From LIST processing.		
02B2.....	During SYSTEM command operation.	41E2	5B51

Disk BASIC Exits

These exits are made from Level II during the Execution Phase whenever a token in the range of **BC - FA** is encountered. Tokens with those values are assigned to statements which are executed entirely by Disk BASIC. When a token in the given range is found control is passed indirectly through the Verb Action Routine List (see chapter 4) to the appropriate Disk BASIC Exit in the Communications Region. Control is returned to Level II at the end of the verb routine's processing.

TOKEN	VERB	CR ADDRESS	DISK BASIC ADDRESS
E6	CVI	4152	5E46
BE	FN	4155	558E
E7	CVS	4158	5E49
B0	DEF	415B	5655
E8	CVD	415E	5E4C
E9	EOF	4161	61EB
EA	LOC	4164	6231
EB	LOF	4167	6242
EC	MKI$	416A	5E2D
ED	MKS$	416D	5E30
EE	MKD$	4170	5E33
85	CMD	4173	56C4
C7	TIME$	4176	5714
A2	OPEN	4179	6349
A3	FIELD	417C	60AB
A4	GET	417F	627C
A5	PUT	4182	627B
A6	CLOSE	4185	606F
A7	LOAD	4188	5F7B
A8	MERGE	418B	600B
A9	NAME	418E	6346
AA	KILL	4191	63C0
NONE	&	4194	58B7
AB	LSET	4197	60E6
AC	RSET	419A	60E5
C5	INSTR	419D	582F
AD	SAVE	41A0	6044
9C	LINE	41A3	5756
C1	USR	41A9	5679

Disk Tables

The most frequently used disks on the Model I series are 5 1/4' single sided single density mini-floppy drives. A variety of other units are available and could be used, however some hardware and software modifications would be necessary. Examples of other units would be: 5 1/4' dual headed and dual density drives; 8' single and dual headed plus single and dual density units; and various hard disks with capacities up to 20 Mbytes.

The terms single and dual headed refer to the number of read/write heads in a unit. Most micro-computer systems use single headed drives but dual headed drives are now becoming more commonplace. A dual headed drive has twice the capacity of a single headed unit because two disk surfaces can be accessed rather than one.

Dual density describes the recording method used. In single density mode each bit cell consists of a clock pulse followed by a data pulse while in dual density recording clock pulses may be omitted if the data pulse is repetitious. Using this method more sectors can be written on a track than in single density format. The recording method used is dictated by the controller and the software, but with dual density drives clock pulses may be omitted and the timing is more critical, hence not all drives can be used for dual density.

Eight inch drives are essentially the same as 5 1/4' drives except they usually only come in one track size (77 tracks). As with the smaller units they come in both single and dual density. Since their radius is larger they have more sectors per track. Track capacities for 8' drives are typically: 26 - 128 byte sectors / track; 15 - 256 byte sectors / track; 8 - 512 byte sectors / track; 4 - 1024 byte sectors / track.

Track capacities for 5 1/4' single density are: 20 - 128 byte sectors / track; 10 - 256 byte sectors / track; 5 - 512 byte sectors / track; and 2 - 1024 byte sectors / track. Dual density 5 1/4' drives have capacities of: 32 - 128 byte sectors / track; 18 - 256 byte sectors / track; 08 - 512 byte sectors / track; and 4 - 1024 byte sectors / track.

Hard disks are too varied to classify. Basically a hard disk has more capacity, faster access time, higher transfer rates, but the disk itself may not be removeable. Without a removeable disk file backup can be a serious problem, a second hard disk is an expensive solution.

Shown below is a diagram of a 5 1/4' 35 track diskette.

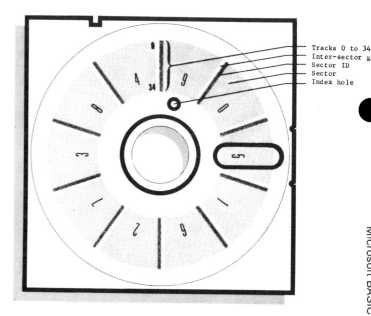

Tracks 0 to 34
Inter-sector g
Sector ID
Sector
Index hole

Each diskette has 35, 40, 77, or 80 tracks depending on the drive used. Each track has 10 sectors of 256 bytes. Sector sizes can vary from 2 to 1024 bytes per sector. But the software must be modified to handle anything other than 256, because that is the size assumed by DOS. The Model I uses a semi IBM compatible sector format. It is not 100% compatible because track and sector numbers on IBM diskettes are numbered from 1 not 0 as in TRSDOS.

DOS uses a file directory to keep a record of file names and their assigned tracks and sectors. The directory occupies all 10 sectors of track number 11. It is composed of three parts: a disk map showing available sectors (track 11, sector 1); a file name in use index that allows the directory to be searched from an advanced starting point (called the Hash Index Table track 11, sector 2); and the directory sectors themselves (track 11 sector 3 thru track 11 sector 10).

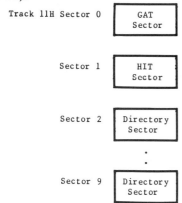

Track 11H Sector 0 — GAT Sector

Sector 1 — HIT Sector

Sector 2 — Directory Sector

Sector 9 — Directory Sector

As well as the directory track there is one other special area on a diskette. Track 0 sector 0 contains a system loader used during the disk IPL sequence to load DOS. The loader is read into RAM locations 4200 - 4300 by the ROM IPL code which then passes control to it so that the DOS can be loaded.

Disk Track Format

Before any diskette can be used it must be initialized rmatted either the FORMAT or COPY (BACKUP if using TRSDOS) utility programs. Formatting initializes the diskette which is orginally magnetically erased. The formatting operation writes the sector addresses for every addressable sector plus synch bytes which will be used by the controller to aid it locating specific addresses. In addition the formatting operation specifies the sector size, the number of sectors per track, and the physical order of the sectors .

Mini-floppys are usually formatted with 128, 256, 512, or 1024 byte sectors although other sizes may be formatted. DOS uses the following track format:

Position	Number of Bytes	Contents
Index	14	FF
	6	00
	1	FE (Address marker)
	1	Track Number
	1	Head Number
One	1	Sector Number
Sector.	1	Sector Length Code :
		00 = 128 bytes
Ten per		01 = 256 bytes
track.		02 = 512 bytes
		03 = 1024 bytes
Sector	2	CRC
order is	11	FF : Sector 0 only, 12
0,5,1,6,	1	A0 : bytes of FF all others
2,7,3,8,	1	FA (Data Field Mark)
4,9.	256	Data
	2	CRC
	12	FF : Except the last (9)
	6	00 : which is followed by
	FE	130 bytes of FF

GAT Sector   (Track 11 Sector 1)

Previously we mentioned the file directory system used by DOS. It is based in part on the ability to dynamically

assign disk space on an as-needed basis. Conversely, it must be possible to reuse space which has been released and is no longer needed. The basic vehicle used for keeping track of assigned and available disk space is the Granuale Allocation Table (GAT). Obviously, GAT data must be stored outside the machine if a permanent record is to be maintained. The GAT sector is used for this storage.

With the disk descripton there was a definition for a track and sector. These terms will now be re-defined into the DOS term granule. A granule is 5 sectors or half of a track. It is the minimum unit of disk space that is allocated or de-allocated. Granules are numbered from 0 to N, where N is a function of the number of tracks on a diskette. A record of all granules assigned is maintained in the GAT sector. Recalling the disk dimensions mentioned earlier we can compute the number of granules on a diskette as:

$$Granule = (Number\ of\ tracks\ *\ 10)\ /\ 5$$

Using a 35 track drive with the default DOS disk values of 10 sectors per track and 5 sectors per granule this gives 70 granules per diskette.

The GAT sector is divided into three parts. The first part is the actual GAT table where a record of GAT's assigned is maintained. Part two contains a track lock out table, and part three system initialization information.

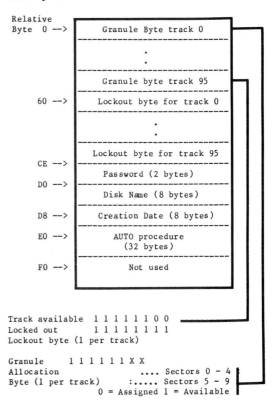

Relative Byte	
0 -->	Granule Byte track 0
	.
	Granule byte track 95
60 -->	Lockout byte for track 0
	.
	Lockout byte for track 95
CE -->	Password (2 bytes)
D0 -->	Disk Name (8 bytes)
D8 -->	Creation Date (8 bytes)
E0 -->	AUTO procedure (32 bytes)
F0 -->	Not used

```
Track available  1 1 1 1 1 1 0 0
Locked out       1 1 1 1 1 1 1 1
Lockout byte (1 per track)

Granule          1 1 1 1 1 1 X X
Allocation            .... Sectors 0 - 4
Byte (1 per track)    :.... Sectors 5 - 9
             0 = Assigned  1 = Available
```

Hash Index Table   (Track 11 Sector 2)

The Hash Index is a method used to rapidly locate a file without searching all of the directory sectors until it is found. Each file has a unique value computed from its name. This value is called the Hash Code. A special sector in the directory contains the Hash Codes for all

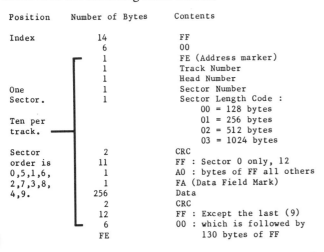

active files on a diskette. When a file is created, its Hash Code is stored in the hash sector in a position that corresponds to the directory for that file. Note, the hash position does not give the file position, just its directory sector position. When a file is KILL'd it code is removed from the hash sector.

Files are located by first computing their hash value, the Hash Index Sector is then searched for this value. if it is not found then the file does not exist. If the code is found then its position in the Hash Index Sector is used to compute the address for the directory sector containing the file name entry.

Hash code values range from **01** to **FF**. They are computed from an 11 character file name that has been left justified, blank filled. Any file name extension is the last three characters of the name. The code used for computing a hash value is shown below:

```
        LD      B,11        NO. OF CHARS TO HASH
        LD      C,0         ZERO HASH REGISTER
LOOP    LD      A,(DE)      GET ONE CHAR OF NAME
        INC     DE          BUMP TO NEXT CHAR
        XOR     C           HASH REG. XOR. NEXT CHAR
        RLCA                2*(HR. XOR. NC)
        LD      C,A         NEW HR
        DJNZ    LOOP        HASH ALL CHARS
        LD      A,C         GET HASH VALUE
        OR      A           DON'T ALLOW ZERO
        JMP     DONE        EXIT, HASH IN A
        INC     A           FORCE HASH TO 1
DONE    .                   EXIT, HASH IN A
        .
```

Space for codes in the Hash Sector is assigned sequentially beginning at an arbitrary point. If the hash sector is full a DOS error code of **1A** is given otherwise the sector is scanned in a circular manner until the first available (zero) entry is found.

Not all words in the Hash Sector are used. Addresses in the range 10 - 1F, 30 - 3F, 50 - 5F are excluded. Only those addresses ending in the digits 00 - 07, 20 - 27 etc are assigned. This speeds the computation of the directory sector number from the hash code value address. The Hash Sector is shown below.

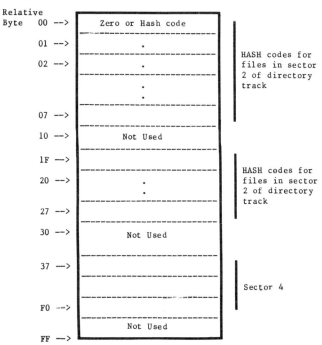

Disk DCB

Each disk file has associated with it a 32 byte DCB which is defined in the user's memory space. When the file is opened the DCB must contain the file name, a name extension if any, and an optional drive specification. As part of the OPEN processing the DCB is initialized for READ and WRITE operations by copying portions of the directory entry into the DCB. After initialization the DCB appears as shown.

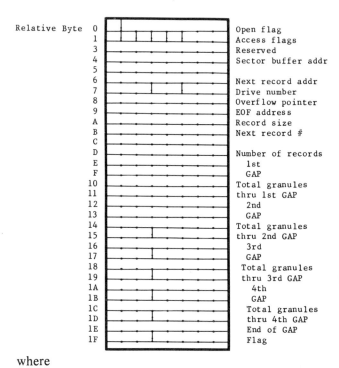

where

```
BYTE   0  bits 0-6 : reserved
          bit  7   : 0 = file not opened
                     1 = file opened

BYTE   1  bits 0-2 : access permission flag.
          bit  3   : reserved
          bit  4   : 0 = sector buffer available
                     1 = flush sector buffer befor using
          bit  5   : 0 = look for record in current buffer
                     1 = unconditionally read next sector
          bit  6   : reserved
          bit  7   : 0 = sector I/O
                     1 = logical record I/O
BYTE   2      reserved
BYTE   3 - 4  sector buffer address in LSB/MSB order
BYTE   5      pointer to next record in buffer
BYTE   6      drive number
BYTE   7      bits 0-3  sector number - 2 of  overflow entry
              bits 3-4  reserved
              bits 5-7  offset/16 to primary entry in directory
BYTE   8      pointer to end of file in last sector
BYTE   9      record size
BYTE  10 - 11 next record number in LSB/MSB format
BYTE  12 - 13 number of records in file
BYTE  14 - 15 first GAP
BYTE  16 - 17 total granules assigned thru first
BYTE  18 - 19 second GAP
BYTE  20 - 21 total granules assigned thru second GAP
BYTE  22 - 23 third GAP
BYTE  24 - 25 total granules assigned thru third GAP
BYTE  26 - 27 fourth GAP
BYTE  28 - 29 total granules assigned thru fourth GAP
BYTE  30 - 31 end of GAP string flag (FFFF)
```

Directory Sector (Track 11 Sector 3 - Track 11 Sector 9)

Directory sectors contain file descriptions used when accessing a disk file. These descriptions contain among other things the file name, passwords, and a list of the disk addresses occupied by the file. The directory sectors are divided into eight fixed-length partitions of thirty two bytes each. Each partition contains one file description. Empty partitions are indicated by a flag in the first byte of the partition.

Space in the directory is assigned when a file is initially created using a DOS OPEN or INIT call. There is no particular order in the way space is assigned because the directory sector number used is determined by a hash code derived from the file name. Partition space in the sector is assigned in sequential order.

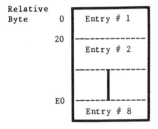

```
BYTE 0    bits 0-2 = file access control flags
          000 - unrestricted access
          001 - KILL/RENAME/WRITE/READ/EXECUTE access
          010 - RENAME/WRITE/READ/EXECUTE access
          011 - reserved
          100 - WRITE/READ/EXECUTE access
          101 - READ/EXECUTE access
          110 - EXECUTE access only
          111 - restricted file no access

          bit 3  = 0, file is displayable. 1, file is invisible.
          bit 4  = 0, this entry is available. 1, entry is
          bit 5  = reserved
          bit 6  = 0, user file. 1, SYSTEM file.
          bit 7  = 0, primary entry. 1, overflow entry.

BYTE 1    used for overflow entries only.
          Bits 0 - 3 byte offset/10 in primary sector to the entry
          for this file
          Bits 4 - 7 sector number - 2 of primary entry.
BYTE 2    Reserved
BYTE 3    Bits 0 - 7  byte offset to end of file in last sector.
BYTE 4    Bits 0 - 7  record length.

BYTES 5 - 12    File name in ASCII, left justified, blank filled.
BYTES 13 - 15   File name extension in ASCII left justified, blank filled.
BYTES 16 - 17   Update password (encoded).
BYTES 18 - 19   Access password (encoded).
BYTES 20 - 21   Last sector number in file. LSB/MSB order.
BYTES 22 - 31   Five two-byte entries called Granule Assignment
                Pairs (GAPs). Each GAP consists of a starting track number
                (byte 1) and a count of the number of consecutively
                asssigned granules (byte 2). A string of these GAP's in
                proper order define the disk addresses assigned
                to a file. The end of a GAP string will be signaled by
                a FF in bytes 1 and 2 if there are no more than five
                GAP assigned, for an FE followed by the disk address of
                another directory sector containing the remainder of
                the GAP's. The directory entry containing the overflow
                GAP's is called an overflow entry and contains only the
                continuation of the GAP string. There is no limit to the
                number of overflow entries that may be assigned.
                GAP bytes are formatted sa shown below
```

1st Byte: Bits 0 - 7 contain one of the following:
a) If the contents of 1st byte is less than FE it is assumed to be a track number.
b) An FF if there are no more GAP's. This is the end of a GAP string
c) An FE if there are more GAP entries in an overflow sector. The next byte contains the overflow sector address.

2nd Byte: The intrepretation of this byte depends on the contents of the preceeding byte. If = FF, then this byte is not contains an FF.
If preceeding byte = FE, then:
holds in bits 0 - 3 the sector number - 2 of overflow sector.
bits 4 - 7 the byte offset/10 in the overflow sector to the entry with the remainder of the GAPs'.
If preceeding byte < FE, then this byte has in bits 0 - 3 the number of consecutive granules minus 1. This value varies from 0 up to 1r.
Bit 4 = a flag indicating whether the first or second granule in the starting track has been assigned. If bit 4 = 0, then the first granule was assigned. if bit 4 = 1, then the second granule starts with sector.
5) was assigned.

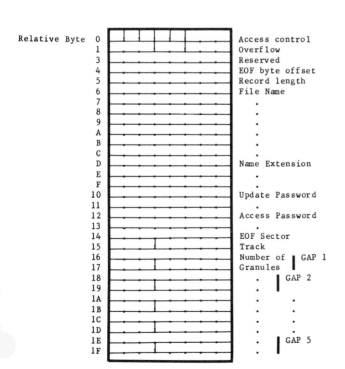

Following is an example of a GAP string:

```
byte 22: 23    file starts on track 23
byte 23: 06    there are 7 granules assigned
               TRK (23) S(0-9), TRK (24) S(0-9)
               TRK (25) S(0-0), TRK (26) S(0-4)
----------------------------------------------
byte 24: 15    file continues on track 15
byte 25: 23    for 4 granules
               TRK (15) S(5-9), TRK (16) S(0-9)
               TRK (17) S(0-4)
----------------------------------------------
byte 26: FF    end of GAP string
byte 27: FF    end of GAP string
----------------------------------------------
```

Chapter 4

Addresses & Tables

Adddress
(Hex)

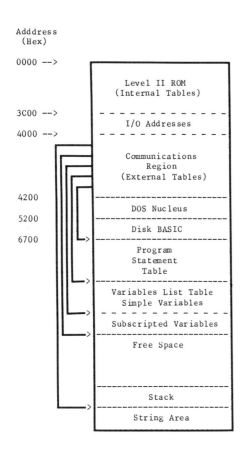

Level II Internal Tables

Internal tables are those lists and tables that are resident in the Level II system. Since they are ROM resident their contents and address are fixed. They are used by BASIC for syntax analysis, during expression evaluation, for data conversions, and while executing such statements as FOR and IF.

Reserved Word List   (1650 - 1821)

This table contains all of the word reserved for use by the BASIC interpreter. Each entry contains a reserved word with bit 8 turned on. During the Input Phase the incoming line is scanned for words in this list. Any occurance of one is replaced by a token representing it. The token is computed as 80 plus the index into the table where the word was found. A list of those words and their token values follows:

Word	Token	Word	Token	Word	Token
END.........80		FOR.......81		RESET.....82	
SET.........83		CLS.......84		*CMD.......85	
RANDOM......86		NEXT......87		DATA......88	
INPUT.......89		DIM.......8A		READ......8B	
LET.........8C		GOTO......8D		RUN.......8E	
IF..........8F		RESTORE...90		GOSUB.....91	
RETURN......92		REM.......93		STOP......94	
ELSE........95		TRON......96		TROFF.....97	
DEFSTR......98		DEFINT....99		DEFSNG....9A	
DEFDBL......9B		*LINE.....9C		EDIT......9D	
ERROR.......9E		RESUM.....9F		OUT.......A0	
ON..........A1		*OPEN.....A2		*FIELD....A3	
*GET........A4		*PUT......A5		*CLOSE....A6	
*LOAD.......A7		*MERGE....A8		*NAME.....A9	
*KILL.......AA		*LSET.....AB		*RSET.....AC	
*SAVE.......AD		SYSTEM....AE		LPRINT....AF	
*DEF........B0		POKE......B1		PRINT.....B2	
CONT........B3		LIST......B4		LLIST.....B5	
DELETE......B6		AUTO......B7		CLEAR.....B8	
CLOAD.......B9		CSAVE.....BA		NEW.......BB	
TAB(........BC		TO........BD		*FN.......BE	
USING.......BF		VARPTR....C0		USR.......C1	
ERL.........C2		ERR.......C3		STRING$...C4	
INSTR.......C5		POINT.....C6		*TIME$....C7	
MEM.........C8		INKEY$....C9		THEN......CA	
NOT.........CB		STEP......CC		+.........CD	
-...........CE		*.........CF		/.........D0	
UP ARROW....D1		AND.......D2		OR........D3	
>...........D4		=.........D5		<.........D6	
SGN.........D7		INT.......D8		ABS.......D9	
FRE.........DA		INP.......DB		POS.......DC	
SQR.........DD		RND.......DE		LOG.......DF	
EXP.........E0		COS.......E1		SIN.......E2	
TAN.........E3		ATN.......E4		PEEK......E5	
*CVI........E6		*CVS......E7		*CVD......E8	
*EOF........E9		*LOC......EA		*LOF......EB	
*MKI$.......EC		*MKS$.....ED		CINT......EF	
CSNG........F0		CDBL......F1		FIX.......F2	
LEN.........F3		STR$......F4		VAL.......F5	
ASC.........F6		CHR$......F7		LEFT$.....F8	
RIGHT$......F9		*MID$.....FA		´.........FB	

* Disk BASIC tokens

Precedence Operator Values (189A - 18A0)

This table contains numeric values used to determine the order of arithmetic operations when evaluating an expression. As the expression is scanned each operator/operand pair plus the precedence value for the previous operand is stored on the stack. When an operator of higher precedence than the preceeding one is found the current operation is performed giving an intermediate value that is carried forward on the stack. The values shown for relational operations are computed rather than being derived from a table look-up.

Operator	Function	Precedence Value
UP ARROW	(Exponent)	7F
*	(Multiplication)	7C
/	(Division)	7C
+	(Addition)	79
–	(Subtraction)	79
ANY	(Relational)	64
AND	(Logical)	50
OR	(Logical)	46
<=	(Relational)	06
<>	(Relational)	05
>=	(Relational)	03
<	(Relational)	04
=	(Relational)	02
>	(Relational)	01

Arithmetic Routines (18AB - 18C8)

There are really three tables back-to-back here. They are used during expression evaluation to compute intermediate values when a higher precedence operator is found.

Arithmetic Routine Addresses

	Integer	Single Precision	Double Precision	String
Addition	0BD2	0716	0C77	298F
Subtraction	0BC7	0713	0C70	NONE
Multiplication	0BF2	0847	0DA1	NONE
Division	2490	08A2	0DE5	NONE
Comparison	0A39	0A0C	0A78	NONE

Data Conversion Routines (18A1 - 18AA)

These routines convert the value in WRA1 from one mode to another. They are called by the expression evaluator when an intermediate computation has been made, and the result needs to be make compatible with the rest of the expression.

Conversion Routine Addresses

Destination Mode	Address
String	0AF4
Integer	0A7F
Single Precision	0AB1
Double Precision	0ADB
Verb Action Addresses	

Verb Action Routines (1822 - 1899)

There are two Verb Action Address Lists. The first one is used by the execution driver when beginning execution of a new statement. It contains address of of verb routines for the tokens 80 - BB. The first token of the statement is used as an index in the range of 0 - 60 into the table at 1822 - 1899 to find the address of the verb routine to be executed. If the statement does not begin with a token control goes to assignment statement processing. The second table contains the addresses of verb routines which can only occur on the right side of an equals sign. If during the expression evaluation stage a token in the range of D7 - FA is encountred it is used as an index into the table at 1608 - 164F, where the address of the verb routine to be executed is found. There is no address list for the tokens BC - D6 because they are associated with and follow other tokens that expect and process them.

(Table Address 1822 – 1899)

Token	Verb	Address	Token	Verb	Address
80	END	1DAE	81	FOR	1CA1
82	RESET	0138	83	SET	0135
84	CLS	01C9	85	CMD	4135
86	RANDOM	01D3	87	NEXT	22B6
88	DATA	1F05	89	INPUT	219A
8A	DIM	2608	8B	READ	21EF
8C	LET	1F21	8D	GOTO	1EC2
8E	RUN	1EA3	8F	IF	2039
90	RESTORE	1D91	91	GOSUB	1EB1
92	RETURN	1EDE	93	REM	1F07
94	STOP	1DA9	95	ELSE	1F07
96	TRON	1DF7	97	TROFF	1DF8
98	DEFSTR	1E00	99	DEFINT	1E03
9A	DEFSNG	1E06	9B	DEFDBL	1E09
9C	LINE	41A3	9D	EDIT	2E60
9E	ERROR	1FF4	9F	RESUME	1FAF
A0	OUT	2AFB	A1	ON	1FC6
A2	OPEN	4179	A3	FIELD	417C
A4	GET	417F	A5	PUT	4182
A6	CLOSE	4185	A7	LOAD	4188
A8	MERGE	418B	A9	NAME	418E
AA	KILL	4191	AB	LSET	4197
AC	RSET	419A	AD	SAVE	41A0
AE	SYSTEM	02B2	AF	LPRINT	2067
B0	DEF	41B5	B1	POKE	2CB1
B2	PRINT	206F	B3	CONT	1DE4
B4	LIST	2B2E	B5	LLIST	2B29
B6	DELETE	2BC6	B7	AUTO	2008
B8	CLEAR	1E7A	B9	CLOAD	2C1F
BA	CSAVE	2BF5	BB	NEW	1B49

(Table Address 1608 – 164F)

TOKEN	VERB	Address	TOKEN	VERB	Address
D7	SGN	098A	D8	INT	0B37
D9	ABS	0977	DA	FRE	27D4
DB	INP	2AEF	DC	POS	27A5
DD	SQR	13E7	DE	RND	14C9
DF	LOG	0809	E0	EXP	1439
E1	COS	1541	E2	SIN	1547
E3	TAN	15A8	E4	ATN	15BD
E5	PEEK	2CAA	E6	CVI	4152
E7	CVS	4158	E8	CVD	415E
E9	EOF	4161	EA	LOC	4164
EB	LOF	4167	EC	MKI$	416A
ED	MKS$	416D	EE	MKD$	4170
EF	CINT	0A7F	F0	CSNG	0AB1
F1	CDBL	0DAB	F2	FIX	0B26
F3	LEN	2A03	F4	STR$	2836
F5	VAL	2AC5	F6	ASC	2A0F
F7	CHR$	2A1F	F8	LEFT$	2A61
F9	RIGHT$	2A91	FA	MID$	2A9A

Error Code Table   (18C9 - 18F6)

Error codes printed under Level II are intrepreted by using the error number as in index into a table of two letter error abbreviations. The format of the error code table is as follows:

Error Number	Code	Cause	Originating Address
0	NF	NEXT WITHOUT FOR	22C2
2	SN	SYNTAX ERROR (NUMEROUS CAUSES)	DA,2C7,EEF 1C9E,1D32,1E0E 1E66,2022,235B 2615,2AE9,2DE2
4	RG	RETURN WITHOUT GOSUB	1EEC
6	OD	OUT OF DATA (READ)	2214,22A2
8	FC	NUMEROUS	1E4C
A	OV	NUMERIC OVERFLOW	7B2
C	OM	OUT OF MEMORY	197C
E	UL	MISSING LINE NUMBER	1EDB
10	BS	INDEX TOO LARGE	273F
12	DD	DOUBLY DEFINED SYMBOL	2735
14	0/	DIVISION BY 0	8A5,DE9,1401
16	ID	INPUT USE INCORRECT	2833
18	TM	VAIRABLE NOT A STRING	AF8
1A	OS	OUT OF STRING SPACE	28DD
1C	LS	STRING TOO LONG	29A5
1E	ST	LITERAL STRING POOL TABLE FULL	28A3
20	CN	CONTINUE NOT ALLOWED	1DEB
22	NR	RESUME NOT ALLOWED	198C
24	UE	INVALID ERROR CODE	2005
26	UE	INVALID ERROR CODE	2005
28	MO	OPERAND MISSING	24A2
2A	FD	DATA ERROR ON CASSETTE	218C
2C	L3	DISK BASIC STATEMENT ATTEMPTED UNDER LEVEL II	12DF

Level II External Tables

External tables used by Level II are those which are kept in RAM. They are kept there because their contents and size, as well as their address, may change. A pointer to each of the External tables is maintained in the Communications Region.

Mode Table   (4101 - 411A)

This table is used by the BASIC intrepreter to determine the data type mode (integer, string, single or double precision) for each variable. Although it never moves its contents may change when a DEF declaration is encountered, and therefore it must be in RAM. It is the only RAM table with a fixed address and consequently there is no pointer to it in the Communications Region. The table is 26 decimal words long and is indexed by using the first character of a variable name as an index. Each entry in the table contains a code indicating the variable type e.g. 02 - integer, 03 - string, 04 - single precision, 08 - double precision.

The mode table is initialized during the IPL sequence to 04 for all variables. It appears as:

Address	Letter	Type	Address	Letter	Type
4101	A	04	4102	B	04
4103	C	04	4104	D	04
4105	E	04	4106	F	04
4107	G	04	4108	H	04
4109	I	04	410A	J	04
410B	K	04	410C	L	04
410D	M	04	410E	N	04
410F	O	04	4110	P	04
4111	Q	04	4112	R	04
4113	S	04	4114	T	04
4115	U	04	4116	V	04
4117	W	04	4118	X	04
4119	Y	04	411A	Z	04

Program Statement Table (PST)

The Program Statement Table contains BASIC statements entered as a program. Since it is RAM resident and its orgin may change from system to system there is a pointer to it in the Communications Region at address **40A4**. As each line is entered it is tokenized and stored in the PST. Statements are stored in ascending order by line number regardless of the order in which they are entered. Each entry begins with a two byte pointer to the next line followed by a two byte integer equivalent of the line number then the text of the BASIC statement. The body of the statement is terminated with a single byte of zeros called the End Of Statement or EOS flag. The ending address of the PST is contained in **40F9**. It is terminated by two bytes of zeros.

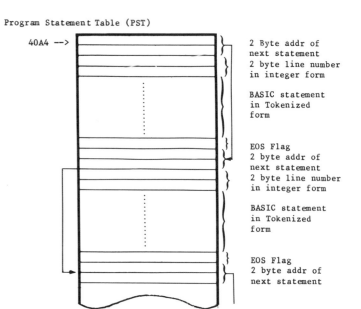

Program Statement Table (PST)

Shown below are two statements and their representation in the PST:

```
100    A = COS ( 1.6 )
110    IF A > .5 THEN 500
```

44

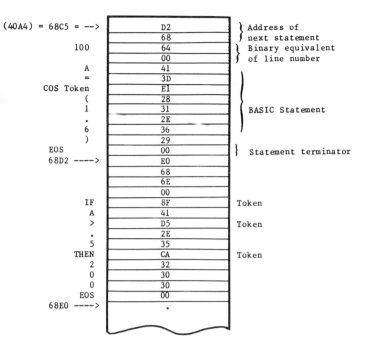

Variable List Table (VLT)

This table contains all variables assigned to a BASIC program. Internally the table is divided into two sections. Section one contains entries for all non-subscripted and string variables while section two contains the values for all subscripted variables. Like the PST the VLT is RAM resident and it has two pointers in the Communications Region. Location **40F9** contains the address of the first section, and **40FB** contains the address of section two. The starting address of the VLT is considered as the end of the PST.

Regardless of which section a variable is defined in, the first three bytes of each entry have the same format. Byte one has a type code (2,3,4,or 8), which doubles as the length of the entry. Bytes two and three contain the variable name in last/first character order. Following this is the value itself in LSB/MSB order, or if it as a string variable a pointer to the string in the String Area.

Section two contains all dimensioned arrays. These entries have the same three byte header followed by a another header which defines the extents of the array. The array is stored after the second header in column-major order.

Variables are assigned space in the VLT as they are encountered (in a DIM statement or in any part of an assignment statement). There is no alphabetical ordering. Because space is assigned on demand it is possible for previously defined variables to be moved down. For example, if A, B, and C(5) were defined followed by D, C(5) would be moved down because section one would be increased for D. This would force section two to be moved.

```
(40F9) -->   Simple &
             String
             Variables
           ---------------
(40FB) -->   Dimensioned
             Variables
```

Arrays are stored in column-major order. In that order the left most index varies the fastest. For example the array A(2,3) would be stored in memory as:

A(0,0)
A(1,0)
A(2,0)
.
.
.
A(0,3)
A(1,3)
A(2,3)

An index for any element can be computed using the formula:

$$INDEX = (((LRI*0)+URI)*LMI)+UMI)*LLI)+ULI$$

where

LRI = limit of right index
LMI = limit of middle index
LLI = limit of left index

URI = user's current right index
UMI = user's current middle index
ULI = user's current left index

The code used to compute these indexes may be found at address **2595** to **27C8**.

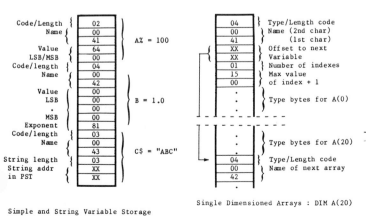

Simple and String Variable Storage

Single Dimensioned Arrays : DIM A(20)

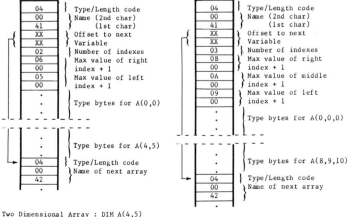

Two Dimensional Array : DIM A(4,5)

Three Dimensional Array : DIM A(8,9,10)

Literal String Pool (40D2)

This table is used by BASIC to keep track of intermediate strings which result from operations such as string addition or some print operations. The table has eleven three byte entries which are assigned sequentially. The start of the table has a two byte pointer to the next available entry. It is initialized during IPL to point to the head of the list.

Each entry contains the length and the address of a string which is usually (although not necessarily) in the PST. Entries are assigned in a top down fashion and released in a bottom up manner. A pointer to the next available entry is kept in **40B3**. If the table overflows an ST error is given.

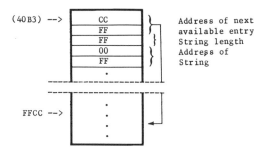

Literal String Pool

Communications Region (4000 - 4200)

The Communications Region has been defined as RAM locations **4000** to **4200**. These addresses give the definition an air of precision that is not warranted. In reality only a portion of the area is used in the sense given to the term Communications Region. Those boundaries were chosen because they represent the end of ROM and the approximate starting address of DOS in RAM. In a Level II system without disk there would be no DOS and the RAM tables such as the PST, VLT, etc. would begin at a much lower address. But they would still be above **4200** so it is safe to think of that region as reserved.

The Communications Region has many uses other than those mentioned so far. The following diagram shows the major areas discussed up to this point. Following it is a description of all bytes in the Communications Region and their known use.

Communications Region

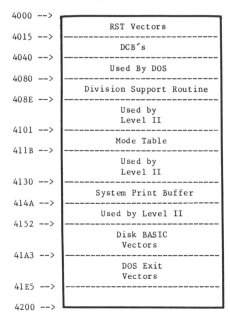

Address	Level II Contents	DOS Contents	Description
4000	JP 1C96	....	RST 8 VECTOR
4003	JP 1D78	....	RST 10 VECTOR
4006	JP 1C90	....	RST 18 VECTOR
4009	JP 25D9	....	RST 20 VECTOR
400C	RET	JP 4BA2	RST 28 DOS REQUEST PROCESSING
400F	RET	JP 44B4	LOAD DEBUG (LD A,XX/RST 28)
4012	DI/RET	CALL 4518	RST 38 INTERRUPT SERVICE CALL
4015	....		KEYBOARD DCB (8 BYTES)
401D	....		VIDEO DCB (8 BYTES)
4025	....		PRINTER DCB (8 BYTES)
402D	JP 5000	JP 4400	MAKE SYS1 (10) DOS REQUEST
4030	RST 0	LD A,A3	DOS REQUEST CODE FOR SYS1
4032	LD A,0	RST 28	WRITE ´DOS READY´ MSG
4033	RET	JP 44BB	CALL DEVICE DRIVER ALA DOS
4036	....		KEYBOARD WORK AREA USED BY SYS0 AND KEYBOARD DRIVER
403D	....		DISPLAY CONTROL WORD (U/L CASE)
403E	....		USED BY DOS
403F	....		USED BY DOS
4040	....		SYSTEM BST´S
4041	....		SECONDS
4042	....		MINUTES
4043	....		HOURS
4044	....		YEAR
4045	....		DAY
4046	....		MONTH
4047	....		LOAD ADDRESS FOR SYSTEM UTILITIES 2 BYTES, INITIALIZED TO 5200 BY SYS0/SYS
4049	....		MEMORY SIZE. COMPUTED BY SYS0/SYS
404A	....		RESERVED
404B	....		CURRENT INTERRUPT STATUS WORD
404C	....		INTERRUPT SUBROUTINE MASK
404D	....		RESERVED (INTERRUPT BIT 0)
404F	....		RESERVED (INTERRUPT BIT 1)
4051	....		COMMUNICATIONS INTERRUPT SUBROUTINE
4053	....		RESERVED (INTERRUPT BIT 3)
4055	....		RESERVED (INTERRUPT BIT 4)
4057	....		RESERVED (INTERRUPT BIT 5)
4059		45F7	ADDR OF DISK INTERRUPT ROUTINE
405B		4560	ADDR OF CLOCK INTERRUPT ROUTINE
405D	....		STACK DURING IPL
407D	....		START OF STACK DURING ROM IPL
407E	....		RESERVED
407F	....		RESERVED
4080	....		SUBTRACTION ROUTINE USED BY DIVISION CODE. CODE IS MOVED FROM ´18F7´ - ´1904´ DURING NON-DISK IPL OR BY BASIC UTILITY FOR DISK SYSTEMS.

408E	CONTAINS ADDRESS OF USER SUBROUTINE.
4090	RANDOM NUMBER SEED
4093	IN A,00
4096	OUT A,00
4099	HOLDS LAST CHAR TYPED AFTER BREAK
409A	FLAG (SIGNALS RESUME ENTERED)
409B	NO. OF CHARS. IN CURRENT PRINT LINE
409D	OUTPUT DEVICE CODE (1-PRINTER 0-VIDEO, MINUS 1-CASSETTE)
409D	SIZE OF DISPLAY LINE (VIDEO)
409E	SIZE OF PRINT LINE
409F	RESERVED
40A0	ADDR OF STRING AREA BOUNDARY
40A2	CURRENT LINE NUMBER
40A4	ADDR OF PST
40A6	CURSOR POSITION
40A7	ADDR OF KEYBOARD BUFFR.
40A9	0 IF CASSETTE INPUT, ELSE NON-ZERO
40AA	RANDOM NUMBER SEED
40AB	VALUE FROM REFRESH REGISTER
40AC	LAST RANDOM NUMBER (2 BYTES)
40AE	FLAG: 0 - LOCATE NAMED VARIABLE -1 - CREATE ENTRY FOR NAMED VARIABLE
40AF	TYPE FLAG FOR VALUE IN WRA1. 2 - INTEGER 3 - STRING 4 - SINGLE PRECISION 8 DOUBLE PRECISION
40B0	HOLDS INTERMEDIATE VALUE DURING EXPRESSION EVALUATION
40B1	MEMORY SIZE
40B2	RESERVED
40B3	ADDR OF NEXT AVAILABLE LOC. IN LSPT.
40B5	LSPT (LITERAL STRING POOL TABLE)
40D2	END OF LSPT
40D3	THE NEXT 3 BYTES ARE USED TO HOLD THE LENGTH AND ADDR OF A STRING WHEN IT IS MOVED TO THE STRING AREA.
40D6	POINTER TO NEXT AVAILABLE LOC. IN STRING AREA.
40D8	1: INDEX OF LAST BYTE EXECUTED IN CURRENT STATEMENT. 2: EDIT FLAG DURING PRINT USING
40DA	LINE NO. OF LAST DATA STATEMENT READ
40DC	FOR FLAG (1 = FOR IN PRGORESS 0 = NO FOR IN PROGRESS)
40DD	0 DURING INPUT PHASE, ZERO OTHERWISE
40DE	READ FLAG: 0 = READ STATEMENT ACTIVE 1 = INPUT STATEMENT ACTIVE ALSO USED IN PRINT USING TO HOLD SEPERATOR BETWEEN STRING AND VARIABLE
40DF	HOLDS EXECUTION ADDR FOR PGM LOADED WITH DOS REQUEST
40E1	AUTO INCREMENT FLAG 0 = NO AUTO MODE NON-ZERO HOLDS NEXT LINE NUMBER
40E2	CURRENT LINE NUMBER IN BINARY (DURING INPUT PHASE)
40E4	AUTO LINE INCREMENT
40E6	DURING INPUT: ADDR OF CODE STRING FOR CURRENT STATEMENT. DURING EXECUTION: LINE NO. FOR CURRENT STATEMENT
40E8	DURING EXECUTION: HOLDS STACK POINTER VALUE WHEN STATEMENT EXECUTION BEGINS
40EA	LINE NO. IN WHICH ERROR OCCURED
40EC	LINE NO. IN WHICH ERROR OCCURED.
40ED	LAST BYTE EXECUTED IN CURRENT STATEMENT
40EF	ADDR OF POSITION IN ERROR LINE
40F0	ON ERROR ADDRESS
40F2	FLAG. FF DURING ON ERROR PROCESSING CLEARED BY RESUME ROUTINE
40F3	ADDR OF DECIMAL POINT IN PBUF
40F5	LAST LINE NUMBER EXECUTED SAVED BY STOP/END
40F7	ADDR OF LAST BYTE EXECUTED DURING ERROR
40F9	ADDR OF SIMPLE VARIABLES
40FB	ADDR OF DIMENSIONED VARIABLES
40FD	STARTING ADDRESS OF FREE SPACE LIST (FSL)
40FF	POINTS TO BYTE FOLLOWING LAST CHAR READ DURING READ STMNT EXECUTION
4101	VARIABLE DECLARATION LIST. THERE ARE 26 ENTRIES (1 FOR EACH LETTER OF THE ALPHABET) EACH ENTRY CONTAINS A CODE INDICATING DEFAULT MODE FOR VARIABLES STARTING WITH THAT LETTER.
411A	END OF DECLARATION LIST
411B	TRACE FLAG (0 = NO TRACE, NON-ZERO = TRACE)

411C	TEMP STORAGE USED BY NUMERIC ROUTINES WHEN UNPACKING A FLOATING POINT NUMBER. USUALLY IT HOLDS THE LAST BYTE SHIFTED OUT OF THE LSB POSITION
411D	WRA1 - LSB OF DBL PREC. VALUE
411E	WRA1 - DBL PREC. VALUE
411F	WRA1 - DBL PREC. VALUE
4120	WRA1 - DBL PREC VALUE
4121	WRA1 - LSB OF INTEGER SINGLE PREC
4122	WRA1
4123	WRA1 - MSB FOR SINGLE PREC
4124	WRA1 - EXPONENT FOR SINGLE PREC
4125	SIGN OF RESULT DURING MATH & ARITHMETIC OPERATIONS
4126	BIT BUCKET USED DURING DP ADDITION
4127	WRA2 - LSB
4128	WRA2
4129	WRA2
412A	WRA2
422B	WRA2
412C	WRA2
412D	WRA2 - MSB
412E	WRA2 - EXPONENT
412F	NOT USED
4130	START OF INTERNAL PRINT BUFFER USED DURING PRINT PROCESSING
4149	LAST BYTE OF PRINT BUFFER
414A	TEMP. STORAGE USED BY DBL PRECISION DIVISION ROUTINE. HOLDS DIVISOR
4151	END OF TEMP AREA

*
*
* LOCATIONS 4152 THRU 41E2 CONTAIN DOS EXITS AND DISK BASIC EXITS. ON NON-DISK
* SYSTEMS THESE LOCATIONS ARE INITIALIZED TO RETURNS (RET´S) WHILE ON DISK
* BASED SYSTEMS THEY WILL BE INITIALIZED AS SHOWN.
*

4152	...RET. .JP 5E46.....	DISK BASIC EXIT (CVI)
4155	...RET. .JP 558E.....	DISK BASIC EXIT (FN)
4158	...RET. .JP 5E49.....	DISK BASIC EXIT (CVS)
415B	...RET. .JP 5655.....	DISK BASIC EXIT (DEF)
415E	...RET. .JP 5E4C.....	DISK BASIC EXIT (CVD)
4161	...RET. .JP 61EB.....	DISK BASIC EXIT (EOF)
4164	...RET. .JP 6231.....	DISK BASIC EXIT (LOC)
4167	...RET. .JP 6242.....	DISK BASIC EXIT (LOF)
416A	...RET. .JP 5E20.....	DISK BASIC EXIT (MKI$)
416D	...RET. .JP 5E30.....	DISK BASIC EXIT (MKS$)
4170	...RET. .JP 5E33.....	DISK BASIC EXIT (MKD$)
4173	...RET. .JP 56C4.....	DISK BASIC EXIT (CMD)
4176	...RET. .JP 5714.....	DISK BASIC EXIT (TIME$)
4179	...RET. .JP 6349.....	DISK BASIC EXIT (OPEN)
417C	...RET. .JP 60AB.....	DISK BASIC EXIT (FIELD)
417F	...RET. .JP 627C.....	DISK BASIC EXIT (GET)
4182	...RET. .JP 627B.....	DISK BASIC EXIT (PUT)
4185	...RET. .JP 606F.....	DISK BASIC EXIT (CLOSE)
4188	...RET. .JP 5F7B.....	DISK BASIC EXIT (LOAD)
418B	...RET. .JP 600B.....	DISK BASIC EXIT (MERGE)
418E	...RET. .JP 6346.....	DISK BASIC EXIT (NAME)
4191	...RET. .JP 63C0.....	DISK BASIC EXIT (KILL)
4194	...RET. .JP 58B7.....	DISK BASIC EXIT (&)
4197	...RET. .JP 60E6.....	DISK BASIC EXIT (LSET)
419A	...RET. .JP 60E5.....	DISK BASIC EXIT (RSET)
419D	...RET. .JP 582F.....	DISK BASIC EXIT (INSTR)
41A0	...RET. .JP 6044.....	DISK BASIC EXIT (SAVE)
41A3	...RET. .JP 5756.....	DISK BASIC EXIT (LINE)
41A6	...RET. .JP 5679.....	DISK BASIC EXIT (USR)

THE FOLLOWING ADDRESSES ARE THE DOS EXIT ADDRESSES.

41A9	...RET. .JP XXXX.....	DOS EXIT FROM
41AC	...RET. .JP 5FFC.....	DOS EXIT FROM 1A1C
41AF	...RET. .JP 598E.....	DOS EXIT FROM 0368
41B2	...RET. .JP 6033.....	DOS EXIT FROM ROM address 1AA1
41B5	...RET. .JP 5BD7.....	DOS EXIT FROM ROM address 1AEC
41B8	...RET. .JP 5B8C.....	DOS EXIT FROM ROM address 1AF2
41BB	...RET. .JP 60A1.....	DOS EXIT FROM ROM address 1B8C
41BE	...RET. .JP 577C.....	DOS EXIT FROM ROM address 2174
41C1	...RET. .JP 59CD.....	DOS EXIT FROM ROM address 032C
41C4	...RET. .JP XXXX.....	DOS EXIT FROM ROM address 0358
41C7	...RET. .JP 5F78.....	DOS EXIT FROM ROM address 1EA6
41CA	...RET. .JP 5A15.....	DOS EXIT FROM ROM address 206F
41CD	...RET. .JP 5B9A.....	DOS EXIT FROM ROM address 2103
41D0	...RET. .JP 5B99.....	DOS EXIT FROM ROM address 2103
41D3	...RET. .JP 5B65.....	DOS EXIT FROM ROM address 2108
41D6	...RET. .JP 5784.....	DOS EXIT FROM ROM address 219E
41DC	...RET. .JP 5E63.....	DOS EXIT FROM ROM address 222D
41DF	...RET. .JP 579C.....	DOS EXIT FROM ROM address 2278
41D2	...RET. .JP 5B51.....	DOS EXIT FROM ROM address 02B2

DCB Descriptions

The keyboard, video, and printer DCB'S (Device Control Blocks) are defined in ROM at locations @@EQ2 06E7 - 06FF. They are moved to the address show in the Communications Region during the IPL sequence.

Video DCB (Address 401D)

Relative Byte

0	0	0	0	0	0	1	1	1	Device type (7)
1	0	1	0	0	1	0	0	0	Driver address
2	0	0	0	0	0	1	0	1	(0458)
3	0	0	0	0	0	0	0	0	Next character address
4	0	0	1	1	1	1	0	0	3C00 =< X < 3FFF
5	0	0	0	0	0	0	0	0	0/value 0 = Supress cursor
6	0	1	0	0	0	1	0	0	value = last char under cursor
7	0	1	0	0	1	1	1	1	RAM buffer addr (4F44)

Keyboard DCB (Address 4015)

Relative Byte

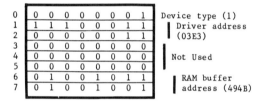

0	0	0	0	0	0	0	0	1	Device type (1)
1	1	1	1	0	0	0	1	1	Driver address
2	0	0	0	0	0	0	1	1	(03E3)
3	0	0	0	0	0	0	0	0	
4	0	0	0	0	0	0	0	0	Not Used
5	0	0	0	0	0	0	0	0	
6	0	1	0	0	1	0	1	1	RAM buffer
7	0	1	0	0	1	0	0	1	address (494B)

Printer DCB (Address 4025)

Relative Byte

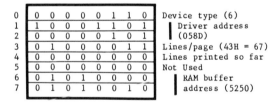

0	0	0	0	0	0	1	1	0	Device type (6)
1	1	0	0	0	1	1	0	1	Driver address
2	0	0	0	0	0	1	0	1	(058D)
3	0	1	0	0	0	0	1	1	Lines/page (43H = 67)
4	0	0	0	0	0	0	0	0	Lines printed so far
5	0	0	0	0	0	0	0	0	Not Used
6	0	1	0	1	0	0	0	0	RAM buffer
7	0	1	0	1	0	0	1	0	address (5250)

Interrupt Vectors

Interrupts are a means of allowing an external event to interrupt the CPU and redirect it to execute some specific portion of code. The signal that causes this to happen is called an interrupt and the code executed in response to that interrupt is called a service routine. After the service routine executes it returns control of the CPU to the point where the interrupt occurred and normal processing continues.

In order for interrupts to occur the system must be primed to accecpt them. When the system is primed it is ENABLED which is shorthand for the instruction used to enable the interrupt system (EI-Enable Interrupts). A system that is not enabled is DISABLED and again that is shorthand for the disable instruction (DI-Disable Interrupts). Besides priming the system for interrupts there must be some outside event to stimulate the interrupt. On Level II systems that could be a clock or a disk. Actually both of them generate interrupts - the clock gives one every 25 milliseconds, and the disk on demand for certain operations.

When running a Level II system without disks the interrupts are disabled. It is only when DOS is loaded that interrupts are enabled and service routines to support those interrupts are loaded. Interrupts are disabled at the start of the IPL sequence that is common to Level II and DOS. For Level II they will remain off, but on a DOS system they will be enabled at the end of the initilization in SYS0/SYS.

When an interrupt occurs two things happen. First a bit indicating the exact cause of the interrupt is set in byte 37E0. Second an RST 56H instruction is executed. As a result of the RST (which is like a CALL) the address of the next instruction to be executed is saved on the stack (PUSH'd) and control is passed to location 0038. Stored at 00 38 is a JP 4012. During the IPL sequence 4012 was initialized to:

```
4012    DI    Disable further interupts
4013    RET   Return to point of interupt
```

for non-disk systems or:

```
4012    CALL 4518   Service Interupt
```

for disk systems

The service routine at 4518 examines the contents of 37E0 and executes a subroutine for each bit that is turned on and for which DOS has a subroutine. The format of the interrupt status word at 37E0 is:

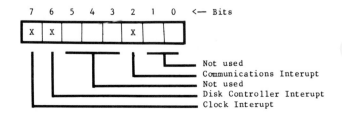

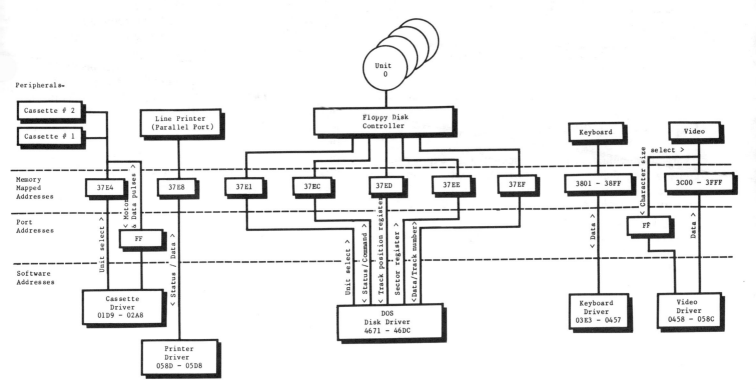

Memory Mapped I/0

DOS maintains an interrupt service mask at **404C** that it uses to decide if there is a subroutine to be executed for each of the interrupt status. As released **404C** contains a **C0** which indicates subroutines for clock and disk interrupts.

The service routine at **4518** combines the status byte and the mask byte by AND'ing them together. The result is used as a bit index into a table of subroutine addresses stored at **404D - 405C**. Each entry is a two byte address of an interrupt subroutine. Bit 0 of the index corresponds to the addess at **404D/404E**, bit 1 **404F/4050**, etc.

The service routine runs disabled. It scans the interrupt status from left to right jumping to a subroutine whenever a bit is found on. All registers are saved before subroutine entry and a return address in the service routine is PUSH'd onto the stack so a RET instruction can be used to exit the subroutine. When all bits in the status have been tested control returns to the point of interrupt with interrupts enabled.

Stack Frame Configurations

Level II usually uses the Communications Region for temporary storage. There are special cases, however where that is not possible because a routine may call itself (called recursion) and each call would destroy the values saved by the previous call. In those cases the stack is used to save some of the variables. Of course an indexed table could be used, but in these cases the stack serves the purpose.

FOR Statement Stack Frame

All variable addresses associated with a FOR loop are carried on the stack until the loop completes. When a NEXT statement is processed, it searches the stack looking for a FOR frame with the same index address as the current one. The routine that searches the stack is at location **1936**. Its only parameter is the address of the current index which is passed in the DE register set. The stack is searched backwards from its current position to the beginning of the stack. If a FOR frame with a matching index address is not found an NF error is generated. The stack frame searched for is given below.

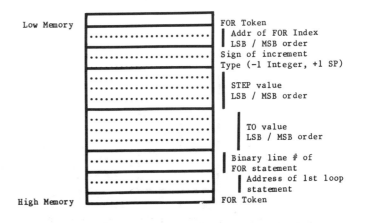

49

GOSUB Stack Configuration

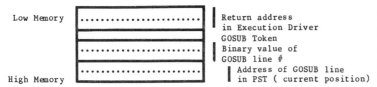

```
Low Memory    .....................  | Return address
              .....................  | in Execution Driver
                                       GOSUB Token
              .....................  | Binary value of
                                       GOSUB line #
              .....................  | Address of GOSUB line
High Memory                          | in PST ( current position)
```

Expression Evaluation

Expression evaluation involves scanning an expression and breaking it intó seperate operations which can be executed in their proper order according to the hierarchary of operators. This means a statement must be scanned and the operations with the highest heiracherial value (called precedence value) must be performed first. Any new terms which result from those operations must be carried forward and combined with the rest of the expression.

The method used for evaluation is an operator precedence parse. An expression is scanned from left to right. Scanning stops as soon as an operator token or EOS is found. The variable to the left of the operator (called the current variable), and the operator (any arithmetic token for - * / or exp) are called a 'set', and are either:

a) pushed onto the stack as a set or,

b) if a precedence break is detected the operation between the previous set pushed onto the stack and the current variable is performed. The result of that operation then becomes the current variable and the previous set is removed from the stack. After the computation another attempt is made to push the new current variable and operator onto the stack as a set.

This step is repeated until the new set is pushed or there are no more sets on the stack with which to combine the current value. In that case the expression has been evaluated.

The variable/operator sets that are pushed on the stack have the following format:

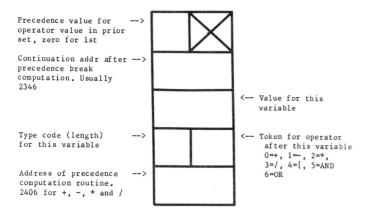

```
Precedence value for    -->  ┌──────────┬──────┐
operator value in prior │          │  ╳   │
set, zero for 1st       ├──────────┴──────┤
                             │                 │
Continuation addr after -->  │                 │
precedence break             │                 │
computation. Usually    ├─────────────────┤
2346                         │                 │  <-- Value for this
                             │                 │      variable
                        ├──────────┬──────┤
Type code (length)      -->  │          │      │  <-- Token for operator
for this variable            │          │      │      after this variable
                        ├──────────┴──────┤      0=+, 1=-, 2=*,
Address of precedence   -->  │                 │      3=/, 4=[, 5=AND
computation routine.         │                 │      6=OR
2406 for +, -, * and /  └─────────────────┘
```

The test for precedence break is simple. If the operator (the token where the scan stopped) has the same or a lower precedence value as the precedence value for the last set pushed on the stack then a break has occured, and an intermediate computation is required. The computation is

performed automatically by POPing the last set. When this occurs control is transferred to a routine (usually at **2406**) which will perform the operation specified in the set between that value (the one from the set on the stack), and the current variable. The result then becomes the current variable. When the computation is finished control returns to a point where the precedence break test is repeated. This time the set which caused the last break is not there, so the test will be between the same operator as before and the operator in the previous set. If there is no previous set then the current variable and operator are pushed as the next set. Note, an EOS or a non-arithmetic token are treated as precedence breaks.

Assuming no break occurs the curent variable and operator are pushed on the stack as the next set, and the scan of the expession continues from the point where it left off. Let's take an example. Assume we have the expression,

A equals B plus C * D / E 5

Scanning begins with the first character to the right of the equals sign and will stop at the first token (plus). B plus would be pushed as the first set because: a) there was no prior set so there could not have been a precedence break, and b) the scan stopped on an arithmetic token (plus).

The next scan would stop at the *. Again the variable/operator pair of C* would be pushed this time as set 2 although for slightly different reasons than before. The * precedence value is higher than the plus precedence value already pushed so there is no break. At this time the stack contains,

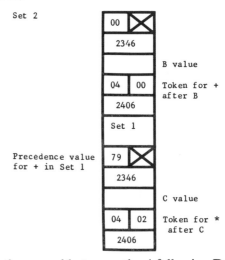

```
Set 2                    ┌──────┬──────┐
                         │  00  │  ╳   │
                         ├──────┴──────┤
                         │   2346      │
                         ├─────────────┤
                         │             │  B value
                         ├──────┬──────┤
                         │  04  │  00  │  Token for +
                         ├──────┴──────┤  after B
                         │   2406      │
                         ├─────────────┤
                         │   Set 1     │
Precedence value         ├──────┬──────┤
for + in Set 1           │  79  │  ╳   │
                         ├──────┴──────┤
                         │   2346      │
                         ├─────────────┤
                         │             │  C value
                         ├──────┬──────┤
                         │  04  │  02  │  Token for *
                         ├──────┴──────┤  after C
                         │   2406      │
                         └─────────────┘
```

Scan three would stop on the / following D. This time there would be a precedence break because * and / have the same values. Consequently set 2 would be POP'd from the stack and control passes to the precedence break routine at **2406** (other routines may be used depending on the operation to be peformed - ckeck the listing for details). Here the operation between set 2 (C*) and the current value (D) would be performed. This would result in a new current value that will be called M. M equals C * D

After the multiplication control goes back to **2346** (continuation after break processing) where the rules from above are used. This time the current value is pushed as set 2 because it has a higher precedence value (/) than that

50

in set 1 (plus). Now the stack contains

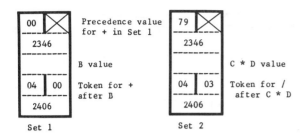

After pushing set 2 the scan continues, stopping at the operator. It has a higher precedence value than the (/) in set 2 so a third set is added to the stack giving:

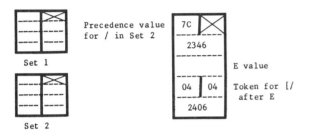

The next scan is made and an EOS is found following the 5 (which is now the current value). As mentioned earlier an EOS or non-arithmetic token is an automatic precedence break, so set 3 is POP'd from the stack and E 5 is computed and becomes the current value. Control passes to 2346 where the rules for pushing the next set are applied and set 2 get's POP'd because the current operator is an EOS. Set 2 (M/) and th current value are operated on giving a current value of

M / E 5   or
C * D / E 5

Again control goes to 2346 which forces set 1 to be POP'd because the current operator is an EOS. When the set is POP'd control goes to the computation routine where the current value and set 1 are operated on. This yields a current value of

B plus C * D / E 5

Now control goes to 2346 and this time the stack is empty causing control to be returned to the caller. The expression has been evaluated and its value is left in WRA1.

DOS Request Codes

DOS request codes provide a mechanism for executing system level commands from within a program. The way they work is to cause the DOS overlay module SYSX/SYS associated with the request to be loaded into 4200 - 5200 and executed. When the request has been satisfied control is returned to the caller as though a subroutine call had been made.

DOS functions may be executed by loading a DOS request code into the a register and executing a RST 28 instruction. Because of the way DOS processes these request codes the push on the stack that resulted from the RST instruction is lost, and control will be returned to the next address found on the stack - rather than to the address following the RST instruction. For example,

```
LD  A,VAL    LOAD DOS  FUNTION CODE
RST   28     EXECUTE DOS FUNCTION
 .                THIS IS WHERE WE WANT TO RETURN
                  TO
 .           BUT WILL NOT BECAUSE OF THE WAY
 .           THE STACK IS MANAGED BY DOS
```

This will not work because the return address (stored on the stack by the RST 28) has been lost during processing. Instead the following sequence should be used:

```
        LD    A,VAL    LOAD REQUEST CODE
        CALL  DOS      PUT RETURN ADDR ON STACK
              .
              .
              .
DOS     RST   28       EXECUTE DOS FUNCTION
                       ALL REGISTERS ARE PRESERVED
                       WE WILL AUTOMATICALLY RET TO
                       CALLER OF DOS
```

The request code value loaded into the A-register must contain the sector number minus 2 of the directory sectory for the overlay to be loaded and a code specifying the exact operation to be performed. The format of the request code is:

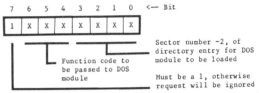

As it is presently implemented the file pointed to by the first entry in the specified directory sector will be loaded. There is no way for example, to load the file associated with the 3rd or 4th entry. A list of the system overlay modules and their functions follows. These descriptions are incomplete. See the individual modules for a complete description.

MODULE	DIRECTORY SECTOR MINUS 2	REQUEST CODE	SUB-FUNCTIONS
SYS1	1	93	10 - write 'DOS READY'
		AC	20 - write 'DOS READY'
		BC	30 - scan input string
		C3	40 - move input string to DCB
		D3	50 - scan and move input string
		E3	60 - append extension to DCB
		F3	70 - reserved
SYS2	2	94	10 - OPEN file processing
		A4	20 - INIT file processing
		B4	30 - create directory overflow entry
		C4	40 -
		D4	50 - reserved
		E4	60 -
		F4	70 -
SYS3	3	95	10 - CLOSE file processing
		A5	20 - KILL file processing
		B5	30 -
		C5	40 - reserved
		D5	50 -
		E5	60 - load SYS3/SYS
		F5	70 - format diskette
SYS4			
SYS5			

Chapter 5

A BASIC SORT Verb

Contained in this chapter is a sample assembly program that demonstrates the use of the ROM calls and tables described in the previous chapters. In this example DOS Exits and Disk BASIC Exits are used to add a SORT verb to BASIC.

In this case a SORT verb will be added so that the statement

100 SORT I$, O$, K1$

be used to read and sort a file specified by the string I$. O$ and K1$ are strings which specify the output file name and the sort key descriptors. The procedure for doing this is simple. First we must modify the Input Phase to recognize the word SORT and replace it with a token. This can be accomplished by using one of the DOS Exits.

A DOS Exit is taken during the Input Phase immediately after the scan for reserved words. We will intercept this exit to make a furthur test for the word SORT and replace it with a token. Processing will then continue as before. Before using any DOS Exit study the surrounding code to determine exact register usage. In this case it is important to note that the length of the incoming line is in the BC register when the exit is taken. If the subroutine compresses the line (by replacing the word SORT with a token) then its length will have changed and the new length must replace the orginal contents of BC.

A second modification must be made to the Execution Driver, or somewhere in its chain, to recognize the new token value and branch to the SORT action routine. This presents a slight problem because there are no DOS Exits in the execution driver before calling the verb routine, and since the driver code and its tables are in ROM they cannot be changed. In short there is no easy way to incorporate new tokens into the Execution Phase.

The solution is to borrow a Disk BASIC token and piggy-back another token behind it. Then any calls to the verb routine associated with the borrowed token must be intercepted and a test make for the piggy-backed token. If one is found control goes to the SORT verb routine otherwise it passes to the assigned verb routine. In this example the tokenq FA will be borrowed and another FA will be tacked behind it giving a token FAFA.

This example is incomplete because the LIST function has not been modified to recognize the sort token. If a LIST command is issued the verb MIDMID will be given for the SORT verb. There is one more detail that needs attention before discussing the verb routine. Using the memory layout figure in Chapter 1 we can see that there is no obvious place to load an assembly language program without interfering somehow with one of BASIC's areas. Depending on where we loaded our verb routine it could overlay the String Area, or the Stack, or maybe even reach as low as the PST or VLT. Of course we might get lucky and find an area in the middle of the Free Space List that never gets used but thats too risky.

BASIC has a facility for setting the upper limit of the memory space it will use. By using this feature we can reserve a region in high memory where our verb routine can be loaded without disturbing any of BASIC's tables. Now for the details of verb routine.

Because a sort can be a lengthy piece of code only the details that pertain to DOS Exits, Disk BASIC, and some of the ROM calls from Chapter 2 will be illustrated. The verb routine has two sections. The first section will be called once to modify the DOS and Disk BASIC exit addresses (also called vectors) in the Communications Region to point to locations within the verb routine. The vector addresses must be modified after BASIC has been entered on a DOS system because they are initialized by the BASIC command. The second section has two parts.

Part one is the DOS Exit code called from the Input Scanner. Part two is the verb action routine for the SORT verb. It is entered when a FA token is encountered during the Execution Phase.

The system being used will be assumed to have 48K of RAM, at least 1 disk, and NEWDOS 2.1. The verb routine will occupy locations E000 - FFFF. The entry point for initializing the vectors will be at qt22E000. All buffers used will be assigned dynamically in the stack portion of the Free Space List. The verb routine will be loaded before exiting DOS and entering Level II BASIC. Although it could be loaded from the BASIC program by using the CMD'LOAD.....' feature of NEWDOS.

```
1. IPL
2. LOAD,SORT       :(load verb into    E000 - FFFF 1)
3. BASIC,57344     :(protect verb area)


100 DEF USR1(0) = &HE000 : initialization entry point
110 A = USR1(0)          : initialize vectors

RUN                      : initialize the sort

100 I$="SORTIN/PAY:1"    : (sort input file)
110 O$="SORTOUT/PAY:1"   : (sort output file)
120 K$="A,A,100-120"     : (sort key: ascending order ASCII
                         : key, sort field is 100 - 120)
130 SORT I$, O$,K$       : (sort file)

RUN

00100          ORG     0E000H
00110 ; INITIAL ENTRY POINT TO INITIALIZE DOS EXIT AND
00120 ; DISK BASIC ADDRESSES.
00130          LD      HL,(41B3H)    ; ORGINAL DOS EXIT VALUE
00140          LD      (ADR1+1),HL   ; IS STILL USED AFTER OUR
00150 ;                              ; PROCESSING
00160          LD      HL,(41DAH)    ; ORGINAL DISK BASIC ADDR FOR
00170 ;                              ; MID$ TOKEN (FA)
00180          LD      (ADR2+1),HL   ; SAVE IN CASE FA TOKEN FOUND
00190          LD      HL,NDX
00200          LD      (41B3H),HL
00210          LD      HL,NDB
00220 ;                              ; OUR ADDR
00230          LD      (41DAH),HL
00240 ;                              ; FA TOKEN W/OUR ADDR
00250          RET                   ; RET TO EXECUTION DRIVER
00260 ;*  GET ADDRESS OF VARIABLE
00270 ;* THIS SECTION OF CODE IS ENTERED AS A DOS EXIT DURING THE
00280 ;* INPUT PHASE. IT WILL TEST FOR A 'SORT' COMMAND AND REPLACE
00290 ;* IT WITH A 'FAFA' TOKEN. THE ORGINAL DOS EXIT ADDR HAS BEEN
00300 ;* SAVED AND WILL BE TAKEN AT ADR1.
00310 ;*
00320 NDX      CALL    SAV           ; SAV ALL REGISTERS
00330          LD      IX,SORT-1     ; TEST STRING
00340          LD      B,3           ; NO. OF CHARS TO MATCH
00350 NDX1     INC     HL            ; START OF LOOP
00360          INC     IX            ; BUMP TO NEXT TEST CHAR
00370          LD      A,(IX+0)      ; GET A TEST CHAR
00380          CP      (HL)          ; COMPARE W/INPUT STRING
00390          JR      NZ,OUT        ; STOP WHEN FIRST MIS-MATCH
00400          DJNZ    NDX1          ; ALL 4 CHARS MUST MATCH
00410 ;*
00420 ;* WE HAVE A MATCH. NOW REPLACE THE WORD 'SORT' WITH A TOKEN
00430 ;* 'FAFA' AND COMPRESS THE STRING
00440 ;*
00450          INC     HL            ; FIRST CHAR AFTER 'SORT'
00460          PUSH    HL            ; SAVE FOR COMPRESSION CODE
00470          LD      BC,-3         ; BACKSPACE INPUT STRING
00480          ADD     HL,BC         ; START OF WORD 'SORT'
00490          LD      (HL),0FAH     ; TOKEN REPLACES 'S'
00500          INC     HL            ; NEXT LOC IN INPUT STRING
00510          LD      (HL),0FAH     ; TOKEN REPLACES 'O'
00520          INC     HL            ; NEXT LOC IN INPUT STRING
00530          POP     DE            ; STRING ADDR AFTER SORT
```

```
00540          EX      DE,HL         ; SO WE CAN USE RST 10
00550 ;*                             ; TO FETCH NEXT CHAR
00560 ;* NOW COMPRESS THE INPUT STRING
00570 ;*
00580          LD      BC,3          ; SET COUNT OF CHARS IN
00590 ;*                             ; EQUAL TO NO SKIPPED OVER
00600 NDX2     RST     10H           ; GET NEXT CHAR, DISCARD
00610 ;*                             ; BLANKS
00620          LD      (DE),A        ; MOVE IT DOWN
00630          INC     DE            ; BUMP SOURCE ADDR
00640          INC     C             ; COUNT 1 CHAR IN LINE
00650          OR      A             ; TEST FOR END OF STRING
00660          JR      NZ,NDX2       ; NOT END, LOOP
00670          LD      (DE),A        ; EACH LINE MUST END WITH
00680 ;*                             ; 3 BYTES OF ZEROS
00690          INC     DE            ; BUMP TO LAST BYTE
00700          LD      (DE),A        ; STORE 3 RD ZERO
00710          INC     C             ; THEN SET BC = LENGTH OF
00720          INC     C             ; LINE + 1
00730          INC     C             ; SO BASIC CAN MOVE IT
00740          LD      (TEMP),BC     ; SAVE NEW LINE LENGTH
00750          CALL    RES           ; RESTORE REGISTERS
00760          LD      BC,(TEMP)     ; NEW LINE LENGTH TO BC
00770 OUT      JR      ADR1          ; EXIT
00780          CALL    RES           ; RESTORE REGISTERS
00790 ADR1     JP      0             ; CONTINUE ON TO ORGINAL
00800 ;*                             ; DOS EXIT
00810 ;* DISK BASIC EXIT FOR FA TOKEN. TEST FOR SORT TOKEN FAFA
00820 ;*
00830 NDB      CALL    SAV           ; SAVE ALL REGISTERS
00840          INC     HL            ; SKIP TO CHAR AFTER TOKEN
00850          LD      A,(HL)        ; TEST FOR SECOND 'FA'
00860          CP      0FAH          ; IS FOLLOWING CHAR A FA
00870          JR      Z,NDB1        ; Z IF SORT TOKEN
00880          CALL    RES           ; RESTORE REGISTERS
00890 ADR2     JP      0             ; CONTINUE WITH MID$ PROCESSING
00900 ;*
00910 ;* WE HAVE A SORT TOKEN
00920 ;*
00930 NDB1     INC     HL            ; SKIP OVER REST OF TOKEN
00940          CALL    GADR          ; GET ADDR OF 1ST PARAM
00950          LD      (PARM1),DE    ; SAV ADDR OF INPUT FILE NAME
00960          RST     08            ; LOOK FOR COMMA
00970          DEFM    ','           ; SYMBOL TO LOOK FOR
00980          CALL    GADR          ; GET ADDR OF 2ND PARAM
00990          LD      (PARM2),DE    ; SAV ADDR OF OUTPUT FILE NAME
01000          RST     08            ; LOOK FOR COMMA
01010          DEFM    ','           ; SYMBOL TO LOOK FOR
01020          CALL    GADR          ; GET ADDR OF SORT KEYS
01030          LD      (PARM3),DE    ; SAV ADDR OF SORT KEY
01040          LD      (TEMP),HL     ; SAVE ENDING POSITION
01050 ;*                             ; IN CURRENT STATEMENT
01060 ;*
01070 ;* NOW, BLANK FILL I/O DCBS
01080 ;*
01090          LD      IX,DCBL       ; LIST OF DCB ADDRS
01100          LD      C,2           ; NO OF DCBS TO BLALNK
01110          LD      A,20H         ; ASCII BLANK
01120 L1       LD      L,(IX+0)      ; LSB OF DCB ADDR
01130          LD      H,(IX+1)      ; MSB OF DCB ADDR
01140          LD      B,32          ; NO OF BYTES TO BLANK
01150 L2       LD      (HL),A        ; BLANK LOOP
01160          INC     HL
01170          DJNZ    L2            ; LOOP TILL BLANKED
01180          INC     IX            ; BUMP TO NXT DCB ADDR
01190          INC     IX            ; BUMP AGAIN
01200          DEC     C             ; ALL DCBS BLNKD
01210          JR      NZ,L1         ; NO
01220 ;*
01230 ; YES, MOVE FILE NAMES TO DCB AREAS
01240 ;*
01250          LD      HL,(PARM1)    ; ADDR OF INPUT FILE NAME STRNG
01260          LD      DE,DCBI       ; INPUT DCB
01270          CALL    29C8H         ; MOVE NAME TO DCB
01280          LD      HL,(PARM2)    ; ADDR OF OUTPUT FILE NAME
01290          LD      DE,DCBO       ; OUTPUT DCB
01300          CALL    29C8H         ; MOVE NAME TO DCB
01310          LD      HL,(PARM3)    ; GET ADDR OF KEY STRING
01320          INC     HL            ; SKIP OVER BYTE COUNT
01330          LD      C,(HL)        ; GET LSB OF STRNG ADDR
01340          INC     HL            ; BUMP TO REST OF ADDR
01350          LD      H,(HL)        ; GET MSB OF STRNG ADDR
01360          LD      L,C           ; NOW HL = STRNG ADDR
01370          CALL    1E3DH         ; MUST BE ALPHA
01380          JR      NC,YA1        ; OK
01390          JP      ERROR         ; INCORRECT SORT ORDER
01400 YA1      LD      (ORDER),A     ; SAVE SORT ORDER (A/D)
01410          INC     HL            ; SKIP TO TERMINAL CHAR
01420          RST     08            ; TEST FOR COMMA
01430          DEFM    ','
01440          CALL    1E3DH         ; MUST BE ALPHA
01450          JR      NC,YA5        ; OK
```

```
01460        JP     ERROR
01470 YA5    LD     (TYPE),A           ; SAVE TYPE (A/B)
01480        INC    HL                 ; SKIP TO TEMINAL CHAR
01490        RST    8                  ; TEST FOR COMMA
01500        DEFM   ','
01510        CALL   0E6CH              ; GET RECORD SIZE
01520        LD     DE,(4121H)         ; GET SIZE FROM WRA1
01530        LD     (SIZE),DE          ; SAVE IT
01540        RST    20H                ; MUST BE AN INTEGER
01550        JP     M,YA10             ; MINUS IF INTEGER
01560        JP     ERROR
01570 YA10   RST    08                 ; LOOK FOR COMMA
01580        DEFM   ','
01590        CALL   0E6CH              ; GET STARTING POSITION
01600        LD     DE,(4121H)         ; GET POS FROM WRA1
01610        LD     (START),DE         ; SAVE IT
01620        RST    08                 ; LOOK FOR -
01630        DEFM   '-'                ; CHAR TO TEST FOR
01640        CALL   0E6CH              ; GET ENDING POS OF KEY
01650        LD     DE,(4121H)         ; GET VALUE FROM WRA1
01660        LD     (END),DE           ; SAVE ENDING POS
01670        LD     HL,(TEMP)          ; RESTORE CURRENT LINE ADDR
01680 ;*                               ; TO EOS ON RETURN
01690        CALL   RES                ; RESTORE REGISTERS
01700        LD     HL,(TEMP)          ; RESTORE EOS ADDR
01710        RET                       ; RETURN TO BASIC
01720 ;*
01730 ;*
01740 ;*
01750 SORT   DEFM   'S'                ; S OF SORT
01760        DEFB   0D3H               ; TOKEN FOR OR OF SORT
01770        DEFM   'T'                ; T OF SORT
01780 ;*
01790 ;*     SAVE ALL REGISTERS
01800 ;*
01810 SAV    EX     DE,HL
01820        EX     (SP),HL            ; SAV DE/RTN ADDR TO HL
01830        PUSH   BC
01840        PUSH   AF
01850        PUSH   IX
01860        PUSH   DE                 ; SAV ORGINAL HL
01870        EX     DE,HL              ; RESTORE HL RET ADDR TO DE
01880        PUSH   DE                 ; RET ADDR TO STK
01890        RET                       ; RET TO CALLER
01900 ;*
01910 ;*     RESTORE ALL REGISTERS
01920 ;*
01930 RES    POP    HL                 ; RTN ADDR TO HL
01940        POP    DE                 ; REAL HL
```

```
01950        POP    IX
01960        POP    AF
01970        POP    BC
01980        EX     (SP),HL            ; RTN ADDR TO STK
01990        EX     DE,HL
02000        RET
02010        JP     (HL)               ; RTN TO CALLER
02020 ;*
02030 ;*     GET THE ADDRESS OF THE NEXT VARIABLE INTO DE
02040 ;*
02050 GADR   LD     A,(HL)             ; GET NEXT CHAR FROM INPUT
02060 ;*                               ; STRNG, TST FOR LITERAL
02070 ;*     CP     22H                ; IS IT A QUOTE -START OF
02080 ;*                               ; A LITERAL-
02090        JR     NZ,GADR2           ; NO, GO FIND ADDR OF VAR
02100        CALL   2866H              ; YES, GO BUILD A LSPT ENTRY
02110        JR     GADR5              ; THEN JOIN COMMON CODE
02120 GADR2  CALL   2540H              ; GET ADDR OF NEXT VARIABLE
02130 GADR5  RST    20H                ; IS IT A STRING
02140        LD     DE,(4121H)         ; ADDR OF NEXT VAR
02150        RET    Z                  ; RET IF STRING VAR
02160        POP    HL                 ; CLEAR STACK
02170        POP    HL                 ; CLEAR STACK
02180        LD     A,2                ; ERROR CODE FOR SYNTAX ERR
02190        JP     1997H              ; GO TO ERROR ROUTINE
02200 ;*
02210 ;*     ERROR EXIT
02220 ;*
02230 ERROR  CALL   RES                ; RESTORE REGISTERS
02240        POP    HL                 ; CLEAR STACK
02250        LD     A,2                ; SYNTAX ERROR CODE
02260        JP     1997H              ; PRINT ERROR MESSAGE
02270 ;*
02280 ;*
02290 ;*
02300 DCBL   DEFW   DCBI
02310        DEFW   DCBO
02320 PARM1  DEFW   0                  ; INPUT FILE NAME STRING ADD
02330 PARM2  DEFW   0                  ; OUTPUT FILE NAME STRING AD
02340 PARM3  DEFW   0                  ; KEY STRING ADDR
02350 TYPE   DEFB   0                  ; RECORD TYPE (A/B/C)
02360 ORDER  DEFB   0                  ; SORT ORDER (A/D)
02370 SIZE   DEFW   0                  ; RECORD SIZE
02380 START  DEFW   0                  ; STARTING POSITION OF KEY
02390 END    DEFW   0                  ; ENDING POSITION OF KEY
02400 TEMP   DEFW   0                  ; HOLDS EOS ADDR
02410 DCBI   DEFS   32                 ; INPUT DCB
02420 DCBO   DEFS   32                 ; OUTPUT DCB
02430        END
```

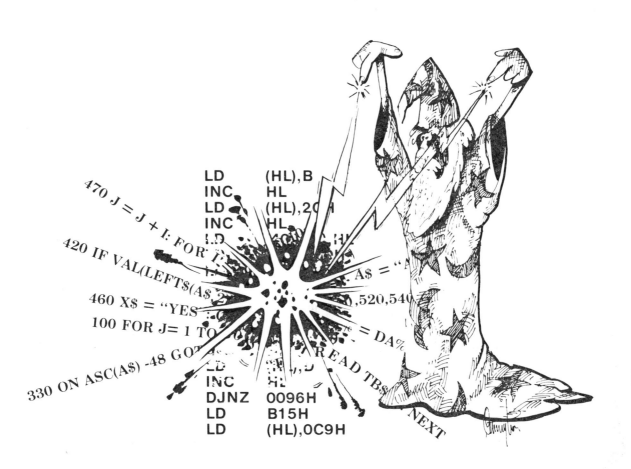

Chapter 6

BASIC Overlay Routine

This example shows how the tables in the Communications Region can be manipulated so that a BASIC program can load and execute overlays. The overlay program will add statements to an executing BASIC program while preserving all the current variables. The calling sequence to be used is:

```
100   DEF USR1=&HE000  : Address of of overlay program
        .               : Main body of application program
        .
        .
300   F$="FILE1/BAS"    : File containing overlay
310   Z=USR1(500)       : Replace lines 500 thru the end
                        : of the program with the
                        : statement from FILE1/BAS.)
320 GOSUB 500           : Execute the overlay
        .
        .
        .
500 REM START OF OVERLAY AREA
        .
        .
        .
```

The operating assumptions for this example will be the same as those in chapter 5. Note, overlay files containing the ASCII file must have been saved in the A mode.

The program itself will be considerably different, however. For instance, there will be no use of DOS Exits. This means that the CR will not need modifica-tion so there will be no need for an initial entry point. One parameter will be passed in the calling sequence while the other one will have an agreed name so that it can be located in the VLT.

When a BASIC program is executing there are three major tables that it uses. First is the PST where the BASIC statements to be executed have been stored. Second is the VLT where the variables assigned to the program are stored, and the third table is the FSL which represents available memory. All of these tables occur in the order mentioned. The problem we need to overcome in order to support overlays is to find a way to change the first table while maintaining the contents of the second one. A diagram of memory showing the tables follows.

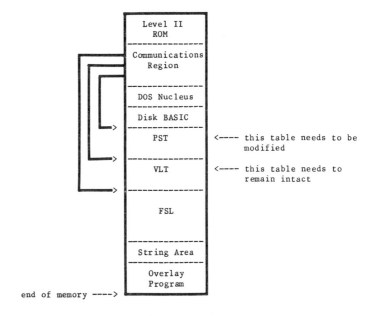

```
        ┌─────────────────┐
        │   Level II      │
        │     ROM         │
        │-----------------│
        │ Communications  │
        │    Region       │
        │-----------------│
        │  DOS Nucleus    │
        │-----------------│
        │  Disk BASIC     │
        │-----------------│
        │      PST        │  <---- this table needs to be
        │-----------------│         modified
        │      VLT        │  <---- this table needs to
        │-----------------│         remain intact
        │                 │
        │      FSL        │
        │                 │
        │-----------------│
        │  String Area    │
        │-----------------│
        │    Overlay      │
        │    Program      │
end of memory ---->└──────┘
```

Fortunately this can be accomplished quite easily. By moving the VLT to the high end of FSL we can seperate it from the PST. Then the overlay statements can be read from disk and added to the PST. Obviously the PST would either grow or shrink during this step unless the overlay being loaded was exactly the same size as the one before it. After the overlay statements have been added the VLT is moved back so it is adjacent to the PST. Then the pointers to the tables moved are updated and control is returned to the BASIC Execution Driver

The overlay loader used in this example assumes that the file containing the overlay statements is in ASCII format. This means that each incoming line must be tokenized before being moved to the PST. To speed up processing the loader could be modified to accept tokenized files.

There is no limit to the number of overlays that can be loaded. The program will exit with an error if a line number less than the starting number is detected. The loader does not test for a higher level overlay destroy-ing a lower one, this would be disasterous - as the return path would be destroyed.

A sample program to load three seperate overlays is given as an example.

```
100 A = 1.2345
110 B = 1
120 IF B = 1 THEN F$ = "FILE1"
130 IF B = 2 THEN F$ = "FILE2"
140 IF B = 3 THEN F$ = "FILE3"
150 Z = USR1(500)
160 GOSUB 500
170 B = B + 1
180 IF B > 3 THEN 110
190 GOTO 120
```

```
500 PRINT"OVERLAY #1 ENTERED"
510 PRINT A
520 C = 25                                        Contents
530 D = 30                                         of File 1
540 E = C+D+A
550 PRINT"C = ";
560 PRINT"D = ";D
570 PRINT"E = ";E
580 RETURN
```

```
500 PRINT"OVERLAY #2 ENTERED"
510 PRINT A
520 C = C + 1
530 D = D + 1
540 E = E + 1                                      Contents
550 REM                                            of File 2
560 REM
570 REM
580 REM
590 PRINT"C, D, E ";C,D,E
600 RETURN
```

```
500 PRINT"OVERLAY #3 ENTERED"
510 A = A + 1                                      Contents
520 PRINT"A = ";A                                  of File 3
530 RETURN
```

```
00100        ORG     0F000H
00110 OPEN   EQU     4424H        ; DOS ADDRESS
00120 READ   EQU     4436H        ; DOS ADDRESS
00130 ERN    EQU     12           ; DISK DCB ADDRESS
00140 NRN    EQU     10           ; DISK DCB ADDRESS
00150 EOF    EQU     8            ; DISK DCB ADDRESS
00160 ;*
00170 ;*     ENTRY POINT FOR OVERLAY LOADING OF BASIC PROGRAMS
00180 ;*
00190        PUSH    AF           ; SAVE ALL REGISTERS
00200        PUSH    BC
00210        PUSH    DE
00220        PUSH    HL
00230        LD      HL,-1        ; INITIALIZE SECTOR COUNT
00240        LD      (RCOUNT),HL  ; TO MINUS 1
00250        LD      HL,00        ; SO WE CAN LOAD CSP
00260        ADD     HL,SP        ; LOAD CSP
00270        LD      (CSP),HL     ; SAVE FOR RESTORATION
00280        LD      DE,(4121H)   ; LINE NO TO START OVERLAY
00290        LD      (LINE),DE    ; SAVE FOR FUTURE REF
00300        LD      A,(40AFH)    ; FUNCTION VALUE TYPE
00310        LD      (TYPE),A     ; MUST BE RESTORED AT END
00320 ;*
00330 ;*     BLANK FILL DCB BEFORE MOVING NAME INTO IT
00340 ;*
00350        LD      B,32         ; NO. OF BYTES TO BLANK
00360        LD      HL,DCB       ; DCB ADDR
00370        LD      A,20H        ; ASCII BLANK
00380 BFL    LD      (HL),A       ; MOVE ONE BLANK
00390        INC     HL           ; BUMP TO NEXT WORD
00400        DJNZ    BFL          ; LOOP TILL DCB FILLED
00410 ;*
00420 ;*     GET OVERLAY FILE NAME FROM VARIABLE F$
00430 ;*     MOVE IT INTO THE BLANKED DCB
00440 ;*
00450        LD      HL,LFN       ; STRING FOR COMMON VAR NAME
00460        CALL    2540H        ; GET ADDR OF F$
00470        RST     20H          ; MAKE SURE IT'S A STRING
00480        JR      Z,OK         ; ZERO IF STRING
00490        JP      ERR          ; WRONG TYPE OF VARIABLE
00500 OK     LD      HL,(4121H)   ; GET ADDR OF F$ INTO HL
00510        LD      DE,DCB       ; DCB ADDR
00520        CALL    29C8H        ; MOVE F$ NAME TO DCB
00530 ;*
00540 ;*     INITIALIZE ALL LOCAL VARIABLES
00550 ;*
00560        LD      A,0          ; SET PASS FLAG TO ZERO
```

```
00570        LD      (PF),A       ; PASS FLAG
00580        LD      (FI),A       ; SECTOR BUFFER INDEX
00590 ;*
00600 ;*  LOCATE ADDR OF VARIABLE ASSIGND TO FUNCTION CALL. IT
00610 ;*  MUST BE RECOMPUTED AFTER THE OVERLAY HAS BEEN LOADED
00620 ;*  BECAUSE THE VLT WILL HAVE BEEN MOVED. NEXT, ALLOCATE
00630 ;*  SPACE IN THE FSL FOR THE SECTOR BUFFER USED FOR
00640 ;*  READING THE OVERLAY FILE.
00650 ;*
00660        LD      HL,00        ; SO WE CAN LOAD CSP
00670        ADD     HL,SP        ; HL = CSP
00680        PUSH    HL           ; SAVE CSP
00690        LD      BC,20        ; AMT TO BACKSPACE CSP
00700        ADD     HL,BC        ; GIVES CSP - 20  OR ADDR
00710 ;*                          ; OF FUNCTION VARIABLE
00720        LD      (VARADR),HL  ; SAVE STK ADDR OF VAR
00730        POP     HL           ; RESTORE CSP TO HL
00740        LD      BC,-256      ; AMT OF SPACE TO ALLOCTAT
00750 ;*                          ; IN FSL FOR SECTOR BUFFR
00760        ADD     HL,BC        ; COMPUTE NEW CSP
00770        LD      (BADDR),HL   ; START OF SECTOR BUFFER
00780        LD      SP,HL        ; IS ALSO NEW CSP
00790        PUSH    HL
00800        LD      DE,(40F9H)   ; CURRENT END OF PST
00810        LD      (CEPST),DE   ; SAVE FOR COMPUTATIONS
00820        LD      HL,(40FBH)   ; START OF ARRAYS
00830        XOR     A            ; CLEAR CARRY
00840        SBC     HL,DE        ; COMPUTE OFFSET FROM START
00850 ;*                          ; OF VLT TO START OF ARRAYS
00860        LD      (LSVLT),HL   ; SAVE OFFSET
00870 ;*
00880 ;*
00890 ;*
00900        LD      DE,(LINE)    ; FIND ADDR OF LINE WHERE
00910        CALL    1B2CH        ; OVERLAY STARTS IN PST
00920        LD      (40F9H),BC   ; MAKE IT TEMP END OF PST
00930 ;*
00940 ;*  COMPUTE LENGTH OF VLT
00950 ;*
00960        LD      DE,(CEPST)   ; ORGINAL END OF PST
00970        LD      HL,(40FDH)   ; START OF FSL
00980        XOR     A            ; CLEAR CARRY
00990        SBC     HL,DE        ; GIVES LNG -1 OF VLT
01000        INC     HL           ; CORRECT FOR -1
01010        LD      (LVLT),HL    ; SAVE LENGHT OF VLT
01020        POP     HL           ; RESTORE CSP TO HL
01030        LD      BC,-50       ; ASSUMED STK LENG NEEDED
01040        ADD     HL,BC        ; GIVE END OF TEMP VLT
01050        LD      BC,(LVLT)    ; NOW, SUBTRACT LENGTH OF
01060        XOR     A            ; VLT FROM END TO GET START
01070        SBC     HL,BC        ; ADDRESS
01080        LD      (SNVLT),HL   ; SAVE END OF TEMP VLT
01090        PUSH    HL           ; SO WE CAN
01100        POP     DE           ; LOAD IT INTO DE
01110        LD      HL,(CEPST)   ; START OF OLD PST
01120        LD      BC,(LVLT)    ; SIZE OF VLT
01130        LDIR                 ; MOVE VLT TO TEMP LOC.
01140 ;*
01150 ;*  BEGIN OVERLAY LOADING
01160 ;*
01170        LD      DE,DCB       ; DCB FOR OVERLAY FILE
01180        LD      HL,(BADDR)   ; SECTOR BUFF ADDR
01190        LD      BC,0         ; SPECIFY SECTOR I/O
01200        CALL    OPEN         ; OPEN OVERLAY FILE
01210 LOOP   CALL    GNL          ; GET NEXT LINE FROM FILE
01220        JR      Z,OUT        ; ZERO IF NO MORE LINES
01230 ;*                          ; IN OVERLAY FILE
01240        CALL    ATOB         ; ADD LINE TO PST
01250        JR      LOOP         ; LOOP TILL FILE EXHAUSTED
01260 ;*
01270 ;*  OVERLAY STATEMENTS HAVE BEEN ADDED. RESET POINTERS
01280 ;*  TO VLT AFTER MOVING IT DOWN (ADJACENT TO PST).
01290 ;*
01300 OUT    LD      HL,(SNVLT)   ; START OF TEMP VLT
01310        LD      DE,(40F9H)   ; CURRENT END OF PST
01320        INC     DE           ; LEAVE TWO BYTES
01330        INC     DE           ; OF ZEROS AT END OF PST
01340        LD      (40F9H),DE   ; SAVE START ADDR OF NEW VLT
01350        LD      BC,(LVLT)    ; LENGTH OF VLT
01360        LDIR                 ; MOVE VLT TO END OF PST
01370        INC     DE           ; GIVES ADDR OF FLS
01380        PUSH    DE           ; SAVE FSL ADDR
01390        LD      HL,(40F9H)   ; START OF VLT
01400        LD      BC,(LSVLT)   ; PLUS LNG OF SIMP VAR
01410        ADD     HL,BC        ; GIVES ADDR OF ARRAYS PTR
01420        LD      (40FBH),HL   ; SAVE NEW ARRAYS POINTER
01430        POP     HL           ; HL = NEW FSL ADDR
01440        LD      (40FDH),HL   ; UPDATE FSL
01450 ;*
01460 ;*  COMPUTE DISTANCE VLT HAS MOVED AND UPDATE THE ADDR OF
01470 ;*  THE FUNCTION VARIABLE BEING CARRIED ON THE STACK.
01480 ;*
```

```
01490        LD      DE,(CEPST)      ; ORGIANL START OF VLT
01500        LD      HL,(40F9H)      ; CURRENT START OF VLT
01510        RST     18H             ; COMPARE THE ADDRESSES
01520        JR      NC,UP           ; NEW VLT WAS MOVED UP
01530        PUSH    HL              ; REVERSE OPERANDS
01540        PUSH    DE
01550        XOR     A               ; CLEAR CARRY
01560        POP     HL              ; RERSTORE OPERANDS
01570        POP     DE
01580        JR      UP1             ; GO COMPUTE DISTANCE
01590 UP     XOR     A               ; CLEAR CARRY FOR SUB
01600 UP1    SBC     HL,DE           ; COMPUTE AMT VLT HAS MOVED
01610        PUSH    HL              ; SAVE DISTANCE
01620        LD      HL,(VARADR)     ; THEN ADD IT TO ADDR
01630        LD      C,(HL)          ; CARRIED ON STK
01640        INC     HL              ; BUMP TO MSB OF ADDR
01650        LD      B,(HL)          ; BC = ADDR OF VAR THAT WAS
01660 ;*                             ;   CARRIED ON STK
01670        POP     HL              ; GET DISPLACEMENT
01680        ADD     HL,BC           ; GET NEW ADDR (BECAUSE VLT
01690 ;*                             ;   HAS BEEN MOVED
01700        PUSH    HL              ; SO WE CAN LOAD IT INTO
01710        POP     DE              ; LOAD NEW ADDR INTO DE
01720        LD      HL,(VARADR)     ; REFETCH STK ADDR
01730        LD      (HL),E          ; LSB OF FUNCTION VAR ADDR
01740        INC     HL              ; NEXT BYTE ADDR ON STK
01750        LD      (HL),D          ; MSB OF FUNCTION VAR ADDR
01760 ;*
01770 ;*     RESET TYPE TO IT'S ORGINAL VALUE
01780 ;*
01790        LD      A,(TYPE)        ; GET MODE FLAG WHEN ENTERED
01800        LD      (40AFH),A       ; RESTORE MODE TO ORGIANL
01810        LD      HL,(CSP)        ; RESET CSP
01820        LD      SP,HL           ; TO IT'S ORGINAL VALUE
01830        POP     HL              ; RESTORE REGISTERS
01840        POP     DE
01850        POP     BC
01860        POP     AF
01870        RET                     ; RETURN TO BASIC
01880 ;*
01890 ;*     GNL - GETS NEXT LINE OF BASIC PROGRAM FROM A FILE
01900 ;*             MOVES IT TO BASIC LINE BUFFER AREA AND THEN
01910 ;*             TOKENIZES IT.
01920 ;*             FILE IS ASSUMED TO BE IN ASCII FORMAT. LINES ARE
01930 ;*             TERMINATED BY A CARRIAGE RET. (0D).
01940 ;*
01950 GNL    LD      A,(PF)          ; GET PASS FLAG
01960        OR      A               ; IS IT TIME TO READ SECTOR
01970        JR      NZ,GNL5         ; NO IF NON-ZERO
01980 GNL3   LD      A,0             ; RESET SECTOR BUFF INDEX
01990        LD      (FI),A          ; TO ZERO
02000        LD      HL,(RCOUNT)     ; PREPARE TO TEST FOR
02010        INC     HL              ; END OF FILE. BUMP COUNT
02020        LD      (RCOUNT),HL     ; OF SECTORS READ
02030        LD      BC,0            ; READ NEXT SECTOR
02040        LD      DE,DCB          ; OVERLAY DCB ADDR
02050        LD      HL,(BADDR)      ; SECTOR BUFF ADDR
02060        CALL    READ            ; READ NEXT SECTOR
02070        LD      A,1             ; RESET PASS FLAG
02080        LD      (PF),A          ; TO DATA IN BUFFER
02090 GNL5   LD      DE,(RCOUNT)     ; NOW TEST FOR END OF FILE
02100        LD      HL,(DCB+ERN)    ; LAST SECTOR NO FROM DCB
02110        XOR     A               ; CLEAR CARRY FOR SUB
02120        SBC     HL,DE           ; HAS LAST SECTOR BEEN READ
02130        JR      NZ,GNL10        ; NON-ZERO IF NOT LAST SECT
02140        LD      A,(DCB+EOF)     ; IN LAST SECTOR. END OF D
02150        LD      B,A             ; DATA REACHED YET?
02160        LD      A,(FI)          ; CURRENT SECTOR INDEX
02170        SUB     B               ; MUST BE LE TO EOD INDEX
02180        JR      C,GNL10         ; CARRY IF NOT END OF DATA
02190        XOR     A               ; SIGNAL END OF FILE
02200        RET                     ; RET TO MAIN PGM
02210 GNL10  LD      HL,(BADDR)      ; SECTOR BUFF ADDR
02220        LD      A,(FI)          ; CURRENT BUFF INDEX
02230        LD      C,A             ; FOR 16 BIT AIRTH
02240        LD      B,0             ; DITTO
02250        ADD     HL,BC           ; CURRENT LINE ADDR IN BUFF
02260        LD      DE,(40A7H)      ; BA~ ; LINE BUFF ADDR
02270 GNL15  LD      A,(HL)          ; MOVE LINE FROM SECT BUFF
02280        LD      (DE),A          ; TO BASIC LINE BUFF
02290        INC     DE              ; BUMP DEST ADDR
02300        INC     C               ; COUNT 1 CHAR MOVED
02310        JR      C,GNL3          ; JMP IF LINE OVERFLOWS
02320 ;*                             ;   SECTOR
02330        INC     HL              ; NO OVERFLOW, BUMP FETCH
02340        SUB     0DH             ; ADDR. TEST FOR END OF LINE
02350        JR      NZ,GNL15        ; LOOP TILL END OF LINE
02360        DEC     DE              ; BKSPC 1 CHAR IN LINE BUFF
02370        LD      (DE),A          ; AND TERM IT WITH A ZERO
02380        LD      A,C             ; SAVE ENDING BUFF INDEX
02390        LD      (FI),A          ; FOR NEXT LINE
02400        OR      A               ; SIGNAL MORE DATA

02410        RET                     ; RET TO CALLER
02420 ;*
02430 ;*     TOKENIZE LINE IN BUFFER. THEN ADD IT TO PST
02440 ;*
02450 ATOB   LD      HL,(40A7H)      ; LINE BUFFER ADDR
02460        CALL    1E5AH           ; GET BINARY LINE NO
02470        PUSH    DE              ; SAVE IT
02480        PUSH    HL              ; SAVE LINE BUFF ADDR
02490        LD      HL,(LINE)       ; BEG OVERLAY LINE NO
02500        RST     18H             ; COMPARED W/CURRENT LINE
02510        JR      Z,ATOB5         ; OK IF EQUAL
02520        JR      NC,ERR          ; ERR IF INCOMMING LESS
02530 ;*                             ;   THAN OVERLAY LINE NO
02540 ATOB5  POP     HL              ; RESTORE LINE ADDR
02550        CALL    1BC0H           ; TOKENIZE LINE
02560        LD      HL,(40F9H)      ; CURRENT END OF PST
02570        PUSH    HL              ; SAVE ADDR OF THIS LINE
02580        ADD     HL,BC           ; ADD LNG OF NEW LINE
02590        LD      (40F9H),HL      ; START OF NEXT LINE
02600        PUSH    HL              ; SO WE CAN
02610        POP     DE              ; LOAD IT INTO DE
02620 ;*
02630 ;*     UPDATE POINTER TO NEXT LINE IN NEW LINE BEING ADDED.
02640 ;*     THEN MOVE BINARY LINE NO. FOR THIS LINE TO PST.
02650 ;*
02660        POP     HL              ; ADDR OF THIS LINE IN PST
02670        LD      (HL),E          ; LSB OF ADDR NEXT LINE
02680        INC     HL
02690        LD      (HL),D          ; MSB OF ADDR NEXT LINE
02700        INC     HL              ; START OF BIN LINE NO
02710        POP     DE              ; BINARY LINE NO
02720        LD      (HL),E          ; LSB OF LINE NO
02730        INC     HL
02740        LD      (HL),D          ; MSB OF LINE NO
02750        INC     HL              ; BUMP TO FIRST CHAR IN LINE
02760        EX      DE,HL           ; DE = PST FOR LINE
02770        LD      HL,(40A7H)      ; TOKENIZED LINE ADDR
02780        DEC     HL
02790        DEC     HL
02800 ATOB10 LD      A,(HL)          ; GET A TOKENIZED BYTE
02810        LD      (DE),A          ; MOVE IT TO PST
02820        INC     HL
02830        INC     DE
02840        OR      A               ; TEST OF EOS
02850        JR      NZ,ATOB10       ; JMP IF NOT END OF STAT.
02860        LD      (DE),A          ; OF MACHINE ZEROS
02870        INC     DE
02880        LD      (DE),A
02890        RET                     ; RET TO CALLER
02900 ;*
02910 ;*     ERROR PROCESSNG - RECOVER STACK SPACE
02920 ;*
02930 ERR    POP     AF              ; CLEAR STACK
02940        POP     AF              ; CLEAR STACK
02950        POP     AF              ; CLEAR STACK
02960        LD      HL,0            ; DEALLOCATE SECTOR BUFFER
02970        ADD     HL,SP           ; CSP
02980        LD      BC,256          ; SIZE OF SECTOR BUFF
02990        ADD     HL,BC           ; COMPUTE NEW CSP
03000        LD      SP,HL           ; SETUP NEW CSP
03010 ERR10  POP     AF              ; CLEAR STACK
03020        POP     AF              ; CLEAR STACK
03030        POP     AF              ; CLEAR STACK
03040        POP     AF              ; CLEAR STACK
03050        POP     AF              ; CLEAR STACK
03060        LD      A,2             ; CODE FOR SYNTAX ERROR
03070        JP      1997H           ; GIVE ERR, RTN TO BASIC
03080 ;*
03090 ;*     CONSTANTS AND COUNTERS
03100 ;*
03110 LINE   DEFW    0               ; OVERLAY LINE NO
03120 CSP    DEFW    0               ; HOLDS CSP ON ENTRY
03130 TYPE   DEFB    0               ; ORGINAL DATA TYPE
03140 LFN    DEFM    'F$'            ; COMMON VARIABLE NAME
03150        DEFB    0
03160 DCB    DEFS    32              ; OVERLAY DCB
03170 BADDR  DEFW    0               ; SECTOR BUFF ADDR ON STK
03180 VARADR DEFW    0               ; VARIABLE ADDR ON STK
03190 CEPST  DEFW    0               ; CURRENT END OF PST
03200 LVLT   DEFW    0               ; LENGTH OF VLT
03210 SNVLT  DEFW    0               ; START ADDR OF NEW VLT
03220 LSVLT  DEFW    0               ; LENGTH OF SIMP VAR VLT
03230 PF     DEFB    0               ; PASS FLAG
03240 FI     DEFB    0               ; SECTOR BUFF INDEX
03250 RCOUNT DEFW    -1              ; COUNT OF SECTORS READ
03260        END
```

Chapter 7 ====================

BASIC Decoded: New ROMs

The comments in chapter 8 are based on the original three chip ROM set, if you have a 2 chip ROM configuration your dissassembly will probably be slightly different.

Differences between the latest 'MEM SIZE ?' ROMs and the old ROMs are given below. Locations with an asterisk next to them have different contents than the next chapter.

When running a Disassembler be careful to check the page sequence where differences occur.

This comment chapter was designed to be used in conjunction with a disassembler that produces 62 lines per page. The Apparat NEWDOS plus Disassembler was used during the books production.

```
0050    0D       DEC  --- Enter no shift (0D)                      * ASCII values
0051    0D       DEC  --- Enter shift (0D)
0052    1F       RRA  --- Clear no shift (1F)
0053    1F       RRA  --- Clear shift (1F)
0054    01015B   LD   --- BREAK ns (01) / BREAK shift (01) / up arrow ns (5B)
0057    1B       DEC  --- Up arrow shift (1B)
0058    0A       LD   --- Down arrow no shift (0A)
0059    *00      NOP  --- Down arrow shift (00)
005A    08       EX   --- Left arrow no shift (08)
005B    1809     JR   --- Left arrow shift (18) / right arrow no shift (09)
005D    19       ADD  --- Right arrow shift (19)
005E    2020     JR   --- Space no shift (20) / space shift (20)

00FC    *210E01  LD   --- Address of 'R/S L2 BASIC' message

0105    4D       LD   --- M                                        * MEM SIZE
0106    45       LD   --- E
0107    4D       LD   --- M
0108    *2053    JR   --- Space, S
010A    *49      LD   --- I
010B    *5A      LD   --- Z
010C    *45      LD   --- E
```

```
010D    *00        NOP    --- Message terminator
010E    *52        LD     --- R                              * R/S L2 BASIC
010F    *2F        CL     --- /
0110    *53        LD     --- S
0111    *204C      JR     --- Space, L
0113    *322042    LD     --- 2, space, B
0116    *41        LD     --- A
0117     53        LD     --- C
0118    *49        LD     --- I
0119    *43        LD     --- C
011A    *OD        DEC    --- Carriage return
011B    *00        NOP    --- Message terminator
011C    *C5        PUSH   --- Save active row address
011D    *010005    LD     --- Delay count value
0120    *CD6000    CALL   --- Delay for 7.33 milliseconds      * Debounce routine
0123    *C1        POP    --- Restore row address
0124    *OA        LD     --- And reload original flags from active row
0125    *A3        AND    --- Then combine current flag lists with original flag bits
0126    *C8        RET    --- Rtn to caller if zero because row was not active on 2nd test
0127    *7A        LD     --- Otherwise we have a legimately active row
0128    *07        RLCA   --- Row index * 2
0129    *07        RLCA   --- Row index * 4
012A    *C3FE03    JP     --- Return to rest of keyboard driver routine

0248    *0660      LD     --- Now, delay for 476/703 microseconds

024F    *0685      LD     --- Then delay for 865/975 microseconds

02E2    *20ED      JR     --- If no match, skip to next program on cassette
02E4    *23        INC    --- We have a character match. Bump to next char of typed in name.

03FB    *C31C01    JP     --- Go to debounce routine. If legimate char rtn to 3FE, else rtn to
caller.

0683    *20F1      JR     --- Loop thru block move routine 128 times

1225     E7        RST    --- Double precision or string
1226    *300B      JR     --- Jmp if double precision

124D    *B7        OR     --- Set status flags

1265    *F24312    JP     --- No change in this comment

2067     3E01      LD     --- A = device code for printer            * LPRINT routine
2069     329C40    LD     --- Set current system device to printer
206C    *C37C20    JP
206F     CDCA41    CALL   --- DOS Exit                                * PRINT routine
2072    *FE23      CP     --- Test for #
2074    *2006      JR     --- Jmp if not PRINT #
2076    *CD8402    CALL   --- Write header on cassette file          * PRINT # routine
2079    *329C40    LD     --- Set current system device to cassette
207C    *2B        DEC    --- Backspace over previous symbol in code string
207D    *D7        RST    --- Re-examine previous char in code string
207E    *CCFE20    CALL   --- If end of string write a Carrige Return
2081    *CA6921    JP     --- If end of string turn off cassette and return
2084    *F620      OR     --- Not end of string.  Convert possible 40 to 60
2086    *FE60      CP     --- Then test for @
2088    *201B      JR     --- Jmp if not PRINT @
208A    *CD012B    CALL   --- Evaluate @ expression, result in DE   * PRINT @ routine
208D    *FE04      CP     --- A = MSB, test for @ value > 1023
```

208F	*D24A1E	JP	--- FC error if @ position > 1023
2092	*E5	PUSH	--- Save current code string addr
2093	*21003C	LD	--- HL = starting addr of video buffer
2096	*19	ADD	--- All tab position
2097	*222040	LD	--- And save addr in video DCB as cursor addr
209A	*7B	LD	--- Then get position within line
209B	*E63F	CP	--- And truncate it to 63
209D	*32A640	LD	--- Then save as current position within line
20A0	*E1	POP	--- Restore code string addr (starting addr of item list)
20A1	*CF	RST	--- But make sure a comma follows the tab position
20A2	*2C	INC	--- DC 2C ´,´
20A3	*18C7	JR	--- Go get first variable from item list
20A5	*7E	LD	--- Reload next element from code string
20A6	*FEBF	CP	--- Test for USING token
20A8	*CABD2C	JP	--- Jmp if USING token
20AB	*FEBC	CP	--- Test for TAB token
20AD	*CA3721	JP	--- Jmp if TAB token
20B0	*E5	PUSH	--- Save current code string addr
20B1	*FEC2	CP	--- Test for a comma
20B3	*2853	JR	--- Go get next item if a comma
20B5	*FE3B	CP	--- Not comma, test for semi-colon
20B7	*285E	JR	--- Go get next item if semi-colon
20B9	CD3723	CALL	--- Evaluate next item to be printed
20BC	*E3	EX	--- Save current code string addr HL = addr of current item
20F6	*C37C20	JP	--- And loop till end of statement (EOS)
213A	*E67F	AND	--- Result in A-reg. Do not let it exceed 127
2166	*C38120	JP	--- Process next of PRINT TAB statement
226A	*00	NOP	--- Remove
226B	*00	NOP	--- Erroneous
226C	*00	NOP	--- Test
226D	*00	NOP	--- For
226E	*00	NOP	--- FD error
2C1F	*D6B2		--- Test for CLOAD? * CLOAD routine
2C21	*2802		--- Jmp if CLOAD?
2C23	*AF		--- Signal CLOAD
2C24	*012F23		--- 2C25: CPL A=-1 if CLOAD?, 0000 if CLOAD
2C27	*F5		--- 2C26: INC HL position to file name Save CLOAD? / CLOAD flag
2C28	*7E		--- Get next element from code string. Should be file name
2C29	*B7		--- Set status flags
2C2A	*2807		--- Jmp if end of line
2C2C	*CD2723		--- Evaluate expression (get file name)
2C2F	*CD132A		--- Get addr of file name into DE
2C32	*1A		--- Get file name
2C33	*6F		--- And move it to L-reg
2C34	*F1		--- Restore CLOAD? / CLOAD flags
2C35	*B7		--- Set status register according to flags
2C36	*67		--- H=CLOAD?/CLOAD flag, L=file name
2C37	*222141		--- Save flag and file name in WRA1
2C3A	*CC4D1B		--- If CLOAD call NEW routine to initialize system variables
2C3D	*210000		--- This will cause the drive to be selected when
2C40	*CD9302		--- We look for leader and synch byte
2C43			--- Restore CLOAD? / CLOAD flag, file name
2FFB	*DEC3		--- These instructions
2FFD	*C344B2		--- Are not used by Level II

Chapter 8

BASIC Decoded: Old ROMs

How to use this book

Unlike most books, this book is made to come apart. Due to the unique nature of the subject matter and the use to which it will be put, its pages may be removed and inserted into a three ring binder. The pages are pre-drilled, and the binding is such that the pages may be removed with little effort.

Each page has 62 lines of comments. This exactly matches the Apparat disassembler's output format. Any printer that will print 66 lines per eleven inch length page, will print the disassembler's output so that it may be lined-up with the comments exactly. Remove the pages and insert them into a three ring binder.

The comments and memory locations are for the original three chip ROM sets, please see chapter 7 for differences on later 2 chip sets.

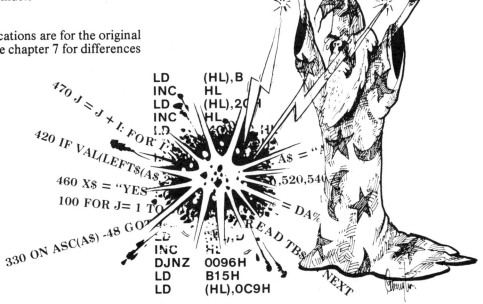

```
0000 F3        DI      --- Power on IPL entry -Turn off clock/disk interrupts
0001 AF        XOR     --- Clear A-reg, status
0002 C37406    JP      --- Go to beginning of IPL sequence
0005 C30040    JP      --- ****************************** Compare *****
0008 C30040    JP      --- RST 08 (JP 1C96) Compare value following cont-->
000B E1        POP      . These instructions are not
000C E9        JP       . used by Level II
000D C39F06    JP      --- Jmp to load & execute sector loader
0010 C30340    JP      --- RST 10 (JP 1D78) Load and examine next char
0013 C5        PUSH    --- Save BC - Keyboard routine
0014 0601      LD      --- B = Entry code
0016 182E      JR      --- Go to driver entry routine (3C2)
0018 C30640    JP      --- RST 18 (JP 1C90H)  Compare DE:HL
001B C5        PUSH    --- Save BC - Display routine, printer routine
001C 0602      LD      --- B = Entry code
001E 1826      JR      --- Go to driver entry routine (3C2)
0020 C30940    JP      --- RST 20 (JP 25D9H)  Determine data type.
0023 C5        PUSH    --- Save BC
0024 0604      LD      --- B = Entry code
0026 181E      JR      --- Go to driver entry routine (3C2)
0028 C30C40    JP      --- RST 28 (Non DOS - Ret; DOS 2.0 - JP 4BA2H)
002B 111540    LD      --- Load keyboard DCB addr into DE ** Scan keyboard *
002E 18E3      JR      --- Jmp to keyboard driver
0030 C30F40    JP      --- RST 30 (Non DOS - Rtn  DOS 2.0 - JP 44B4H)
0033 111D40    LD      --- Load video DCB addr into DE ***** Video display  *
0036 18E3      JR      --- Jmp to video driver
0038 C31240    JP      --- RST 38 (Non DOS - DI, Rtn  DOS 2.0 -     cont-->
003B 112540    LD      --- Load printer DCB ptr ****************************
003E 18DB      JR      --- Jmp to printer driver
0040 C3D905    JP      --- Go see what's being typed
0043 C9        RET      . These instructions are
0044 00        NOP      .  not used
0045 00        NOP      .   by Level II
0046 C3C203    JP      --- Go to driver entry routine
0049 CD2B00    CALL    --- Strobe keyboard ******* Wait for keyboard input *
004C B7        OR      --- Test if any key active
004D C0        RET     --- Go if key active
004E 18F9      JR      --- Loop till some key pressed
0050 0D        DEC     --- ENTER, no shift (0D) ************** see note--> *
0051 0D        DEC     --- ENTER, shift (0D)
0052 1F        RRA     --- CLEAR, no shift (1F)
0053 1F        RRA     --- CLEAR, shift (1F)
0054 01015B    LD      --- BREAK ns (01), BREAK shift (01), UP arrow ns (5B)
0057 1B        DEC     --- Up arrow, shift (1B)
0058 0A        LD      --- Down arrow, no shift (0A)
0059 1A        LD      --- Down arrow, shift (00)
005A 08        EX      --- Left arrow, no shift (08)
005B 1809      JR      --- Left arrow, shift (18): Right arrow, ns (09)
005D 19        ADD     --- Right arrow, shift (19)
005E 2020      JR      --- Space, ns (20): Space, shift (20)
0060 0B        DEC     --- Decrement cycle count *** Delay **** see note--> *
0061 78        LD      --- Test if count zero
0062 B1        OR      --- Combine LSB/MSB of count
0063 20FB      JR      --- Loop until delay count exhausted
0065 C9        RET     --- Rtn to caller
0066 310006    LD      --- Reset IPL entry ****************** Reset ******
0069 3AEC37    LD      --- Get controller status            see note-->
006C 3C        INC     --- Test for controller present
006D FE02      CP      --- Status usually FF if no EI
006F D20000    JP      --- NC if controller addressable. Join common IPL code
```

```
0005  *  ********************************************************
0008  :  RST 08 with next input symbol.
      :  Syntax error if unequal




002B  *  **********************************************************


0033  *  **********************************************************

0038  :  JP(4518H)    Entry pt. for all interrupts
003B  *  **********************************************************




0049  *  **********************************************************



0050  *  Table for keyboard routine at 3E3H ************************
      *
      *  ASCII values for ENTER, CLEAR, BREAK, UP ARROW,
      *  DOWN ARROW, LEFT ARROW, RIGHT ARROW and SPACE




0060  *  Delay for ((BC-1) * 26 + 17) * 2.255  T-states *************



0066  *  **********************************************************
      :  Status = 00 - If EI (Expansion Interface) present and DISK
      :           80 - If EI and DISK not ready              :ready
      :           FF - If EI off or not present
```

64

0072 C3CC06	JP	---	No disk go to BASIC 'READY' prompt
0075 118040	LD	---	Here on power on or reset with no disk ***********
0078 21F718	LD	---	Move initialization data to communication area
007B 012700	LD	---	Number of bytes to move
007E EDB0	LDIR	---	Move ROM 18F7-191D to RAM 4080-40A6 see note-->
0080 21E541	LD	---	Continue with comm. region initialization
0083 363A	LD	---	3A to 41E5 LD A,(2C00)
0085 23	INC	---	Bump to 41E6
0086 70	LD	---	0 to 41E6
0087 23	INC	---	Bump to 41E7
0088 362C	LD	---	2C to 41E7
008A 23	INC	---	HL = 41E8. Set input buffer pointer (40A7)
008B 22A740	LD	---	to keyboard buffer area (41E8)
008E 112D01	LD	---	Addr field for JP instr
0091 061C	LD	---	Initialize 4152-41A5 to JP 12D this gives an L3
0093 215241	LD	---	Error if disk basic commands are attempted
0096 36C3	LD	---	C3 to 4152 gives (JP)
0098 23	INC	---	Bump to LSB of address field
0099 73	LD	---	2D to 4153 gives (JP 2D) 23
009A 23	INC	---	Bump to MSB of address field
009B 72	LD	---	01 to 4154 gives (JP 012D)
009C 23	INC	---	Bump to addr. of next JP instr
009D 10F7	DJNZ	---	Repeat 28 times (84 locations)
009F 0615	LD	---	loop count for DOS EXIT RETURNS
00A1 36C9	LD	---	C9 to 41A6 gives (RETURN INSTRUCTION)
00A3 23	INC	-	41A9: Ret Clear DOS EXIT vectors
00A4 23	INC	-	: to RETURNS
00A5 23	INC	-	41E2: Ret
00A6 10F9	DJNZ	---	repeat: (gives JP 012D) in locs 4152 - 41A5
00A8 21E842	LD	---	Load HL with addr so we can store
00AB 70	LD	---	0 to 42E8
00AC 31F841	LD	---	Stack addr. during IPL is 41F8
00AF CD8F1B	CALL	---	Initialize BASIC printers and variables
00B2 CDC901	CALL	---	Clear screen
00B5 210501	LD	---	'MEMORY SIZE ?' message pntr
00B8 CDA728	CALL	---	Output message
00BB CDB31B	CALL	---	Print '? ' and wait for user input
00BE 38F5	JR	---	If break was hit, ask again
00C0 D7	RST	---	Examine a character from response
00C1 B7	OR	---	Set status flags
00C2 2012	JR	---	Jmp if not end of response
00C4 214C43	LD	---	If CR only entered, then determine cont-->
00C7 23	INC	---	Start at 17220 and work towards 65535 testing for
00C8 7C	LD	---	LSB of next test addr :memory
00C9 B5	OR	---	Combine w/MSB of next test addr
00CA 281B	JR	---	Memory up thru 65535 scanned. cont-->
00CC 7E	LD	---	Fetch original contents of memory test location
00CD 47	LD	---	Save it for restoration
00CE 2F	CPL	---	Complement it (gives test pattern)
00CF 77	LD	---	Store test pattern
00D0 BE	CP	---	Compare contents of mem loc with test pattern
00D1 70	LD	---	Restore original value
00D2 28F3	JR	---	Address exists. Go test for min amt of memory
00D4 1811	JR	---	Address non-existant. Bump to next addr & test
00D6 CD5A1E	CALL	---	Get binary equivalent of value :again
00D9 B7	OR	---	into DE/A
00DA C29719	JP	---	SN error if NZ
00DD EB	EX	---	HL = memory size
00DE 2B	DEC	---	Size minus one . Test memory size value
00DF 3E8F	LD	---	Comparison value . make sure it's there.

```
0075 * ****************************************************************

007E : Load division support routine.  Initialize comm. region to:
     : 4080 - 408D     Division support routine
     : 408E 1E4A       Address of user subroutine
     : 4090 E64DDB     Random number seed
     : 4093 IN A,(00)  INP skeleton instruction
     : 4095 RET
     : 4096 OUT A,00   OUTP skeleton instruction.
     : 4098 RET
     : 4099    00      Last character typed
     : 409A    00      Error count
     : 409B    00      Count of chars in current line
     : 409C            Output device type
     : 40AD    00      Size of display line (64 characters)
     : 409E    30      Line size during PRINT

     : 40A0 - 434C     Start of string area
     : 40A2 FEFF       Initial BASIC line number
     : 40A4 42E9       Address of PROGRAM STATEMENT TABLE (PST)




00C4 : mem. size dynamically



00CA : Go test for min amt required
```

00E1	46	LD	--- Fetch contents of memory and save in B reg
00E2	77	LD	--- Store test pattern
00E3	BE	CP	--- Compare test pattern stored with pattern in A reg
00E4	70	LD	--- Restore original value of memory location
00E5	20CE	JR	--- Specified memory size not present, ask again
00E7	2B	DEC	--- Amt of memory - 2
00E8	111444	LD	--- DE = 17428 (dec.)
00EB	DF	RST	--- Test for a minimum amount of mem (17428)
00EC	DA7A19	JP	--- OM error if C. Insufficient memory
00EF	11CEFF	LD	--- Load constant for default size of see note-->-
00F2	22B140	LD	--- Save memory size
00F5	19	ADD	--- Subtract size of string area from see note-->-
00F6	22A040	LD	--- Save starting addr of string area
00F9	CD4D1B	CALL	--- Initialize all BASIC variables and pointers
00FC	211101	LD	---´RADIO . . .BASIC´ message pntr
00FF	CDA728	CALL	--- Output message
0102	C3191A	JP	--- Go to ready routine
0105	4D	LD	--- M ** ´MEMORY SIZE´ message **********************
0106	45	LD	--- E
0107	4D	LD	--- M
0108	4F	LD	--- O
0109	52	LD	--- R
010A	59	LD	--- Y
010B	2053	JR	--- Space, S
010D	49	LD	--- I
010E	5A	LD	--- Z
010F	45	LD	--- E
0110	00	NOP	--- 00 - message terminator
0111	52	LD	--- R ** ´RADIO SHACK LEVEL II BASIC´ message ********
0112	41	LD	--- A
0113	44	LD	--- D
0114	49	LD	--- I
0115	4F	LD	--- O
0116	2053	JR	--- Space, S
0118	48	LD	--- H
0119	41	LD	--- A
011A	43	LD	--- C
011B	4B	LD	--- K
011C	204C	JR	--- Space, L
011E	45	LD	--- E
011F	56	LD	--- V
0120	45	LD	--- E
0121	4C	LD	--- L
0122	2049	JR	--- Space, I
0124	49	LD	--- I
0125	2042	JR	--- Space, B
0127	41	LD	--- A
0128	53	LD	--- S
0129	49	LD	--- I
012A	43	LD	--- C
012B	0D	DEC	--- 0D - carriage return
012C	00	NOP	--- 00 - end of message terminator
012D	1E2C	LD	--- Code for L3 error ***********************
012F	C3A219	JP	--- Jump to error routine and print L3 error
0132	D7	RST	--- Position to next character ** (POINT/SET/RESET) *
0133	AF	XOR	--- A = 0 if POINT entered else POINT (x,y)
0134	013E80	LD	--- 0135 LD A,80 SET routine A = -1 SET (x,y)
0137	013E01	LD	--- 0138 LD A,01 RESET routine A = +1 RESET (x,y)
013A	F5	PUSH	--- Save flag indicating POINT/SET/RESET entry
013B	CF	RST	--- Examine next char, look for (

00EF : string area (50 dec. bytes)

00F5 : ending memory addr.

0105 * ***

0111 * ***

012D * ***

0132 * ***

Addr	Code	Mnemonic	Comment
013C	28CD	JR	--- 13C: DC 28 (for RST 08
013E	1C	INC	--- 13D: CALL 2B1C go evaluate 1st variable (x)
013F	2B	DEC	--- Result in A-reg
0140	FE80	CP	--- Compare x coordinate to 128 dec.
0142	D24A1E	JP	--- FC error if x => 128
0145	F5	PUSH	--- Save x coordinate
0146	CF	RST	--- Examine next symbol in input string
0147	2C	INC	--- Make sure its a , (comma)
0148	CD1C2B	CALL	--- Go evaluate 2nd variable (y)
014B	FE30	CP	--- Result in A-reg. Compare to 48 dec.
014D	D24A1E	JP	--- FC error if y => 48
0150	16FF	LD	--- Prepare to divide y coordinate by 3 giving Q+R
0152	14	INC	<----: D = Q
0153	D603	SUB	. : Divide by compound subtraction
0155	30FB	JR	---->: Loop till remainder < 3
0157	C603	ADD	--- Make remainder positive :
0159	4F	LD	--- And store it in C :
015A	F1	POP	--- A = x coordinate :
015B	87	ADD	--- Times 2 see note ---> :
015C	5F	LD	--- E = 2 times x :
015D	0602	LD	--- B = shift count :
015F	7A	LD	<----: Right shift D/E (Q,2*x) :
0160	1F	RRA	. : Two places so that
0161	57	LD	. : Bit 1 of E is left in the
0162	7B	LD	. : Carry. This bit will be
0163	1F	RRA	. : zero if we're on the first column
0164	5F	LD	. : of a rectangular box, and one if
0165	10F8	DJNZ	---->: we're on the 2nd column.
0167	79	LD	--- Now, compute position of point within
0168	8F	ADC	--- the word according to the formula
0169	3C	INC	--- (2*R)+1+(0 or 1 for column 1 or 2)
016A	47	LD	--- Save bit position count
016B	AF	XOR	--- Clear A and carry flag then
016C	37	SCF	--- force CARRY on.
016D	8F	ADC	<---: Build a bit mask to position a one over
016E	10FD	DJNZ	--->: the point we're looking for. Save mask in C.
0170	4F	LD	--- Compute word address for box, store in DE
0171	7A	LD	--- Mask for bit we want
0172	F63C	OR	--- A = Q from y/3
0174	57	LD	--- Restore so that DE = addr of box we want
0175	1A	LD	--- Fetch the bits for this box
0176	B7	OR	--- and ret the status flag
0177	FA7C01	JP	--->: Jump if graphics word
017A	3E80	LD	-- : Else, make it a graphics word
017C	47	LD	<---: B = bits for this display box
017D	F1	POP	--- Get entry point flag
017E	B7	OR	--- And test it
017F	78	LD	--- A = bits for this box
0180	2810	JR	--- Jump if POINT called
0182	12	LD	--- Restore box contents
0183	FA8F01	JP	--- Jump if SET called else
0186	79	LD	--- This must be a RESET call
0187	2F	CPL	--- Turn bit to be RESET off
0188	4F	LD	--- Save mark with bit off in C reg
0189	1A	LD	--- Fetch box from memory
018A	A1	AND	--- Turn specified bit off
018B	12	LD	--- And restore. Then we're
018C	CF	RST	--- Done, prepare to exit after testing for)
018D	29	ADD	--- DC)
018E	C9	RET	--- Return to caller

```
0150 : Compute the memory address for the specified point.  Graphics
     : area in memory ranges from 3C00 - 3FFF.  Each six bit (2X3)
     : box is represented by an 8 bit byte starting at 3D00.  The
     : boxes are stored in memory as a string of 6 bits, right
     : justified in the byte.  The bits in the byte are numbered
     : from right to left (as you would expect) starting at 0 and
     : going thru 5.  Bits 6 & 7 are unused.
     : Rectangular coordinates within the box are represented in
     : the box ´byte´ as follows:  bits 0 & 1 represent the first
     : row, points 0 and one respectively; bits 2 & 3 correspond
     : to the second row, bits 0 and 1, respectively; etc.
```

```
018F  B1       OR      --- SET continues **** Turn on bit in box ************
0190  18F9     JR      --- Restore box and rtn to caller
0192  A1       AND     --- POINT continues ** Isolate bit we're testing for**
0193  C6FF     ADD     --- If bit was on, overflow will occur
0195  9F       SBC     --- A = 0 if bit off,  = -1 if bit on
0196  E5       PUSH    --- Save current code string address
0197  CD8D09   CALL    --- Save 00 (false) or -1 (true) as current value
019A  E1       POP     --- Restore code string addr
019B  18EF     JR      --- Test for closing paren & return to caller
019D  D7       RST     --- INKEY$ routine * Position to next char in code str
019E  E5       PUSH    --- Save current code string addr
019F  3A9940   LD      --- Get last char typed during keyboard scan (shift
01A2  B7       OR      --- Set status flags                          @ key)
01A3  2006     JR      --- Jmp if shift @ key strunk else
01A5  CD5803   CALL    --- Scan keyboard once
01A8  B7       OR      --- Set status flags for result
01A9  2811     JR      --- Jmp if no input
01AB  F5       PUSH    --- Save char typed
01AC  AF       XOR     --- Clear A-reg status flags
01AD  329940   LD      --- Clear shift @ key character
01B0  3C       INC     --- A = 1, size of character string to be built
01B1  CD5728   CALL    --- Make sure there is room for char string, cont-->
01B4  F1       POP     --- A = char typed
01B5  2AD440   LD      --- HL = addr of string in literal string pool area
01B8  77       LD      --- Save character
01B9  C38428   JP      --- Move string to literal string pool area
01BC  212819   LD      --- Load address of 'READY' message and **************
01BF  222141   LD      --- move to current string variable point
01C2  3E03     LD      --- Data type = String
01C4  32AF40   LD      --- Set current type to string
01C7  E1       POP     --- Message address to HL
01C8  C9       RET     --- Rtn to caller
01C9  3E1C     LD      --- Clear screen ************** Home cursor command **
01CB  CD3A03   CALL    --- Send to video
01CE  3E1F     LD      --- Clear screen command
01D0  C33A03   JP      --- Send to video then return
01D3  ED5F     LD      --- Load current refresh addr **** RANDOM routine ****
01D5  32AB40   LD      --- Save random value                   : see note -->
01D8  C9       RET     --- Rtn to caller
01D9  2101FC   LD      --- Set bit 0 of 4 bit data latch *******************
01DC  CD2102   CALL    --- OUT (FF) 01
01DF  060B     LD      --- B = count for delay loop
01E1  10FE     DJNZ    --- B = count for delay loop = 80 US
01E3  2102FC   LD      --- Set bit 1 of 4 bit data latch
01E6  CD2102   CALL    --- OUT (FF) 02
01E9  060B     LD      --- B = count for delay loop          see note -->
01EB  10FE     DJNZ    --- Delay 3.25X10-6 * 11 * 2.26 = 80 US
01ED  2100FC   LD      --- Clear bits 0 and 1 of 4 bit data latch
01F0  CD2102   CALL    --- OUT (FF) 00
01F3  065C     LD      --- B = delay loop count  92
01F5  10FE     DJNZ    --- Delay = 3.25X10-6 * 92 * 2.26 = 676 US
01F7  C9       RET     --- Rtn to caller
01F8  E5       PUSH    --- Entry to turn off cassette *********************
01F9  2100FB   LD      --- HL = command to turn off cassette
01FC  181B     JR      --- Go to cassette driver
01FE  7E       LD      --- Get next token from input string **************
01FF  D623     SUB     --- Test for #
0201  3E00     LD      --- A = unit 0 if care of no # x specification
0203  200D     JR      --- Jmp if not #
0205  CD012B   CALL    --- Get unit number in DE                    cont-->
```

```
018F  *  ****************************************************************

0192  *  ****************************************************************




019D  *  ****************************************************************









01B1  :  Save length, addr at 4023






01BC  *  ****************************************************************






01C9  *  ****************************************************************




01D3  *  (Uses refresh register contents)****************************


01D9  *  ****************************************************************


01E1  :  Write one bit on cassette.  Assume motor has been turned
      :  on.  Called to write clock pulses  Requires three steps
      :  consisting of an
      :          OUT (FF) 01
      :          OUT (FF) 02
      :          OUT (FF) 00
      :  Total time for clock pulse is 836 US




01F8  *  ****************************************************************


01FE  *  ****************************************************************




0205  :  (as integer in 'current' area) in DE
```

72

0208 CF	RST	--- Look for comma following unit number
0209 2C	INC	- DC 2C Comma
020A 7B	LD	--- Convert unit from
020B A2	AND	--- - XX to its positive
020C C602	ADD	--- Equivalent
020E D24A1E	JP	--- FC error if NC
0211 3D	DEC	--- A = positive value for unit number
0212 32E437	LD	--- Entry to define drive **** Select cassette unit **
0215 E5	PUSH	--- Save current code string address
0216 2104FF	LD	--- Code to turn on cassette
0219 CD2102	CALL	--- Turn drive on/off
021C E1	POP	--- Restore code string addr
021D C9	RET	--- Rtn to caller
021E 2100FF	LD	--- Mask for preserving video controller flags
0221 3A3D40	LD	--- Get video control bits (32/64 char)
0224 A4	AND	--- Combine with cassette
0225 B5	OR	--- Control bits :controller)
0226 D3FF	OUT	--- Write reg A to port 255 (cassette/video
0228 323D40	LD	--- Save new value as current control value
022B C9	RET	--- Return to caller
022C 3A3F3C	LD	--- Blink ´*´ when reading cassette ****** cont --> *
022F EE0A	XOR	--- Gives 2A/20/2A . . . *, ,*, ,. . .
0231 323F3C	LD	--- Store new display value
0234 C9	RET	--- Rtn to caller
0235 C5	PUSH	--- Entry to read cassette *************** cont --> *
0236 E5	PUSH	--- Saves callers register
0237 0608	LD	--- B = number of bits to read
0239 CD4102	CALL	--- Read 1 bit. Assembled into a byte in the A-reg
023C 10FB	DJNZ	--- Loop till 8 bits (one byte) read
023E E1	POP	--- Restore caller´s
023F C1	POP	--- register
0240 C9	RET	--- Return
0241 C5	PUSH	--- Read 1 data bit from cassette ********* cont --> *
0242 F5	PUSH	--- Save caller´s registers
0243 DBFF	IN	<--: Begin tape motion. Stop when first start pulse
0245 17	RLA	. : Input and test for clock pulse :is sensed
0246 30FB	JR	. : Not there, loop till it shows up
0248 0641	LD	--->: Now delay for 476 micro seconds
024A 10FE	DJNZ	--- After sensing start pulse
024C CD1E02	CALL	--- Reset outsig flip/flop so we can read data pulse
024F 0676	LD	--- Then delay for 865 micro seconds before reading
0251 10FE	DJNZ	--- The data pulse
0253 DBFF	IN	--- Read data pulse
0255 47	LD	--- Save it as B
0256 F1	POP	--- A = prior bits for this byte
0257 CB10	RL	--- Shift data bit into carry flag
0259 17	RLA	--- Combine this data bit with others
025A F5	PUSH	--- Save byte thus far
025B CD1E02	CALL	--- Reset outsig flip/flop
025E F1	POP	--- Restore data byte
025F C1	POP	--- Other registers
0260 C9	RET	--- And return
0261 CD6402	CALL	--- Call 0264 to write clock pulse
0264 E5	PUSH	--- Entry to write byte
0265 C5	PUSH	--- Save caller´s registers
0266 D5	PUSH	--- BC
0267 F5	PUSH	-- DE see note ---->
0268 0E08	LD	--- C = no of bits to write
026A 57	LD	--- D = data word to be written bit by bit
026B CDD901	CALL	--- Write clock bit

```
0212 * ****************************************************

022C * Fetch display word that holds an *     **********************

0235 * Reads one byte then returns ********************************

0241 * Called 8 times to read one byte ***************************

0265 : Writing a byte is done by serially writing each bit in
     : the byte.  Each bit is preceeded by a clock pulse followed
     : by another pulse if the bit is a one or no pulse if the
     : bit is a zero.  The time from the clock pulse to the bit
     : pulse is approx 1 millisecond
```

026E	7A	LD	--- Get byte to be written
026F	07	RLCA	--- Set status (carry) if upper bit is one else no
0270	57	LD	--- Save shifted data byte : carry
0271	300B	JR	--- Jmp if high bit is zero see note -->
0273	CDD901	CALL	--- Else write a one bit
0276	0D	DEC	--- Count of bits written from this byte
0277	20F2	JR	--- Not done, go write clock pulse then test data bit
0279	F1	POP	--- Restore caller's register : AF
027A	D1	POP	--- DE
027B	C1	POP	--- BC
027C	E1	POP	--- and HL
027D	C9	RET	--- Rtn to caller
027E	0687	LD	--- B = count of times to delay *********************
0280	10FE	DJNZ	--- Delay 3.25 * 10-6 * 135 * 2.26 = 991 US
0282	18F2	JR	--- Go count no of bits written
0284	CDFE01	CALL	--- Get unit no and turn on motor *******************
0287	06FF	LD	--- Entry to write leader and sync byte
0289	AF	XOR	--- A = data word to write (all zeroes)
028A	CD6402	CALL	--- Write 256 zeros
028D	10FB	DJNZ	--- Count one byte of zeroes written. Loop till 256
028F	3EA5	LD	--- Trailer byte is A5 : bytes written
0291	18D1	JR	--- Write trailer byte as A5 and rtn to caller
0293	CDFE01	CALL	--- Get unit no., turn on motor *********************
0296	E5	PUSH	--- Entry to find leader and sync byte
0297	AF	XOR	--- Zero A, status flags
0298	CD4102	CALL	<--: Read cassette
029B	FEA5	CP	. : Until a flag of 'A5' is found. We should skip
029D	20F9	JR	-->: over 256 bytes of zeroes before getting there
029F	3E2A	LD	--- A = ASCII *
02A1	323E3C	LD	--- Display * *
02A4	323F3C	LD	--- On screen
02A7	E1	POP	--- Restore code string addr
02A8	C9	RET	--- Rtn to caller
02A9	CD1403	CALL	--- Go read 2 bytes from cassette ********* cont --> *
02AC	22DF40	LD	--- Save execution address
02AF	CDF801	CALL	--- Turn off drive
02B2	CDE241	CALL	--- DOS Exit (JP 5B51)
02B5	318842	LD	--- Set CSP below assumed load address
02B8	CDFE20	CALL	--- Print CR
02BB	3E2A	LD	--- A = ASCII *
02BD	CD2A03	CALL	--- Print '*'
02C0	CDB31B	CALL	--- Wait for input from keyboard should be file name
02C3	DACC06	JP	--- Jmp if BREAK key hit :to load
02C6	D7	RST	--- Examine next character in input stream
02C7	CA9719	JP	--- SN error if EOS
02CA	FE2F	CP	--- It is a '/'
02CC	284F	JR	--- Jump if '/'
02CE	CD9302	CALL	--- Start up cassette. see note-->
02D1	CD3502	CALL	<--: Read 1 byte
02D4	FE55	CP	. : Test for U
02D6	20F9	JR	-->: Loop till an ASCII 'U' is read
02D8	0606	LD	. : B = number of characters to match
02DA	7E	LD	<----: Get a character from type in 2C0
02DB	B7	OR	. : : Test for zero, end of name
02DC	2809	JR	. : : Go start load, else
02DE	CD3502	CALL	. : : Read 1 byte from cassette and
02E1	BE	CP	. : : Compare with type
02E2	20ED	JR	. : : Bump to next char of type
02E4	23	INC	--->: : If no match, skip to next prog on cassette
02E5	10F3	DJNZ	----->: Loop till 6 chars match or end of cont -->

75

0271 : (Go delay for approx 1 ms)

027E * ***

0284 * ***

0293 * ***

02A9 * Load an assembler program from cassette ********************

     : Position to first data byte by skipping
     : over leader until a U is found

02E5 : type in command

Addr	Code	Mnemonic	Comment
02E7	CD2C02	CALL	--- Blink * on video during load
02EA	CD3502	CALL	--- Read a byte
02ED	FE78	CP	<-------: Now test if byte is an upper case 8
02EF	28B8	JR	. : Yes, read next two bytes and save cont -->
02F1	FE3C	CP	. : Is it a <
02F3	20F5	JR	. : No, read till '78' or '3C' found
02F5	CD3502	CALL	. : Read number of bytes to load
02F8	47	LD	. : Save count of bytes to load
02F9	CD1403	CALL	. : Read following two bytes (addr) into HL
02FC	85	ADD	. : Cksum starts with addr
02FD	4F	LD	. : Save 8 bit cksum
02FE	CD3502	CALL	<--: . : Read a byte
0301	77	LD	. : . : Store it
0302	23	INC	. : . : Bump store address
0303	81	ADD	. : . : Cksum data byte
0304	4F	LD	. : . : Save cksum
0305	10F7	DJNZ	-->: . : Count 1 byte loaded
0307	CD3502	CALL	. : Read cksum
030A	B9	CP	. : Compare w/computed cksum
030B	28DA	JR	. : Cksum OK, keep loading till a '78' found
030D	3E43	LD	. : Cksum error. Display a C
030F	323E3C	LD	. : Store C in video memory
0312	18D6	JR	------->: Scan till start of next program
0314	CD3502	CALL	--- Read one byte from cassette *********************
0317	6F	LD	--- Save LSB see note-->
0318	CD3502	CALL	--- Read another byte from cassette
031B	67	LD	--- Save as MSB
031C	C9	RET	--- Rtn to caller
031D	EB	EX	--- DE = input response address **********************
031E	2ADF40	LD	--- 40DF = will hold execution address
0321	EB	EX	--- HL = input addr DE = execution addr location
0322	D7	RST	--- Test for CR if not CR then
0323	C45A1E	CALL	--- Convert ASCII to binary. Result in DE
0326	208A	JR	--- Jmp if no digits found
0328	EB	EX	--- Else digit is execution address
0329	E9	JP	--- Jmp to addr given in /XXXX cmnd
032A	C5	PUSH	--- Output (A) to screen, printer or tape ***********
032B	4F	LD	--- Save character to output
032C	CDC141	CALL	--- Rtn if non-DOS
032F	3A9C40	LD	--- Get device type code
0332	B7	OR	--- Set status flags according to dev type
0333	79	LD	--- A = char to be written
0334	C1	POP	--- Restore callers BC
0335	FA6402	JP	--- Write to tape
0338	2062	JR	--- Write to printer
033A	D5	PUSH	--- Write to video
033B	CD3300	CALL	--- Print
033E	F5	PUSH	--- Save character written
033F	CD4803	CALL	--- Test for display memory full
0342	32A640	LD	--- Update cursor position (0 - 3FH)
0345	F1	POP	--- Restore character written
0346	D1	POP	--- Restore caller's DE
0347	C9	RET	--- Rtn to caller
0348	3A3D40	LD	--- Get video control word ************************
034B	E608	AND	--- Test for 32/64 char line
034D	3A2040	LD	--- Addr if cursor
0350	2803	JR	--- Jump if 64 characters/line
0352	0F	RRCA	--- Force cursor position
0353	E61F	AND	--- to be between 3C00
0355	E63F	AND	--- and 3FFF

02EF : in 40DF. Wait for input

0314 * **
0317 : Read 2 bytes from cassette and assemble as a 16 bit value

031D * **

032A * **
    :   :----------------------:
    : -1 : cassette   :
    : 0 : video   :
    : +1 : printer   :
    :----------------------:

0348 * **

```
0357  C9        RET      --- Rtn to caller
0358  CDC441    CALL     --- DOS Exit (JP  59CD)    ****************************
035B  D5        PUSH     --- Save callers DE
035C  CD2B00    CALL     --- Scan keyboard
035F  D1        POP      --- Restore callers DE
0360  C9        RET      --- Rtn to caller
0361  AF        XOR      --- Keyboard input routine ***************************
0362  329940    LD       --- Zero last char typed following break.
0365  32A640    LD       --- And current cursor position.
0368  CDAF41    CALL     --- DOS Exit  (JP  598E)
036B  C5        PUSH     --- Save BC
036C  2AA740    LD       --- Buffer = 41E8 (usually)
036F  06F0      LD       --- Length of buffer = 240
0371  CDD905    CALL     --- Go see what´s being typed into buffer
0374  F5        PUSH     --- Save flags
0375  48        LD       --- C = input length
0376  0600      LD       --- BC = input length
0378  09        ADD      --- HL = end of input area ptr
0379  3600      LD       --- Flag end of input with a 00H
037B  2AA740    LD       --- HL= input area ptr
037E  F1        POP      --- Restore flags
037F  C1        POP      --- Restore BC
0380  2B        DEC      --- HL = input area ptr - 1          see note-->
0381  D8        RET      --- Return w/carry set if BREAK key hit
0382  AF        XOR      --- Else clear all status flags
0383  C9        RET      --- Rtn with HL = input buffer -1
0384  CD5803    CALL     --- Go scan keyboard *****************************
0387  B7        OR       --- Test for any key depressed
0388  C0        RET      --- Exit if key pressed
0389  18F9      JR       --- Else, loop till some entry made
038B  AF        XOR      --- Clear A then ********************************
038C  329C40    LD       --- Set output device = video
038F  3A9B40    LD       --- Get printer carriage position
0392  B7        OR       --- Set status flags
0393  C8        RET      --- Return if printer buffer empty
0394  3E0D      LD       --- Load char to print (carriage ret)
0396  D5        PUSH     --- Save caller´s DE
0397  CD9C03    CALL     --- Call print driver
039A  D1        POP      --- Restore caller´s DE
039B  C9        RET      --- Rtn to caller
039C  F5        PUSH     --- Save callers registers *********** see note --> *
039D  D5        PUSH     --- DE
039E  C5        PUSH     --- and BC
039F  4F        LD       --- C = character to be printed
03A0  1E00      LD       --- E = new char/line count of ´C´, ´D´, or ´A´
03A2  FE0C      CP       --- Test for skip to next line              :printed
03A4  2810      JR       ------>: Jmp if skip to next line
03A6  FE0A      CP       --     : Test for a line feed (A)
03A8  2003      JR       -->:   : Not LF, test for ´D´ carriage ret
03AA  3E0D      LD       -- :   : Set next char to LP carriage ret
03AC  4F        LD       -- :   : Save LP carriage ret char
03AD  FE0D      CP       <--:--: Test for second type of carriage ret
03AF  2805      JR       -- :   Jmp if ´A´ or ´D´ carriage ret
03B1  3A9B40    LD       -- :   Get count of characters in current line
03B4  3C        INC      -- :   Bump count for next char going out
03B5  5F        LD       -- :   Move count to E-reg so we can
03B6  7B        LD       <--:   Use common code
03B7  329B40    LD       --- Save updated count of chars/this line
03BA  79        LD       --- Get char to be printed in A
03BB  CD3B00    CALL     --- Call line printer driver
```

0358 * ***

0361 * ***

0380 : (Required for RST 16 routine)

0384 * ***

038B * ***

039C * Call print driver on entry. Char to be printed in **********
      : A-reg. If A = ´C´, skip on line and reset count of
      : characters in current line. If A = ´A´ or ´D´ print
      : carriage return and reset character count for this line

```
03BE C1       POP        --- Restore caller's register, BC
03BF D1       POP        --- DE
03C0 F1       POP        --- and AF
03C1 C9       RET        --- Rtn to caller
03C2 E5       PUSH       --- Driver entry routine ************** see note--> *
03C3 DDE5     PUSH       --- Save registers            B = entry code
03C5 D5       PUSH       --- Load DCB addr             DE = DCB addr
03C6 DDE1     POP        --- into IX
03C8 D5       PUSH       --- Save original contents of DE
03C9 21DD03   LD         --- HL = return address
03CC E5       PUSH       --- Push return address onto stack
03CD 4F       LD         --- Save char to be sent to device
03CE 1A       LD         --- Fetch 1st word from DCB
03CF A0       AND        --- Isolate device code bits
03D0 B8       CP         --- and compare w/entry code (B). If unequal
03D1 C23340   JP         --- goto driver via DOS Exit
03D4 FE02     CP         --- Clear status flags
03D6 DD6E01   LD         --- HL = driver address from DCB
03D9 DD6602   LD         --- Load MSB of driver addr
03DC E9       JP         --- Go to driver routine
03DD D1       POP        --- Return from driver routine
03DE DDE1     POP        --- Restore registers, IX
03E0 E1       POP        --- HL
03E1 C1       POP        --- and BC
03E2 C9       RET        --- Rtn to caller
03E3 213640   LD         --- Keyboard driver routine *********** see note--> *
03E6 010138   LD         --- BC = row A0 ptr
03E9 1600     LD         --- D = column index
03EB 0A       LD         --- Load row N
03EC 5F       LD         --- 8 column bits
03ED AE       XOR        --- XOR with previous
03EE 73       LD         --- Store column bits in buffer
03EF A3       AND        --- then test for active row
03F0 2008     JR         --- Go if key active in row N
03F2 14       INC        --- Bump row index
03F3 2C       INC        --- Seven byte buffer indexed by row
03F4 CB01     RLC        --- Step address from 3801 - 3840
03F6 F2EB03   JP         --- Try next row
03F9 C9       RET        --- No key depression - return
03FA 5F       LD         --- Save column bits *****************************
03FB 7A       LD         --- Row index 0 - 6
03FC 07       RLCA       --- Row * 2
03FD 07       RLCA       --- Row * 4
03FE 07       RLCA       --- Row * 8
03FF 57       LD         --- Save in D
0400 0E01     LD         --- Start with bit 0
0402 79       LD         --- Mask
0403 A3       AND        --- Test for non-zero column
0404 2005     JR         --- Go if found
0406 14       INC        --- Bump column number
0407 CB01     RLC        --- Align mask
0409 18F7     JR         --- Try again
040B 3A8038   LD         --- Load shift bit
040E 47       LD         --- Shift bit to B
040F 7A       LD         --- Row * 8 + column (0 - 7)
0410 C640     ADD        --- Row * 8 + column (0 - 7) + 64 decimal
0412 FE60     CP         --- Test for first 4 row (@,A-Z)
0414 3013     JR         --- Go if last 3 rows, numeric & special characters
0416 CB08     RRC        --- Shift to C
0418 3031     JR         --- Go if no shift
```

03C2 * Entered on RST 14,1C,24 *************************************

03E3 * HL = keyboard work area ptr *******************************

03FA * ***

Address	Code	Mnemonic	Comment
041A	C620	ADD	--- Set lower case
041C	57	LD	--- Adjusted character
041D	3A4038	LD	--- Get row 6 column bits
0420	E610	AND	--- Test for down arrow or CR
0422	2828	JR	--- Go if no down arrow or CR
0424	7A	LD	--- Reload adjusted value for key struck
0425	D660	SUB	--- Adjust to ASCII CR
0427	1822	JR	--- Go to return
0429	D670	SUB	--- Test for last row (ENTER - SPACE)
042B	3010	JR	--- Go if last row
042D	C640	ADD	--- Readjust for rows 4, 5
042F	FE3C	CP	--- Convert rows 4, 5
0431	3802	JR	--- Jmp if (0-1-2-3-4-5-6-7-8-9-:-;-,) key struck
0433	EE10	XOR	--- Invert row 5 bits
0435	CB08	RRC	--- Ret if shift key down
0437	3012	JR	--- Jmp if no
0439	EE10	XOR	--- then re-invert row 5 bits
043B	180E	JR	--- Go to output
043D	07	RLCA	--- (Now (ROW * 8 + COLUMN - 48) * 2)
043E	CB08	RRC	--- Test for shift
0440	3001	JR	--- Go if no shift
0442	3C	INC	--- Now (ROW*8 + COLUMN-48) * 2 + 5 = COLUMN * 2 + 1
0443	215000	LD	--- Table of codes for last row
0446	4F	LD	--- Ret C to value from 43D or 442
0447	0600	LD	--- depending on shift. Set B = 0
0449	09	ADD	--- Index into table
044A	7E	LD	--- Get ASCII - like code
044B	57	LD	--- Save character
044C	01AC0D	LD	--- Load delay count
044F	CD6000	CALL	--- Delay 20 milliseconds
0452	7A	LD	--- A = ASCII - like character
0453	FE01	CP	--- Is it BREAK?
0455	C0	RET	--- Go if not
0456	EF	RST	--- Yes, BREAK
0457	C9	RET	--- Return
0458	DD6E03	LD	--- HL=cursor position ptr ************ see note--> *
045B	DD6604	LD	--- Load MSB of current video buffer addr
045E	383A	JR	--- Jmp if return last char request
0460	DD7E05	LD	--- Get cursor on/off flag
0463	B7	OR	--- Set status flags for cursor on/off
0464	2801	JR	-->: Jmp if cursor off
0466	77	LD	-- : Move char overlaid by cursor to character buffer
0467	79	LD	<--: Get char to be displayed
0468	FE20	CP	--- Compare with space
046A	DA0605	JP	--- Jump if control character
046D	FE80	CP	--- Test for graphics word or compression code
046F	3035	JR	--- Jump if graphic or space compression character
0471	FE40	CP	--- Compare w/letter A
0473	3808	JR	--- Jmp if not alphabetic @ - Z
0475	D640	SUB	--- Subtract A to get 0 - 26 value for alpha
0477	FE20	CP	--- Test for lower case
0479	3802	JR	-->: Jmp if not lower case
047B	D620	SUB	-- : Convert lower case to upper case
047D	CD4105	CALL	<--: Add new char to video display. Roll screen if
0480	7C	LD	--- Force addr of next char to :necessary
0481	E603	AND	--- be in the range 3C00 <= X <3FFF
0483	F63C	OR	--- Force MSB of buffer addr to 3C - 3F
0485	67	LD	--- Move updated MSB of buffer addr to HL
0486	56	LD	--- Get value of char at cursor position
0487	DD7E05	LD	--- Get cursor on/off flag

0458 * Display driver routine - Load LSB if current video **********
     :   buffer addr.

048A B7	OR	---	Get status flags for cursor
048B 2805	JR	--->:	Jmp if cursor off
048D DD7205	LD	-- :	Else save character to be replaced by cursor
0490 365F	LD	-- :	Move (_) cursor to addr of next char position
0492 DD7503	LD	<---:	Save addr of next character
0495 DD7404	LD	---	Position on screen in DCB (3,4)
0498 79	LD	---	Restore last character displayed
0499 C9	RET	---	Rtn to caller
049A DD7E05	LD	---	Get cursor on/off switch see note-->
049D B7	OR	---	Set status flags for switch
049E C0	RET	---	If cursor on, exit with character
049F 7E	LD	---	It overlaid in A-reg else
04A0 C9	RET	---	Get last char displayed
04A1 7D	LD	---	Get LSB of current video buffer addr. ** cont--> *
04A2 E6C0	AND	---	Remove lower six bits giving value of XX00,
04A4 6F	LD	---	XX40, XX80, or XXC0. 64 char/line assumed
04A5 C9	RET	---	Rtn with new video buffer addr. in HL.
04A6 FEC0	CP	---	Check for space compression code *****************
04A8 38D3	JR	---	Graphic
04AA D6C0	SUB	---	Subtract conversion bias
04AC 28D2	JR	---	Jmp if 0 blanks to be displayed
04AE 47	LD	---	B = count of blanks to be displayed
04AF 3E20	LD	---	A = blank
04B1 CD4105	CALL	---	Display a blank
04B4 10F9	DJNZ	---	Loop till B blanks displayed
04B6 18C8	JR	---	Update pointer to video buffer and exit
04B8 7E	LD	---	Load char of current position and ** see note--> *
04B9 DD7705	LD	---	Save cursor on/off in DCB
04BC C9	RET	---	Rtn to caller
04BD AF	XOR	---	Set cursor flag off
04BE 18F9	JR	---	Update video DCB and exit
04C0 21003C	LD	---	Hl = start of video area ******* Home cursor *****
04C3 3A3D40	LD	---	Force 64 characters/line
04C6 E6F7	AND	---	Clear 32 char/line bit in command word
04C8 323D40	LD	---	Save command word
04CB D3FF	OUT	---	Send command word to video controller
04CD C9	RET	---	Rtn to caller
04CE 2B	DEC	---	Backspace one char in line ********* see note--> *
04CF 3A3D40	LD	---	Get status of video controller
04D2 E608	AND	---	Test for 32/64 char per line
04D4 2801	JR	---	Go if 64 characters/line
04D6 2B	DEC	---	Backspace one more word if 64 char/line
04D7 3620	LD	---	Replace previous char with a blank
04D9 C9	RET	---	Rtn to caller
04DA 3A3D40	LD	---	Get status of video controller ***** see note--> *
04DD E608	AND	---	Isolate number of chars/line
04DF C4E204	CALL	---	Call backspace cursor twice if 32 char line
04E2 7D	LD	---	Save LSB of current cursor position
04E3 E63F	AND	---	Backspace LSB of cursor to previous line
04E5 2B	DEC	---	Then backspace cursor 1 character
04E6 C0	RET	---	Rtn if cursor on same line
04E7 114000	LD	---	Else skip down one line
04EA 19	ADD	---	by adding 64 to current cursor addr
04EB C9	RET	---	then rtn to caller
04EC 23	INC	---	Bump current cursor *************** see note--> *
04ED 7D	LD	---	addr by 1, fetch LSB of addr
04EE E63F	AND	---	and test for overflow into next line
04F0 C0	RET	---	No overflow, rtn to caller
04F1 11C0FF	LD	---	Upward linefeed, add a
04F4 19	ADD	---	minus 64 to current cursosr addr

049A : Return either current character or last character
     : replaced by cursor

04A1 * Backspace pointer in video buffer to start of ***************
     : current line. 64 char/line assumed

04A6 * **

04B8 * cont-->   use as cursor flag ********************************
     : note--> Turn cursor on/off (control code processing)

04C0 * **

04CE * Backspace cursor on video (control char processing) *********

04DA * Backspace cursor. Left arrow (control char processing) *****

04EC * Advance cursor. Right arrow (control char processing) ******

```
04F5  C9        RET       --- Rtn to caller
04F6  3A3D40    LD        --- Get video control word **************************
04F9  F608      OR        --- Turn on 32 char/line mode
04FB  323D40    LD        --- Restore video control word
04FE  D3FF      OUT       --- Select 32 char/line
0500  23        INC       --- Increment current position in video buffer
0501  7D        LD        --- Force LSB to
0502  E6FE      AND       --- an even value when in 32 char/line mode
0504  6F        LD        --- Restore updated line addr to HL
0505  C9        RET       --- Rtn to caller
0506  118004    LD        --- Return addr after processing ****** see note--> *
0509  D5        PUSH      --- To stack                         :control character
050A  FE08      CP        --- Backspace and erase character
050C  28C0      JR        --- Jmp if backspace
050E  FE0A      CP        --- Not backspace, test for A
0510  D8        RET       --- Ignore if control code < A (hex) except for 08
0511  FE0E      CP        --- Test for turn on cursor
0513  384F      JR        --- Jmp if A-D (carriage return)
0515  28A1      JR        --- Jmp if turn on cursor
0517  FE0F      CP        --- Test for turn off cursor
0519  28A2      JR        --- Jmp if turn off cursor
051B  FE17      CP        --- Test for select 32 char/line
051D  28D7      JR        --- Jmp if 32 select 32 char/line
051F  FE18      CP        --- Left arrow
0521  28B7      JR        --- Jmp if left arrow
0523  FE19      CP        --- Right arrow
0525  28C5      JR        --- Jmp if right arrow
0527  FE1A      CP        --- Down arrow
0529  28BC      JR        --- Jmp if down arrow
052B  FE1B      CP        --- Up arrow
052D  28C2      JR        --- Jmp if up arrow
052F  FE1C      CP        --- Home cursor
0531  288D      JR        --- Jmp if home cursor
0533  FE1D      CP        --- Beginning of line
0535  CAA104    JP        --- Jmp if backspace to start of current line
0538  FE1E      CP        --- Erase to end of line
053A  2837      JR        --- Jmp if delete rest of line
053C  FE1F      CP        --- Clear to end of frame
053E  283C      JR        --- Jmp if CLEAR rest of screen
0540  C9        RET       --- Ignore all others
0541  77        LD        --- Send character to display memory *** see note--> *
0542  23        INC       --- Bump to next addr in display memory
0543  3A3D40    LD        --- Get status word for video
0546  E608      AND       --- Isolate characters/line flag
0548  2801      JR        --->: Jmp if 32 char/line
054A  23        INC       --  : 64 char/line. Bump one more word to     cont-->
054B  7C        LD        <--: Now, test if end of display mem reached
054C  FE40      CP        --- If MSB of next avail word = 40, then end of mem
054E  C0        RET       --- Rtn if not out of memory                  :reached
054F  11C0FF    LD        --- DE = -64
0552  19        ADD       --- Backspace mem ptr 1 line. Prepare to roll screen
0553  E5        PUSH      --- Save starting mem addr of botom line up one line
0554  11003C    LD        --- DE = addr 1st line
0557  21403C    LD        --- HL = addr of 2nd line
055A  C5        PUSH      --- Save BC
055B  01C003    LD        --- BC = count of chars to move (15 lines)
055E  EDB0      LDIR      --- Move screen up one line
0560  C1        POP       --- Restore BC
0561  EB        EX        --- HL = addr of 16th (last) line
0562  1819      JR        --- Go blank out 16th line
```

04F6 * **

0506 * Process control characters for video All characters < 20H **

0541 * Moves new char to display buffer **************************

054A : next addr in display mem

```
0564 7D      LD      --- Get LSB of current char position
0565 E6C0    AND     --- And force its address to the start
0567 6F      LD      --- Of the current line            see note -->
0568 E5      PUSH    --- Save starting line addr for current character
0569 114000  LD      --- DE = number of characters (words) in a line
056C 19      ADD     --- Gives starting addr for next line
056D 7C      LD      --- Now, test MSB of next line addr
056E FE40    CP      --- Test for end of screen
0570 28E2    JR      --- Jmp if end of screen (scroll up one line)
0572 D1      POP     --- DE = starting addr for current line
0573 E5      PUSH    --- Erase to end of line.  HL = starting addr for next
0574 54      LD      --- Compute ending addr                        :line
0575 7D      LD      --- For line blanking code below
0576 F63F    OR      --- Take addr in HL,
0578 5F      LD      --- round it up to the next line
0579 13      INC     --- number then
057A 1804    JR      --- Jmp to the line blanking code
057C E5      PUSH    --- Erase to end of frame
057D 110040  LD      --- Test addr for end of loop check
0580 3620    LD      <---: Move a blank to current char pos in line
0582 23      INC       . : Bump to next char pos
0583 7C      LD        . : Test if end of line.  Compare
0584 BA      CP        . : MSB of current addr to 40base16
0585 20F9    JR      --->: Loop if not end of line
0587 7D      LD      --- Then compare LSB of
0588 BB      CP      --- addresses
0589 20F5    JR      --- Loop if not end of line
058B E1      POP     --- Restore HL - (current char position addr)
058C C9      RET     --- Rtn to caller
058D 79      LD      --- Print driver routine ** Get char to be printed ***
058E B7      OR      --- Set status flags
058F 2840    JR      --- If zero, then get printer status and return
0591 FE0B    CP      --- Skip to top of form code          see note-->
0593 280A    JR      --- Yes, go issue line feeds till next page reached
0595 FE0C    CP      --- Test for conditional skip to top of form
0597 201B    JR      ------>: Jmp if data char
0599 AF      XOR     ---    : Then clear A (gives null char to be printed)
059A DDB603  OR      ---    : Get number of lines/page
059D 2815    JR      ---    : If zero, don't skip any lines
059F DD7E03  LD      ---    : Get count of lines per page and
05A2 DD9604  SUB     ---    : subtract lines printed this page so far, gives
05A5 47      LD      ---    : B = no. of lines to skip to top of next page
05A6 CDD105  CALL    <--: : Get printer status
05A9 20FB    JR      --->: : Loop till not busy
05AB 3E0A    LD        . : : Get a line feed character
05AD 32E837  LD        . : : Send it to the printer
05B0 10F4    DJNZ    --->: : Loop till we're at top of next page
05B2 1818    JR      ---    : Reset line count for new page & rtn to caller
05B4 F5      PUSH    <----: Save print status
05B5 CDD105  CALL    <---: Get print status
05B8 20FB    JR      --->: Loop till not busy
05BA F1      POP     --- Get character to print
05BB 32E837  LD      --- Send it to printer
05BE FE0D    CP      --- Carriage return?
05C0 C0      RET     --- Rtn to caller if data char
05C1 DD3404  INC     --- Bump count of lines printed this page
05C4 DD7E04  LD      --- Fetch line count for this page
05C7 DDBE03  CP      --- And compare to no. of lines per page
05CA 79      LD      --- Restore print char to A (carriage ret)
05CB C0      RET     --- Exit if page not full
```

0567 : (Control code processing)

058D * ***
     :   Carriage control codes
     :   A = line feed + CR
     :   B = skip to top of form
     :   C = conditional skip to top of form
     :   D = CR

```
05CC  DD360400  LD    --- Page full, reset line count for next page to zero
05D0  C9        RET   --- Rtn to caller
05D1  3AE837    LD    --- Get printer status word ************************
05D4  E6F0      AND   --- Isolate status
05D6  FE30      CP    --- Test for printer selected and ready
05D8  C9        RET   --- Rtn with status zero if selected & ready
05D9  E5        PUSH  --- Input routine HL points to input area ** cont--> *
05DA  3E0E      LD    --- Code to turn on cursor        HL=Start of buffer
05DC  CD3300    CALL  --- Turn  on cursor               B=Buffer size
05DF  48        LD    --- C = buffer size               Exit with carry if
05E0  CD4900    CALL  <---: Return when key is pressed         BREAK hit
05E3  FE20      CP      . : Test for SPACE
05E5  3025      JR      . : Not a space but diplayable if NC
05E7  FE0D      CP      . : Test for carriage ret.
05E9  CA6206    JP      . : Jmp if CR
05EC  FE1F      CP      . : Test for CLEAR
05EE  2829      JR      . : Jmp if CLEAR
05F0  FE01      CP      . : Test for BREAK
05F2  286D      JR      . : Jmp if BREAK
05F4  11E005    LD      . : Push rtn addr of 05E0 onto stack in case
05F7  D5        PUSH    . : character is none of the following
05F8  FE08      CP      . : Test for backspace and erase char.
05FA  2834      JR      . : Jmp if backspace / erase
05FC  FE18      CP      . : Backspace cursor
05FE  282B      JR      . : Jmp if backspace
0600  FE09      CP      . : Horizontal tab
0602  2842      JR      . : Jmp if horizontal tab
0604  FE19      CP      . : Select 32 char/line
0606  2839      JR      . : Jmp if line size selection
0608  FE0A      CP      . : Test for line feed
060A  C0        RET     . : Return to 5E0 if not a line feed
060B  D1        POP     . : Remove 5E0 as a rtn addr
060C  77        LD      . : He hit a printable character (save it)
060D  78        LD      . : 240 - count of characters fetched
060E  B7        OR      . : Set status
060F  28CF      JR      . : If end of buffer ignore unless BRK or CR
0611  7E        LD      . : Reload char just entered
0612  23        INC     . : Bump buffer address
0613  CD3300    CALL    . : Print the character just received
0616  05        DEC     . : Count 1 char received
0617  18C7      JR    --->: Get next character
0619  CDC901    CALL  --- He hit CLEAR : CLS   Clear screen
061C  41        LD    --- Reset count of characters transmitted
061D  E1        POP   --- Reset buffer address
061E  E5        PUSH  --- Save buffer origin on stk
061F  C3E005    JP    --- Go get next character (first char of buffer)
0622  CD3006    CALL  --- Go wait for next key
0625  2B        DEC   --- Backup to previous character (one before CR)
0626  7E        LD    --- Fetch it and test for a LF
0627  23        INC   --- Restore buffer addr to next avail position
0628  FE0A      CP    --- Was previous char a line feed
062A  C8        RET   --- yes, rtn
062B  78        LD    --- No, test for buffer full.  A = count of chars
062C  B9        CP    --- Received minus size of buffer
062D  20F3      JR    --- Loop if room for more data
062F  C9        RET   --- Rtn (buffer full)
0630  78        LD    --- B = characters received  C = size of buffer ******
0631  B9        CP    --- Test if buffer full
0632  C8        RET   --- Exit if buffer full
0633  2B        DEC   --- Backspace to previous character
```

05D1 * **

05D9 * Accept keyboard input ***********************************

0630 * **

```
0634 7E      LD      --- And fetch it
0635 FE0A    CP      --- Test for a line feed
0637 23      INC     --- Bump to last character received
0638 C8      RET     --- Exit if previous char was a line feed
0639 2B      DEC     --- Backspace over last char in buffer
063A 3E08    LD      --- Backspace screen command
063C CD3300  CALL    --- Print backspace
063F 04      INC     --- Adjust char received count
0640 C9      RET     --- Exit
0641 3E17    LD      --- Send position command ***************************
0643 C33300  JP      --- To video control unit and exit
0646 CD4803  CALL    --- Go wait for next key ****************** cont--> *
0649 E607    AND     --- Isolate lower 3 bits of ASCII value
064B 2F      CPL     --- Gives inverse of value
064C 3C      INC     --- Gives value  1 <= X <= 8
064D C608    ADD     --- Clears upper bits of counter
064F 5F      LD      --- Save count of blanks to add
0650 78      LD      <---: Get amt of space left in buffer
0651 B7      OR        . : Test for full buffer
0652 C8      RET       . : Exit if buffer full
0653 3E20    LD        . : Load an ASCII space into A-reg
0655 77      LD        . : Store space in buffer
0656 23      INC       . : Bump to next location in buffer
0657 D5      PUSH      . : Save callers DE
0658 CD3300  CALL      . : Display blank
065B D1      POP       . : Restore DE
065C 05      DEC       . : Decrement count of bytes left in buffer
065D 1D      DEC       . : Count one spaced added to buffer
065E C8      RET       . : Exit if specified number of blanks added
065F 18EF    JR      --->: Else loop till buffer full or count zero
0661 37      SCF     --- CARRY flag set if BREAK hit. *********** cont--> *
0662 F5      PUSH    --- He hit a  CR                          see note-->
0663 3E0D    LD      --- A = CR terminates buffer
0665 77      LD      --- Save terminator in buffer
0666 CD3300  CALL    --- Print it (CR)
0669 3E0F    LD      --- Cursor off code
066B CD3300  CALL    --- Turn cursor off via driver call
066E 79      LD      --- C = buffer size
066F 90      SUB     --- Minus (buffer size - chars processed)
0670 47      LD      --- Gives chars in buffer
0671 F1      POP     --- Restore status flag carry                cont-->
0672 E1      POP     --- HL = start of buffer address
0673 C9      RET     --- Return to original caller
0674 D3FF    OUT     --- 0 to cassette ************** Video controller ****
0676 21D206  LD      --- Addr. of video/keyboard/printer DCB's
0679 110040  LD      --- Start of communications region
067C 013600  LD      --- Setup for block move
067F EDB0    LDIR    --- Move 6D2-707 to 4000-4035
0681 3D      DEC     --- Change value being sent to port FF to FFFD, . . .
0682 3D      DEC     --- FFFB, .  .  .  .
0683 20F1    JR      --- Go thru this 128 times
0685 0627    LD      --- 0 to A
0687 12      LD      --- 0 to 4036-4062
0688 13      INC     --- Bump destination pntr
0689 10FC    DJNZ    --- Go if not done
068B 3A4038  LD      --- Test keyboard for BREAK
068E E604    AND     --- BREAK key hit
0690 C27500  JP      --- Go if BREAK
0693 317D40  LD      --- New stack area
0696 3AEC37  LD      --- Load disk status
```

```
0641 * ************************************************************

0646 * No. of blanks to produce **** HT key during input ***********
     :                              Pad buffer with specified
     :                              number of blanks or until
     :                              buffer is full.
     :                              Number of blanks added is:
     :                              HT 0  - 8 :  HT 5  - 3
     :                                 1  - 7 :     6  - 2
     :                                 2  - 6 :     7  - 1
     :                                 3  - 5 :     8  - 0
     :                                 4  - 4 :

0661 * Else reset *** BREAK key during input ***********************
0662 :                    CR during input

0671 : Set if BREAK  -  Not set if CR

0674 * ************************************************************
```

0699 3C	INC	--- Test for Expansion Interface
069A FE02	CP	--- and disk drive
069C DA7500	JP	--- Go if no disk
069F 3E01	LD	--- Unit select mask for drive 0
06A1 32E137	LD	--- Select drive 0
06A4 21EC37	LD	--- Addr of disk command / status register
06A7 11EF37	LD	--- Addr of disk data register
06AA 3603	LD	--- 3 to disk command register = restore, position
06AC 010000	LD	--- Delay count :to track 0
06AF CD6000	CALL	--- Delay for approx 3 seconds
06B2 CB46	BIT	--- Test if controller busy,
06B4 20FC	JR	--- Loop till not busy
06B6 AF	XOR	--- 0 to A
06B7 32EE37	LD	--- 0 to sector register
06BA 010042	LD	--- BC = addr of buffer area
06BD 3E8C	LD	--- A = read command
06BF 77	LD	-- Read sector 0, track 0 into 4200 - 4455
06C0 CB4E	BIT	--- Test if data ready
06C2 28FC	JR	--- Go if no data avail
06C4 1A	LD	--- Get next byte from disk
06C5 02	LD	-- Transfer data to 4200+
06C6 0C	INC	--- Bump buffer pntr
06C7 20F7	JR	--- Go if not 256 bytes
06C9 C30042	JP	--- Done, transfer to TRSDOS loader
06CC 01181A	LD	--- Addr of BASIC READY routine (rtn addr) ***********
06CF C3AE19	JP	--- Initialize BASIC's variables & pntrs ** cont--> *
06D2 C3961C	JP	* 4000 *--- RST 08 vector JP 1C96 (compare) **********
06D5 C3781D	JP	* 4003 *--- RST 10 vector JP 1D78 (get next char)
06D8 C3901C	JP	* 4006 *--- RST 18 vector JP 1C90 (compare DE:HL)
06DB C3D925	JP	* 4009 *--- RST 20 vector JP 25D9 (test data type)
06DE C9	RET	* 400C *--- RST 28 vector RET (JP 4BA2 for DOS)
06DF 00	NOP	*
06E0 00	NOP	*
06E1 C9	RET	* 400F *--- RST 30 vector RET (JP 44B4 for DOS)
06E2 00	NOP	*
06E3 00	NOP	* 4012 *--- RST 38 vector DI/RET (JP 4518 for DOS)
06E4 FB	EI	* :Interrupt entry point vector
06E5 C9	RET	*
06E6 00	NOP	*
06E7 01E303	LD	* 4015 *--- Keyboard DCB ***************************
06EA 00	NOP	*
06EB 00	NOP	* Driver addr = 3E3
06EC 00	NOP	*
06ED 4B	LD	*
06EE 49	LD	* 401D *--- Video DCB ******************************
06EF 07	RLCA	*
06F0 58	LD	*
06F1 04	INC	*
06F2 00	NOP	* Driver addr = 458
06F3 3C	INC	*
06F4 00	NOP	*
06F5 44	LD	*
06F6 4F	LD	* 4025 *--- Line printer DCB **********************
06F7 068D	LD	*
06F9 05	DEC	*
06FA 43	LD	* Driver addr = 58D
06FB 00	NOP	*
06FC 00	NOP	*
06FD 50	LD	*
06FE 52	LD	**

```
06CC  *  *********************************************************
06CF  *  then goto 1A18 (BASIC READY routine)
06D2  *  The contents of 6D2 - 707 are moved to location
      *  4000 - 4035 in the Communications Region
      *  during the first stage of the IPL sequence



06E7  *  *********************************************************



06EE  *  *********************************************************



06F6  *  *********************************************************



06FE  *  *********************************************************
```

06FF	C30050	JP	* 402D *--- Changed by SYS 0 to JP 4400
0702	C7	RST	* 4030 *--- Changed by SYS 0 to LD A,A3
0703	00	NOP	*
0704	00	NOP	* 4043 *--- Changed by SYS 0 to RST 28
0705	3E00	LD	* 4033 *--- Changed by SYS 0 to 44BB
0707	C9	RET	*
0708	218013	LD	--- Address of the single precision routines *********
070B	CDC209	CALL	--- Load a SP number pointed to by HL into BC/DE
070E	1806	JR	--- Go add SP no. in registers to 4121 - 4124
0710	CDC209	CALL	--- Load current value into BC/DE :
0713	CD8209	CALL	--- Invert sign of value in WRA1 : see notes -->
0716	78	LD	--- Get exponent for register value :
0717	B7	OR	--- Set status flags for exponent
0718	C8	RET	--- If exponent = 0, then no. in registers is zero
0719	3A2441	LD	--- Now, get exponent of the other number
071C	B7	OR	--- and test its exponent
071D	CAB409	JP	--- Exit if it is zero.
0720	90	SUB	--- A = current exp - Reg. exp = bits to scale
0721	300C	JR	--- Register value has smallest exp. & therefore is
0723	2F	CPL	--- smaller. Make diff in exponents positive. Also
0724	3C	INC	--- reverse registers and current values so that
0725	EB	EX	--- smallest one is in registers.
0726	CDA409	CALL	--- Put SP no. in '4121-4124' onto stack
0729	EB	EX	--- Restore HL to addr of second value
072A	CDB409	CALL	--- Put SP no. in registers into '4121 - 4124'
072D	C1	POP	--- Load SP no. saved on stack at 0726 above.
072E	D1	POP	--- If difference in exponent > 24, then no. cannot be
072F	FE19	CP	--- added because of difference in magnitude.
0731	D0	RET	--- Save number of places to right shift register
0732	F5	PUSH	--- value so its exponent = exponent of current value
0733	CDDF09	CALL	--- Turn on MS bit of both values to be added. Save
0736	67	LD	--- sign determination in H. A = no. of bit position
0737	F1	POP	--- to right shift BC/CE scale value in registers so
0738	CDD707	CALL	--- it is equivalent to current value. Go unpack
073B	B4	OR	--- value in BC/DE. Set status flags for sign of
073C	212141	LD	--- Load addr of WRA1 :register value
073F	F25407	JP	--- Jump if value in registers is negative.
0742	CDB707	CALL	--- Add a SP no in CDE to SP no. pointed to by
0745	D29607	JP	--- HL. Sum in CDE. Jump if coefficient
0748	23	INC	--- same size else
0749	34	INC	--- increase exponent by 1
074A	CAB207	JP	--- error if exponent overflows to zero.
074D	2E01	LD	--- L = number of bits to shift
074F	CDEB07	CALL	--- Right shift coefficient 1 place.
0752	1842	JR	--- Go normalize value & rtn to caller
0754	AF	XOR	--- Clear A, status flags ************** see note-->
0755	90	SUB	--- 0-exponent = -exponent
0756	47	LD	--- Save negative of exponent
0757	7E	LD	--- Load LSB of mem. value
0758	9B	SBC	--- Minus LSB of reg. value
0759	5F	LD	--- E = new LSB reg. value
075A	23	INC	--- Bump to middle byte of mem. value
075B	7E	LD	--- Load middle byte of mem. value
075C	9A	SBC	--- Subtract middle byte of reg. value
075D	57	LD	--- D = new MSB of reg. value
075E	23	INC	--- Bump to MSB of mem. value
075F	7E	LD	--- Load MSB of mem. value
0760	99	SBC	--- Minus MSB of reg. value
0761	4F	LD	--- C = new MSB of reg. value
0762	DCC307	CALL	--- If carry go convert reg. value to cont-->

0708 * Single precision addition routines (5 entry points) ********

0708: This entry point loads a .5 into BC/DF
      then adds it to the value in WRA1
070B: This entry point loads a SP value, pointed to by HL
    : into and then adds it to WRA1
0710: Loads SP value pointed to by HL into BC/DE. Then
    : inverts the sign of WRA1 value, before adding
    : BC/DE and WRA1
0713: This entry point inverts the sign of the value
    : in WRA1 before adding it to BC/DE
0716: Adds WRA1 to BC/DE, leaves sum in WRA1

0754 * Adds a negative SP value in BC/DE to a positive *************
    : SP value pointed to by HL. Result left in BC/DE

    : its positive equivalent

98

```
0765 68      LD      --- L = exponent of original reg. value  see note-->
0766 63      LD      --- H = least sig. byte
0767 AF      XOR     --- Clear A, status.
0768 47      LD      <---: B = count of bytes tested
0769 79      LD       . : Load next byte of new reg. value(MSB/middle/LSB)
076A B7      OR       . : Test if MSB is zero
076B 2018    JR       . : Jmp if MSB non-zero (go normalize reg. value)
076D 4A      LD       . : This is a circular              see note-->
076E 54      LD       . : Left shift of 8 bits
076F 65      LD       . : C <-- D <-- H
0770 6F      LD       . : H <-- L <-- A
0771 78      LD       . : Zero in B gets propagated until a non-zero byte
0772 D608    SUB      . : or all 3 bytes of reg. value have tested
0774 FEE0    CP       . : Test if all 3 bytes of value tested
0776 20F0    JR      --->: Jmp if no
0778 AF      XOR     --- Yes, value is zero
0779 322441  LD      --- Zero exponent
077C C9      RET     --- Rtn to caller
077D 05      DEC     <---: Count 1 left shift ************** see note--> *
077E 29      ADD      . : Shift HL left 1 bit
077F 7A      LD       . : Then shift D left 1 bit
0780 17      RLA      . : Picking up any carry from HL
0781 57      LD       . : Restore shifted D
0782 79      LD       . : Then shift C left 1 bit
0783 8F      ADC      . : Picking up any carry from D
0784 4F      LD       . : Restore shifted C
0785 F27D07  JP      --->: Loop till CDHL is normalized
0788 78      LD      --- A = count of bits shifted left
0789 5C      LD      --- Save HL so we can
078A 45      LD      --- use it for addr of exponent
078B B7      OR      --- Test count of bits shifted
078C 2808    JR      --->: Jump if reg value already normalized or negative
078E 212441  LD       . : HL = addr. of original exponent of reg. value
0791 86      ADD      . : Add shifted count to bias
0792 77      LD       . : Store result as exponent
0793 30E3    JR       . : Set exponent to zero if value < 2**24
0795 C8      RET      . : Rtn with WRA1 = zero if exponent is zero
0796 78      LD      <---: Load least sig. byte of value
0797 212441  LD      --- Addr. of exponent to HL          see note-->
079A B7      OR      --- Test if any bits in LSB
079B FCA807  CALL    --->: if so go test for overflow
079E 46      LD       . : otherwise load the exponent into B
079F 23      INC      . : Bump to 4025 (contains sign of result)
07A0 7E      LD       . : then load the sign. Isolate it so
07A1 E680    AND      . : that it can be combined with new exponent
07A3 A9      XOR      . : Clear sign bit of MSB
07A4 4F      LD       . : B=exponent, C=MSB, D=next MSB, E=LSB
07A5 C3B409  JP       . : Store SP number in BC, DE into 4121-4124.
07A8 1C      INC     <---: Bump least sig. byte ************* see note--> *
07A9 C0      RET     --- Exit if no overflow
07AA 14      INC     --- Go on to next byte.  Bump it
07AB C0      RET     --- Exit if no overflow
07AC 0C      INC     --- Go on to next byte.  Bump it
07AD C0      RET     --- Exit if no overflow
07AE 0E80    LD      --- Set value to -0
07B0 34      INC     --- Bump exponent
07B1 C0      RET     --- Exit if we havef not overflowed
07B2 1E0A    LD      --- OV error code
07B4 C3A219  JP      --- Output OV error message
07B7 7E      LD      --- Load LSB of memory value
```

```
      : Part I of integer to SP conversion
      : On entry C=MSB,D=middle byte,E=MSB of integer to be converted
      : If both bytes are zero, set the exponent to zero (4124),
      : the other three bytes are already zero.  If the integer
      : is not zero, locate the first non-zero byte and go to
      : 785-77D to normalize (shift it left until the most
      : significant bit is 1) it.
076D  : ------- Rotate reg. value left 8 bits.
      :     :    If entire value is zero set exponent to zero & exit
      :     :    C <-- D <-- H <-- L <-- A


077D  * Part II of integer to SP conversion
      : Shift CDHL left as a single unit the MS bit of
      : L->H, MS bit of H->D, MS bit of D->C.  Shifting
      : stops when the MS bit of C is shifted into bit
      : 15.  A count of the number of shifts necessary
      : is kept in B as a negative number.


      : Part III of integer to SP conversion. Clear sign
      : of mantissa (it was set neg during the normalization
      : process above).  Setup registers for storing
      : result.


07A8  * Return to caller for negative
      : numbers, zeros have been
      : converted to all ones.  Now,
      : convert all the trailing zeros
      : (which are now ones) back to
      : zeros.  Also used to test for
      : overflow when creating a
      : SP number.


      : Add 3 bytes of a SP number in C D/E
```

07B8	83	ADD	--- Add to LSB of register value
07B9	5F	LD	--- Save new LSB
07BA	23	INC	--- Bump to middle byte of memory value
07BB	7E	LD	--- Load middle byte of memory value : see note-->
07BC	8A	ADC	--- Add middle byte of register value
07BD	57	LD	--- Save new middle byte
07BE	23	INC	--- Bump to MSB of memory value
07BF	7E	LD	--- Load MSB of memory value
07C0	89	ADC	--- Add MSB of register value
07C1	4F	LD	--- Save new MSB
07C2	C9	RET	--- Rtn to caller
07C3	212541	LD	--- Reset sign flag so that *********** see note--> *
07C6	7E	LD	--- mantissa will have a negative sign
07C7	2F	CPL	--- Invert the sign flag
07C8	77	LD	--- Store sign flag
07C9	AF	XOR	--- Zero A
07CA	6F	LD	--- then save it
07CB	90	SUB	--- Complement B (0 - B)
07CC	47	LD	--- Save new value of B
07CD	7D	LD	--- Reload zero into A
07CE	9B	SBC	--- Complement E (0 - E)
07CF	5F	LD	--- Save new value for E
07D0	7D	LD	--- Reload A with zero
07D1	9A	SBC	--- Complement D (0 - D)
07D2	57	LD	--- Save new D value
07D3	7D	LD	--- Reload A with zero
07D4	99	SBC	--- Complement C (0 - C)
07D5	4F	LD	--- Save new C value
07D6	C9	RET	---Rtn to caller *********** Unpack a SP number ******
07D7	0600	LD	<--: On entry, A = no bits to right shift
07D9	D608	SUB	---:>: If carry, then shift right (A) bits,
07DB	3807	JR	. : : else shift number right one byte
07DD	43	LD	. : : This code thru 07E2
07DE	5A	LD	. : : shifts 00CDE such
07DF	51	LD	. : : that afterwards we have E00CD
07E0	0E00	LD	-->: : Loop to see if must right shift another byte
07E2	18F5	JR	<----: Make shift count positive
07E4	C609	ADD	--- And move it to L
07E6	6F	LD	--- Clear status flags
07E7	AF	XOR	--- Decrement shift count
07E8	2D	DEC	--- Exit if done
07E9	C8	RET	--- Now, right shift BCDE one bit at a time as a unit
07EA	79	LD	--- Right shift C one positionn, put bit 0 of C into
07EB	1F	RRA	--- Restore C :carry
07EC	4F	LD	--- Now, right shift D one place. Bit 0 of C becomes
07ED	7A	LD	--- Bit 0 of D to carry : bit 8 of D
07EE	1F	RRA	--- Restore D
07EF	57	LD	--- Right shift E one bit. Bit 0 of D becomes bit 8
07F0	7B	LD	--- Bit 0 of E to carry : of E
07F1	1F	RRA	--- Restore E
07F2	5F	LD	--- Finally right shift B one bit.
07F3	78	LD	--- Bit 0 of E becomes
07F4	1F	RRA	--- bit 7 of B. Bit 0 of B is lost.
07F5	47	LD	--- Loop till (L) bits shifted. cont-->
07F6	18EF	JR	**
07F8	00	NOP	--- 07F8 - 07FB = SP 1.0
07F9	00	NOP	---
07FA	00	NOP	---
07FB	81	ADD	--- Count of following SP values (03)
07FC	03	INC	--- Coefficients for power series used in LN comp

```
     :          To 3 bytes of a SP number pointed
     :          to by HL - One of the numbers must
     :          have been scaled so its exponent is
     :          the same as the other.  A carry
     :          from a LSB is added to the MSB, etc.
     :          On exit A=MSB, carry flag set if
     :          coefficient has increased and there-
     :          fore the exponent must be adjusted.
     :          Zero otherwise. Sum left in C D/E


07C3 * This routine converts a 4 byte negative integer into its ****
     : twos complement positive equivalent so it can be converted
     : to SP state, the SP sign flag (4125) is also
     : complemented.  This will insure a negative coefficient after
     : normalization.




* 07D7 * **********************************************************




07F6 : Integer portion left in C/D/E.  Fractional part left in B.
07F8 * **********************************************************
```

```
07FD AA        XOR        --- 07FD - 0800 = .5988
07FE 56        LD         ---
07FF 19        ADD        ---
0800 80        ADD        --- 0801 - 0804 =   .96145
0801 F1        POP        ---
0802 227680    LD         --- 0805 - 0808 =   2.88539
0805 45        LD         ---
0806 AA        XOR        ---
0807 3882      JR         ---
0809 CD5509    CALL       --- Test sign of current SP number **** LOG routine **
080C B7        OR         --- Set status flags according to sign   : see note-->
080D EA4A1E    JP         --- Error if value is negative
0810 212441    LD         --- HL = addr of exponent of current value
0813 7E        LD         --- A = exponent of current value
0814 013580    LD         --- BC/DE = .707092
0817 11F304    LD         --- (approx ln 2)
081A 90        SUB        --- Scale value so it's <1
081B F5        PUSH       --- Save scale factor
081C 70        LD         --- Force exponent of current value to be same as
081D D5        PUSH       --- constant in BC/DE
081E C5        PUSH       --- Save constant in BC/DE on stack
081F CD1607    CALL       --- Add constant in BC/DE to current value
0822 C1        POP        --- Restore constant
0823 D1        POP        --- into BC/DE
0824 04        INC        --- Bump exponent.  Multiply constant by 2**1 or
0825 CDA208    CALL       --- Divide 1.4141 (approx ln 4) by scaled value +
0828 21F807    LD         --- HL = add of SP 1.0                      : ln 2
082B CD1007    CALL       --- Load BC/DE with 1.0 and subtract from current
082E 21FC07    LD         --- Addr of table of 3 S.P. values          :value
0831 CD9A14    CALL       --- Call series routine to evaluate sum     cont-->
0834 018080    LD         --- BC = -.5
0837 110000    LD         ---
083A CD1607    CALL       --- Add (-.5) to current value
083D F1        POP        --- Restore scale factor from 81A above
083E CD890F    CALL       --- Scale current value to original magnitude
0841 013180    LD         --- Load BC/DE with .693115
0844 111872    LD         --- then multiply sum from series by .693115
0847 CD5509    CALL       --- Test sign & exponent ****************** cont--> *
084A C8        RET        --- Exit if exponent is zero
084B 2E00      LD         --- L = 00 means add exponents
084D CD1409    CALL       --- Add exponents together. Set most sig bit of MSB
0850 79        LD         --- for each value.
0851 324F41    LD         --- 414F = MSB of register value
0854 EB        EX         ---
0855 225041    LD         --- 4150 - 4151 = next MSB of register value
0858 010000    LD         --- BC = 00
085B 50        LD         --- DE = 00
085C 58        LD         ---
085D 216507    LD         --- Integer to SP conversion called after
0860 E5        PUSH       --- multiplication to convert result to SP.
0861 216908    LD         --- We will go there after unpacking the SP
0864 E5        PUSH       --- numbers. Now, put 869 on stk twice so
0865 E5        PUSH       --- we'll unpack each SP number.
0866 212141    LD         --- HL = address of current value
0869 7E        LD         --- Test LSB for zero
086A 23        INC        --- HL = addr. of next MSB
086B B7        OR         --- A = LSB of current SP value
086C 2824      JR         --- Jmp if LSB is zero (do a circular     cont-->
086E E5        PUSH       --- Save addr of next MSB
086F 2E08      LD         --- L = count of bits to right shift      cont-->
```

```
0809 * ****************************************************************
     * Method used:
     * 1. Test sign of value. If negative exit with FC error.
     * 2. Scale the value so it is between 0.5 and 1. Save the
     *    count of bits used for scaling
     * 3. Recompute scaled value as
     *      x = 1 - (2 ln 2 / ( x + ln 2))
     * 4. Evaluate
     *      ((x**2 * c0 + c1) x**2 + c2)x
     * 5. Subtract 0.5 from final term of series
     * 6. Add the shift count to the result of step 5
     * 7. Multiply result of step 6 by ln 2
```

```
     : of coeff. (I)*value(I)**2I+2 for I=-2
```


```
0847 * of current SP number *****************************************
     : Single precision multiplication-------
     : Multiply BC/DE by current value.  Use shift and add method.
     : Unpack each number first then we shift and add.
```

```
086C : right shift of one byte) then go get next byte.

086F : SP number ( or until it's right justified
```

```
0871 1F      RRA      <--: Right shift LSB 1 position
0872 67      LD        . : Save shifted LSB
0873 79      LD        . : Load MSB into A
0874 300B    JR        . : Jmp there when no one bit shifted from LSB
0876 E5      PUSH      . : else save shifted LSB and count
0877 2A5041  LD        . : Addr of middle & LSB bytes of orig register value
087A 19      ADD       . : Add to total thus far far (compound add)
087B EB      EX        . : and leave sum in proper register
087C E1      POP       . : Restore shifted LSB and shift count
087D 3A4F41  LD        . : then add MSB of original register value
0880 89      ADC       . : to the accumulated total
0881 1F      RRA       . : Right shift MSB
0882 4F      LD        . : Save shifted MSB            see notes-->
0883 7A      LD        . : Load middle byte so
0884 1F      RRA       . : we can right shift it 1 bit
0885 57      LD        . : Save shifted middle byte
0886 7B      LD        . : Load LSB and
0887 1F      RRA       . : right shift it 1 bit
0888 5F      LD        . : then move it back
0889 78      LD        . : Load exponent
088A 1F      RRA       . : Right shift it
088B 47      LD        . : and restore it
088C 2D      DEC       . : Decrement count of bits tested
088D 7C      LD        . : Restore original LSB value to A
088E 20E1    JR       -->: Loop till all 8 bits tested
0890 E1      POP      --- Restore HL to addr. of next byte
0891 C9      RET      --- And rtn
0892 43      LD       ****************************************** see note--> *
0893 5A      LD       ---      Left circular shift BC/DE one byte.  B is
0894 51      LD       ---      lost and C is replaced by A.  Shift appears
0895 4F      LD       ---      as follows:  A      BC/DE
0896 C9      RET      ---      A->C C->D D->E E->B
0897 CDA409  CALL     --- Move value in WRA1 onto stack                    *
089A 21D80D  LD       --- Addr of floating pt. 10.
089D CDB109  CALL     --- Load flt. pt. 10 into BC/DE and move into
08A0 C1      POP      --- Reload original value        :(4121 - 4124)
08A1 D1      POP      --- of WRA1 into BC/DE
08A2 CD5509  CALL     --- Single precision division routine ****** cont--> *
08A5 CA9A19  JP       --- Error - division by zero attempted
08A8 2EFF    LD       --- L = FF means subtract exponents
08AA CD1409  CALL     --- Compute new exponent by addition.  Set most sig.
08AD 34      INC      --- bit of each value, ret sign of result in 4125.
08AE 34      INC      --- Add 2 to exponent of dividend
08AF 2B      DEC      --- HL = 4123 = MSB of current value
08B0 7E      LD       --- Load MSB of value in WRA1
08B1 328940  LD       --- 4089 = MSB of current value
08B4 2B      DEC      --- HL = addr of next most sig byte
08B5 7E      LD       --- A = next most sig byte
08B6 328540  LD       --- 4085 = most sig byte of current value
08B9 2B      DEC      --- HL = addr of least sig byte
08BA 7E      LD       --- Load LSB and move it to
08BB 328140  LD       --- 4081 = next most sig byte of current value
08BE 41      LD       --- B = most sig byte of register value
08BF EB      EX       --- DE = 4122, HL = MSB/LSB register value
08C0 AF      XOR      --- now, set
08C1 4F      LD       --- MSB, next MSB
08C2 57      LD       --- LSB of register value
08C3 5F      LD       --- to zero
08C4 328C40  LD       --- Zero count of times doubling B/HL overflows
08C7 E5      PUSH     --- Save divisor in BC/HL on stack
```

```
     :          Examine current value for ones by using a
     :          right shift and test carry method.  For
     :          each one bit found, add the register value
     :          (now in 414F - 4151) to the current value
     :          repeat process until all bits positions in
     :          current value have been tested.


     :          Get MSB register value and add to MSB
     :          current value, then continue.

     :          Right justify current value in registers to get
     :          integer equivalent of value.  Right shift
     :          D/E. Shift D first, bit 1 goes to carry
     :          which will be picked up when E is shifted.
     :          Result is left in BC/DE as an un-normalized
     :          floating point number.  4124 (exponent of
     :          current value holds adjusted exponent).




0892 * Called by single precision multiplying *********************
     : while unpacking SP numbers before multiplying them


0897 * *****************************************************************


08A2 * Test sign of value in WRA1 *********************************
```

Addr	Code	Instr	Comment
08C8	C5	PUSH	--- BC = most sig byte of reg value/00
08C9	7D	LD	--- A=LSB register value. Now compute dividend-divisor
08CA	CD8040	CALL	--- Subtract current value from reg. value cont-->
08CD	DE00	SBC	--- On exit A=0, carry=1 if reg value<current value
08CF	3F	CCF	--- Reset carry so carry=1 if reg value>current value
08D0	3007	JR	--->: Jmp if reg value<current value. Go double
08D2	328C40	LD	-- : Save count of times B/HL overflows :divisor
08D5	F1	POP	-- : Clear last division from stack
08D6	F1	POP	— : We ddn´t need it
08D7	37	SCF	-- : Set carry flag.
08D8	D2C1E1	JP	<—-: 8D9: POP BC Restore last divisor so
08DB	79	LD	--- 8DA: POP HL We can double it
08DC	3C	INC	--- but first test for possible overflow
08DD	3D	DEC	--- by division out of HL into BC
08DE	1F	RRA	--- Test bit 0 of C, if it is on
08DF	FA9707	JP	--- Done: Go normalize result
08E2	17	RLA	--- Clear poss CARRY ON
08E3	7B	LD	--- Shift E left one position. cont-->
08E4	17	RLA	--- Pick up bit 8 of A-reg.
08E5	5F	LD	--- Restore shifted E. Most sig. bit in CARRY
08E6	7A	LD	--- Shift D left one position
08E7	17	RLA	--- Pick up bit 8 from E becomes bit 0 of D
08E8	57	LD	--- Restore shifted D. Most sig. bit in CARRY
08E9	79	LD	--- Shift C left one position
08EA	17	RLA	--- Pick up bit 8 from D becomes bit 0 of C
08EB	4F	LD	--- Restore shifted C
08EC	29	ADD	--- Now, double the divisor so that eventually it
08ED	78	LD	--- will exceed the dividend. When it does, the
08EE	17	RLA	--- quotient plus reminder will be in B/HL as reg.
08EF	47	LD	--- values. Carry any overflow from shifting HL left
08F0	3A8C40	LD	--- one place to B. Then shift B left one place. Keep
08F3	17	RLA	--- count of overflow amt of B in 408C as a bit
08F4	328C40	LD	--- string. i.e. the number of ones equals the
08F7	79	LD	--- number of times overflow occurred
08F8	B2	OR	--- now combine all bytes
08F9	B3	OR	--- of the register value and
08FA	20CB	JR	--- loop until divisor overflows
08FC	E5	PUSH	--- Save HL
08FD	212441	LD	--- Exponent of saved value
0900	35	DEC	--- Decrement it by 1 for: (A**X)/(B**Y)=(A/B)**(X-Y)
0901	E1	POP	--- Restore HL
0902	20C3	JR	--- Continue with shift and decrement loop
0904	C3B207	JP	--- OV error (exponent has gone to zero)
0907	3EFF	LD	--- Computes new exponent for flt. pt. multiplication*
0909	2EAF	LD	--- 090A: XOR A Zero A, clear flags
090B	212D41	LD	--- HL = addr of MSB for WRA2 DP value
090E	4E	LD	--- C = MSB, saved value : see note -->
090F	23	INC	--- HL = addr of exponent for WRA2 DP value
0910	AE	XOR	--- Make exp pos/neg depending on entry used
0911	47	LD	--- Save exponent in B
0912	2E00	LD	--- Mask for testing exponent sign of WRA1 (force
0914	78	LD	--- Refetch exponent & test for for zero : sign +)
0915	B7	OR	--- Set status flags
0916	281F	JR	--- WRA1 value is zero
0918	7D	LD	--- Not zero. Get exponent for WRA1 value
0919	212441	LD	--- Which we already know is non-zero
091C	AE	XOR	--- Combine sign of exp WRA1 with mask cont --> *
091D	80	ADD	--- Now, add the exponents for the two values to be
091E	47	LD	--- multiplied and save in B-reg. Addition should
091F	1F	RRA	--- produce a carry. Now test for presence.

08CA : (4081-4089). Result in B/HL

08E3 : Shift C/D/E left as one unit. Bits carried out of E are
     : shifted into D, etc.

0907 * **

     : When entered at 0917 it is the callers
     : responsibility to load the L register
     : according to the sign of the value
     : in WRA1. L = 0 if WRA1 >= 0,
     : L = FF if WRA1 < 0

091C * in L. Note : The second entry at 0917

```
0920 A8        XOR  B          ---     Of carry by shifting it into bit 8 and doing
0921 78        LD   A,B        ---     an exclusive OR with new exponent   see note->
0922 F23609    JP   P,0936H    --- Jmp if sum of exponent is out of range
0925 C680      ADD  80H        --- Reload new exponent into A and turn on bit 8
0927 77        LD   (HL),A     --- Store new exponent
0928 CA9008    JP   Z,0890H    --- Jmp if value is exactly zero
092B CDDF09    CALL 09DFH      --- Turn on MSB of current value so it can be
092E 77        LD   (HL),A     --- unpacked for repetitive addition.
092F 2B        DEC  HL         --- HL = next most sig byte
0930 C9        RET             --- Return to caller
0931 CD5509    CALL 0955H      --- Go test sign of floating pt. number in WRA1 ******
0934 2F        CPL             --- Reverse the results so A = minus if value +, and
0935 E1        POP  HL         --- is positive if value is minus.
0936 B7        OR   A          --- Set status flags according to new exponent
0937 E1        POP  HL         --- Clear stack
0938 F27807    JP   P,0778H    --- Set current floating point value to zero & return
093B C3B207    JP   07B2H      --- OV error exit
093E CDBF09    CALL 09BFH      --- Load a SP no. from 4121 - 4124 ***** see note--> *
0941 78        LD   A,B        --- B = Exponent, C = MSB, D = Next MSB, E = LSB
0942 B7        OR   A          --- Set status flags according to new exponent
0943 C8        RET  Z          --- Exit if number is zero
0944 C602      ADD  02H        --- Multiply number in registers by 4
0946 DAB207    JP   C,07B2H    --- Error if exponent overflows
0949 47        LD   B,A        --- Restore adjusted exponent
094A CD1607    CALL 0716H      --- Add original value which gives value * 5
094D 212441    LD   HL,4124H   --- 4124 = addr of exp of result. By adding 1 to
0950 34        INC  (HL)       --- it we double it which gives us the original
0951 C0        RET  NZ         --- value * 10
0952 C3B207    JP   07B2H      --- OV error exit
0955 3A2441    LD   A,(4124H)  --- Test sign of SP number. On exit A=-1 if negative
0958 B7        OR   A          --- Set status flags for exponent : A=+1 if positive
0959 C8        RET  Z          --- Exit if exponent is zero
095A 3A2341    LD   A,(4123H)  --- No, get MSB of SP number
095D FE2F      CP   2FH        --- 095E : CPL A
095F 17        RLA             --- Sign bit to carry
0960 9F        SBC  A,A        --- Gives 0 - sign bit
0961 C0        RET  NZ         --- Return with A = all 1'S if MSB negative
0962 3C        INC  A          --- Return with A = +1 if MSB positive
0963 C9        RET             --- Rtn to caller
0964 0688      LD   B,88H      --- B = 80 + number of bits to convert ***************
0966 110000    LD   DE,0000H   --- Zero register used in normalization routine
0969 212441    LD   HL,4124H   --- Addr of exponent for WRA1
096C 4F        LD   C,A        --- C = MSB of integer
096D 70        LD   (HL),B     --- Save initial exponent
096E 0600      LD   B,00H      --- B must be zero before entering     see note-->
0970 23        INC  HL         --- Normalization routine. Bump
0971 3680      LD   (HL),80H   --- to sign word of WRA1 rtn it positive
0973 17        RLA             --- Set CARRY to sign of integer value
0974 C36207    JP   0762H      --- Go normalize
0977 CD9409    CALL 0994H      --- Convert a negative value *************** cont--> *
097A F0        RET  P          --- Rtn if positive, else determine data type
097B E7        RST  20H        --- Test data type
097C FA5B0C    JP   M,0C5BH    --- Integer, convert to + value,              cont-->
097F CAF60A    JP   Z,0AF6H    --- TM error if Z
0982 212341    LD   HL,4123H   --- We have a SP, or a DP number. Make it positive
0985 7E        LD   A,(HL)     --- by setting the sign bit (bit 8) of the MSB to
0986 EE80      XOR  80H        --- zero. Set current value to zero if current
0988 77        LD   (HL),A     --- value is +, all ones otherwise
0989 C9        RET             --- Rtn to caller
098A CD9409    CALL 0994H      --- Go test sign of current value ****** see note--> *
```

0921 : (Which should have bit 8 zero since it produced the carry
     : we're testing.)

0931 * ***

093E * Multiply a SP number by 10 ************************************
     : First, add 2 to exponent which is equivalent to multiplying
     : by 4 then add the original quantity which yields value * 5.

0964 * ***

          :   Start of integer to SP conversion.
          :   Store exponent bits in 4124.
          :   Set sign flag (4125) for positive
          :   coefficient. Set C = MSB,
          :   D = LSB of integer. Set carry to
          :   Sign of MSB. Call normalization
          :   routine. If entered at 0969 B must
          :   be set to 80 + no of bits in integer value
0977 * to its positive equivalent ***---Test sign of current value *

097C : SP if it has overflowed & rtn to caller

098A * A = +1 if positive, all ones if negative. ********************
110

098D	6F	LD	--- Set up HL as follows: HL = 00 00 if current value
098E	17	RLA	--- if positive. HL = FF FF if current val is negative
098F	9F	SBC	--- gives A=0 if carry is zero or A=FF if
0990	67	LD	--- CARRY is set. Move flag to H
0991	C39A0A	JP	--- Save HL as current value, cont-->
0994	E7	RST	--- Determine current data type *********** cont--> *
0995	CAF60A	JP	--- TM error if Z (string)
0998	F25509	JP	--- Jump if SP or DP. Determine sign & rtn to caller
099B	2A2141	LD	--- Load integer value in HL
099E	7C	LD	--- Combine LSB and MSB in
099F	B5	OR	--- order to test if zero
09A0	C8	RET	--- Exit if integer value zero
09A1	7C	LD	--- A = MSB of integer
09A2	18BB	JR	--- Go test sign & rtn to caller cont-->
09A4	EB	EX	--- **
09A5	2A2141	LD	--- Save HL
09A8	E3	EX	--- Value to be moved onto stack
09A9	E5	PUSH	--- Rtn addr to HL, stack = (4121)
09AA	2A2341	LD	--- Rtn addr to stack
09AD	E3	EX	--- 2nd value to be moved onto stack
09AE	E5	PUSH	--- Rtn addr back to stack
09AF	EB	EX	--- Restore HL
09B0	C9	RET	--- Rtn to caller
09B1	CDC209	CALL	--- Load a SP no. pointed to by HL into BC/DE. *******
09B4	EB	EX	--- Then move it to WRA1 value area. On exit
09B5	222141	LD	--- save HL (points to byte following exponent). On
09B8	60	LD	--- exit, B = exponent, C = MSB, D = next MSB, E =
09B9	69	LD	--- LSB, HL = addr of byte following exponent.
09BA	222341	LD	--- Save LSB and next LSB in WRA1
09BD	EB	EX	--- Restore HL to original contents
09BE	C9	RET	--- Return to caller
09BF	212141	LD	--- Load a SP number from 4121 - 4124 or addr in HL **
09C2	5E	LD	--- E = LSB (4121) :see note -->
09C3	23	INC	--- Bump to next byte
09C4	56	LD	--- D = next MSB (4122)
09C5	23	INC	--- Bump to next byte
09C6	4E	LD	--- C = MSB (4123)
09C7	23	INC	--- Bump to next byte
09C8	46	LD	--- B = exponent (4124)
09C9	23	INC	--- Bump to byte following exponent
09CA	C9	RET	--- Rtn to caller
09CB	112141	LD	--- Source address of a SP number ********** cont--> *
09CE	0604	LD	--- Number of bytes to remove
09D0	1805	JR	--- Move to address specified in HL and rtn to caller
09D2	EB	EX	--- Move routine ********************* see note--> *
09D3	3AAF40	LD	--- Get type specification (which is also the length
09D6	47	LD	--- Length of field to move
09D7	1A	LD	--- Load a byte from source field
09D8	77	LD	--- Store it in destination field see note-->
09D9	13	INC	--- Bump source addr
09DA	23	INC	--- Bump destination addr
09DB	05	DEC	--- Count 1 byte moved
09DC	20F9	JR	--- Jmp if more bytes to move
09DE	C9	RET	--- else rtn to caller
09DF	212341	LD	--- Turn on most significant bit of a SP number *****
09E2	7E	LD	--- Get MSB
09E3	07	RLCA	--- Bit 7 to CARRY
09E4	37	SCF	--- Turn on bit 7 and reposition number, also original
09E5	1F	RRA	--- sign bit to CARRY.
09E6	77	LD	--- Restore number with MSB on

```
0991 : rtn type to integer & return to caller.
0994 * Test sign of current numeric value: on entry A = +1
     : if positive or all ones if negative.




09A2 :  on rtn A = all 1'S (negative), +1 (positive)
09A4 * Store 4121 - 4124 (WRA1) on stack *************************




09B1 * ***********************************************************




09BF * ***********************************************************
     * 09BF: This entry point loads a SP number
     * from WRA1 into BC/DE
     * 09C2: This entry point loads a SP number
     * pointed to by HL into BC/DE.


     *         On entry HL points to the LSB of a SP value
     *         On exit HL points to the byte following the exponent
09CB * Move a SP no. from (HL) to 4121 - 4124 *********************

09D2 * Entry pt. when HL = source addr & DE = dest. addr. **********

     :              Move number of bytes in type/
     :              length specification from
     :              location given in DE to address
     :              specified in HL.




09DF * ***********************************************************
```

112

09E7 3F	CCF	---	Complement bit zero and position it into bit 7
09E8 1F	RRA	---	(sign & MS bit) of MSB
09E9 23	INC	---	HL = 4125 = sign of result -determined below
09EA 23	INC	---	Gives HL - 4125
09EB 77	LD	---	Save complement of original sign in 4125
09EC 79	LD	---	Turn on most significant bit of most significant
09ED 07	RLCA	---	byte for the SP value in BC/DE
09EE 37	SCF	---	then force CARRY so we can
09EF 1F	RRA	---	restore byte with bit 7 = 1, original sign bit to
09F0 4F	LD	---	Restore C = MSB :CARRY
09F1 1F	RRA	---	Original sign bit to bit 7 set sign flag as
09F2 AE	XOR	---	sign of both #'s equal, then
09F3 C9	RET	---	4125 = 80, else 00.
09F4 212741	LD	---	Destination addr for numeric value of variable ***
09F7 11D209	LD	---	Return addr
09FA 1806	JR	---	Move value in WRA1 to WRA2
09FC 212741	LD	---	Addr of WRA2
09FF 11D309	LD	---	Move value in WRA1 to WRA2
0A02 D5	PUSH	---	Force rtn addr to 9D3 see note-->
0A03 112141	LD	---	Addr of current variable in WRA1
0A06 E7	RST	---	Determine data type of variable
0A07 D8	RET	---	Exit to move routine if INT, STR, or SP
0A08 111D41	LD	---	Addr of double precision variable
0A0B C9	RET	---	Exit to move routine
0A0C 78	LD	---	Compare a SP number in BC/DE with ****** cont--> *
0A0D B7	OR	---	Test exponent of register value
0A0E CA5509	JP	---	Jump if exponent (and rest of number) are zero.
0A11 215E09	LD	---	Rtn addr when exiting from this routine
0A14 E5	PUSH	---	To stack
0A15 CD5509	CALL	---	Test sign of MSB of SP number. A = MSB of SP
0A18 79	LD	---	number in registers.
0A19 C8	RET	---	Exit if (4121 - 4124) does not hold a SP number
0A1A 212341	LD	---	Addr of MSB of WRA1 value
0A1D AE	XOR	---	Compare MSB of (4121) to MSB of value in register
0A1E 79	LD	---	Reload MSB of register value
0A1F F8	RET	---	Exit if signs are different
0A20 CD260A	CALL	---	Compare SP mo. in BC/DE with that in 4121 - 4124.
0A23 1F	RRA	---	Get CARRY flag from comparison and combine with
0A24 A9	XOR	---	sign bit of value in registers.
0A25 C9	RET	---	Rtn to caller
0A26 23	INC	---	HL = addr of exponent WRA1 **********************
0A27 78	LD	---	A = exponent of register value
0A28 BE	CP	---	Compare exponents
0A29 C0	RET	---	Exit if different :
0A2A 2B	DEC	---	Gives addr of MSB for WRA1 :
0A2B 79	LD	---	A=MSB of register value :
0A2C BE	CP	---	Compare MSB : see note-->
0A2D C0	RET	---	Exit if not equal :
0A2E 2B	DEC	---	Gives addr of middle for WRA1 :
0A2F 7A	LD	---	A = middle byte of reg value :
0A30 BE	CP	---	Compare next most MSB :
0A31 C0	RET	---	Exit if unequal :
0A32 2B	DEC	---	Gives addr of LSB for WRA1 :
0A33 7B	LD	---	A = LSB of register value
0A34 96	SUB	---	Compare LSB of values. Exit if not equal
0A35 C0	RET	---	Exit if not equal
0A36 E1	POP	---	Numbers are equal
0A37 E1	POP	---	Clear 095E from stack and
0A38 C9	RET	---	Rtn to caller of 0A0C
0A39 7A	LD	---	Prepare to test signs ** Compare integer values **

09F4 * ***

0A02 : (Move 4DAF bytes from 4121 to 4127)

0A0C * One in 4121 - 4124. Signs must be alike. On exit negative
      : if signs unlike or quantity in memory > value in registers.

0A26 * ***

0A29 : Compare a SP no. in BC/DE with a SP no. in 4121 - 4124 must
      : have same signs. Do not compare exponents. Begin by com-
      : paring the exponent of each number, working down to the LSB.
      : Exit as soon as a mix-match if found. HL = addr of byte
      : that mis-compared. If the numbers are
      : Identical exit with HL = 411F, A = 0, FLAGS = 0.
      : If unequal C = 0 (memory) = or < register value
      :   C = 1 (memory) > register value

0A39 * ***

114

0A3A	AC	XOR	--- Compare sign of D to sign of H see note-->
0A3B	7C	LD	--- Prepare for subtraction
0A3C	FA5F09	JP	--- Jmp if signs unequal
0A3F	BA	CP	--- Else, compare MSB´s
0A40	C26009	JP	--- Jmp if unequal
0A43	7D	LD	--- Prepare to compare LSB of integer
0A44	93	SUB	--- Compare LSB´s
0A45	C26009	JP	--- Jmp it unequal
0A48	C9	RET	--- Rtn - Values are equal. A=00
0A49	212741	LD	--- Addr of WRA1 value **** Compare two DP values ****
0A4C	CDD309	CALL	--- Move value pointed to by saved location 4127-412E
0A4F	112E41	LD	--- Now get addr of the exponent for the value moved
0A52	1A	LD	--- Load the exponent
0A53	B7	OR	--- Set status flags according to exponent
0A54	CA5509	JP	--- If exponent zero, test sign of MSB & rtn to caller
0A57	215E09	LD	--- Push rtn addr of 95E onto stack in case WRA1 and
0A5A	E5	PUSH	--- WRA2 values not equal
0A5B	CD5509	CALL	--- Test WRA1 value for zero. Skip if zero at 0A61
0A5E	1B	DEC	--- DE = addr of MSB of moved value
0A5F	1A	LD	--- Load MSB
0A60	4F	LD	--- and move it to C
0A61	C8	RET	--- Exit if MSB of WRA1 value is zero
0A62	212341	LD	--- HL = addr of MSB for current value
0A65	AE	XOR	--- Compare sign of moved & current values
0A66	79	LD	--- Restore MSB of WRA2 value (moved value)
0A67	F8	RET	--- Exit if signs different
0A68	13	INC	--- DE = current value exponent addr
0A69	23	INC	--- HL = saved value exponent addr
0A6A	0608	LD	--- Prepare to compare current and saved values
0A6C	1A	LD	<--: Begin comparing values byte for byte
0A6D	96	SUB	. : by subtracting WRA1 from WRA2
0A6E	C2230A	JP	. : Jump if unequal
0A71	1B	DEC	. : Backspace WRA2 1 byte
0A72	2B	DEC	. : Backspace WRA1 1 byte
0A73	05	DEC	. : Count number of bytes compared
0A74	20F6	JR	---> Loop till all bytes compared
0A76	C1	POP	--- Values are equal, clear rtn addr of 95E from stack
0A77	C9	RET	--- and rtn to caller
0A78	CD4F0A	CALL	--- Compare current to saved value ***** see note--> *
0A7B	C25E09	JP	--- Set status flag if unequal
0A7E	C9	RET	--- Equal. Return with A=00, status = 0
0A7F	E7	RST	--- Test data type ***************** CINT routine ****
0A80	2A2141	LD	--- HL = addr of LSB of SP value in WRA1
0A83	F8	RET	--- Already an integer
0A84	CAF60A	JP	--- TM error if Z (string)
0A87	D4B90A	CALL	--- If double precision, call CSNG
0A8A	21B207	LD	--- Address of OV error routine becomes
0A8D	E5	PUSH	--- Rtn addr in case of error
0A8E	3A2441	LD	--- Get exponent of current value in WRA1
0A91	FE90	CP	--- and test if > 16 : 16 bits)
0A93	300E	JR	--->: Jump if exponent>16 (integer has more than
0A95	CDFB0A	CALL	-- : Convert A +SP number to its integer equivalent
0A98	EB	EX	-- : Integer value in DE to HL
0A99	D1	POP	-- : Clear error rtn or addition operand from stack
0A9A	222141	LD	-- : Return integer value in HL to WRA1
0A9D	3E02	LD	-- : Integer flag
0A9F	32AF40	LD	-- : Set data type to integer
0AA2	C9	RET	-- : Rtn to original caller
0AA3	018090	LD	<---: BC/DE = -2**16 ****************************
0AA6	110000	LD	--- in SP format

0A3A : Compare integer values in DE/HL. If signs are unlike, rtn
     : with status of -1. If DE>HL then rtn A=-1, if DE<HL then
     : A=+1, if DE=HL then A=00.

0A49 * **

0A78 * Compare two DP values ************************************

0A7F * **

0AA3 * **

0AA9	CD0C0A	CALL	--- Compare current value to -2**16
0AAC	C0	RET	--- If values not identical exit
0AAD	61	LD	--- If so, set current value to integer,-2**16
0AAE	6A	LD	--- and rtn to caller
0AAF	18E8	JR	--- Rtn type to integer, value to 8000, & return
0AB1	E7	RST	--- Test data type ************* CSNG routine ********
0AB2	E0	RET	--- Already single
0AB3	FACC0A	JP	--- Jump if integer
0AB6	CAF60A	JP	--- TM error if Z (string)
0AB9	CDBF09	CALL	--- Load a first half of DP value from WRA1 into BC/DE
0ABC	CDEF0A	CALL	--- Flag current value as single precision
0ABF	78	LD	--- Get exponent for DP value
0AC0	B7	OR	--- Set status flags
0AC1	C8	RET	--- Test exponent, exit if zero (DP value is zero)
0AC2	CDDF09	CALL	--- Turn on MSB of value in WRA1 & register value
0AC5	212041	LD	--- HL = middle addr of DP value in WRA1
0AC8	46	LD	--- Load middle part of DP. Value becomes LSB
0AC9	C39607	JP	--- Convert reg part of DP no to SP value & rtn
0ACC	2A2141	LD	--- Convert integer to single precision ************
0ACF	CDEF0A	CALL	--- Flag WRA1 as SP
0AD2	7C	LD	--- A = MSB of integer
0AD3	55	LD	--- D = LSB of integer
0AD4	1E00	LD	--- E = Rest of value (equals zero)
0AD6	0690	LD	--- B = initial max exponent
0AD8	C36909	JP	--- Go normalize then rtn to caller
0ADB	E7	RST	--- Test data type *************** See note --> ****
0ADC	D0	RET	--- Already double
0ADD	CAF60A	JP	--- Jump if string
0AE0	FCCC0A	CALL	--- Call if integer (convert integer to SP)
0AE3	210000	LD	--- Zero last 4 bytes of WRA1
0AE6	221D41	LD	--- These bytes hold the
0AE9	221F41	LD	--- tail end of a DP value
0AEC	3E08	LD	--- Double precision flag
0AEE	013E04	LD	--- 0AEF LD A,04 Single precision flag
0AF1	C39F0A	JP	--- Store A in type flag & return
0AF4	E7	RST	--- Test data type **********************************
0AF5	C8	RET	--- Return with no error message if a string
0AF6	1E18	LD	--- TM error code if not a string
0AF8	C3A219	JP	--- Output TM error message
0AFB	47	LD	--- Convert a positive SP number to integer **********
0AFC	4F	LD	--- Move exponent from A to BC,
0AFD	57	LD	--- D
0AFE	5F	LD	--- and E
0AFF	B7	OR	--- Test value of exponent
0B00	C8	RET	--- Exit if value of number is zero
0B01	E5	PUSH	--- Save error rtn addr
0B02	CDBF09	CALL	--- Load current SP value into BC/DE
0B05	CDDF09	CALL	--- Prepare current value and register value for
0B08	AE	XOR	--- arithmetic operation see note-->
0B09	67	LD	--- H = sign of value. Bit 8 = 0 if +, 1 if -
0B0A	FC1F0B	CALL	--- Jmp if value negative
0B0D	3E98	LD	--- A = max. exponent allowed
0B0F	90	SUB	--- Exponent - bias = no. of bits to right cont-->
0B10	CDD707	CALL	--- Get integer equivalent of no. in CDE cont-->
0B13	7C	LD	--- A = original sign. Bit 8 = 0 if +, 1 if -
0B14	17	RLA	--- Shift sign into carry
0B15	DCA807	CALL	--- If neg. convert trailing ones to zeroes
0B18	0600	LD	--- Zero exponent
0B1A	DCC307	CALL	--- If number was neg. make it a neg. integer
0B1D	E1	POP	--- Restore caller's HL

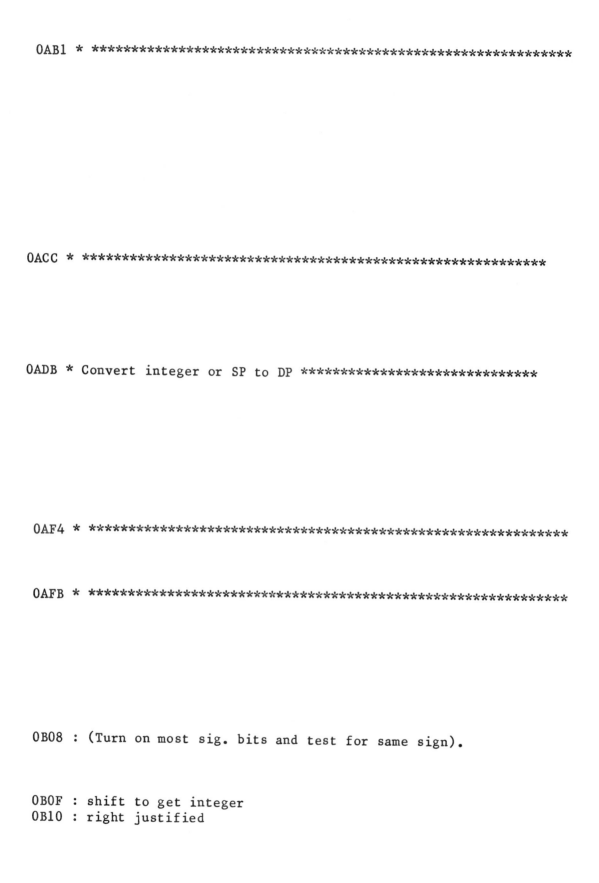

```
0AB1 * *******************************************************

0ACC * **********************************************************

0ADB * Convert integer or SP to DP ******************************

0AF4 * ************************************************************

0AFB * ************************************************************

0B08 : (Turn on most sig. bits and test for same sign).

0B0F : shift to get integer
0B10 : right justified
```

0B1E	C9	RET	--- Rtn to caller
0B1F	1B	DEC	--- Decrement middle and LSB of SP value *** cont--> *
0B20	7A	LD	--- then combine new
0B21	A3	AND	--- middle & LSB. If they were zero the cont-->
0B22	3C	INC	--- Test for FFFF (middle & LSB were 0)
0B23	C0	RET	--- Exit if they were not zero
0B24	0B	DEC	--- Else decrement MSB
0B25	C9	RET	--- Then exit
0B26	E7	RST	--- Determine data type ********* Fix routine ********
0B27	F8	RET	--- Finished if an integer
0B28	CD5509	CALL	--- Test sign of current value (floating point)
0B2B	F2370B	JP	--- Jmp if it's positive
0B2E	CD8209	CALL	--- Clear sign bit of current value (make it +)
0B31	CD370B	CALL	--- Convert a SP or DP value to integer. Do not round
0B34	C37B09	JP	--- Convert integer part of no. back to cont-->
0B37	E7	RST	--- Convert SP or DP to integer - Determine data type*
0B38	F8	RET	--- Done, already an integer
0B39	301E	JR	--- Jump if double precision
0B3B	28B9	JR	--- TM error if Z (string)
0B3D	CD8E0A	CALL	--- Convert from SP to integer & return to caller
0B40	212441	LD	--- HL = addr of current SP value *******************
0B43	7E	LD	--- A = exponent of current value
0B44	FE98	CP	--- Test if more than 16 bits in integer position
0B46	3A2141	LD	--- A = least sig byte of current value
0B49	D0	RET	--- Exit if more than 16 bits in integer position
0B4A	7E	LD	--- A = exponent see note-->
0B4B	CDFB0A	CALL	--- Convert SP to integer. This gives integer
0B4E	3698	LD	--- equivalent of number.
0B50	7B	LD	--- Now, convert number back to SP
0B51	F5	PUSH	--- Move 8 bits of integer value
0B52	79	LD	--- From E to A then save it on stk.
0B53	17	RLA	--- Then position sign from bit 8 of C in CARRY then
0B54	CD6207	CALL	--- Normalize number & adjust exponent
0B57	F1	POP	--- Restore 8 bits of integer value
0B58	C9	RET	--- Rtn to caller.
0B59	212441	LD	--- Double precision to integer ********************
0B5C	7E	LD	--- Get exponent
0B5D	FE90	CP	--- and compare to bias
0B5F	DA7F0A	JP	--- Jump if number will have less than 16 cont-->
0B62	2014	JR	--- Jump if number will have more than 16 cont-->
0B64	4F	LD	--- C = exponent = 90 Number will have 16 bits of int
0B65	2B	DEC	--- Backspace to MSB of WRA1
0B66	7E	LD	--- A = most sig byte
0B67	EE80	XOR	--- Complement sign bit of MSB
0B69	0606	LD	--- Test for a minus zero. If sum of A plus all
0B6B	2B	DEC	--- successive bytes is zero, then value is zero.
0B6C	B6	OR	--- Backspace to next byte of DP value
0B6D	05	DEC	--- Examined all bytes
0B6E	20FB	JR	--- No, loop
0B70	B7	OR	--- Set status flags for OR of all bytes in DP value
0B71	210080	LD	--- HL = integer - 0
0B74	CA9A0A	JP	--- Rtn value to - 0, type to integer and return to
0B77	79	LD	--- DP exponent to A-reg caller
0B78	FEB8	CP	--- Compare to 56(base 10)
0B7A	D0	RET	--- Error - more than 56 bits in DP no.
0B7B	F5	PUSH	--- Save exponent
0B7C	CDBF09	CALL	--- Load BC/DE with first part of a DP number
0B7F	CDDF09	CALL	--- Turn on most sig bit. Determine sign of result
0B82	AE	XOR	--- Test sign of value. If + then status = +, else
0B83	2B	DEC	--- HL=4123=MSB current value addr :negative

```
------  ---------------------------------------------------------------
0B1F * Round down a SP number  **********************************
0B21 : result will be FFFF.


0B26 * **************************************************************



0B34 : SP or DP then return
0B37 * **************************************************************


0B40 * **************************************************************


       :      Isolate the integer portion of a SP number.
       :      Leave the integer in the A-register.  Convert
       :      the integer to a SP number and leave it in WRA1
       :      returns with NO CARRY if called with a DP value in WRA1.




0B59 * **************************************************************

0B5F : bits of precision. Use SP to integer conversion routine.
0B62 : bits of precision
```

```
0B84  36B8    LD      --- Max exponent to exponent area
0B86  F5      PUSH    --- Save sign of value
0B87  FCA00B  CALL    --- If negative, convert trailing ones to zeroes
0B8A  212341  LD      --- HL = addr of MSB of DP value
0B8D  3EB8    LD      --- A = exponent (max) for DP number
0B8F  90      SUB     --- Subtract current exponent gives no.      cont-->
0B90  CD690D  CALL    --- Unpack and right justify value
0B93  F1      POP     --- Restore sign
0B94  FC200D  CALL    --- If negative, convert trailing zeroes to ones
0B97  AF      XOR     --- Clear A
0B98  321C41  LD      --- Ret sign of mantissa
0B9B  F1      POP     --- Restore original exponent
0B9C  D0      RET     --- Error if more than 56 bits in mantissa
0B9D  C3D80C  JP      --- Normalize result and exit
0BA0  211D41  LD      --- HL=addr of LSB of DP value ********* see note--> *
0BA3  7E      LD      <---: Fetch a byte from list
0BA4  35      DEC       .  : Decrement byte in list
0BA5  B7      OR        .  : Test byte as originally fetched
0BA6  23      INC       .  : Bump to next item in list
0BA7  28FA    JR      --->: Loop till non-zero byte found
0BA9  C9      RET     --- Rtn to caller
0BAA  E5      PUSH    --- Save callers HL******************** see note-> **
0BAB  210000  LD      --- Zero accumulator register
0BAE  78      LD      --- Test quantity in BC, if
0BAF  B1      OR      --- zero, move zeros to DE & exit
0BB0  2812    JR      ------>: Jump if BC zero
0BB2  3E10    LD        .   : A = 16 = no. of times to shift left
0BB4  29      ADD     <-----:--: Shift result left 1 position
0BB5  DA3D27  JP        .   :  : BS error if C
0BB8  EB      EX        .   :  : Prepare to shift multiplican left
0BB9  29      ADD       .   :  : 1 place. Shift it and
0BBA  EB      EX        .   :  : move it back to DE
0BBB  3004    JR      --->:   :  : If no carry, has not found a 1,don't add
0BBD  09      ADD       .  :  :  : Else add multiplier to result thus far
0BBE  DA3D27  JP        .  :  :  : BS error if C
0BC1  3D      DEC     <---:  :  : Have we shifted 16 times
0BC2  20F0    JR      -------:->: No, loop
0BC4  EB      EX      <------: Move answer to DE
0BC5  E1      POP     --- Restore caller's HL
0BC6  C9      RET     --- Return to caller
0BC7  7C      LD      --- Test sign of value in HL ********** see note--> *
0BC8  17      RLA     --- And save in B.  B = 0
0BC9  9F      SBC     --- If HL +, all one's if HL neg.
0BCA  47      LD      --- Move sign flag to B
0BCB  CD510C  CALL    --- Convert HL to it's one's compliment     cont-->
0BCE  79      LD      --- Zero to A. Setup A for sign of difference. If HL
0BCF  98      SBC     --- was +, then A=+0, if was -, then A=-1
0BD0  1803    JR      --- Use addition routine. If result        cont-->
0BD2  7C      LD      --- Set B = sign of HL **************** see note--> *
0BD3  17      RLA     --- Sign bit to CARRY
0BD4  9F      SBC     --- B = 0 if HL +, else -1
0BD5  47      LD      --- Repositioned sign bit to B
0BD6  E5      PUSH    --- Save HL in case we must convert it to SP
0BD7  7A      LD      --- MSB of register value so we can test sign
0BD8  17      RLA     --- Set A = sign of DE
0BD9  9F      SBC     --- A = 0 if HL +, else -1
0BDA  19      ADD     --- Add the two integers.  Add sign of result to sum
0BDB  88      ADC     --- of the signs
0BDC  0F      RRCA    --- Sign of result to bit 7 and
0BDD  AC      XOR     --- combine with sign of HL
```

OB8F : of places to right shift to get integer

OBA0 * Convert trailing ones to a neg. DP value to zeroes **********

OBAA * Binary multiplication of two 16 bit quantities in BC and DE**
     : Result is left in DE. Uses shift and add method. Called
     : from BASIC interpreter when computing addr of a subscripted
     : variable.

OBC7 * Binary subtraction for two 16 bit values in HL and DE.*******

OBCB : so we use addition routine

OBD0 : underflows convert to SP.
OBD2 * Binary addition for two integers in HL & DE. Result left in**
     : HL. If result overflows, convert both quantities to SP and
     : add. Determine overflow as follows:
     : C = carry after addition   C = 0 -- No overflow
     :   C = 1 --- then if
     :   :
     :   ----------!----------
     :   :   :
     :   A = 0, B = 0   A <> B
     :   then overflow   negative no.

```
0BDE  F2990A    JP     --- No overflow. Flag result as integer,      cont-->:
0BE1  C5        PUSH   --- Save sign flag on stk
0BE2  EB        EX     --- Original DE to HL for conversion purposes.
0BE3  CDCF0A    CALL   --- Convert original value of DE to SP. Save it in
0BE6  F1        POP    --- 4121 - 4124. Clear stk.
0BE7  E1        POP    --- Restore original quanitiy in HL. It was wiped by
0BE8  CDA409    CALL   --- Move converted value of DE to stack         : add.
0BEB  EB        EX     --- Restore HL
0BEC  CD6B0C    CALL   --- Convert HL to single precision
0BEF  C38F0F    JP     --- Add single precision equivalent of HL & DE
0BF2  7C        LD     --- Test value of HL ****************** see note--> *
0BF3  B5        OR     --- If
0BF4  CA9A0A    JP     --- Zero, exit with result (0) in HL
0BF7  E5        PUSH   --- Save original value in case we need to
0BF8  D5        PUSH   --- convert them to SP.
0BF9  CD450C    CALL   --- Set result to integer type.  Convert any neg.
0BFC  C5        PUSH   --- value to +.  BC = sign of result (pushed one).
0BFD  44        LD     --- B = MSB of value 2
0BFE  4D        LD     --- BC = value 2
0BFF  210000    LD     --- HL = accumulator
0C02  3E10      LD     --- No. of times to shift left.
0C04  29        ADD    <-------:  Shift answer and test for
0C05  381F      JR        .    :  overflow.  CARRY if so.
0C07  EB        EX        .    :  No overflow, shift DE left
0C08  29        ADD       .    :  one bit and test for a binary
0C09  EB        EX        .    :  one (CARRY).
0C0A  3004      JR     ---->:  :  No CARRY, no binary one
0C0C  09        ADD       .  :  :  Add original value in HL to
0C0D  DA260C    JP     --------:->:  Accumulator for each binary one
0C10  3D        DEC    <---:  :  :  in DE.
0C11  20F1      JR     -------->:  :  Have we shifted DE 16 places, no loop
0C13  C1        POP    ---           :  Yes, get sign of result
0C14  D1        POP    ---           :  Original value in DE
0C15  7C        LD     ---           :  Now test true sign of result
0C16  B7        OR     ---           :  Set status flags according to result
0C17  FA1F0C    JP     ---           :  Jump if answer is negative.   see note-->
0C1A  D1        POP    ---           :  Clear stack,
0C1B  78        LD     ---           :  get sign of result to A
0C1C  C34D0C    JP     ---           :  Convert HL to proper sign,        cont-->
0C1F  EE80      XOR    ---           :  Clear sgn bit & test rest of value for 0
0C21  B5        OR     ---           :  If zero, we have a negative number,else
0C22  2813      JR     ---           :  Convert it to single precision etc.
0C24  EB        EX     ---           :  :C26 POP BC Clear sign of result  note-->
0C25  01C1E1    LD     <---------:  : C27 POP HL Restore original HL value
0C28  CDCF0A    CALL   --- Convert original HL to single precision
0C2B  E1        POP    --- HL = original DE
0C2C  CDA409    CALL   --- Move converted HL to stack
0C2F  CDCF0A    CALL   --- Convert DE (now in HL) to single precision
0C32  C1        POP    --- Load converted HL value from stack
0C33  D1        POP    --- into BC/DE
0C34  C34708    JP     --- Do single precision multiplication
0C37  78        LD     --- Get sign flag of result *************************
0C38  B7        OR     --- Rtn status flags to sign of result
0C39  C1        POP    --- Clear stack in case we exit
0C3A  FA9A0A    JP     --- If sign was suppose to be negative, exit
0C3D  D5        PUSH   --- Save original DE
0C3E  CDCF0A    CALL   --- Convert result to single precision
0C41  D1        POP    --- Restore original DE
0C42  C38209    JP     --- Rtn sign and return to caller
0C45  7C        LD     --- Get sign of MSB from 2nd operand **** see note-->*
```

```
     :         store in 4121 & return.




OBF2 * Integer multiplication.  DE = first value, HL = 2nd value.***
     : Result is left in HL.  If the signs of both operands are
     : equal, then the result has the same sign.  If either sign is
     : different, the result is set negative.  Any negative values
     : are converted to their positive equivalents before the
     : multiplication is started.  Method used is shift and add.
     : For each 1 found in DE, the original contents of HL are
     : added to an accumulator register (HL in this case) and
     : shifted left.  Process is repeated 16 times (must test all
     : 16 bits in DE).  If overflow occurs, convert both values to
     : SP and use SP multiplication routine.




     OC17 : (May have overflowed.)


     OC1C : save result and return to caller.
OC1F * ***********************************************************


  OC24 : Number has overflowed. Convert to SP to re-multiply.




OC37 * *************************************************************



     :      : If HL is negative convert it to its one's complement.
OC45 * *** : If DE is negative convert it also. *******************
```

124

0C46	AA	XOR	--- And combine with sign from 1st operand.
0C47	47	LD	--- B = + if signs are equal (+,+) or (-,-), cont-->
0C48	CD4C0C	CALL	--- Test sign of HL operand. If neg. convert to pos.
0C4B	EB	EX	--- Switch HL/DE so we can test sign of DE cont-->
0C4C	7C	LD	--- Get sign byte of value in DE.
0C4D	B7	OR	--- Set status flags according to sign of value in DE
0C4E	F29A0A	JP	--- Flag as integer, result to 4121. Rtn to caller
0C51	AF	XOR	--- Clear A, CARRY
0C52	4F	LD	--- Zero C : Convert a negative :
0C53	95	SUB	--- Convert LSB : integer to its one's :
0C54	6F	LD	--- And restore : complement positive :
0C55	79	LD	--- Zero to A : equivalent :
0C56	9C	SBC	--- Convert MSB
0C57	67	LD	--- And restore
0C58	C39A0A	JP	--- Set data type to integer(02), cont-->
0C5B	2A2141	LD	--- Get binary value of integer *********************
0C5E	CD510C	CALL	--- Convert to a positive value
0C61	7C	LD	--- Make sure value is LE 2**15
0C62	EE80	XOR	--- If bit 15 is not zero, and the remainder
0C64	B5	OR	--- of the word is zero then value > 2**15
0C65	C0	RET	--- Rtn if integer = or < 32768
0C66	EB	EX	--- Value is > 2**15. Move it to DE
0C67	CDEF0A	CALL	--- Set SNG precision flag
0C6A	AF	XOR	--- Set exponent to zero
0C6B	0698	LD	--- Maximum exponent for SP values
0C6D	C36909	JP	--- Convert value to SP and rtn to caller
0C70	212D41	LD	--- Double precision subtraction routine. ** cont--> *
0C73	7E	LD	--- Load MSB of saved value
0C74	EE80	XOR	--- Invert sign
0C76	77	LD	--- And restore
0C77	212E41	LD	--- HL=addr of exponent in WRA2 *********** cont--> *
0C7A	7E	LD	--- Load exponent from WRA2
0C7B	B7	OR	--- Set status flags for exponent
0C7C	C8	RET	--- Exit if WRA2 value zero
0C7D	47	LD	--- B = Exponent WRA2 value
0C7E	2B	DEC	--- Backspace to MSB of WRA2
0C7F	4E	LD	--- C = MSB WRA2 number
0C80	112441	LD	--- DE = addr exponent of WRA1 value
0C83	1A	LD	--- Load exponent of value in WRA1
0C84	B7	OR	--- Set status flags
0C85	CAF409	JP	--- Jump if WRA1 value is zero
0C88	90	SUB	--- Else, compare exponents : WRA1 - WRA2
0C89	3016	JR	--- Jump if WRA1 exponent > WRA2 exponent cont-->
0C8B	2F	CPL	--- Make diff. in exponent positive
0C8C	3C	INC	--- Current number is larger than saved number
0C8D	F5	PUSH	--- Save difference in exponents
0C8E	0E08	LD	--- Now, swap the two numbers so that WRA1 = WRA2
0C90	23	INC	--- And visa-versa
0C91	E5	PUSH	--- HL = addr of exponent WRA2
0C92	1A	LD	--- Swap WRA1 and WRA2 double precision numbers
0C93	46	LD	--- Load a byte from WRA1
0C94	77	LD	--- Load a byte from WRA2 : Force larger
0C95	78	LD	--- WRA1 byte to WRA2 : number into
0C96	12	LD	--- WRA2 byte to WRA1 : WRA1
0C97	1B	DEC	--- Decrement WRA1 addr.
0C98	2B	DEC	--- Decrement WRA2 addr.
0C99	0D	DEC	--- Count 1 byte moved
0C9A	20F6	JR	--- Loop till 8 bytes of SP numbers moved
0C9C	E1	POP	--- Restore addr. of WRA2 to HL
0C9D	46	LD	--- B = exponent of new WRA2 number

OC47 : negative if unlike (+,-)

OC4B : Convert to + if its negative.

OC58 : Save value in 4121/4122 & return
OC5B * **

OC70 * Addr of saved DP value ***************************************

OC77 * Double precision addition routine. Add current value to
     : saved value.

OC89 : There are less bits in integer portion so it is smaller

0C9E 2B	DEC		--- HL = addr. of MSB of WRA2 value
0C9F 4E	LD		--- C = MSB new WRA2 number
0CA0 F1	POP		--- A = difference in exponents
0CA1 FE39	CP		--- Is diff in exponent more than 56 bits
0CA3 D0	RET		--- Exit if difference in exponent more than 56 bits
0CA4 F5	PUSH		--- Save diff. in exponents
0CA5 CDDF09	CALL		--- Turn on most significant bit in MSB of WRA1
0CA8 23	INC		--- HL = addr. of bit bucket zeroed
0CA9 3600	LD		--- during normalization. Zero it
0CAB 47	LD		--- Save sign flag for WRA2
0CAC F1	POP		--- Restore exponent diff.
0CAD 212D41	LD		--- HL = addr of MSB for saved value
0CB0 CD690D	CALL		--- Scale (right justify) saved value so its exponent
0CB3 3A2641	LD		--- = current value then the two numbers can be added
0CB6 321C41	LD		--- Get last 8 bits shifted out of WRA2 value
0CB9 78	LD		--- Get sign flag for WRA2 value
0CBA B7	OR		--- Set status flags according to WRA2 sign
0CBB F2CF0C	JP		--- Signs are different, must substract
0CBE CD330D	CALL		--- Add DP number in (4127-412D) to (411D-4123)
0CC1 D20E0D	JP		--- If no CARRY, adjust sign of result and exit
0CC4 EB	EX		--- There was CARRY, increment exponent of current
0CC5 34	INC		--- value, error if overflow
0CC6 CAB207	JP		--- Jump to OV error message routine
0CC9 CD900D	CALL		--- Then right shift coefficient, position
0CCC C30E0D	JP		--- Adjust sign of result and return
0CCF CD450D	CALL		--- Subtract saved value from current ***** cont--> *
0CD2 212541	LD		--- HL = Sign flag for result
0CD5 DC570D	CALL		--- If CARRY, then get one's complement of the diff.
0CD8 AF	XOR		--- Initial counter value
0CD9 47	LD	<-----:	Zero B for normalization loop below
0CDA 3A2341	LD	. :	Fetch MSB and
0CDD B7	OR	. :	Test for zero
0CDE 201E	JR	------->:	If non-zero, go shift left until cont-->
0CE0 211C41	LD	. : :	HL = addr of LSB-1 for DP value in WRA1
0CE3 0E08	LD	. : :	C = no. of bytes to shift
0CE5 56	LD	<---: : :	Get next byte to be moved
0CE6 77	LD	. : : :	Save current byte
0CE7 7A	LD	. : : :	Save byte to be moved to suceeding addr
0CE8 23	INC	. : : :	Bump to next byte in WRA1
0CE9 0D	DEC	. : : :	Have we shifted entire DP no. left one byte
0CEA 20F9	JR	--->: : :	No, loop
0CEC 78	LD	. : :	Yes, in case no. is zero, don't loop forever
0CED D608	SUB	. : :	Have we shifted the LSB all the way to the
0CEF FEC0	CP	. : :	exponent (8 bytes)
0CF1 20E6	JR	----->: :	No, continue looking for a non-zero MSB
0CF3 C37807	JP	--- :	Yes, zero exponent & return
0CF6 05	DEC	<---: :	Maintain count of bytes & bits shifted left *
0CF7 211C41	LD	.: :	Addr of LSB of 8 byte no.to shift left 1 bit
0CFA CD970D	CALL	.: :	Shift number left one place
0CFD B7	OR	.: :	Test bit 7 of MSB
0CFE F2F60C	JP	<-->:<--:	Continue shifting until bit 7 = 1
0D01 78	LD		--- Test count of places shifted left
0D02 B7	OR		--- Set status flags for count
0D03 2809	JR		--- Jmp if value already normalized
0D05 212441	LD		--- HL=address of exponent
0D08 86	ADD		--- Add count of bits shifted left to bias
0D09 77	LD		--- Save new exponent
0D0A D27807	JP		--- If no overflow, set exponent to zero
0D0D C8	RET		--- and rtn to caller
0D0E 3A1C41	LD		--- Get MSB of current value

```
OCCF * Difference replaces current *******************************
     : Normalize the difference.  Test the MSB, if zero shift entire
     :    number left one byte.  When MSB is non-zero shift number
     :    left one bit at a time until a one is shifted into bit 7
     :    of the MSB.


OCDE : A 1 appears in bit 7. Else shift entire number left one byte
     : starting at the LSB shifting towards the exponent.




OCF6 * ***********************************************************
```

0D11	B7	OR	---	Set status flags
0D12	FC200D	CALL	---	If value is negative, reset trailing zeroes to
0D15	212541	LD	---	Get sign of result :ones
0D18	7E	LD	---	into A register
0D19	E680	AND	---	Isolate sign of result flag
0D1B	2B	DEC	---	Backspace to sign of mantissa
0D1C	2B	DEC	---	gives HL-2
0D1D	AE	XOR	---	Set sign of result to mantissa of result
0D1E	77	LD	---	Restore MSB with correct sign
0D1F	C9	RET	---	Ret to caller
0D20	211D41	LD	---	HL = Addr of LSB for current DP value ***********
0D23	0607	LD	---	Current DP value
0D25	34	INC	---	Bump LSB
0D26	C0	RET	---	Exit if no overflow :
0D27	23	INC	---	Else add CARRY to :
0D28	05	DEC	---	Next byte until no : see note-->
0D29	20FA	JR	---	Overflow :
0D2B	34	INC	---	Bump exponent :
0D2C	CAB207	JP	---	OV error code
0D2F	2B	DEC	---	Number has become negative
0D30	3680	LD	---	Reset MSB=80, rest of byte=00
0D32	C9	RET	---	Rtn
0D33	212741	LD	---	Addr of augment ******************************
0D36	111D41	LD	---	Addr of addend
0D39	0E07	LD	---	No. of bytes to add
0D3B	AF	XOR	---	Clear CARRY flag :
0D3C	1A	LD	<----:	Do addition :
0D3D	8E	ADC	. :	Begin with LSB and work : see note-->
0D3E	12	LD	. :	Towards MSB. Move :
0D3F	13	INC	. :	result to WRA1 (4121-4124). Number
0D40	23	INC	. :	must be unpacked before starting addition
0D41	0D	DEC	. :	Count 1 byte added
0D42	20F8	JR	---->:	Loop till all bytes added
0D44	C9	RET	---	Rtn to caller
0D45	212741	LD	---	Start of WRA2 value ***********************
0D48	111D41	LD	---	Start of WRA1 value
0D4B	0E07	LD	---	No. of bytes to subtract
0D4D	AF	XOR	---	Clear CARRY flag
0D4E	1A	LD	<----:	Get a current LSB and :
0D4F	9E	SBC	. :	Subtract a saved LSB :
0D50	12	LD	. :	From it. Result replaces : see note-->
0D51	13	INC	. :	Current value. Bump fetch :
0D52	23	INC	. :	addresses for WRA1 & WRA2 :
0D53	0D	DEC	. :	Count bytes subtracted
0D54	20F8	JR	---->:	Loop till all bytes subtracted
0D56	C9	RET	---	Then rtn
0D57	7E	LD	---	Set sign flag to E ***********************
0D58	2F	CPL	---	Indicating one's complement
0D59	77	LD	---	Restore sign flag
0D5A	211C41	LD	---	HL = addr of LSB of current DP #
0D5D	0608	LD	---	No. of bytes to complement
0D5F	AF	XOR	---	Zero A & clear CARRY flag :
0D60	4F	LD	---	Save zero so it can be reloaded :
0D61	79	LD	<---:	Reload zero, leave CARRY untouched : see note-->
0D62	9E	SBC	. :	Complement a byte :
0D63	77	LD	. :	And restore it :
0D64	23	INC	. :	Bump to next byte of number
0D65	05	DEC	. :	Done 8 bytes
0D66	20F9	JR	---->:	No, loop
0D68	C9	RET	---	Yes, exit

```
0D20  *  ***************************************************************
      :  Add 1 to a DP number in WRA1
      :  Begin by adding 1 to the LSB.  If overflow (result = 0), add
      :  the CARRY to next byte, etc.  If there is overflow out of
      :  the exponent then the number has overflowed.




0D33  *  ***************************************************************
      :  Add two double precision numbers.
      :  Add coefficients only, do not add exponents.  Address of one
      :  number in DE, and other in HL.  Sum replaces the number
      :  pointed to by HL
      :




0D45  *  ***************************************************************
      :  Subtract two double precision numbers
      :  Contents of (411D - 4123) are subtracted from (4127 - 412D).
      :  Result replaces (411D - 4123).




0D57  *  ***************************************************************
      :  This routine converts a positive DP value in WRA1
      :  to its one's complement equivalent
```

0D69	71	LD	--- Save MSB see note-->
0D6A	E5	PUSH	--- Save starting addr of value starting
0D6B	D608	SUB	--- with MSB. Is shift count => 8
0D6D	380E	JR	--- No, go to bit shift routine
0D6F	E1	POP	--- Restore HL to start of array
0D70	E5	PUSH	--- Save start of array
0D71	110008	LD	--- D = count of bytes to move (shift right 1 byte)
0D74	4E	LD	<----: Now, right shift array one byte, zero filling
0D75	73	LD	. : on the left. C = byte being shifted
0D76	59	LD	. : E = previous byte shifted out (initially zero).
0D77	2B	DEC	. : Decrement addr
0D78	15	DEC	. : Decrement count
0D79	20F9	JR	---->: Loop till 7 bytes shifted
0D7B	18EE	JR	--- Loop till shift count < 8
0D7D	C609	ADD	--- Continuation of unpacking routine above cont--> *
0D7F	57	LD	--- D = number of positions to shift right
0D80	AF	XOR	--- Zero A
0D81	E1	POP	--- HL = addr of MSB
0D82	15	DEC	--- Count no. of places shifted
0D83	C8	RET	--- Exit from unpacking routine if done shifting
0D84	E5	PUSH	--- Save addr of MSB
0D85	1E08	LD	--- No. of bytes to shift
0D87	7E	LD	--- Get a btye, shift it right. Bit 0 to CARRY will
0D88	1F	RRA	--- become bit 7 of following byte
0D89	77	LD	--- Restore shifted byte
0D8A	2B	DEC	--- Bump to next byte
0D8B	1D	DEC	--- Shifted all bytes
0D8C	20F9	JR	--- No, loop
0D8E	18F0	JR	--- Yes, go test if shifted the correct no. of places
0D90	212341	LD	--- Addr of exponent *********************** cont--> *
0D93	1601	LD	--- Number of bits to right shift
0D95	18ED	JR	--- Jump to shift routine. Rtn to caller at D83
0D97	0E08	LD	--- No. of bytes to shift left ************ cont--> *
0D99	7E	LD	--- Fetch a LSB
0D9A	17	RLA	--- Shift left 1 so bit 7 goes to CARRY
0D9B	77	LD	--- And CARRY goes to bit 0.
0D9C	23	INC	--- Restore shifted value.
0D9D	0D	DEC	--- Bump to next most LSB. Count a byte shifted
0D9E	20F9	JR	--- Jump if 8 bytes not shifted
0DA0	C9	RET	--- Else rtn
0DA1	CD5509	CALL	--- Double precision multiplication ******* cont--> *
0DA4	C8	RET	--- Exit if value zero
0DA5	CD0A09	CALL	--- Adjust exponent. New exponent to 4124.
0DA8	CD390E	CALL	--- Move current value to 414A - 4150 cont--->
0DAB	71	LD	--- Zero 411C
0DAC	13	INC	--- DE = 414A = start addr of moved SP value
0DAD	0607	LD	--- B = count of bytes to add
0DAF	1A	LD	--- Fetch a byte - starting at LSB
0DB0	13	INC	--- Position to next byte
0DB1	B7	OR	--- Test current byte for zero
0DB2	D5	PUSH	--- Save current byte address : 1 byte position
0DB3	2817	JR	--- If current byte zero, shift entire value right
0DB5	0E08	LD	--- No of times to right shift a byte
0DB7	C5	PUSH	--- Save count of bytes processed, initially B=7,C=8
0DB8	1F	RRA	--- Right shift LSB so we
0DB9	47	LD	--- can test if current bit 0 is a one, if so
0DBA	DC330D	CALL	--- add two unpacked SP numbers. cont--->
0DBD	CD900D	CALL	--- Right shift sum 1 place.
0DC0	78	LD	--- Restore shifted LSB so we can test
0DC1	C1	POP	--- rest of bits, then load number of bits

0D69 : Unpack a DP number addr of value (starting with MSB) in HL.
     : C = MSB, A-reg = no. of bits to right shift. Value is right
     : shifted. Shift is byte at a time until shift count < 0
     : then it becomes bit at a time.

0D7D * Bit shift portion of right just. for DP value ***************

0D90 * Right shift a DP number pointed to by HL one bit. ***********

0D97 * Left shift a DP number pointed to by HL left one bit.********

0DA1 * Uses repetative addition. Test exponent of current value. **

0DA8 : (Temp storage), zero current value

0DBA : Add current value to saved value. Sum left in current value

0DC2	0D	DEC	--- to test. Count 1 bit tested
0DC3	20F2	JR	--- Loop till all bits in current byte tested
0DC5	D1	POP	--- then load addr of next byte to test
0DC6	05	DEC	--- Have all bytes been right justified
0DC7	20E6	JR	--- No, loop
0DC9	C3D80C	JP	--- Yes, normalized result and rtn to caller
0DCC	212341	LD	--- HL = addr of WRA1. A = 0
0DCF	CD700D	CALL	--- Right shift WRA1 one byte
0DD2	18F1	JR	--- Then continue with shift/add loop
0DD4	00	NOP	--- Double precision 10 *****************************
0DD5	00	NOP	---
0DD6	00	NOP	---
0DD7	00	NOP	---
0DD8	00	NOP	---
0DD9	00	NOP	---
0DDA	2084	JR	---
0DDC	11D40D	LD	--- Addr of double precision 10
0DDF	212741	LD	--- Destination address
0DE2	CDD309	CALL	--- Move a DP 10 to WRA2
0DE5	3A2E41	LD	--- ********** Double precision division ** cont--> *
0DE8	B7	OR	--- Prepare test for zero exponent
0DE9	CA9A19	JP	--- /0 error if Z (division by zero)
0DEC	CD0709	CALL	--- Compute new exponent. Set WRA1 negative
0DEF	34	INC	--- Restore exponent of
0DF0	34	INC	--- WRA1 to original value
0DF1	CD390E	CALL	--- Move WRA1 value to 414A - 4150 (dividend)
0DF4	215141	LD	--- HL = addr of exponent of moved value
0DF7	71	LD	--- Zero exponent
0DF8	41	LD	--- Zero B-reg
0DF9	114A41	LD	<---: Addr of LSB of moved WRA1 (dividend)
0DFC	212741	LD	. : Addr of LSB of WRA2 (divisor)
0DFF	CD4B0D	CALL	. : Subtract divisor from dividend
0E02	1A	LD	. : Difference moved to 414A-4151
0E03	99	SBC	. : If value in WRA2 was > 414A-4151
0E04	3F	CCF	. : Decrease MSB of 414A-4151 value
0E05	380B	JR	. : Jmp if divisor greater than dividend cont-->
0E07	114A41	LD	. : DE = addr of moved WRA1 value (dividend)
0E0A	212741	LD	. : HL = addr of WRA2 (divisor)
0E0D	CD390D	CALL	. : Add them together, sum to 414A
0E10	AF	XOR	. : Clear all status flags so we don't exit
0E11	DA1204	JP	. : E12: LD (DE),A Save new exponent (dividend)
0E14	3A2341	LD	. : E13: INC B Signal 1 subtraction
0E17	3C	INC	. : Then load MSB
0E18	3D	DEC	. : for dividend.
0E19	1F	RRA	. : CARRY into sign pos.
0E1A	FA110D	JP	. : Done. Go normalize result
0E1D	17	RLA	. : Restore CARRY flag
0E1E	211D41	LD	. : HL = addr of original dividend
0E21	0E07	LD	. : No. of bytes to shift
0E23	CD990D	CALL	. : Shift entire dividend left one bit
0E26	214A41	LD	. : HL = addr of moved divisor
0E29	CD970D	CALL	. : Shift the moved dividend left one cont-->
0E2C	78	LD	. : Get subtraction count
0E2D	B7	OR	. : Set status flags
0E2E	20C9	JR	--->: Jmp if divisor < dividend
0E30	212441	LD	. : Else divisor > dividend. Divide divisor
0E33	35	DEC	. : by 2 by decrementing exponent
0E34	20C3	JR	--->: Then repeat subtraction. If divisor goes to
0E36	C3B207	JP	--- Zero we have an OV error
0E39	79	LD	--- Restore MSB of WRA2 value. We need the C-register!

ODD4 * **

ODE5 * Get exponent of divisor **********************************
     : Divide WRA1 by WRA2 uses subtraction/shift method

OE05 : else, add difference back to moved current value

OE29 : bit left so they are in synch

OE39 * **

```
0E3A 322D41   LD      --- Load MSB of WRA2
0E3D 2B       DEC     --- HL = MSB of current value
0E3E 115041   LD      --- DE addr of temp storage area for current SP value
0E41 010007   LD      --- B=no. of bytes to move. C=value to move to current
0E44 7E       LD      --- Get a byte of the current value            :value
0E45 12       LD      --- Move it to 4150 - 414A
0E46 71       LD      --- Zero a byte of current value
0E47 1B       DEC     --- Decrement all addresses.  We started at the MSB
0E48 2B       DEC     --- and must work down towards the LSB.
0E49 05       DEC     --- Have we moved 7 bytes
0E4A 20F8     JR      --- No, loop
0E4C C9       RET     --- Yes, rtn to caller
0E4D CDFC09   CALL    --- Move current value ******************** cont--> *
0E50 EB       EX      --- HL = end of current value
0E51 2B       DEC     --- Backup to get exponent
0E52 7E       LD      --- Load exponent
0E53 B7       OR      --- And test for zero
0E54 C8       RET     --- Exit if not a flt. pt. no. or value is zero
0E55 C602     ADD     --- Adjust exponent for following addition
0E57 DAB207   JP      --- Error if exponent overflow
0E5A 77       LD      --- Save adjusted exponent
0E5B E5       PUSH    --- and addr of exponent of saved value
0E5C CD770C   CALL    --- Add current to saved value          see note-->
0E5F E1       POP     --- Restore addr of exponent
0E60 34       INC     --- Adjust it
0E61 C0       RET     --- and rtn if no overflow
0E62 C3B207   JP      --- OV error if exponent is zero
0E65 CD7807   CALL    --- Zero exponent of SP value ** ASCII TO BINARY ** **
0E68 CDEC0A   CALL    --- Flag as DP
0E6B F6AF     OR      --- E6C: XOR A
0E6D EB       EX      --- Save HL (current input symbol)
0E6E 01FF00   LD      --- Initialize HL=00, B=0, C=-0
0E71 60       LD      --- Zero H
0E72 68       LD      --- and L
0E73 CC9A0A   CALL    --- Flag as integer.  Zero accumulator
0E76 EB       EX      --- Restore addr of current input symbol to HL, DE=00
0E77 7E       LD      --- Fetch 1st char of digit
0E78 FE2D     CP      --- Test for minus sign
0E7A F5       PUSH    --- Save MSD as sign
0E7B CA830E   JP      --- Jump if minus sign (bump to next char)
0E7E FE2B     CP      --- Test for +
0E80 2801     JR      --- Jump if plus sign (bump to next char)
0E82 2B       DEC     --- Compensate for increment at RST 10
0E83 D7       RST     --- Re-examine current character
0E84 DA290F   JP      --- Jump if character is numeric
0E87 FE2E     CP      --- Test for decimal point
0E89 CAE40E   JP      --- Jump if decimal point
0E8C FE45     CP      --- Test for E
0E8E 2814     JR      --- Jump if E exponential type SP
0E90 FE25     CP      --- Test for %
0E92 CAEE0E   JP      --- Jump if % force integer
0E95 FE23     CP      --- Test for #
0E97 CAF50E   JP      --- Jump if # force double precision
0E9A FE21     CP      --- Test for !
0E9C CAF60E   JP      --- Jump if ! force single precision
0E9F FE44     CP      --- Test for D
0EA1 2024     JR      --- Jump if not D else exponential type DP
0EA3 B7       OR      --- If D ret A-reg non-zero for E, status = 0
0EA4 CDFB0E   CALL    --- Convert digit to SP or DP      :E or D processing
0EA7 E5       PUSH    --- Save HL so it can be used to hold       cont-->
```

```
0E4D * to saved location ****************************************
      :                This routine multiplies the current DP
      :                value by 2 by adding it to itself. First
      :                current value is moved to saved location
      :                then DP add routine adds current value
      :                to saved value.



0E5C : (DP   result left in current location)



****** **********************************************************
```

0EA8	21BD0E	LD	--- Place rtn addr of EBD on stk and
0EAB	E3	EX	--- Restore HL = next input character. Stack = EBD
0EAC	D7	RST	--- Examine next char in input stream. Look for sign
0EAD	15	DEC	--- If any of the following tests are true. D=-1
0EAE	FECE	CP	--- Control goes to EBD. Else we fall into EBD.
0EB0	C8	RET	--- Return if - (minus) token (D = -1)
0EB1	FE2D	CP	--- Not minus token, test for ASCII minus
0EB3	C8	RET	--- Return if - character (D = -1)
0EB4	14	INC	--- D = 0 if + sign follows -1 if - sign follows
0EB5	FECD	CP	--- Test for plus (+) token
0EB7	C8	RET	--- Return if + token (D = 0)
0EB8	FE2B	CP	--- Not a + token, test for ASCII plus
0EBA	C8	RET	--- Return if + character (D = 0)
0EBB	2B	DEC	--- Backspace input pointer to E or D
0EBC	F1	POP	--- Remove EBD address from stack
0EBD	D7	RST	--- Examine next character in input stream
0EBE	DA940F	JP	--- Jmp if next character is numeric
0EC1	14	INC	--- Finalize exponential number ----:D = 0 if - sign
0EC2	2003	JR	--->: Jmp if exponent positive :D = +1 if + sign
0EC4	AF	XOR	. : Clear A-reg
0EC5	93	SUB	. : A = - value off exponent
0EC6	5F	LD	. : E = Exponent
0EC7	E5	PUSH	<---: Save current position in code string
0EC8	7B	LD	--- E = exponent
0EC9	90	SUB	--- B=count of numbers beyond the dec. pt. cont-->
0ECA	F40A0F	CALL	<---: Multiply no. by 10
0ECD	FC180F	CALL	. : Divide no. by 10 for each mult. and cont-->
0ED0	20F8	JR	--->: Loop till value scaled according to number
0ED2	E1	POP	--- Restore addr of next symbol :in A reg
0ED3	F1	POP	--- Get possible sign
0ED4	E5	PUSH	--- Preserve addr of next symbol
0ED5	CC7B09	CALL	--- Value was preceeded by a minus sign
0ED8	E1	POP	--- Restore code string addr
0ED9	E7	RST	--- Determine type of data conversion
0EDA	E8	RET	--- Return if not single precision
0EDB	E5	PUSH	--- Save code string addr
0EDC	219008	LD	--- Return addr
0EDF	E5	PUSH	--- Save on stack
0EE0	CDA30A	CALL	--- Make sure value is not exacly -2**16. cont-->
0EE3	C9	RET	--- Goto 0890
0EE4	E7	RST	--- Determine data type *****************************
0EE5	0C	INC	--- C = 0
0EE6	20DF	JR	--- Fall thru if integer followed by ., or cont-->
0EE8	DCFB0E	CALL	--- If not DP convert to single precision
0EEB	C3830E	JP	--- Go get next digit
0EEE	E7	RST	--- Determine data type ******************* cont--> *
0EEF	F29719	JP	--- SN error if P (not an integer)
0EF2	23	INC	--- Bump to next element in code string
0EF3	18D2	JR	--- Go finalize number and return
0EF5	B7	OR	--- Force A-reg non-zero ******** # found ! found **
0EF6	CDFB0E	CALL	--- Convert value to SP or DP
0EF9	18F7	JR	--- Rtn to caller
0EFB	E5	PUSH	--- Save current position in input string ***********
0EFC	D5	PUSH	--- Save integer part of number in input string
0EFD	C5	PUSH	--- BC = 00 00
0EFE	F5	PUSH	--- Save flags indicating data type, A = lng
0EFF	CCB10A	CALL	--- Convert current value to single precision
0F02	F1	POP	--- Restore flags
0F03	C4DB0A	CALL	--- Convert current value to double precision
0F06	C1	POP	--- Restore B = 00/00

0EC9 : A-reg = no. off times to divide/multiply

0ECD : addition at 0F6B - 0F6F. A reg automatically
     : bumped by 0F18

0EE0 : If so Set type to integer. Value to 8000

0EE4 * **

0EE6 : dec. pt. first char.

0EEE * % found - finalize value and exit *************************

0EFF5 * **

0EFB * **

0F07	D1	POP	--- Restore integer part of number
0F08	E1	POP	--- Restore current position in input string
0F09	C9	RET	--- Return
0F0A	C8	RET	--- Multiply a SP or DP number by 10 ****** cont--> *
0F0B	F5	PUSH	--- Save caller's AF
0F0C	E7	RST	--- Determine data type
0F0D	F5	PUSH	--- Save data type
0F0E	E43E09	CALL	--- Single: multiply current value by 10
0F11	F1	POP	--- Reload data type
0F12	EC4D0E	CALL	--- Double: multiply current value by 10
0F15	F1	POP	--- Restore caller's AF
0F16	3D	DEC	--- and decrement count of times multiplied
0F17	C9	RET	--- Rtn to caller
0F18	D5	PUSH	--- Divide current SP or DP value by 10 *************
0F19	E5	PUSH	--- Save caller's registers
0F1A	F5	PUSH	--- DE / HL / AF
0F1B	E7	RST	--- Determine data type
0F1C	F5	PUSH	--- A = type
0F1D	E49708	CALL	--- Divide current value by 10
0F20	F1	POP	--- Reload type so we'll skip other call
0F21	ECDC0D	CALL	--- Double: divide current value by 10
0F24	F1	POP	--- Restore users registers
0F25	E1	POP	--- AF / HL
0F26	D1	POP	--- and DE then incrementM
0F27	3C	INC	--- Count of times divided
0F28	C9	RET	--- Rtn to caller
0F29	D5	PUSH	--- DE = 00 00 **************************************
0F2A	78	LD	--- B = 00
0F2B	89	ADC	--- CARRY is always set when entered, see note-->
0F2C	47	LD	--- B = 0 for integer conversion. Count of cont-->
0F2D	C5	PUSH	--- Save 0 or count
0F2E	E5	PUSH	--- Save position in input string
0F2F	7E	LD	--- Refetch current character
0F30	D630	SUB	--- A= 0 - 9
0F32	F5	PUSH	--- Save binary value for current digit
0F33	E7	RST	--- Determine data type we're converting to
0F34	F25D0F	JP	--- Jump if not an integer. A = current digit
0F37	2A2141	LD	--- ASCII to integer conversion
0F3A	11CD0C	LD	--- DE = 3277
0F3D	DF	RST	--- Compare current value to 3277
0F3E	3019	JR	--- Jump, value >= 3277
0F40	54	LD	--- DE = current value
0F41	5D	LD	--- Multiply by 10
0F42	29	ADD	--- * 2
0F43	29	ADD	--- * 4
0F44	19	ADD	--- * 5
0F45	29	ADD	--- * 10
0F46	F1	POP	--- Reload current digit
0F47	4F	LD	--- Binary value of current digit
0F48	09	ADD	--- Add units digit
0F49	7C	LD	--- Now test sign of value thus far
0F4A	B7	OR	--- Ret status flags
0F4B	FA570F	JP	--- Jump if value exceeds 2 ** 15
0F4E	222141	LD	--- Save binary value
0F51	E1	POP	--- Restore HL, BC, and DE
0F52	C1	POP	--- B=count of digits after dec. pt. cont-->
0F53	D1	POP	--- Possible sign flags
0F54	C3830E	JP	--- Get next digit
0F57	79	LD	--- A = current digit
0F58	F5	PUSH	--- Save so it can be converted to SP then cont-->

0F0A * Exit if integer ***

    0F18

0F29 * **

0F2B : C = 00 for SP, = FF for integer
0F2C : integers for SP conversion after decimal point

0F52 : C=FF until a dec. pt. encountered

0F58 : added to current value after current value is converted to SP

140

0F59	CDCC0A	CALL	--- Convert current value to SP
0F5C	37	SCF	--- So we'll bypass calls to convert to DP
0F5D	3018	JR	--- Jump if double
0F5F	017494	LD	--- ASCII to SP Load a SP 16X10E6 into BC/DE
0F62	110024	LD	--- 16X10E6 to current SP no. in (4121 - 4124)
0F65	CD0C0A	CALL	--- Compare
0F68	F2740F	JP	--- Jmp if current value >2E16 go convert to DP
0F6B	CD3E09	CALL	--- Multiply current value by 10 cont-->
0F6E	F1	POP	--- A = current digit
0F6F	CD890F	CALL	--- Convert current digit to SP format cont-->
0F72	18DD	JR	--- Go get next digit. Count of digits cont-->
0F74	CDE30A	CALL	--- Initialize DP 411D,411F. Flag value as DP
0F77	CD4D0E	CALL	--- Multiply current SP value by 10
0F7A	CDFC09	CALL	--- Move DP no. in (4121 - 4126) to (4127 - 412E)
0F7D	F1	POP	--- A = binary value for current digit
0F7E	CD6409	CALL	--- Convert current digit to SP
0F81	CDE30A	CALL	--- Initialize DP cells 411D, 411F to zero
0F84	CD770C	CALL	--- Add current SP digit to current SP value
0F87	18C8	JR	--- Go get next digit
0F89	CDA409	CALL	--- Save current value (4121-4123) on stk ** note--> *
0F8C	CD6409	CALL	--- Convert value in A-reg to a single prec. value
0F8F	C1	POP	--- Load current SP value into BC/DE
0F90	D1	POP	--- B = exponent, C = MSB, D = next MSB, C = LSB
0F91	C31607	JP	--- Add value in registers to current cont-->
0F94	7B	LD	--- A = exponent thus far ************* see note--> *
0F95	FE0A	CP	--- Compare with 10
0F97	3009	JR	--- If => 10. Force it to a constant 32
0F99	07	RLCA	--- Then multiply current value by 10
0F9A	07	RLCA	--- *4
0F9B	83	ADD	--- +1 gives times 5
0F9C	07	RLCA	--- *2 gives times 10
0F9D	86	ADD	--- Fetch current digit (in ASCII)
0F9E	D630	SUB	--- Convert it to its binary equivalent cont-->
0FA0	5F	LD	--- Current digit to E
0FA1	FA1E32	JP	--- 0FA2 = LD E,32
0FA4	C3BD0E	JP	--- Get next digit from input string. Rtn to F94
0FA7	E5	PUSH	--- Save code string addr **************************
0FA8	212419	LD	--- Load addr of IN message
0FAB	CDA728	CALL	--- Output message
0FAE	E1	POP	--- Restore code string addr
0FAF	CD9A0A	CALL	--- Save value in HL as current value ***** cont--> *
0FB2	AF	XOR	--- Signal no editing when converting
0FB3	CD3410	CALL	--- Initialize print bufffer
0FB6	B6	OR	--- Set status to NON-ZERO for test at 0FE7
0FB7	CDD90F	CALL	--- Convert current value to ASCII
0FBA	C3A628	JP	--- Output value & rtn to caller
0FBD	AF	XOR	--- Clear edit flags ***************** see note--> *
0FBE	CD3410	CALL	--- Output buffer addr to HL. Edit flags to 40D8
0FC1	E608	AND	--- Test if sign requested in output
0FC3	2802	JR	--->: Jmp if no leading + sign required
0FC5	362B	LD	-- : Plus sign
0FC7	EB	EX	<---: Save addr of output buffer in DE
0FC8	CD9409	CALL	--- Determine sign of current value
0FCB	EB	EX	--- Restore output buffer addr to HL
0FCC	F2D90F	JP	--- Jmp if value is positive
0FCF	362D	LD	--- Minus sign to PBUF
0FD1	C5	PUSH	--- Save count of #'s before & after decimal point
0FD2	E5	PUSH	--- Current position in print buffer
0FD3	CD7B09	CALL	--- Convert a neg. number to its positive equivalent
0FD6	E1	POP	--- Restore print buffer address

141

OF6B : We´ll divide out multiplication later

OF6F : & add to number thus far
OF72 : after dec. pt. in B-reg

OF89 * *****   Converts the 8 bit value in the A-reg to a SP *******
      :   number and adds it to the current value in WRA1

OF91 : value (4121 - 4124). Rtn to caller
OF94 * ***** Accumulate value for exponent in E-reg. Do not *******
      :   let it exceed 50 (base 10). Called when processing
      :   exponents for E or D type values.

OF9E : and add to current value

OF94 * ***

OFAF * Set type to integer ********* Convert no. in HL to ASCII ****
      :   and write to video

OFBD * ***** Convert binary to ASCII. Build print buffer using ****
      :   edit flags in A. On entry
      :   B = count of #´s before
      :   C = count of #´s after

0FD7	C1	POP	--- Restore counter
0FD8	B4	OR	--- Combine 41 with positive MSB
0FD9	23	INC	--- HL = 4131H
0FDA	3630	LD	--- ASCII zero to next position in print buffer
0FDC	3AD840	LD	--- A = edit flags
0FDF	57	LD	--- Save edit flags in D
0FE0	17	RLA	--- Prepare to test bit 2**15 (print using) call
0FE1	3AAF40	LD	--- A = type/length of current variable
0FE4	DA9A10	JP	--- Jmp if called from PRINT USING
0FE7	CA9210	JP	--- Jmp to exit if edit flag is zero
0FEA	FE04	CP	--- Test data type
0FEC	D23D10	JP	--- Jmp if SNG or DOUBLE
0FEF	010000	LD	--- BC = flag for no commas or dec. pts.
0FF2	CD2F13	CALL	--- Convert integer number to ASCII in work area
0FF5	213041	LD	--- Start of ASCII buffer :(current value)
0FF8	46	LD	--- B = first ASCII character in buffer
0FF9	0E20	LD	--- Blank
0FFB	3AD840	LD	--- Get editing parameter word. See if we must test
0FFE	5F	LD	--- for and identify numbers out of range.
0FFF	E620	AND	--- Test if leading *'s wanted
1001	2807	JR	--- Do not test for out of range numbers.
1003	78	LD	--- If first char in PBUF <> blank, cont-->
1004	B9	CP	--- Compare PBUF(1) with blank, if not equal replace
1005	0E2A	LD	--- PBUF(1) with an *. C = *
1007	2001	JR	--- Number has not overflowed
1009	41	LD	--- Number has overflowed
100A	71	LD	--- Replace PBUF(1) with *
100B	D7	RST	--- If no range checks, unconditionally cont-->
100C	2814	JR	--- Jump if binary zero (end of buffer)
100E	FE45	CP	--- Test for E
1010	2810	JR	--- Jump if E
1012	FE44	CP	--- Test for D : Scan print buffer
1014	280C	JR	--- Jump if D : looking for an E, 0,
1016	FE30	CP	--- Test for 0 : ., or end of print
1018	28F0	JR	--- Jump if ASCII zero : buffer. Replace zeroes
101A	FE2C	CP	--- Test for comma : with blanks.
101C	28EC	JR	--- Jump if comma
101E	FE2E	CP	--- Test for decimal point
1020	2003	JR	--- Jump if not decimal point
1022	2B	DEC	--- We have a decimal point, end of line or a D or E
1023	3630	LD	--- Backspace to previous byte and replace it with an
1025	7B	LD	--- A = edit flags :ASCII 0
1026	E610	AND	--- Test for leading $ insertion
1028	2803	JR	--- No
102A	2B	DEC	--- Yes, backspace one more byte
102B	3624	LD	--- And insert a $
102D	7B	LD	--- Refetch edit flags
102E	E604	AND	--- Test if sign follows value
1030	C0	RET	--- No, rtn
1031	2B	DEC	--- Yes, backspace print buffer
1032	70	LD	--- Save sign
1033	C9	RET	--- then rtn
1034	32D840	LD	--- Save edit flags ********************************
1037	213041	LD	--- HL = Starting addr of line buffer (PBUF)
103A	3620	LD	--- Blank if first char. in print buffer
103C	C9	RET	--- Rtn to caller
103D	FE05	CP	--- Convert SP or DP to ASCII ************* cont--> *
103F	E5	PUSH	--- Save current position in PBUF
1040	DE00	SBC	--- A = 4 if SP, A = 8 if DP
1042	17	RLA	--- A = 8 if SP, A = 10 if DP

1003 : then number has overflowed

100B : replace 1st char in buffer with a blank.

1034 * ***

103D * Set CARRY if double precision ****************************

Addr	Code	Mnem	Comment
1043	57	LD	--- D = Adjust type flag
1044	14	INC	--- D = 9 (SP), D = B (DP)
1045	CD0112	CALL	--- Scale no. to 99,999 < X < 999,999
1048	010003	LD	--- After scaling, A = count of times DP value scaled
104B	82	ADD	--- Up (positive), or down (negative)
104C	FA5710	JP	--->: Jmp if scaled down more than 9 or 11 places
104F	14	INC	-- : D = A (SP) or C (DP)
1050	BA	CP	-- : Test if value was not scaled at all
1051	3004	JR	--->: Jmp if scaled up or down
1053	3C	INC	-- : A = no. of digits in value
1054	47	LD	-- : Save in B
1055	3E02	LD	-- : Force exponent to zero
1057	D602	SUB	<--: Compute exponent value
1059	E1	POP	--- Restore PBUF addr
105A	F5	PUSH	--- Save exponent
105B	CD9112	CALL	--- Initialize commas & dec. pt. routine
105E	3630	LD	--- Put an ASCII zero into current pos. in print
1060	CCC909	CALL	--- Increment HL if no scalinng was done :buffer
1063	CDA412	CALL	--- Convert binary to ASCII. Result to PBUF
1066	2B	DEC	--- Backspace PBUF to previous char see note-->
1067	7E	LD	--- Load previous char
1068	FE30	CP	--- Compare to an ASCII zero
106A	28FA	JR	--- Loop till a non-zero char. found
106C	FE2E	CP	--- Test for dec. pt.
106E	C4C909	CALL	--- Call if not decimal point (increment cont-->
1071	F1	POP	--- Restore exponent
1072	281F	JR	--- Jump if exponent is zero
1074	F5	PUSH	--- Save exponent
1075	E7	RST	--- Test data type
1076	3E22	LD	--- This will become a D or
1078	8F	ADC	--- E depending on whether value is SP or DP
1079	77	LD	--- Save exponent designation
107A	23	INC	--- Bump to first pos. of exponent in buffer
107B	F1	POP	--- Reload exponent value
107C	362B	LD	--- + (exponent)
107E	F28510	JP	--- Jmp if exponent is positive
1081	362D	LD	--- - (exponent)
1083	2F	CPL	--- Convert negative exponent
1084	3C	INC	--- to its positive equivalent
1085	062F	LD	--- B = start of ASCII values 0, 1, 2 9
1087	04	INC	--- Start of divide by 10 using compound cont-->
1088	D60A	SUB	--- Subtract 10 until
108A	30FB	JR	--- Remainder < 10. B = quoitent
108C	C63A	ADD	--- Convert remainder to an ASCII digit
108E	23	INC	--- Bump to next pos. in PBUF
108F	70	LD	--- 1st digit of exponent
1090	23	INC	--- Bump to next pos. in PBUF
1091	77	LD	--- 2nd digit of exponent
1092	23	INC	--- Bump to next pos. in PBUF
1093	3600	LD	--- 00 marks end of ASCII number
1095	EB	EX	--- DE = ending addr. of PBUF
1096	213041	LD	--- HL = starting addr. of PBUF
1099	C9	RET	--- Ret. to caller
109A	23	INC	--- Bump to next location in PBUF ********* cont--> *
109B	C5	PUSH	--- B = count of #'s before. C = count of #'s after
109C	FE04	CP	--- A = data type. Test for integer/floating point
109E	7A	LD	--- A = edit flags
109F	D20911	JP	--- Jmp if single or double precision
10A2	1F	RRA	--- Position exponential notation flag
10A3	DAA311	JP	--- Jmp if current variable is string, else cont-->

1066 : Backspace PBUF to first non-zero value

106E : HL to first char after dec. pt.)

1087 : subtraction loop: Convert value in A-register

   :   to a true digit ASCII value.
   :   Divide by 10 using compound subtraction

109A * Edit operations for PRINT USING *****************************

10A3 : must be integer

146

Addr	Code	Op	Comment
10A6	010306	LD	--- B = no. of leading digits C = comma cont-->
10A9	CD8912	CALL	--- Test comma flag. If not set zero C
10AC	D1	POP	--- D = count of #'s before dec. pt.
10AD	7A	LD	--- Count to A
10AE	D605	SUB	--- Compare to 5 (max no. digits allowed in integer)
10B0	F46912	CALL	--- Fill PBUF with leading zeroes. If cont-->
10B3	CD2F13	CALL	--- Convert current value (integer) to cont-->
10B6	7B	LD	--- Load count of #'s after dec. pt. into A
10B7	B7	OR	--- and set status flags
10B8	CC2F09	CALL	--- If no trailing #'s, backspace PBUF
10BB	3D	DEC	--- Test if no count given
10BC	F46912	CALL	--- Else add count trailing zeros
10BF	E5	PUSH	--- Save current PBUF addr
10C0	CDF50F	CALL	--- Edit ASCII buffer w/ converted number in it
10C3	E1	POP	--- Restore HL to PBUF addr
10C4	2802	JR	--->: Jmp if sign follows value
10C6	70	LD	-- : No. store a blank after value
10C7	23	INC	-- : Bump to next pos. in PBUF
10C8	3600	LD	<---: Terminate buffer with a byte of zeros
10CA	212F41	LD	--- Start of ASCII print buffer minus 1
10CD	23	INC	--- Bump to next pos. in PBUF note-->
10CE	3AF340	LD	--- A = LSB of addr of dec. pt. in PBUF
10D1	95	SUB	--- Compare to LSB of current PBUF
10D2	92	SUB	--- Then subtract length of field
10D3	C8	RET	--- Exit if start of field located
10D4	7E	LD	--- Not start of field, then fetch char and
10D5	FE20	CP	--- Test for blank
10D7	28F4	JR	--- Loop till start of field or +, -, $ found
10D9	FE2A	CP	--- Test for *
10DB	28F0	JR	--- Ignore blanks and *
10DD	2B	DEC	--- Backspace to previous char so it can be retested
10DE	E5	PUSH	--- Save PBUF addr
10DF	F5	PUSH	--- Save current char
10E0	01DF10	LD	--- Return addr in case of -, +, $
10E3	C5	PUSH	--- to stack
10E4	D7	RST	--- Re-examine char
10E5	FE2D	CP	--- Compare with a -
10E7	C8	RET	--- Exit to 10DF if a minus
10E8	FE2B	CP	--- Not - try a +
10EA	C8	RET	--- Exit to 10DF if a plus
10EB	FE24	CP	--- Not + or -, try $
10ED	C8	RET	--- Exit to 10DF if $
10EE	C1	POP	--- Clear rtn addr. of 10DF
10EF	FE30	CP	--- Test for ASCII 0 (leading 0)
10F1	200F	JR	--->: Jump if not leading 0
10F3	23	INC	-- : Skip next char
10F4	D7	RST	-- : and examine following one
10F5	300B	JR	-- : Jump if not numeric
10F7	2B	DEC	-- : Backspace to last char examined
10F8	012B77	LD	-- : 10F9: DEC HL :Backspace one more char
10FB	F1	POP	-- : 10FA: LD (HL),A :Shift digits up 1 pos.
10FC	28FB	JR	-- : Loop till end of field reached
10FE	C1	POP	-- : Clear stack
10FF	C3CE10	JP	-- : Restart scan
1102	F1	POP	<---: Restore char at start of field
1103	28FD	JR	--- Loop till beginning of field found
1105	E1	POP	--- Restore starting addr of field
1106	3625	LD	--- Replace it with a %
1108	C9	RET	--- Rtn to caller
1109	E5	PUSH	--- Save current PBUF addr. *********** see note--> *

10B0 : more than 5 digits
10B3 : ASCII. Result to PBUF


```
       :              Locate start of field in PBUF and
       :              rtn to caller.  If field starts with
       :              a +, -, or $ goto 10DF before rtning
       :              to caller.  Search for field by starting
       :              at addr. of dec. pt. and backspacing
       :              size of field (D-reg)
```


1109 * *********** Floating point editing **************************

110A	1F	RRA	--- Test bit 0 of edit flags see note-->
110B	DAAA11	JP	--- Jmp if exponential notation on flt. pt. number
110E	2814	JR	--->: Jump if value is SP
1110	118413	LD	. : DE = addr of DP 1X10**16
1113	CD490A	CALL	. : Compare value to 1X10**16
1116	1610	LD	. : D = no. of digits in a DP field
1118	FA3211	JP	----:--:>: Jmp if value < 1X10**16 else
111B	E1	POP	<---:--: : Restore current location in print buffer
111C	C1	POP	. : : : B=count of #'s before, C=count of #'S after
111D	CDBD0F	CALL	. : : : Reenter edit routine till value < 1X10**16
1120	2B	DEC	. : : : Restore buffer addr. current position
1121	3625	LD	. : : : Store a % (start of spaces field)
1123	C9	RET	. : : : Rtn to caller
1124	010EB6	LD	<---: : : BC/DE = 1 X 10E16 ********** see note--> *
1127	11CA1B	LD	. : :
112A	CD0C0A	CALL	. : : Compare edit value to 1 X 10E16
112D	F21B11	JP	------>: : Jmp if edit value > 1X10E16
1130	1606	LD	--- : D = no. of digits to print (size of field)
1132	CD5509	CALL	<-------: Test sign of current value
1135	C40112	CALL	--- Scale SP value to 99,999<X<999,999 cont-->
1138	E1	POP	--- HL = origin of ASCII buffer
1139	C1	POP	--- B=count of #'s before, C=count of #'s afterwards
113A	FA5711	JP	--->: Jmp if value was scaled up (multiplied by 10)
113D	C5	PUSH	-- : Save count of #'s before and after dec. pt.
113E	5F	LD	-- : E=count of times value was divided
113F	78	LD	-- : B=no. of user specified #'s before note-->
1140	92	SUB	-- : D=6
1141	93	SUB	-- : E = no. of times edit value divided by 10
1142	F46912	CALL	-- : Put leading ASCII zeroes into PBUF
1145	CD7D12	CALL	-- : Compute count of dec. pts. and commas
1148	CDA412	CALL	-- : Convert integer of SP number to ASCII
114B	B3	OR	-- : Test count of times value scaled
114C	C47712	CALL	-- : Add trailing zeroes for each time value scaled
114F	B3	OR	-- : Set status flag
1150	C49112	CALL	-- : Place decimal point/commas in numeric buffer
1153	D1	POP	-- : Restore edit counts
1154	C3B610	JP	-- : Go convert fractional portion of no. to ASCII
1157	5F	LD	<---: E=count of times value scaled up (mult. by 10) *
1158	79	LD	--- C=count of digits following dec. pt. cont-->
1159	B7	OR	--- Test count
115A	C4160F	CALL	--- Decrement count of trailing #'s by cont-->
115D	83	ADD	--- A=((no. trailing #'s)-1) + cont-->
115E	FA6211	JP	--->: Jmp if value needs to be scaled down
1161	AF	XOR	-- : Signal no down-scaling
1162	C5	PUSH	<---: Save before & after counters
1163	F5	PUSH	--- Save scale count
1164	FC180F	CALL	<---: Divide current value by 10 (A) times
1167	FA6411	JP	--->: After each division, A-reg is incremented
116A	C1	POP	--- Original scale count
116B	7B	LD	--- A = count of times value multiplied by 10
116C	90	SUB	--- Minus scale value
116D	C1	POP	--- Restore before and after dec. pt. counter
116E	5F	LD	--- Adjusted scale factor
116F	82	ADD	--- Plus size of field (set sign flag)
1170	78	LD	--- A = count of #'s before dec. pt.
1171	FA7F11	JP	--- Jmp no leading digits
1174	92	SUB	--- Else subtract field size (6 for SP, cont-->
1175	93	SUB	--- Then subtract adjusted scale
1176	F46912	CALL	--- Add trailing zeroes
1179	C5	PUSH	--- Save count of #'s before and after dec. pt.

For PRINT USING

1124 * ***** Edit SP value or a DP value <1X10E16 ****************

1135 : On rtn A = times value scaled up or down as + or -

      :   Value was scaled down or not
      :   scaled at all. Adjust scale for
      :   no. of places before dec. pt.

1157 * **
1158 : to print.   Value was scaled up. Adjust scale
      :   for no. of places following dec. pt.
115A : one if its non-zero
115D : (-no. of times value scaled up)

1174 : 10 for DP) from adjusted size

117A	CD7D12	CALL	--- Setup B/C for dec. pt. and comma counters
117D	1811	JR	--- Go edit number before dec. pt.
117F	CD6912	CALL	--- Insert a zero into PBUF *************************
1182	79	LD	--- Save comma counter Will be wiped by call 1294
1183	CD9412	CALL	--- Add dec. pt. to PBUF gives 0
1186	4F	LD	--- Restore comma counter to C-reg
1187	AF	XOR	--- Zero to A-reg
1188	92	SUB	--- Now, get diff. between requested
1189	93	SUB	--- field size and scaled field size
118A	CD6912	CALL	--- Then add that many zeroes to PBUF
118D	C5	PUSH	--- Save count or #'s before and after dec. pt.
118E	47	LD	--- Zero B
118F	4F	LD	--- Zero C
1190	CDA412	CALL	--- Convert integer portion of SP value to integer
1193	C1	POP	--- Restore counters :ASCII
1194	B1	OR	--- Set status for count of #'s after dec. pt.
1195	2003	JR	--- Jmp if digits follow dec. pt.
1197	2AF340	LD	--- Else load addr. of dec. pt. in PBUF
119A	83	ADD	--- Gives no. of digits before dec. pt.
119B	3D	DEC	--- Minus 1
119C	F46912	CALL	--- Add that many zeros to PBUF
119F	50	LD	--- Set D = no. of #'s before
11A0	C3BF10	JP	--- Go edit ASCII value
11A3	E5	PUSH	--- Save current position in PBUF ******* see note--->*
11A4	D5	PUSH	--- Save edit flags
11A5	CDCC0A	CALL	--- Convert integer to single precision
11A8	D1	POP	--- Restore edit flags
11A9	AF	XOR	--- Clear status flags. Force jmp for SP
11AA	CAB011	JP	--- Jmp if single precision SP/DP entry pt.
11AD	1E10	LD	--- E = no. digits to print if DP
11AF	011E06	LD	--- 11B0: LD E,6 E = no. digits to print if SP
11B2	CD5509	CALL	--- Test sign of current value
11B5	37	SCF	--- Force jmp at 11F3 on first pass
11B6	C40112	CALL	--- If current value not zero, go scale it
11B9	E1	POP	--- Restore PBUF addr.
11BA	C1	POP	--- Restore count of #'s before and after
11BB	F5	PUSH	--- Decimal point, save flag for test at 11F3
11BC	79	LD	--- A = count of #'s after
11BD	B7	OR	--- Set status so we can test for zero
11BE	F5	PUSH	--- Save original trailing digit count
11BF	C4160F	CALL	--- If trail count non-zero, decrement it
11C2	80	ADD	--- Combine count of before & after
11C3	4F	LD	--- Save total digit count
11C4	7A	LD	--- Load edit flags
11C5	E604	AND	--- Isolate sign follows value flag
11C7	FE01	CP	--- Gives no CARRY if sign follows
11C9	9F	SBC	--- A = 0 if no sign, FE otherwise
11CA	57	LD	--- Save new edit flag
11CB	81	ADD	--- Adjust count of digits to print if sign follows
11CC	4F	LD	--- Save adjusted count
11CD	93	SUB	--- A = number of times to divide by 10
11CE	F5	PUSH	--- Save divisor count
11CF	C5	PUSH	--- Save char. count
11D0	FC180F	CALL	<---: Divide value by 10 (A) times
11D3	FAD011	JP	--->: Loop till division completed
11D6	C1	POP	--- Restore counter of #'s
11D7	F1	POP	--- Restore division count
11D8	C5	PUSH	--- Then resave
11D9	F5	PUSH	--- Registers and
11DA	FADE11	JP	--- Jmp if any trailing zeros

```
117F :  *********************************************************
```



```
11A3 *  Exponential formatting for PRINT USING *********************
     :  11A3 - Entry pt. INTEGER
     :  11AA - Entry pt. SP/DP
```

```
11DD AF      XOR     --- Clear A, status flags
11DE 2F      CPL     --- Make trailing zero count positive
11DF 3C      INC     --- 2´s complement
11E0 80      ADD     --- Add size of field before dec. pt.
11E1 3C      INC     --- Plus one more
11E2 82      ADD     --- Add size of field (6/SP, 10/DP)
11E3 47      LD      --- B = number of digits before dec. pt.
11E4 0E00    LD      --- Signal no commas
11E6 CDA412  CALL    --- Convert value to ASCII
11E9 F1      POP     --- Restore original count of #´s before
11EA F47112  CALL    --- Add trailing zeros
11ED C1      POP     --- Restore counts of nos. before and after dec. pt.
11EE F1      POP     --- Get count of nos. before dec. pt.
11EF CC2F09  CALL    --- None before, backspace PBUF addr 1 byte
11F2 F1      POP     --- Get first time flag. If set, clear stk,
11F3 3803    JR      --- Add exponet, and join common edit code.
11F5 83      ADD     --- Otherwise, add default field size to + 1 if pos.
11F6 90      SUB     --- Or a - 1 if neg.. Then subtract actual
11F7 92      SUB     --- Number of chars in field to get size of exponet
11F8 C5      PUSH    --- Save BC
11F9 CD7410  CALL    --- Compute and add exponet to PBUF
11FC EB      EX      --- Restore HL
11FD D1      POP     --- Clear stack
11FE C3BF10  JP      --- Go edit ASCII value
1201 D5      PUSH    --- Test magnitude of SP and DP numbers **** cont--> *
1202 AF      XOR     --- Zero A and flags, save zero
1203 F5      PUSH    --- On stk                      see note-->
1204 E7      RST     --- Test data type
1205 E22212  JP      --- Jump if single
1208 3A2441  LD      --- Must be double, get the exponent into A
120B FE91    CP      --- Compute no. of bits in integer portion of number
120D D22212  JP      --- Jmp if 17 or more bits in integer portion of
1210 116413  LD      --- DE=addr of DP 5.5X10E2            :DP value
1213 212741  LD      --- Destination addr
1216 CDD309  CALL    --- Move 5.5X10E8 to saved value location
1219 CDA10D  CALL    --- Multiply 5.5X10E8 times current value
121C F1      POP     --- A = count of times DP value multiplied to scale
121D D60A    SUB     --- A = count - 10                   :it up
121F F5      PUSH    --- Save for testing
1220 18E6    JR      --- Loop till integer portion exceeds 2E16
1222 CD4F12  CALL    --- Compare current value to 999,999, ****** cont--> *
1225 E7      RST     <------: Test data type
1226 EA3412  JP         .  : Jump if not single
1229 014391  LD         .  : BC/DE = SP 99,999 decimal
122C 11F94F  LD         .  :
122F CD0C0A  CALL       .  : Compare current value to 99,999
1232 1806    JR      --->:  : Go test results of comparison
1234 116C13  LD         . :  : DE addr of SP 1.44X10E17
1237 CD490A  CALL       . :  : Compare current value to 1.44X10E17
123A F24C12  JP      <--:--:-->: Jmp if value  > 99,999    see note-->
123D F1      POP        .  :  : A = scaled counter
123E CD0B0F  CALL       .  :  : Multiply current value by 10
1241 F5      PUSH       .  :  : A = - no. of times value multiplied
1242 18E1    JR      ------>:  : Loop till between 999,999 and 99,999
1244 F1      POP     ---        : A = scaled count
1245 CD180F  CALL    ---        : Divide value by 10. It´s > 999,999
1248 F5      PUSH    ---        : Keep count of times divided
1249 CD4F12  CALL    ---        : Loop till value < 999,999
124C F1      POP     <-------- : A = + times divided : - times multiplied
124D D1      POP     --- Restore callers DE
```

```
1201 * Clear times value scaled ************************************

     :              Scale a single or double precision number
     :              so it lies between 99,999 and  999,999.
     :              On exit A = +(times value divided), or
     :              -(times multiplied).




1222 * Rtn in line if value smaller ******************************
          : Scale SP and DP numbers so that 99,999<SP<999,999




123A : (more than 5 digits in integer or less than 17 digits in DP)
```

124E	C9	RET	--- Rtn to caller
124F	E7	RST	--- Test data type ********************************
1250	EA5E12	JP	--- Jump if double precision
1253	017494	LD	--- BC/DE = 999,999 decimal
1256	11F823	LD	---
1259	CD0C0A	CALL	--- Compare current value to 999,999 decimal
125C	1806	JR	--- Test result of comparison
125E	117413	LD	--- DE = address ********************************
1261	CD490A	CALL	--- Compare current value
1264	E1	POP	--- Clear rtn addr so we can go to 1244
1265	F24412	JP	--- Jmp if current value has more than 6 digits in
1268	E9	JP	--- Else rtn to caller :integer
1269	B7	OR	--- Test zero flag ******************** see note--> *
126A	C8	RET	<---: in HL.
126B	3D	DEC	. : Count 1 ASCII zero moved to print buffer
126C	3630	LD	. : Move an ASCII zero
126E	23	INC	. : Bump destination address
126F	18F9	JR	--->: Loop till 'A' ASCII zeroes moved
1271	2004	JR	--- If not done adding trailing zeroes else exit ****
1273	C8	RET	--- Rtn to caller if trailing zeros added
1274	CD9112	CALL	--- Decimal point/commas in numeric buffer
1277	3630	LD	--- Add a trailing ASCII zero to print buffer
1279	23	INC	--- Bump print buffer add
127A	3D	DEC	--- Count of trailing zeroes to add
127B	18F6	JR	--- Go test for completion
127D	7B	LD	--- A = count of times value scaled up or down *******
127E	82	ADD	--- D = no. of digits to print
127F	3C	INC	--- Plus 1 gives no.of digits before dec. pt.
1280	47	LD	--- B = leading digit count
1281	3C	INC	--- Gives leading digits +2 note-->
1282	D603	SUB	--- Divide modulo 3
1284	30FC	JR	<---: Loop till A = -1, -2, or -3
1286	C605	ADD	--->: Add 5 (get positive remainder) gives 4, 3, or 2
1288	4F	LD	--- C = comma counter
1289	3AD840	LD	--- A = edit flags. Test for comma flag
128C	E640	AND	--- Isolate comma bit in edit flag word
128E	C0	RET	--- Exit with C = comma count if commas requested
128F	4F	LD	--- Else force comma count to zero
1290	C9	RET	--- Rtn to caller
1291	05	DEC	--- Count 1 leading digit ***************************
1292	2008	JR	--->: Jmp if all leading digits not stored cont-->
1294	362E	LD	-- : Leading digit stored. Add decimal pt.
1296	22F340	LD	-- : Save addr of dec. pt. in buffer
1299	23	INC	-- : Bump to first char of fractionnal part of number
129A	48	LD	-- : Set C and B to zero to inhibit any more dec. pts.
129B	C9	RET	-- : and commas. Rtn to caller
129C	0D	DEC	<---: Count one char stored **************************
129D	C0	RET	--- Rtn if not end of 3 character group
129E	362C	LD	--- ',' every third digit
12A0	23	INC	--- Bump to next position in buffer
12A1	0E03	LD	--- Reset comma counter
12A3	C9	RET	--- Rtn to caller
12A4	D5	PUSH	--- Save edit flags ********************************
12A5	E7	RST	--- Test data type
12A6	E2EA12	JP	--- Jump if single precision see note-->
12A9	C5	PUSH	--- Save leading digit count/comma counter
12AA	E5	PUSH	--- Save buffer addr
12AB	CDFC09	CALL	--- Move WRA1 to WRA2
12AE	217C13	LD	--- HL = address of DP .5
12B1	CDF709	CALL	--- Move to WRA1

```
124F * **************************************************************


125E * **************************************************************


1269 * Move ´A´ ASCII zeroes to a print buffer.  Address of buffer


1271 * **************************************************************




127D * **************************************************************
     :      Compute the number of digits before the decimal
     :      point, and the number of commas to be included
     :      in first part of number.  On entry D = size of
     :      field (6 or 10), E = scale count.  On exit B =
     :      number of digits before dec. pt., C = number of
     :      commas to include in first part of number.




1291 * **************************************************************
1292 : in PBUF              Count leading digits before dec. pt.




129C * **************************************************************




12A4 * **************************************************************

     : Convert a DP value to its ASCII equivalent in integer
     : portion only
```

156

```
12B4  CD770C      CALL  0C77H     --- Add .5 to value in WRA2. Result to WRA1
12B7  AF          XOR   A         --- Clear status flags
12B8  CD7B0B      CALL  0B7BH     --- Unpack DP value in WRA1. Save in current area.
12BB  E1          POP   HL        --- Restore buffer addr
12BC  C1          POP   BC        --- and counters
12BD  118C13      LD    DE,138CH  --- DE=table of powers of 10 from 1.0X10E15 - 1.0X10E6
12C0  3E0A        LD    A,0AH     --- A=no. of times to dvd current val by a power of 10
12C2  CD9112      CALL  1291H   <-----: Go add a dec point or a comma to buffer
12C5  C5          PUSH  BC        --    : Save count of digits before & after dec point
12C6  F5          PUSH  AF        --    : Save division count
12C7  E5          PUSH  HL         .    : Save current buffer addr
12C8  D5          PUSH  DE         .    : Addr of power table to stack
12C9  062F        LD    B,2FH      .    : B = quotient in ASCII for each division
12CB  04          INC   B       <---:  : B start at 30 (ASCII zero)
12CC  E1          POP   HL         .  : : HL = addr of power table = divisor
12CD  E5          PUSH  HL         .  : : Save it so it can be restored during loop
12CE  CD480D      CALL  0D48H      .  : : Dvd current value (integer) by      cont-->
12D1  30F8        JR    NC,12CBH --->:  : Loop till reminder < current power
12D3  E1          POP   HL         .  : Restore starting addr of current power of 10
12D4  CD360D      CALL  0D36H      .  : Add current power to remainder - make it pos
12D7  EB          EX    DE,HL      .  : Save currennt power addr in DE
12D8  E1          POP   HL         .  : HL = current print buffer addr
12D9  70          LD    (HL),B     .  : Digit to buffer
12DA  23          INC   HL         .  : Bump to next print position
12DB  F1          POP   AF         .  : Restore status flags so we can test  cont-->
12DC  C1          POP   BC         .  : Restore counts
12DD  3D          DEC   A          .  : Count 1 time thru loop
12DE  20E2        JR    NZ,12C2H ----->: Done 10 times , no loop
12E0  C5          PUSH  BC        --- Restore counts
12E1  E5          PUSH  HL        --- and current buffer addr
12E2  211D41      LD    HL,411DH  --- then move last half of DP value
12E5  CDB109      CALL  09B1H     --- into WRA1 as a SP value
12E8  180C        JR    12F6H     --- and convert it to ASCII
12EA  C5          PUSH  BC        --- Convert a SP value to its integer ***** cont--> *
12EB  E5          PUSH  HL        --- Save counts & buffer addr
12EC  CD0807      CALL  0708H     --- Add a .5 to current value.  Result left in BC/DE
12EF  3C          INC   A         --- Bump MSB
12F0  CDFB0A      CALL  0AFBH     --- Convert a + SP number to integer. Result in BC/DE
12F3  CDB409      CALL  09B4H     --- Move SP value in BC/DE to current value.  Integer
12F6  E1          POP   HL        --- portion of original SP value.  Restore HL
12F7  C1          POP   BC        --- Restore buffer addr
12F8  AF          XOR   A         --- Restore counts
12F9  11D213      LD    DE,13D2H  --- DE = addr of integer equivalent of 100,000
12FC  3F          CCF             --- CARRY=first time switch for division loop 12FC-
12FD  CD9112      CALL  1291H     --- Decimal point/commas to numeric buffer      :1327
1300  C5          PUSH  BC        --- Save counts
1301  F5          PUSH  AF        --- Save CARRY flag for count of times thru loop
1302  E5          PUSH  HL        --- Save buffer addr
1303  D5          PUSH  DE        --- Save division table addr
1304  CDBF09      CALL  09BFH     --- Load current SP value into BC/DE
1307  E1          POP   HL        --- HL = addr of integer value of 100,000
1308  062F        LD    B,2FH     --- B =  ASCII (30-1) = (0-1
130A  04          INC   B         --- Gives 30,31,...... which equal ASCII 0,1,2,...
130B  7B          LD    A,E       --- Least sig byte of integer equiv
130C  96          SUB   (HL)      --- Minus least sig. byte of 100,000
130D  5F          LD    E,A       --- Restore difference for next subtration
130E  23          INC   HL        --- Bump to next byte of 100,000
130F  7A          LD    A,D       --- Middle byte of integer equiv        see note-->
1310  9E          SBC   A,(HL)    --- Minus middle byte of 100,000
1311  57          LD    D,A       --- Restore diff. for next subtraction
```

12CE : a power of 10 starting at 10E15 and working down to 10E6

12DB : for 10 times thru

12EA * equivalent. Divide integer equivalent by 100,000 and *******
     : 10,000. Use code at 1335 to convert last 1000 to ASCII

     : This code divides the integer portion of the current value
     : by 100,000 using compound subtraction. A quotient is kept
     : in the B-reg as an ASCII value

```
1312 23      INC     --- Bump to most sig. byte of 100,000
1313 79      LD      --- Most sig. byte of integer equivalent
1314 9E      SBC     --- Minus most sig. byte of 100,000
1315 4F      LD      --- Restore for next subtraction
1316 2B      DEC     --- Reset HL to least
1317 2B      DEC     --- Sig byte of 100,000 constant
1318 30F0    JR      --- Loop till integer equivalent < 100,000
131A CDB707  CALL    --- Add 100,000 to value in C/DE, make remainder pos
131D 23      INC     --- Bump HL to addr of 10,000 constant
131E CDB409  CALL    --- Save remainder as current value
1321 EB      EX      --- Addr of constant 10,000 to DE
1322 E1      POP     --- HL = current PBUF addr
1323 70      LD      --- Save ASCII quotient
1324 23      INC     --- Bump to next position in print buffer
1325 F1      POP     --- Restore CARRY flag (switch)
1326 C1      POP     --- Restore BC so it can be saved later
1327 38D3    JR      --- If CARRY set, reset it and divide        cont-->
1329 13      INC     --- When we fall thru we have divided        cont-->
132A 13      INC     --- Bump DE to point to constant 1000
132B 3E04    LD      --- A = no. of digits
132D 1806    JR      --- Go convert remainder to 4 ASCII digits
132F D5      PUSH    --- Convert integer to ASCII ********** see note--> *
1330 11D813  LD      --- DE = table of descending powers of 10    cont-->
1333 3E05    LD      --- A = no. of ASCII digits to build
1335 CD9112  CALL    --- Add decimal point or commas to buffer
1338 C5      PUSH    --- Save counts
1339 F5      PUSH    --- Save number of digits counter
133A E5      PUSH    --- Save buffer addr
133B EB      EX      --- HL = addr of power table
'33C 4E      LD      --- Load a power of 10 in BC
133D 23      INC     --- Bump to MSB or power
133E 46      LD      --- Load MSB or power
133F C5      PUSH    --- Save power
1340 23      INC     --- Bump to next value in power table
1341 E3      EX      --- HL=value just loaded, addr of next value to stack
1342 EB      EX      --- DE = value loaded - division
1343 2A2141  LD      --- HL = current value (integer)
1346 062F    LD      <--: Divide current value by a power of 10 starting at
1348 04      INC      . : 10,000 dec. and working down to 10.  Remainder
1349 7D      LD       . : from each division is added to the division and
134A 93      SUB      . : the sum becomes the dividend for the next
134B 6F      LD       . : division etc. Division is by compound subtraction
134C 7C      LD       . : Quotient +2F(hex) = ASCII equivalent of quotient.
134D 9A      SBC      . : B - reg = quotient.
134E 67      LD       . : HL = next dividend
134F 30F7    JR      -->: Loop till quotient (HL) less than current power
1351 19      ADD     --- Remainder + divisor = dividend                 :of 10
1352 222141  LD      --- Save next dividend
1355 D1      POP     --- DE = addr of next power of 10
1356 E1      POP     --- Restore addr of output buffer
1357 70      LD      --- ASCII digit to buffer
1358 23      INC     --- Next loc. in print buffer
1359 F1      POP     --- A = count of digits to convert
135A C1      POP     --- Restore counter of #'s before & after dec point
135B 3D      DEC     --- Have we got 5 digits yet
135C 20D7    JR      --- no, loop
135E CD9112  CALL    --- Decimal point/commas to numeric buffer
1361 77      LD      --- Zero terminator PBUF
1362 D1      POP     --- Restore callers DE
1363 C9      RET     --- Rtn to caller *********************************
```

```
1327 : remainder by 10,000
1329 : integer part of SP value by 100,000 and 10,000.  The
     : remainder is positive and has been saved as current value.


132F * Save edit flags *****************************************
1330 : starting at 10,000 dec.
```

```
1363 * ************************************************************
```

1364 00	NOP	---	
1365 00	NOP	---	1364 = 10 X 10E9 DP
1366 00	NOP	---	
1367 00	NOP	---	
1368 F9	LD	---	
1369 02	LD	---	
136A 15	DEC	---	
136B A2	AND	---	
136C FDFF	INDEX	---	
136E 9F	SBC	---	136C = 1 X 10E15 DP
136F 31A95F	LD	---	
1372 63	LD	---	
1373 B2	OR	---	
1374 FEFF	CP	---	
1376 03	INC	---	1374 - 137A = 1 X 10E16 DP
1377 BF	CP	---	
1378 C9	RET	---	
1379 1B	DEC	---	
137A 0EB6	LD	---	
137C 00	NOP	---	137C - 1383 = .5 (double)
137D 00	NOP	---	
137E 00	NOP	---	
137F 00	NOP	---	
1380 00	NOP	---	1380 - 1383 = .5 (single)
1381 00	NOP	---	
1382 00	NOP	---	
1383 80	ADD	---	
1384 00	NOP	---	1384 - 138B = 1 X 10E16 (double)
1385 00	NOP	---	
1386 04	INC	---	
1387 BF	CP	---	
1388 C9	RET	---	
1389 1B	DEC	---	
138A 0EB6	LD	---	138A - 1380 = .502778 (single)
138C 00	NOP	---	138C - 1392 = 1 X 100E15
138D 80	ADD	---	(integer portion of DP value
138E C6A4	ADD	---	
1390 7E	LD	---	
1391 8D	ADC	---	
1392 03	INC	---	
1393 00	NOP	---	1393 - 1399 = 1.0 X 10E14
1394 40	LD	---	(integer portion of DP value
1395 7A	LD	---	
1396 10F3	DJNZ	---	
1398 5A	LD	---	
1399 00	NOP	---	
139A 00	NOP	---	139A - 13A0 = 1.0 X 10E13
139B A0	AND	---	(integer portion of DP value
139C 72	LD	---	
139D 4E	LD	---	
139E 1809	JR	---	
13A0 00	NOP	---	
13A1 00	NOP	---	13A1 - 13A7 = 1.0 X 10E12
13A2 10A5	DJNZ	---	(integer portion of DP value
13A4 D4E800	CALL	---	
13A7 00	NOP	---	
13A8 00	NOP	---	13A8 - 13AE = 1.0 X 10E11
13A9 E8	RET	---	(integer portion of DP value
13AA 76	HALT	---	
13AB 48	LD	---	

161

13AC 17	RLA	---	
13AD 00	NOP	---	
13AE 00	NOP	---	
13AF 00	NOP	--- 13AF - 13B5 = 1.0 X 10E10
13B0 E40B54	CALL	---	(integer part of DP value)
13B3 02	LD	---	
13B4 00	NOP	---	
13B5 00	NOP	---	
13B6 00	NOP	--- 13B6 - 13BC = 1.0 X 10E9
13B7 CA9A3B	JP	---	(integer part of DP value)
13BA 00	NOP	---	
13BB 00	NOP	---	
13BC 00	NOP	--- 13BD - 13C3 = 1.0 X 10E8
13BD 00	NOP	---	(integer part of DP value)
13BE E1	POP	---	
13BF F5	PUSH	---	
13C0 05	DEC	---	
13C1 00	NOP	---	
13C2 00	NOP	---	
13C3 00	NOP	---	
13C4 80	ADD	--- 13C4 - 13CA = 1.0 X 10E7
13C5 96	SUB	---	(integer part of DP value)
13C6 98	SBC	---	
13C7 00	NOP	---	
13C8 00	NOP	---	
13C9 00	NOP	---	
13CA 00	NOP	---	
13CB 40	LD	--- 13CB - 13D1 = 1,000,000
13CC 42	LD	---	(integer part of DP value)
13CD 0F	RRCA	---	
13CE 00	NOP	---	
13CF 00	NOP	---	
13D0 00	NOP	---	
13D1 00	NOP	---	
13D2 A0	AND	--- 13D2 = 100,000
13D3 86	ADD	---	
13D4 011027	LD	--- 13D5 = 10,000
13D7 00	NOP	---	
13D8 1027	DJNZ	--- 13D8 2710: 10000 decimal ********** see note--> *
13DA E8	RET	--- 13DA 03E8: 1000 decimal
13DB 03	INC	---	
13DC 64	LD	--- 13DC 0064: 100 decimal
13DD 00	NOP	---	
13DE 0A	LD	--- 13DD 000A: 10 decimal
13DF 00	NOP	---	
13E0 010021	LD	--- 13E1: NOP **************************************
13E3 82	ADD	--- 13E2: LD HL,982 Addr of neg to pos cont-->
13E4 09	ADD	---	
13E5 E3	EX	--- 13E5: EX (SP), HL Addr of conv routine to stack
13E6 E9	JP	--- 13E6: JP (HL) Rtn to caller
13E7 CDA409	CALL	--- Move current SP value to stack*******************
13EA 218013	LD	--- HL = addr of a SP .5 (exponent)
13ED CDB109	CALL	--- Load a .5 into BC/DE and move it to WRA1
13F0 1803	JR	--- Join common cde used for X ** Y
13F2 CDB10A	CALL	--- Convert integer in 4121-4122 to SP & cont-->
13F5 C1	POP	--- Load value to be raised into
13F6 D1	POP	--- BC/DE.
13F7 CD5509	CALL	--- Test sign of exponent
13FA 78	LD	--- A = MSB of number to be raised
13FB 283C	JR	--- Jmp if exponent zero

```
13D8 * Integer table of powers of 10 *******************************




13E0 * ***********************************************************
13E3 : conversion for floating point numbers


13E7 * *********  SQR routine  *********************************
     * Compute X ** .5 ( uses general power routine at 13F2)


     : store in 4121-4124 ******** X ** Y Routine *****************
     : method used is : e ** (y ln x)
```

13FD F20414	JP	--- Jmp if exponent is positive
1400 B7	OR	--- Test value to be raised
1401 CA9A19	JP	--- Exit if raising 0 to a neg. power
1404 B7	OR	--- Another test of value to be raised
1405 CA7907	JP	--- Raising 0 to a positive power
1408 D5	PUSH	--- Move value to be raised to stack
1409 C5	PUSH	--- both parts
140A 79	LD	--- A = MSB of value to be raised
140B F67F	OR	--- Test sign of base. Set bits 0-6 in case it is
140D CDBF09	CALL	--- Load exponent (power) into BC/DE :negative
1410 F22114	JP	--->: Jump if base is positive
1413 D5	PUSH	-- : Save the exponent on the stack
1414 C5	PUSH	-- : both parts
1415 CD400B	CALL	-- : Get integer portion of exponent cont-->
1418 C1	POP	-- : Then restore exponent as a
1419 D1	POP	-- : SP value in BC/DE
141A F5	PUSH	-- : Save integer portion of exponent
141B CD0C0A	CALL	-- : Compare original exp. to truncated cont-->
141E E1	POP	-- : H = exp (integer)
141F 7C	LD	-- : A = exp
1420 1F	RRA	-- : Set carry if exp. is odd
1421 E1	POP	<---: Load SP version of exp
1422 222341	LD	--- Move to WRA1
1425 E1	POP	--- Get rest of exponent
1426 222141	LD	--- and move to WRA1
1429 DCE213	CALL	--- Call if exponent is odd and base is negative
142C CC8209	CALL	--- Call if exponent is integer & base negative
142F D5	PUSH	--- Save exponent
1430 C5	PUSH	--- both parts
1431 CD0908	CALL	--- Find log of base value. Gives 'ILLEGAL FUNCTION
1434 C1	POP	--- Restore exponent : CALL' if negative base raised
1435 D1	POP	--- Restore exponent : to a power with a fraction
1436 CD4708	CALL	--- Multiply ln(value) * exponent, then cont-->
1439 CDA409	CALL	--- Move exponent to stack *** Compute e ** x ********
143C 013881	LD	--- BC/DE = 1.4427 (approx ln 2 + ln 2)
143F 113BAA	LD	---
1442 CD4708	CALL	--- Multiply exponent value by 1.4427 (2 ln 2)
1445 3A2441	LD	--- A = exponent of product
1448 FE88	CP	--- Test exponent to see if more than 8 cont-->
144A D23109	JP	--- Jmp if more than 8 bits in integer part of #
144D CD400B	CALL	--- Integer portion has less than 8 bits. Get
1450 C680	ADD	--- integer part & put in A reg
1452 C602	ADD	--- then test it
1454 DA3109	JP	--- Jmp if exponent * 2 ln 2 => 126(dec.)
1457 F5	PUSH	--- Save integer + 82
1458 21F807	LD	--- Addr. of SP 1.0
145B CD0B07	CALL	--- Add to INT (EXP * 2 ln 2)
145E CD4108	CALL	--- Multiply by ln 2
1461 F1	POP	--- Clear stack (integerized EXP * 2 ln 2)
1462 C1	POP	--- then load original
1463 D1	POP	--- exponent into BC/DE
1464 F5	PUSH	--- Save integerized EXP * 2 ln 2
1465 CD1307	CALL	--- Subtract original exponent from integerized one
1468 CD8209	CALL	--- Force difference to be positive
146B 217914	LD	--- Addr of 8 coefficients
146E CDA914	CALL	--- Compute series
1471 110000	LD	--- Load integerized equivalent
1474 C1	POP	--- of EXP * 2 ln 2 into BC/DE
1475 4A	LD	--- Zero C
1476 C34708	JP	--- Multiply by sum from series & rtn to caller

1415 : into A. Truncated flt. pt. portion into WRA1.

141B : exp. This tells if exp. is a whole number

1436 : compute e**ln(value) * exponent
1439 * ***

1448 : bits in integer portion
     · Method: 1. Compute x=x * 2 ln 2
     :   2. Isolate the integer portion of x. If it is > than
     :   88 then exit with an overflow error.
     :   3. Using the integer from step 2 compute :
     :   y = (2 ** integer) * 2
     :   4. Add 1 to the integer from step 2
     :   5. Multiply the result of step 4 by ln 2
     :   6. Subtract step 5 result from original value of x,
     :   and invert the sign of result
     :   7. Using the value computed in step 7 for x, evaluate
     :   the series:
     :   (((((((x*c0+c1)x+c2)x+c3)x+c4)x+c5)x+c6)x+c7)
     :   8. Multiply the final term of the series by the value
     :   computed in step 3

1479	08	EX	--- Count of numbers in list (08)
147A	40	LD	--- 147A = -1.41316 * 10E-4 : coefficients used
147B	2E94	LD	--- : in series to compute
147D	74	LD	--- : e ** x
147E	70	LD	--- 147E = 1.32988 * 10E-3 = 1/6
147F	4F	LD	---
1480	2E77	LD	---
1482	6E	LD	--- 1482 = -8.30136 * 10E-3 = -1/5
1483	02	LD	---
1484	88	ADC	---
1485	7A	LD	---
1486	E6A0	AND	--- 1486 = .0416574 = 1/4
1488	2A7C50	LD	---
148B	AA	XOR	--- 148A = - .166665 = 1/3
148C	AA	XOR	---
148D	7E	LD	---
148E	FF	RST	--- 148E = .5
148F	FF	RST	---
1490	7F	LD	---
1491	7F	LD	---
1492	00	NOP	--- 1492 = -1.0
1493	00	NOP	---
1494	80	ADD	---
1495	81	ADD	---
1496	00	NOP	--- 1496 = 1.0
1497	00	NOP	---
1498	00	NOP	---
1499	81	ADD	---
149A	CDA409	CALL	--- Move x value to stack ************* see note--> *
149D	11320C	LD	--- Then push a return address of C32 onto the stack
14A0	D5	PUSH	--- It will compute the last term before returning
14A1	E5	PUSH	--- Save addr. of no. of term, coefficients
14A2	CDBF09	CALL	--- Load value into BC/DE
14A5	CD4708	CALL	--- Square x value
14A8	E1	POP	--- Restore addr of coefficient
14A9	CDA409	CALL	--- Move x value or x ** 2 value to stack
14AC	7E	LD	--- A = no. of terms
14AD	23	INC	--- HL = addr of next coeff.
14AE	CDB109	CALL	--- Load a coeff pointed to HL & move it to cont-->
14B1	06F1	LD	--- 14B2: POP AF. Get count of coefficients left
14B3	C1	POP	--- BC/DE = x value
14B4	D1	POP	--- Saved at 14A9
14B5	3D	DEC	--- Count 1 term computed
14B6	C8	RET	--- Exit if all terms computed
14B7	D5	PUSH	--- BC/DE = x value
14B8	C5	PUSH	--- Save x value on stk so it can be reused
14B9	F5	PUSH	--- Save count of terms remaining to compute
14BA	E5	PUSH	--- HL pointer to next coeff.
14BB	CD4708	CALL	--- Compute: C(I)*x value
14BE	E1	POP	--- Restore coeff. table addr.
14BF	CDC209	CALL	--- Load next coeff. from list in HL into cont-->
14C2	E5	PUSH	--- Save addr of next coeff.
14C3	CD1607	CALL	--- Compute: C(I) * x value + C(I+1)
14C6	E1	POP	--- Restore coefficient table addr.
14C7	18E9	JR	--- Continue series. WRA1 = current term
14C9	CD7F0A	CALL	--- Convert value to Integer ***** RND routine *******
14CC	7C	LD	--- A = MSB argument
14CD	B7	OR	--- Set status flags
14CE	FA4A1E	JP	--- FC error if negative if RND(A) where A is negative
14D1	B5	OR	--- Combine MSB & LSB, set status flags

```
149A  *  ****  General purpose summation routine computes the ********
   :        series SUM ((((x**2 * c0+c1)x**2 +c2)x**2 +...cN)x
   :        for I=0 to N when entered at 149A.  A second entry
   :        point at 14A9 may be used for the series
   :        SUM ((((x*c0+c1)x+c2)x+c3)x+...cN
   :        for I=0 to N. On entry, the x term is in BC/DE.
   :        HL  points to a list containing the number of terms
   :        followed by the coefficients.

14AE  :  WRA1. HL points to the next value coefficient




14BF  :  BC/DE.  HL points to next value afterwards



14C9  *  ****************************************************************
```

Microsoft BASIC Decoded & Other Mysteries

168

14D2	CAF014	JP	--- Jmp if parameter is zero i.e. RND(0)
14D5	E5	PUSH	--- Save parameter (X from RND(X))
14D6	CDF014	CALL	--- Compute RND(0)
14D9	CDBF09	CALL	--- Load the random number into BC/DE
14DC	EB	EX	--- Now, save the random nuumber on the
14DD	E3	EX	--- stack, and load the original parameter into HL
14DE	C5	PUSH	--- Save RND (0) value.
14DF	CDCF0A	CALL	--- Convert original parameter to SP
14E2	C1	POP	--- Load value from RND(0)
14E3	D1	POP	--- Call at 14D6
14E4	CD4708	CALL	--- Then, nmultiply RND(0)*parameter
14E7	21F807	LD	--- HL = addr of a SP 1.0
14EA	CD0B07	CALL	--- Add 1.0 to current value
14ED	C3400B	JP	--- Convert to integer and return to caller
14F0	219040	LD	--- HL = addr of 3 byte flag table ******** RND(0) **
14F3	E5	PUSH	--- Save falg table addr on stack
14F4	110000	LD	--- DE = middle and LSB of starting value
14F7	4B	LD	--- C = MSB of starting value
14F8	2603	LD	--- H = count of times thru outer loop
14FA	2E08	LD	<-------------: L = times thru inner loop
14FC	EB	EX	<------: . : Move middle of LSB current cont -->
14FD	29	ADD	. : . : Double them
14FE	EB	EX	. : . : Then move them back
14FF	79	LD	. : . : Now, get MSB of current value
1500	17	RLA	. : . : Double it
1501	4F	LD	. : . : And move back to its source reg
1502	E3	EX	. : . : Save counters. Get addr of cont -->
1503	7E	LD	. : . : A = flag word
1504	07	RLCA	. : . : Multiply by 2
1505	77	LD	. : . : And restore
1506	E3	EX	. : . : Counters back to HL
1507	D21615	JP	--->: : . : Jmp if flag word has not cont -->
150A	E5	PUSH	. : : . : Flag word overflowed. Save counter
150B	2AAA40	LD	. : : . : Least two significant bytes of seed
150E	19	ADD	. : : . : Add seed to starting value
150F	EB	EX	. : : . : Move new seed to DE
1510	3AAC40	LD	. : : . : MSB of seed
1513	89	ADC	. : : . : Add to MSB of starting value
1514	4F	LD	. : : . : MSB starting value back to cont -->
1515	E1	POP	. : : . : Restore counters
1516	2D	DEC	<--: : . : Count of times thru inner loop
1517	C2FC14	JP	------>: . : Jmp if not 8 times
151A	E3	EX	. . : Save counters HL = addr of flag word
151B	23	INC	. . : Bump to next flag word
151C	E3	EX	. . : And restore counters. cont -->
151D	25	DEC	. . : Count of times thru outer loop
151E	C2FA14	JP	------------->: Jmp if not 3 times
1521	E1	POP	--- Clear flag table addr from stk
1522	2165B0	LD	--- HL = middle and LSB of original seed
1525	19	ADD	--- Add to current value and save
1526	22AA40	LD	--- As new seed value
1529	CDEF0A	CALL	--- Set current data type to single precision
152C	3E05	LD	--- Now, add a 5 to MSB
152E	89	ADC	--- Of current value and
152F	32AC40	LD	--- Save as MSB of seed
1532	EB	EX	--- Move middle and LSB to DE so we have BC/DE
1533	0680	LD	--- B = sign flag and exponent :arrangement
1535	212541	LD	--- HL = sign flag word
1538	70	LD	-- Set sign flag positive
1539	2B	DEC	--- Bump down to exponent

14F0 * ***

:   value to HL

:   flag word into HL

:   overflowed initially

:   source register

:   New flag word addr to stk.

170

Address	Hex	Mnemonic	Comment
153A	70	LD	--- Set exponent to 80 so value will be < 1
153B	4F	LD	--- C = new MSB (computed at 152E)
153C	0600	LD	--- B = 0 : rtn to caller
153E	C36507	JP	--- Normalize value & jmp to 14D9 unless RND(0) then
1541	218B15	LD	--- Addr. of 1.57 (pi/2) ************ COS routine ***
1544	CD0B07	CALL	--- Add 1.5 to current value
1547	CDA409	CALL	--- Save current value on stack ******** SIN routine *
154A	014983	LD	--- BC/DE = SP = 6.28 (2 pi)
154D	11DB0F	LD	---
1550	CDB409	CALL	--- Move 2 pi to WRA1
1553	C1	POP	--- Load value to
1554	D1	POP	--- find SIN of into BC/DE
1555	CDA208	CALL	--- Value / 2 Pi gives x/360
1558	CDA409	CALL	--- Move value / 2 Pi to stack
155B	CD400B	CALL	--- Convert result to integer so we can isolate
155E	C1	POP	--- BC/DE = quotient & remainder of :remainder
155F	D1	POP	--- value / 2 pi
1560	CD1307	CALL	--- Subtract integer part of value from cont-->
1563	218F15	LD	--- Addr of a SP (.250)
1566	CD1007	CALL	--- Subtract .250 from fractional part. Test if < or =
1569	CD5509	CALL	--- Test sign of the difference : to 90 deg
156C	37	SCF	--- Skip sign inversion call at 1582 if positive
156D	F27715	JP	--- Jmp if < than 90 deg. Go add back the .250
1570	CD0807	CALL	--- Add 0.5 to difference : subtracted
1573	CD5509	CALL	--- Test sign of current value. See if > 0.75
1576	B7	OR	--- Set status flags : (< 270 deg)
1577	F5	PUSH	--- And save sign indicator (+ = +1, - = -1)
1578	F48209	CALL	--- If positive, make it negative (gives x - 1.0)
157B	218F15	LD	--- Addr of SP (.250)
157E	CD0B07	CALL	--- Add 0.250 to current value in WRA1
1581	F1	POP	--- Get sign reversal flag
1582	D48209	CALL	--- Set sign of x term according to quadrant
1585	219315	LD	--- Addr of coefficient
1588	C39A14	JP	--- Compute series and rtn to caller
158B	DB0F	IN	--- 158B = SP (1.5) *****************************
158D	49	LD	---
158E	81	ADD	---
158F	00	NOP	--- 158F - 1592 = .25
1590	00	NOP	---
1591	00	NOP	---
1592	7F	LD	---
1593	05	DEC	--- 1593: count of values that follow (05)
1594	BA	CP	--- 1594 - 1597 = SP (39.7107) : Coefficients used
1595	D7	RST	--- : in power series
1596	1E86	LD	--- : to compute SIN
1598	64	LD	--- 1598 -- 159B = SP (-76.575)
1599	2699	LD	---
159B	87	ADD	---
159C	58	LD	--- 159C - 159F = SP (81.6022)
159D	34	INC	---
159E	23	INC	---
159F	87	ADD	---
15A0	E0	RET	--- 15A0 - 15A3 = SP (-41.3417)
15A1	5D	LD	---
15A2	A5	AND	---
15A3	86	ADD	---
15A4	DA0F49	JP	--- 15A4 - 15A7 = SP (6.28319)
15A7	83	ADD	---
15A8	CDA409	CALL	--- Move WRA1 to stack ********* TAN routine *********
15AB	CD4715	CALL	--- Compute SIN(x) see note-->

```
1541  *  ****************************************************************

1547  *  ****************************************************************
      * Method: 1. Assume x < or = 360 deg
      *         2. Recompute x as x = x/360 so that x =< 1
      *         3. If x < or = 90 deg goto step 7
      *         4. If x < or = 180 deg then x = 0.5 - x. Goto step 7
      *         5. If x < or = 270 deg then x = 0.5 - x
      *         6. Recompute x as x = x - 1.0
      *         7. Compute SIN using power series


1560  : original value (isolate fractional part of x)
```

```
158B  *  ****************************************************************
```

```
15A8  *  ****************************************************************
      : Uses the identity TAN(x) = sin(x) / cos(x)
```

15AE C1	POP	BC	--- Restore the original value
15AF E1	POP	HL	--- to BC / DE
15B0 CDA409	CALL	09A4H	--- Move SIN(x)to stack
15B3 EB	EX	DE,HL	--- Gives original value in BC/DE
15B4 CDB409	CALL	09B4H	--- Original value to WRA1
15B7 CD4115	CALL	1541H	--- Compute COS(x)
15BA C3A008	JP	C8A0H	--- Compute SIN(x)/COS(x) & rtn value as TAN(x)
15BD CD5509	CALL	0955H	--- Test sign of tangent ********** ATN Routine *****
15C0 FCE213	CALL	M,13E2H	--- If neg. put pos. to neg, conv. addr cont--->
15C3 FC8209	CALL	M,0982H	--- Convert current value from neg to pos
15C6 3A2441	LD	A,(4124H)	--- Load exponent of tangent
15C9 FE81	CP	81H	--- Test for value greater than one
15CB 380C	JR	C,15D9H	--->: Jmp if value less than 1
15CD 010081	LD	BC,8100H	. : Setup BC/DE as a
15D0 51	LD	D,C	. : floating point + 1
15D1 59	LD	E,C	. : to BC / DE
15D2 CDA208	CALL	08A2H	. : Get reciprocal of tangent
15D5 211007	LD	HL,0710H	. : Addr of subtract routine be called after series
15D8 E5	PUSH	HL	. : Will subtract last term from Pi/2
15D9 21E315	LD	HL,15E3H	<---: HL = addr of SP coefficients
15DC CD9A14	CALL	149AH	--- Evaluate series
15DF 218B15	LD	HL,158BH	--- Addr of 1.5708 (Pi/2) : step 2
15E2 C9	RET		--- Subtract last term from Pi/2 & rtn. On rtn see
15E3 09	ADD	HL,BC	--- 15E3 = count of SP numbers that follow (09) ******
15E4 4A	LD	C,D	--- 15E4 = 2.86623 * 10E-3
15E5 D7	RST	10H	--- : Coefficients used in
15E6 3B	DEC	SP	--- : power series for ATN
15E7 78	LD	A,B	---
15E8 02	LD	(BC),A	--- 15E8 = - .0161657
15E9 6E	LD	L,(HL)	---
15EA 84	ADD	A,H	---
15EB 7B	LD	A,E	---
15EC FEC1	CP	0C1H	--- 15EC = .0429096
15EE 2F	CPL		---
15EF 7C	LD	A,H	---
15F0 74	LD	(HL),H	--- 15F0 = - .0752896
15F1 319A7D	LD	SP,7D9AH	---
15F4 84	ADD	A,H	--- 15F4 = .105586
15F5 3D	DEC	A	---
15F6 5A	LD	E,D	---
15F7 7D	LD	A,L	---
15F8 C8	RET	Z	--- 15F8 = - .142089
15F9 7F	LD	A,A	---
15FA 91	SUB	C	---
15FB 7E	LD	A,(HL)	---
15FC E4BB4C	CALL	PO,4CBBH	--- 15FC = .199936
15FF 7E	LD	A,(HL)	---
1600 6C	LD	L,H	--- 1600 = - .333331
1601 AA	XOR	D	---
1602 AA	XOR	D	---
1603 7F	LD	A,A	---
1604 00	NOP		--- 1604 = 1.0000
1605 00	NOP		---
1606 00	NOP		---
1607 81	ADD	A,C	---
1608 8A	ADC	A,D	--- ********************************* see note--> *
1609 09	ADD	HL,BC	---
160A 37	SCF		--- INT 0B37
160B 0B	DEC	BC	---
160C 77	LD	(HL),A	--- ABS 0977

173

```
15BD  * ****************************************************************
15C0  : on stack to give proper result

      : Method: 1. Test sign of tangent, if negative angle is in 2nd
      :            or 4th quadrant. Set flag to force result positive
      :            on exit. If value is negative invert the sign
      :         2. Test magnitude of tangent. If < 1 goto step 3,
      :            otherwise compute its reciprocal and put rtn addr
      :            on stack that will calculate Pi/2 - series value
      :         3. Evaluate the series :
      :                 (((x**2 *c0+c1)x**2 +c2)...c8)x
      :         4. If flag from step 1 not set then invert sign of
      :            series result.
      :         5. If original value <1 then rtn to caller, or else
      :            compute Pi/2 - value from step 4 - then rtn

15E3  * ****************************************************************
```

```
1608 * Address of embedded functions ******************************
```

160D 09	ADD	---
160E D427EF	CALL	--- 160E: FRE (27D4)
1611 2AF527	LD	--- 1611:1613 INP (2AEF), POS (27F5)
¯614 E7	RST	--- 1614: SQR (13E7)
¯615 13	INC	---
1616 C9	RET	--- 1616: RND (14C9)
1617 14	INC	---
1618 09	ADD	--- 1618: LOG (0809)
1619 08	EX	---
161A 39	ADD	--- 161A: EXP (1439)
161B 14	INC	---
161C 41	LD	--- 161C: COS (1541)
161D 15	DEC	---
161E 47	LD	--- 161E: SIN (1547)
161F 15	DEC	---
1620 A8	XOR	--- 1620: TAN (15A8)
1621 15	DEC	---
1622 BD	CP	--- 1622: ATN (15BD)
1623 15	DEC	---
1624 AA	XOR	--- 1624: PEEK (2CAA)
1625 2C	INC	---
1626 52	LD	--- 1626: CVI (4152)
1627 41	LD	---
1628 58	LD	--- 1628: CVS (4158)
1629 41	LD	---
162A 5E	LD	--- 162A: CVD (415E)
162B 41	LD	---
162C 61	LD	--- 162C: EOF (4161)
162D 41	LD	---
162E 64	LD	--- 162E: LOC (4164)
162F 41	LD	---
1630 67	LD	--- 1630: LOF (4167)
1631 41	LD	---
1632 6A	LD	--- 1632: MKI$ (416A)
1633 41	LD	---
1634 6D	LD	--- 1634: MKS$ (416D)
1635 41	LD	---
1636 70	LD	--- 1636: MKD$ (4170)
1637 41	LD	---
1638 7F	LD	--- 1638: CINT (0A7F)
1639 0A	LD	---
163A B1	OR	--- 163A CSNG (0AB1)
163B 0A	LD	---
163C DB0A	IN	--- 163C: CDBL (0DAB)
163E 260B	LD	--- 163E: FIX (0B26)
1640 03	INC	--- 1640:1642 LEN (2A03), STR$(2836)
1641 2A3628	LD	---
1644 C5	PUSH	--- 1644:1646 VAL (2AC5), ASC(2A0F)
1645 2A0F2A	LD	---
1648 1F	RRA	--- 1648:164A CHR$(2A1F), LEFT$(2A61)
1649 2A612A	LD	---
164C 91	SUB	--- 164C:164F: RIGHT$ (2A91), MID$(2A9A)
164D 2A9A2A	LD	---
1650 C5	PUSH	--- 80 END **************************
1651 4E	LD	---
1652 44	LD	---
1653 C64F	ADD	--- 81 FOR
1655 52	LD	---
1656 D24553	JP	--- 82 RESET
1659 45	LD	---

```
1650  * Reserved word list ****************************************
```

Address	Hex	Instr		Token	Word *** Reserved word list
165A	54	LD	---		
165B	D345	OUT	---	83	SET
165D	54	LD	---		
165E	C34C53	JP	---	84	CLS
1661	C34D44	JP	---	85	CMD
1664	D2414E	JP	---	86	RANDOM
1667	44	LD	---		
1668	4F	LD	---		
1669	4D	LD	---		
166A	CE45	ADC	---	87	NEXT
166C	58	LD	---		
166D	54	LD	---		
166E	C44154	CALL	---	88	DATA
1671	41	LD	---		
1672	C9	RET	---	89	INPUT
1673	4E	LD	---		
1674	50	LD	---		
1675	55	LD	---		
1676	54	LD	---		
1677	C4494D	CALL	---	8A	DIM
167A	D24541	JP	---	8B	READ
167D	44	LD	---		
167E	CC4554	CALL	---	8C	LET
1681	C7	RST	---	8D	GOTO
1682	4F	LD	---		
1683	54	LD	---		
1684	4F	LD	---		
1685	D2554E	JP	---	8E	RUN
1688	C9	RET	---	8F	IF
1689	46	LD	---	90	RESTORE
168A	D24553	JP	---		
168D	54	LD	---		
168E	4F	LD	---		
168F	52	LD	---		
1690	45	LD	---		
1691	C7	RST	---	91	GOSUB
1692	4F	LD	---		
1693	53	LD	---		
1694	55	LD	---		
1695	42	LD	---		
1696	D24554	JP	---	92	RETURN
1699	55	LD	---		
169A	52	LD	---		
169B	4E	LD	---		
169C	D2454D	JP	---	93	REM
169F	D354	OUT	---	94	STOP
16A1	4F	LD	---		
16A2	50	LD	---		
16A3	C5	PUSH	---	95	ELSE
16A4	4C	LD	---		
16A5	53	LD	---		
16A6	45	LD	---		
16A7	D4524F	CALL	---	96	TRON
16AA	4E	LD	---		
16AB	D4524F	CALL	---	97	TROFF
16AE	46	LD	---		
16AF	46	LD	---		
16B0	C44546	CALL	---	98	DEFSTR
16B3	53	LD	---		
16B4	54	LD	---		

				Token	Word *** Reserved word list continued
16B5	52	LD	---		
16B6	C44546	CALL	---	99	DEFINT
16B9	49	LD	---		
16BA	4E	LD	---		
16BB	54	LD	---		
16BC	C44546	CALL	---	9A	DEFSNG
16BF	53	LD	---		
16C0	4E	LD	---		
16C1	47	LD	---		
16C2	C44546	CALL	---	9B	DEFDBL
16C5	44	LD	---		
16C6	42	LD	---		
16C7	4C	LD	---		
16C8	CC494E	CALL	---	9C	LINE
16CB	45	LD	---		
16CC	C5	PUSH	---	9D	EDIT
16CD	44	LD	---		
16CE	49	LD	---		
16CF	54	LD	---		
16D0	C5	PUSH	---	9E	ERROR
16D1	52	LD	---		
16D2	52	LD	---		
16D3	4F	LD	---		
16D4	52	LD	---		
16D5	D24553	JP	---	9F	RESUME
16D8	55	LD	---		
16D9	4D	LD	---		
16DA	45	LD	---		
16DB	CF	RST	---	A0	OUT
16DC	55	LD	---		
16DD	54	LD	---		
16DE	CF	RST	---	A1	ON
16DF	4E	LD	---		
16E0	CF	RST	---	A2	OPEN
16E1	50	LD	---		
16E2	45	LD	---		
16E3	4E	LD	---		
16E4	C649	ADD	---	A3	FIELD
16E6	45	LD	---		
16E7	4C	LD	---		
16E8	44	LD	---		
16E9	C7	RST	---	A4	GET
16EA	45	LD	---		
16EB	54	LD	---		
16EC	D0	RET	---	A5	PUT
16ED	55	LD	---		
16EE	54	LD	---		
16EF	C34C4F	JP	---	A6	CLOSE
16F2	53	LD	---		
16F3	45	LD	---		
16F4	CC4F41	CALL	---	A7	LOAD
16F7	44	LD	---		
16F8	CD4552	CALL	---	A8	MERGE
16FB	47	LD	---		
16FC	45	LD	---		
16FD	CE41	ADC	---	A9	NAME
16FF	4D	LD	---		
1700	45	LD	---		
1701	CB49	BIT	---	AA	KILL
1703	4C	LD	---		

Addr	Hex	Instr
1704	4C	LD
1705	CC5345	CALL
1708	54	LD
1709	D25345	JP
170C	54	LD
170D	D341	OUT
170F	56	LD
1710	45	LD
1711	D359	OUT
1713	53	LD
1714	54	LD
1715	45	LD
1716	4D	LD
1717	CC5052	CALL
171A	49	LD
171B	4E	LD
171C	54	LD
171D	C44546	CALL
1720	D0	RET
1721	4F	LD
1722	4B	LD
1723	45	LD
1724	D0	RET
1725	52	LD
1726	49	LD
1727	4E	LD
1728	54	LD
1729	C34F4E	JP
172C	54	LD
172D	CC4953	CALL
1730	54	LD
1731	CC4C49	CALL
1734	53	LD
1735	54	LD
1736	C4454C	CALL
1739	45	LD
173A	54	LD
173B	45	LD
173C	C1	POP
173D	55	LD
173E	54	LD
173F	4F	LD
1740	C34C45	JP
1743	41	LD
1744	52	LD
1745	C34C4F	JP
1748	41	LD
1749	44	LD
174A	C35341	JP
174D	56	LD
174E	45	LD
174F	CE45	ADC
1751	57	LD
1752	D44142	CALL
1755	28D4	JR
1757	4F	LD
1758	C64E	ADD
175A	D5	PUSH
175B	53	LD
175C	49	LD

Token	Word *** Reserved word list continued
AB	LSET
AC	RSET
AD	SAVE
AE	SYSTEM
AF	LPRINT
B0	DEF
B1	POKE
B2	PRINT
B3	CONT
B4	LIST
B5	LLIST
B6	DELETE
B7	AUTO
B8	CLEAR
B9	CLOAD
BA	CSAVE
BB	NEW
BC	TAB(
BD	TO
BE	FN
BF	USING

				Token	Word *** Reserved word list continued
175D 4E	LD		---		
175E 47	LD		---		
175F D641	SUB		---	C0	VARPTR
1761 52	LD		---		
1762 50	LD		---		
1763 54	LD		---		
1764 52	LD		---		
1765 D5	PUSH		---	C1	USR
1766 53	LD		---		
1767 52	LD		---		
1768 C5	PUSH		---	C2	ERL
1769 52	LD		---		
176A 4C	LD		---		
176B C5	PUSH		---	C3	ERR
176C 52	LD		---		
176D 52	LD		---		
176E D354	OUT		---	C4	STRING$
1770 52	LD		---		
1771 49	LD		---		
1772 4E	LD		---		
1773 47	LD		---		
1774 24	INC		---		
1775 C9	RET		---	C5	INSTR
1776 4E	LD		---		
1777 53	LD		---		
1778 54	LD		---		
1779 52	LD		---		
177A D0	RET		---	C6	POINT
177B 4F	LD		---		
177C 49	LD		---		
177D 4E	LD		---		
177E 54	LD		---		
177F D4494D	CALL		---	C7	TIME$
1782 45	LD		---		
1783 24	INC		---		
1784 CD454D	CALL		---	C8	MEM
1787 C9	RET		---	C9	INKEY4
1788 4E	LD		---		
1789 4B	LD		---		
178A 45	LD		---		
178B 59	LD		---		
178C 24	INC		---		
178D D44845	CALL		---	CA	THEN
1790 4E	LD		---		
1791 CE4F	ADC		---	CB	NOT
1793 54	LD		---		
1794 D354	OUT		---	CC	STEP
1796 45	LD		---		
1797 50	LD		---		
1798 AB	XOR		---	CD	+
1799 AD	XOR		---	CE	-
179A AA	XOR		---	CF	*
179B AF	XOR		---	D0	/
179C DBC1	IN		---	D1	up arrow
179E 4E	LD		---		
179F 44	LD		---		
17A0 CF	RST		---	D2	AND
17A1 52	LD		---	D3	OR
17A2 BE	CP		---	D4	>
17A3 BD	CP		---	D5	=

17A4	BC	CP	---	D6	<
17A5	D347	OUT	---	D7	SGN
17A7	4E	LD	---		
17A8	C9	RET	---	D8	INT
17A9	4E	LD	---	Token	Word *** Reserved word list
17AA	54	LD	---		
17AB	C1	POP	---	D9	ABS
17AC	42	LD	---		
17AD	53	LD	---		
17AE	C652	ADD	---	DA	FRE (String)
17B0	45	LD	---		
17B1	C9	RET	---	DB	INP
17B2	4E	LD	---		
17B3	50	LD	---		
17B4	D0	RET	---	DC	POS
17B5	4F	LD	---		
17B6	53	LD	---		
17B7	D351	OUT	---	DD	SQR
17B9	52	LD	---		
17BA	D24E44	JP	---	DE	RND
17BD	CC4F47	CALL	---	DF	LOG
17C0	C5	PUSH	---	E0	EXP
17C1	58	LD	---		
17C2	50	LD	---		
17C3	C34F53	JP	---	E1	COS
17C6	D349	OUT	---	E2	SIN
17C8	4E	LD	---		
17C9	D4414E	CALL	---	E3	TAN
17CC	C1	POP	---	E4	ATN
17CD	54	LD	---		
17CE	4E	LD	---		
17CF	D0	RET	---	E5	PEEK
17D0	45	LD	---		
17D1	45	LD	---		
17D2	4B	LD	---	E6	CVI
17D3	C35649	JP	---	E7	CVS
17D6	C35653	JP	---	E8	CVD
17D9	C35644	JP	---	E9	EOF
17DC	C5	PUSH	---		
17DD	4F	LD	---		
17DE	46	LD	---	EA	LOC
17DF	CC4F43	CALL	---	EB	LOF
17E2	CC4F46	CALL	---	EC	MKI$
17E5	CD4B49	CALL	---		
17E8	24	INC	---		
17E9	CD4B53	CALL	---	ED	MKS$
17EC	24	INC	---		
17ED	CD4B44	CALL	---	EE	MKD$
17F0	24	INC	---		
17F1	C3494E	JP	---	EF	CINT
17F4	54	LD	---		
17F5	C3534E	JP	---	F0	CSNG
17F8	47	LD	---		
17F9	C34442	JP	---	F1	CDBL
17FC	4C	LD	---		
17FD	C649	ADD	---	F2	FIX
17FF	58	LD	---		
1800	CC454E	CALL	---	F3	LEN
1803	D354	OUT	---	F4	STR$ (Exp)
1805	52	LD	---		

Addr	Code	Mnem			
1806	24	INC	---	Token	Word *** Reserved word list continued
1807	D641	SUB	---	F5	VAL (string)
1809	4C	LD	---		
180A	C1	POP	---	F6	ASC (string)
180B	53	LD	---		
180C	43	LD	---		
180D	C34852	JP	---	F7	CHR$ (esp)
1810	24	INC	---		
1811	CC4546	CALL	---	F8	LEFT$ (string, n)
1814	54	LD	---		
1815	24	INC	---		
1816	D24947	JP	---	F9	RIGHT$ (string, n)
1819	48	LD	---		
181A	54	LD	---		
181B	24	INC	---		
181C	CD4944	CALL	---	FA	MID$ (string, pos, n)
181F	24	INC	---		
1820	A7	AND	---	FB	´
1821	80	ADD	---	End of syntax list ***--Addr verb ***************
1822	AE	XOR	---	1822: 1DAE - END *****************************
1823	1D	DEC	---	
1824	A1	AND	---	1824: 1CA1 - FOR
1825	1C	INC	---	
1826	3801	JR	---	1826: 0138 - RESET
1828	35	DEC	---	1828: 0135 - SET
1829	01C901	LD	---	182A: 01C9 - CLS
182C	73	LD	---	182C: 4173 - CMD
182D	41	LD	---	
182E	D301	OUT	---	182E: 01DC - RANDOM
1830	B6	OR	---	1830: 22B6 - NEXT
1831	22051F	LD	---	1832: 1F05 - DATA
1834	9A	SBC	---	1834: 219A - INPUT
1835	210826	LD	---	1836: 2608 - DIM
1838	EF	RST	---	1838: 21EF - READ
1839	21211F	LD	---	183A: 1F21 - LET
183C	C21EA3	JP	---	183C - 183E: (1EC2 - GOTO, 1EA3 - RUN)
183F	1E39	LD	---	1840: 2039 - IF
1841	2091	JR	---	1842: 1D91 - RESTORE
1843	1D	DEC	---	
1844	B1	OR	---	1844: 1EB1 - GOSUB
1845	1EDE	LD	---	1846: 1EDE - RETURN
1847	1E07	LD	---	1848: 1F07 - REM
1849	1F	RRA	---	
184A	A9	XOR	---	184A: 1DA9 - STOP
184B	1D	DEC	---	
184C	07	RLCA	---	184C: 1F07 - ELSE
184D	1F	RRA	---	
184E	F7	RST	---	184E: 1DF7 - TRON
184F	1D	DEC	---	
1850	F8	RET	---	1850: 1DF8 - TROFF
1851	1D	DEC	---	
1852	00	NOP	---	1852: 1E00 - DEFSTR
1853	1E03	LD	---	1854: 1E03 - DEFINT
1855	1E06	LD	---	1856: 1E06 - DEFSNG
1857	1E09	LD	---	1858: 1E09 - DEFDBL
1859	1EA3	LD	---	185A: 41A3 - LINE
185B	41	LD	---	
185C	60	LD	---	185C: 2E60 - EDIT
185D	2EF4	LD	---	185E: 1FF4 - ERROR
185F	1F	RRA	---	

```
1821 * *****************************************************************
1822 * Routine vector addresses 2 bytes each *********************
```

1860	AF	XOR	---
1861	1F	RRA	--- 1860: 1FAF - RESUME
1862	FB	EI	---
1863	2A6C1F	LD	--- 1862: 26FB - OUT
1866	79	LD	--- 1864: 1F6C - ON
1867	41	LD	--- 1866: 4179 - OPEN
1868	7C	LD	---
1869	41	LD	--- 1868: 417C - FIELD
186A	7F	LD	---
186B	41	LD	--- 186A: 417F - GET
186C	82	ADD	---
186D	41	LD	--- 186C: 4182 - PUT
186E	85	ADD	---
186F	41	LD	--- 186E: 4185 - CLOSE
1870	88	ADC	---
1871	41	LD	--- 1870: 4188 - LOAD
1872	8B	ADC	---
1873	41	LD	--- 1872: 418B - MERGE
1874	8E	ADC	---
1875	41	LD	--- 1874: 418E - NAME
1876	91	SUB	---
1877	41	LD	--- 1876: 4191 - KILL
1878	97	SUB	---
1879	41	LD	--- 1878: 4197 - LSET
187A	9A	SBC	---
187B	41	LD	--- 187A: 419A - RSET
187C	A0	AND	---
187D	41	LD	--- 187C: 41A0 - SAVE
187E	B2	OR	---
187F	02	LD	--- 187E: 02B2 - SYSTEM
1880	67	LD	---
1881	205B	JR	--- 1880: 2067 - LPRINT
1883	41	LD	--- 1882: 415B - CEF
1884	B1	OR	---
1885	2C	INC	--- 1884: 2CB1 - POKE
1886	6F	LD	---
1887	20E4	JR	--- 1886: 206F - PRINT
1889	1D	DEC	--- 1888: 1DE4 - CONT
188A	2E2B	LD	---
188C	29	ADD	--- 188A: 2B2E - LIST
188D	2B	DEC	--- 188C: 2B29 - LLIST
188E	C62B	ADD	---
1890	08	EX	--- 188E: 2BC6 - DELETE
1891	207A	JR	--- 1890: 2008 - AUTO
1893	1E1F	LD	--- 1892: 1E7A - CLEAR
1895	2C	INC	--- 1894: 2C1F - CLOAD
1896	F5	PUSH	---
1897	2B	DEC	--- 1896: 2BF5 - CSAVE
1898	49	LD	---
1899	1B	DEC	--- 1898: 1B49 - NEW
189A	79	LD	---
189B	79	LD	--- + ******************** Precedent operators *****
189C	7C	LD	--- -
189D	7C	LD	--- *
189E	7F	LD	--- /
189F	50	LD	--- up arrow
18A0	46	LD	--- AND
18A1	DB0A	IN	--- OR
18A3	00	NOP	--- 18A1: 0ADB - convert to double precision *********
18A4	00	NOP	--- 18A3: 0000 - This location not used

189A * ***

18A1 * Used by arithmetic routines to do data conversion & *********
     : arithmetic.

190

18A5	7F	LD	--- 18A5: 0AF7 - Convert to Integer
18A6	0A	LD	---
18A7	F40AB1	CALL	--- 18A7: 0AF4 - Test data type. TM error if not string
18AA	0A	LD	--- 18A9: 0AB1 - Convert to single precision
18AB	77	LD	--- 18AB: 0C77 - Double precision add routine
18AC	0C	INC	---
18AD	70	LD	--- 18AD: 0C70 - Double precision subtract routine
18AE	0C	INC	---
18AF	A1	AND	--- 18AF: 0DA1 - Double precision multiply routine
18B0	0D	DEC	---
18B1	E5	PUSH	--- 18B1: 0DE5 - Double precision divide routine
18B2	0D	DEC	---
18B3	78	LD	--- 18B3: 0A78 - Double precision exponential routine
18B4	0A	LD	---
18B5	1607	LD	--- 18B5: 0716 - Single precision add routine
18B7	13	INC	--- 18B7: 0713 - Single precision subtract routine
18B8	07	RLCA	---
18B9	47	LD	--- 18B9: 0847 - Single precision multiply routine
18BA	08	EX	---
18BB	A2	AND	--- 18BB: 08A2 - Single precision divide routine
18BC	08	EX	---
18BD	0C	INC	--- 18BD: 0A0C - Single precision exponential routine
18BE	0A	LD	--- 18BF-18C1: 0BD2/0BC2 Integer add/subtract routines
18BF	D20BC7	JP	---
18C2	0B	DEC	--- 18C3-18C5: 0BF2/2490 Int multiply/divide routines
18C3	F20B90	JP	---
18C6	24	INC	--- 18C7: 0A39 - Integer exponential routine
18C7	39	ADD	---
18C8	0A	LD	---
18C9	4E	LD	--- 0 - NF (NEXT without FOR) ** Error codes *******
18CA	46	LD	---
18CB	53	LD	--- 2 - SN (Syntax error)
18CC	4E	LD	---
18CD	52	LD	--- 4 - RG (RETURN without GOSUB)
18CE	47	LD	---
18CF	4F	LD	--- 6 - OD (Out of DATA)
18D0	44	LD	---
18D1	46	LD	--- 8 - FC (Illegal function call)
18D2	43	LD	---
18D3	4F	LD	--- 10 - OV (Overflow)
18D4	56	LD	---
18D5	4F	LD	--- 12 - OM (Out of memory)
18D6	4D	LD	---
18D7	55	LD	--- 14 - UL (Undefined linenumber)
18D8	4C	LD	---
18D9	42	LD	--- 16 - BS (Subscript out of range)
18DA	53	LD	---
18DB	44	LD	--- 18 - DD (Redimensioned array)
18DC	44	LD	---
18DD	2F	CPL	--- 20 - /0 (Division by zero)
18DE	3049	JR	--- 22 - ID (Illegal direct operation)
18E0	44	LD	---
18E1	54	LD	--- 24 - TM (Type mismatch)
18E2	4D	LD	---
18E3	4F	LD	--- 26 - OS (Out of string space)
18E4	53	LD	---
18E5	4C	LD	--- 28 - LS (String too long)
18E6	53	LD	---
18E7	53	LD	--- 30 - ST (String formula too complex)
18E8	54	LD	---

```
18C9  *  *********************************************************
```

18E9	43	LD	--- 32 - CN (Can't continue)
18EA	4E	LD	---
18EB	4E	LD	--- 34 - NR (No RESUME)
18EC	52	LD	---
18ED	52	LD	--- 36 - RW (RESUME without error)
18EE	57	LD	---
18EF	55	LD	--- 38 - UE (Unprintable error)
18F0	45	LD	---
18F1	4D	LD	--- 40 - MO (Missing operand)
18F2	4F	LD	---
18F3	46	LD	--- 42 - FD (Bad file data)
18F4	44	LD	---
18F5	4C	LD	--- 44 - L3 (Disk BASIC command)
18F6	33	INC	---
18F7	D600	SUB	--- Subtract LSB * Division Support routine * note-> *
18F9	6F	LD	--- and restore value to L
18FA	7C	LD	--- Get middle byte
18FB	DE00	SBC	--- Subtract middle byte
18FD	67	LD	--- and move difference to H
18FE	78	LD	--- Get MSB
18FF	DE00	SBC	--- Subtract MSB
1901	47	LD	--- and move it back
1902	3E00	LD	--- Clear A
1904	C9	RET	--- Rtn to caller
1905	4A	LD	--- 408E : Addr of user subroutine
1906	1E40	LD	---
1908	E64D	AND	--- 4090 : 3 byte table used by RND to keep track
190A	DB00	IN	--- 4093 : Used for INP (XX) : of previous RND
190C	C9	RET	--- 4093 : RET : value
190D	D300	OUT	--- 4096 : Used for OUTP (XX)
190F	C9	RET	--- 4098 : RET
1910	00	NOP	--- 4099 : 00
1911	00	NOP	--- 409A : 00
1912	00	NOP	--- 409B : 00
1913	00	NOP	--- 409C : 00
1914	40	LD	--- 409D : 40
1915	3000	JR	--- 40A0 : Contains initial stack addr used
1917	4C	LD	--- (434C) : for non-disk IPL
1918	43	LD	--- 40A2 : Initial BASIC line number (FFFE)
1919	FEFF	CP	---
191B	E9	JP	--- 40A4 : Initial addr for PST (42E9)
191C	42	LD	---
191D	2045	JR	--- Space, E ******************* ERROR Message ******
191F	72	LD	--- R
1920	72	LD	--- R
1921	6F	LD	--- O
1922	72	LD	--- R
1923	00	NOP	--- Terminator
1924	2069	JR	--- Space, I ******************** IN Message ********
1926	6E	LD	--- N
1927	2000	JR	--- Space, 0 - terminator
1929	52	LD	--- Space, R ******************** READY Message *****
192A	45	LD	--- E
192B	41	LD	--- A
192C	44	LD	--- D
192D	59	LD	--- Y
192E	0D	DEC	--- Carriage ret
192F	00	NOP	--- Terminator
1930	42	LD	--- B *************************** BREAK Message ****
1931	72	LD	--- R

```
18F7  *  Code from 18F7 to 191D is moved  *****************************
      :  to locations 4080 - 40A5 during
      :  the non-disk IPL sequence. This
      :  section of code contains the
      :  division support routine
      :  used for single precision
      :  division, and initial values
      :  for the communications region
      :   locations 408E - 40A4



191D  *  ****************************************************************



1924  *  ****************************************************************


1929  *  ****************************************************************



1930  *  ****************************************************************
```

1932	65	LD	--- E
1933	61	LD	--- A
1934	6B	LD	--- K
1935	00	NOP	--- Message terminator
1936	210400	LD	--- HL = 4 so we can backspace ******** see note--> *
1939	39	ADD	--- Current stack pointer 4 bytes
193A	7E	LD	<---: A = current stk ptr (-4)
193B	23	INC	. : Backspace one more byte in case FOR token
193C	FE81	CP	. : Does current stk ptr(-4) = FOR token :located
193E	C0	RET	. : No, exit with A non-zero if no FOR push
193F	4E	LD	. : C = LSB addr of index variable
1940	23	INC	. : Backspace current stk ptr one more byte
1941	46	LD	. : B = MSB addr of index variable
1942	23	INC	. : HL = addr of FOR index on stk
1943	E5	PUSH	. : Save addr of FOR index pointer on stk
1944	69	LD	. : L = LSB of index addr
1945	60	LD	. : H = MSB of index addr see note-->
1946	7A	LD	. : Test user specified variable addr
1947	B3	OR	. : Set status flags
1948	EB	EX	. : DE = addr of index from stk
1949	2802	JR	. : Jmp, if user specified addr of zero
194B	EB	EX	. : HL = addr of index from stk
194C	DF	RST	. : Compare caller's DE to addr of cont-->
194D	010E00	LD	. : Amt to backspace to next FOR token
1950	E1	POP	. : HL = stk addr of sign of increment flag
1951	C8	RET	. : Exit if FOR index = NEXT index
1952	09	ADD	. : Else, backspace to next possible FOR push
1953	18E5	JR	--->: Keep looking
1955	CD6C19	CALL	--- Make sure there's room in ********** see note--> *
1958	C5	PUSH	--- Source addr (end of list) to stack
1959	E3	EX	--- Source addr (end of list) to HL
195A	C1	POP	--- BC = destination addr (end)
195B	DF	RST	<---: Test for end of move
195C	7E	LD	. : Fetch a byte from source list
195D	02	LD	. : Store in destination list
195E	C8	RET	. : Exit if list moved
195F	0B	DEC	. : Decrement source address
1960	2B	DEC	. : Decrement destination address
1961	18F8	JR	--->: Loop until list moved
1963	E5	PUSH	--- Save code string addr ************* see note--> *
1964	2AFD40	LD	--- Start of free memory ptr.
1967	0600	LD	--- B=00, C=no. of double bytes needed
1969	09	ADD	--- Add 2*no. of bytes required to start of free area
196A	09	ADD	--- HL = end free area
196B	3EE5	LD	--- 196C: PUSH HL, save new free area ptr (starting)
196D	3EC6	LD	--- Now, compute amt. of memory between
196F	95	SUB	--- FFC6 (65478) start of the stack and new starting
1970	6F	LD	--- Free memory pointer by subtracting new starting
1971	3EFF	LD	--- Free mem. addr from FFC6. If free mem. overflows
1973	9C	SBC	--- Beyond start of stk we are out of space.
1974	3804	JR	--- OM error if C-Free space list exceeds 65478,7FFC6
1976	67	LD	--- Now attempt to determine
1977	39	ADD	--- If free space list has
1978	E1	POP	--- Overflowed stack area.
1979	D8	RET	--- No overflow if CARRY
197A	1E0C	LD	--- OM error code
197C	1824	JR	--- Output OM error message
197E	2AA240	LD	--- HL = current line number ************************
1981	7C	LD	--- Combine MSB
1982	A5	AND	--- With LSB

1936 * (Locate FOR push which matches caller's index specified *****

```
      : Called w/DE = addr of NEXT index.  Scans stk backwards
      : looking for a FOR push.  If one found get addr of index
      : and compare w/caller's DE.  If equal exit with A = 0,
      : HL = addr of variable.  If unequal keep scanning till no
      : FOR push found & exit w/A<>0.
```

194C : <———:-: index from the stack

1955 * string area   ******* On entry DE = upper limit **************
      :   This routine moves a variable (string
      :   usually) into another area specified by
      :   the caller.
      :   On entry:
      :   BC = end addr of list to move
      :   DE = start addr of list to move
      :   HL = end of area to move list to.
      :

1963 * Compute amt of space between HL and end of memory FFC6. *****

197E * **
```
```

1983	3C	INC	--- If current line = FFFF then we have cont-->
1984	2808	JR	--- Jmp if BASIC pgm has not been executed. cont-->
1986	3AF240	LD	--- Get error override flag
1989	B7	OR	--- Set status flags
198A	1E22	LD	--- Code for NO RESUME error
198C	2014	JR	--- Output NR error message if no RESUME addr
198E	C3C11D	JP	--- Error while in Input Phase. Re-enter cont-->
1991	2ADA40	LD	--- Load line number for last DATA stmnt
1994	22A240	LD	--- Store it in current line ptr
1997	1E02	LD	--- SN error code
1999	011E14	LD	--- 199A: LD E,14 /0 Error code
199C	011E00	LD	--- 199D: LD E,0 NF Error code
199F	011E24	LD	--- 19A1: LD E,24 RW error code
19A2	2AA240	LD	--- HL = addr of line with error *********************
19A5	22EA40	LD	--- Save error line number
19A8	22EC40	LD	--- Twice
19AB	01B419	LD	--- BC = continuation addr after re-initialization
19AE	2AE840	LD	--- HL = stack ptr for start of statement
19B1	C39A1B	JP	--- Go re-initialize system variables. Rtn to 19B4
19B4	C1	POP	--- BC = 00 00
19B5	7B	LD	--- A = error number
19B6	4B	LD	--- C = error number
19B7	329A40	LD	--- Save error number
19BA	2AE640	LD	--- HL = addr of last byte executed in current line
19BD	22EE40	LD	--- Save addr of last byte executed
19C0	EB	EX	--- Save HL
19C1	2AEA40	LD	--- HL = addr of last line executed
19C4	7C	LD	--- Combine LSB of last line
19C5	A5	AND	--- Executed with MSB of last line
19C6	3C	INC	--- Then test, if line number = FFFF
19C7	2807	JR	--- Line number = FFFF, still in Input Phase
19C9	22F540	LD	--- Save error addr
19CC	EB	EX	--- Restore last byte executed
19CD	22F740	LD	--- Save last byte executed
19D0	2AF040	LD	--- Get ON ERROR address
19D3	7C	LD	--- Combine LSB with MSB so it can be
19D4	B5	OR	--- tested for zero
19D5	EB	EX	--- DE = ON ERROR address
19D6	21F240	LD	--- Addr of flag word during ON ERROR processing
19D9	2808	JR	--- Jmp if no ON ERROR address
19DB	A6	AND	--- Test if RESUME processing in program
19DC	2005	JR	--- Yes, cannot have nested RESUMES
19DE	35	DEC	--- Flag an error so RESUME will work
19DF	EB	EX	--- HL = addr of statement to branch to
19E0	C3361D	JP	--- Goto Execution Driver
19E3	AF	XOR	--- Zero A ***
19E4	77	LD	--- Clear error override flag
19E5	59	LD	--- Error number to E
19E6	CDF920	CALL	--- Position video to next line
19E9	21C918	LD	--- HL = table of error codes
19EC	CDA641	CALL	--- DOS Exit (load & execute BASIC error routine)
19EF	57	LD	--- Zero D
19F0	3E3F	LD	--- A = ASCII '?'
19F2	CD2A03	CALL	--- Print '?'
19F5	19	ADD	--- HL = addr
19F6	7E	LD	--- Get a char. of error code
19F7	CD2A03	CALL	--- Print one char of error code
19FA	D7	RST	--- Get next char of error code
19FB	CD2A03	CALL	--- And print it
19FE	211D19	LD	--- Error message

1983 : not started execution of BASIC pgm
1984 : Still in Input Phase

198E : BASIC ´READY´ routine. --- Load current data line number

19A2 * ***

19E3 * ***

```
1A01 E5      PUSH      --- Save addr of 'ERROR' message
1A02 2AEA40  LD        --- HL = line number of stmnt causing error
1A05 E3      EX        --- Line no. to stk.  HL = addr of 'ERROR' message
1A06 CDA728  CALL      --- Print message shere addr is in HL
1A09 E1      POP       --- HL = binary line no. of STOP/END or line w/error
1A0A 11FEFF  LD        --- DE = 65534 (10)
1A0D DF      RST       --- Is current line no. = 65534
1A0E CA7406  JP        --- Yes, IPL system
1A11 7C      LD        --- No, test for line no. = 0
1A12 A5      AND       --- Combine MSB and LSB
1A13 3C      INC       --- of current line no.
1A14 C4A70F  CALL      --- If non-zero, print current line no.
1A17 3EC1    LD        --- 1A18: POP BC
1A19 CD8B03  CALL      --- Set output device to video ***** Flush current ***
1A1C CDAC41  CALL      --- line buffer. DOS Exit (JP 5FFC)
1A1F CDF801  CALL      --- Off cassette
1A22 CDF920  CALL      --- Skip to next line on video
1A25 212919  LD        --- Ready message
1A28 CDA728  CALL      --- Print 'READY' message
1A2B 3A9A40  LD        --- Get error number
1A2E D602    SUB       --- Test for syntax error
1A30 CC532E  CALL      --- If syntax error, enter EDIT routine
1A33 21FFFF  LD        --- HL = current line no.
1A36 22A240  LD        --- Set current line no. to -1.  Signal      cont-->
1A39 3AE140  LD        --- Auto input flag field - Non zero if auto, 00H
1A3C B7      OR        --- Set status flags                      :if not auto
1A3D 2837    JR        --- Jmp & Print '>' prompt if no auto increment
1A3F 2AE240  LD        --- Else, fetch current line no. into HL
1A42 E5      PUSH      --- Save line number on stack
1A43 CDAF0F  CALL      --- Output a line #
1A46 D1      POP       --- Load current line no. into DE for search routine
1A47 D5      PUSH      --- And leave it on the stack
1A48 CD2C1B  CALL      --- Search for matching line number
1A4B 3E2A    LD        --- '*' (matching line number)
1A4D 3802    JR        --- Jmp if matching line number found
1A4F 3E20    LD        --- Else print a blank
1A51 CD2A03  CALL      --- Print a ' ' or '*'
1A54 CD6103  CALL      --- Accept input into buffer
1A57 D1      POP       --- DE = current line no.
1A58 3006    JR        --->:   Jmp if BREAK not hit
1A5A AF      XOR       <---:-: Else clear AUTO increment flag
1A5B 32E140  LD        -- : : Turn off AUTO increment
1A5E 18B9    JR        -- : : Go to 'READY'
1A60 2AE440  LD        <---: : Get increment value ***************************
1A63 19      ADD       --  :   Add to current line no. and test for overflow
1A64 38F4    JR        ----->: Jmp if line no. exceeds 2**15.   Clear AUTO
1A66 D5      PUSH      --- Save unincremented line no. on stk       :increment
1A67 11F9FF  LD        --- DE = 65529
1A6A DF      RST       --- Compare bumped line no. to 65529
1A6B D1      POP       --- DE = unincremented line no.
1A6C 30EC    JR        --- Jmp if bumped line no. => 65529
1A6E 22E240  LD        --- Save unincremented value as current line no.
1A71 F6FF    OR        --- Set A = -1
1A73 C3EB2F  JP        --- Use EDIT code to load buffer addr       cont-->
1A76 3E3E    LD        --- A = '>' (prompt) ****************** see note--> *
1A78 CD2A03  CALL      --- Print '>'
1A7B CD6103  CALL      --- Accept input, on return HL = buffer addr
1A7E DA331A  JP        --- Jmp if BREAK key hit.  Go get next line
1A81 D7      RST       --- Get a char from buffer, skip blanks & control
1A82 3C      INC       --- Set status flags but save carry          :codes
```

1A19 * ***

1A36 : that execution has not started

1A60 * ***

1A73 : into HL. Then jmp to 1A98
1A76 * Input line no. w/o AUTO increment **************************

1A83 3D	DEC	---	So we can test for end of statement
1A84 CA331A	JP	---	Jmp if end of statement
1A87 F5	PUSH	---	Save status (CARRY)-Get line in binary into DE
1A88 CD5A1E	CALL	---	Backspace input buffer over any trailing blanks
1A8B 2B	DEC	<---:	that follow line number
1A8C 7E	LD	. :	Get next character
1A8D FE20	CP	. :	Check for blank
1A8F 28FA	JR	--->:	Loop till last digit of line number found
1A91 23	INC	---	HL = addr of first char following line number
1A92 7E	LD	---	Fetch first char after line number
1A93 FE20	CP	---	If its a blank then
1A95 CCC909	CALL	---	Bump buffer addr to next char
1A98 D5	PUSH	---	Save binary line number
1A99 CDC01B	CALL	---	Encode input into tokens-BC=length of encoded stmt
1A9C D1	POP	---	DE = line number in binary
1A9D F1	POP	---	Get CARRY flag from fetch at 1A81
1A9E 22E640	LD	---	Encoded statement pointer
1AA1 CDB241	CALL	---	DOS Exit (JP 6033)
1AA4 D25A1D	JP	---	Jmp if no line number. Must be Direct Statement
1AA7 D5	PUSH	---	Save binary line number : or System command
1AA8 C5	PUSH	---	Save length of code string
1AA9 AF	XOR	---	Clear A and
1AAA 32DD40	LD	---	Set INPUT PHASE entered flag
1AAD D7	RST	---	Scan for 1st token
1AAE B7	OR	---	Set status flag
1AAF F5	PUSH	---	Save them
1AB0 EB	EX	---	HL = binary equivalent of line number
1AB1 22EC40	LD	---	Save line number in communications area
1AB4 EB	EX	---	DE = line number for search routine
1AB5 CD2C1B	CALL	---	Search for matching line number
1AB8 C5	PUSH	---	After search, BC = addr of line number cont-->
1AB9 DCE42B	CALL	---	If matching line not found shift closest line up
1ABC D1	POP	---	in memory to make room for new line. cont-->
1ABD F1	POP	---	Restore status from token scan at 1AAD
1ABE D5	PUSH	---	Save addr of line in buffer
1ABF 2827	JR	---	If matching line found, otherwise new cont-->
1AC1 D1	POP	---	DE = addr of last line or line > new line
1AC2 2AF940	LD	---	HL = end of pgm line ptr
1AC5 E3	EX	---	HL = length of code string. cont-->
1AC6 C1	POP	---	BC = length of new line
1AC7 09	ADD	---	HL = new end of pgm line ptr
1AC8 E5	PUSH	---	Save end of pgm addr
1AC9 CD5519	CALL	---	Make sure enough room for new line. Test for PST
1ACC E1	POP	---	HL = end of PST :overflow in stk area
1ACD 22F940	LD	---	New end of PST addr
1AD0 EB	EX	---	HL = addr of line to be moved up
1AD1 74	LD	---	Save MSB of addr of line to moved as cont-->
1AD2 D1	POP	---	DE = new line number in binary
1AD3 E5	PUSH	---	Save addr if line to be moved up
1AD4 23	INC	---	Bump to LSB of line number entry
1AD5 23	INC	---	Bump to MSB of line number entry
1AD6 73	LD	---	DE = binary value of line no for new line. Save
1AD7 23	INC	---	Bump to MSB :LSB
1AD8 72	LD	---	Save MSB of new line in old line nos. position
1AD9 23	INC	---	HL = stmt ptr (past line number)
1ADA EB	EX	---	DE = first data byte addr following line number
1ADB 2AA740	LD	---	HL = input area ptr
1ADE EB	EX	---	DE = input area ptr (fetch addr). cont-->
1ADF 1B	DEC	---	DE = input area ptr - 1
1AE0 1B	DEC	---	DE = input area ptr - 2

1AB8 : in buffer if it exists

1ABC : DE = addr of line in buffer

1ABF : line is to be added

1AC5 : Stack = addr of line to be moved

1AD1 : first byte of line

1ADE : HL = addr of first data position in pgm area (store addr)

```
1AE1 1A       LD      <---: Get a byte of pgm from input buffer
1AE2 77       LD         . : Move it to pgm storage area (PST)
1AE3 23       INC        . : Bump store addr
1AE4 13       INC        . : Bump fetch addr
1AE5 B7       OR         . : Test for end of code string
1AE6 20F9     JR      --->: Jmp if not end of statement to be moved
1AE8 D1       POP     --- DE = addr of line in pgm table
1AE9 CDFC1A   CALL    --- Update line ptrs for all line following new line
1AEC CDB541   CALL    --- DOS Exit (JP 5BD7)
1AEF CD5D1B   CALL    --- Update 40FB, 40FD line ptrs = 40F9
1AF2 CDB841   CALL    --- DOS Exit (JP 5B8C)
1AF5 C3331A   JP      --- Loop back to repeat input sequence
1AF8 2AA440   LD      --- HL = start addr of PST (entered from Disk BASIC)
1AFB EB       EX      --- Move PST addr to HL
1AFC 62       LD      <---: HL = current line ptr *********** see note--> *
1AFD 6B       LD         . : First 2 bytes of each line contains addr of next
1AFE 7E       LD         . : line. An addr of 00 00 terminates      cont-->
1AFF 23       INC        . : Look for end byte
1B00 B6       OR         . : of pgm (0000)
1B01 C8       RET        . : Return if end
1B02 23       INC        . : HL = beginning of stmt ptr               cont-->
1B03 23       INC        . : Skip over 3 & 4th bytes of
1B04 23       INC        . : current line which hold its line no.
1B05 AF       XOR        . : A = 0, status flags cleared
1B06 BE       CP      <--:: Scan for end of current line its        cont-->
1B07 23       INC       .:: When end found, HL+1 will be addr of next line
1B08 20FC     JR      -->:: Loop till end of stmnt found
1B0A EB       EX         . : DE=end of stmt + 1 (ptr to next stmt)   cont->
1B0B 73       LD         . : Move addr of next line to 1st 2 bytes of current
1B0C 23       INC        . : Save LSB of next line addr                 :line
1B0D 72       LD         . : Save MSB of next line addr
1B0E 18EC     JR      --->: Loop till end of pgm found
1B10 110000   LD      --- Initialize starting line to 0 in case * cont--> *
1B13 D5       PUSH    --- none is specified.  Save on stack
1B14 2809     JR      --- Jmp if no line nos. given
1B16 D1       POP     --- Clear temp. starting value
1B17 CD4F1E   CALL    --- Get starting line no. in DE
1B1A D5       PUSH    --- Save starting line no.
1B1B 280B     JR      --->: Jmp if no ending line specified
1B1D CF       RST     --  : Test for dash following line number
1B1E CE11     ADC     --  : 1B1E : DC CE dash token
1B20 FAFFC4   JP      --  : 1B1F : LD DE,FFAF default ending line number
1B23 4F       LD      --  : 1B22 : CALL NZ,1E4F get ending line no into DE
1B24 1EC2     LD      --  : 1B25 : JP NZ,1997 SN Error if no terminator
1B26 97       SUB     --  :
1B27 19       ADD     --  :
1B28 EB       EX      <---: HL = ending line no.
1B29 D1       POP     --- DE = starting line no.
1B2A E3       EX      --- Ending line no to stack. Rtn addr to HL
1B2B E5       PUSH    --- Rtn addr to stk so we can exit below
1B2C 2AA440   LD      --- HL = starting addr of PST ************** cont--> *
1B2F 44       LD      --- DE = Line number to locate
1B30 4D       LD      --- BC = address of current line in PST
1B31 7E       LD      --- A = LSB of addr of next line
1B32 23       INC     --- Bump to MSB of addr of next line
1B33 B6       OR      --- Combine MSB/LSB and set status flags
1B34 2B       DEC     --- Restore HL to start of current line
1B35 C8       RET     --- Exit if end of PST, else
1B36 23       INC     --- Bump HL to point to line number
1B37 23       INC     --- for current line
```

```
1AFC  * Update line pointers for all lines after new line. **********
      * DE = Addr of Program Statement Table
1AFE  : the program.  Get 1st byte of current line and combine w/2nd


1B02  : (Past next stmt ptr and line number)


1B06  : terminated by 00


1B0A  : HL = current line ptr


1B10  * **** Called by LIST/DELETE ********************************
      :       Converts starting and ending line numbers (X - Y) to
      :       binary and saves ending line number on stack.
      :       Then falls into code below to locate pgm table addr for
      :       starting line.  Leaves addr of starting line in BC -
      :       ending line number on stack


1B2C  * Search for matching line routine **************************
      : Exit conditions
      : Line not found. End of PST encountered:
      :               NC/Z/HL = BC
      : Line found: DE=HL/C/Z, BC = addr of line in PST
      :                        HL = addr of next line
      : Line not found. Line number > asked for line number
      :           DE>HL/NC/NZ, BC = addr of current line
      :                        HL = addr of next line
```

```
1B38 7E      LD      --- A = LSB of line no. for current line
1B39 23      INC     --- Bump to MSB
1B3A 66      LD      --- HL = MSB of line no. for current line
1B3B 6F      LD      --- L = LSB of current line number
1B3C DF      RST     --- Subtract line no. in DE from line no. for current
1B3D 60      LD      --- Set HL = starting addr of current line   :statement
1B3E 69      LD      --- L = LSB of start addr of current line
1B3F 7E      LD      --- Now, get addr of next line into HL
1B40 23      INC     --- Bump to MSB of addr of next line
1B41 66      LD      --- H = MSB of addr for next line
1B42 6F      LD      --- Form addr of next line in HL
1B43 3F      CCF     --- CARRY set if current line              cont-->
1B44 C8      RET     --- Line numbers match. Exit C, Z,         cont-->
1B45 3F      CCF     --- No match, reverse CARRY & exit if
1B46 D0      RET     --- line no. in DE < current line number   cont-->
1B47 18E6    JR      --- Loop till end of pgm or line number    cont-->
1B49 C0      RET     --- Syntax error if NEW XX ************** NEW routine *
1B4A CDC901  CALL    --- Clear screen
1B4D 2AA440  LD      --- HL = start of Program Statement Table (PST)
1B50 CDF81D  CALL    --- Turn TRACE OFF
1B53 32E140  LD      --- Clear AUTO INCREMENT flag
1B56 77      LD      --- Initialize PST as empty by
1B57 23      INC     --- zeroing first two bytes
1B58 77      LD      --- Zero 2nd byte
1B59 23      INC     --- then
1B5A 22F940  LD      --- initialize the start of the variable    cont-->
1B5D 2AA440  LD      --- Reload HL with PST addr     *** RUN starts here ***
1B60 2B      DEC     --- and backspace 1.  This will be the
1B61 22DF40  LD      --- beginning execution addr for the program
1B64 061A    LD      --- 26 alpha characters ** RUN line no. starts here ***
1B66 210141  LD      --- Def alpha table entries initialized to 004H
1B69 3604    LD      --- Load one value                     :(single precision)
1B6B 23      INC     --- Bump to next entry
1B6C 10FB    DJNZ    --- Loop till DEC ALPHA table initialized
1B6E AF      XOR     --- Clear A-reg
1B6F 32F240  LD      --- Signal no error for RESUME verb
1B72 6F      LD      --- then
1B73 67      LD      --- Zero HL
1B74 22F040  LD      --- Set ON ERROR address to zero
1B77 22F740  LD      --- Points to next statement following a    cont-->
1B7A 2AB140  LD      --- Highest memory pointer
1B7D 22D640  LD      --- String working area pointer
1B80 CD911D  CALL    --- Restore
1B83 2AF940  LD      --- HL = end of basic pgm
1B86 22FB40  LD      --- Simple variable ptrs
1B89 22FD40  LD      --- Array ptrs
1B8C CDBB41  CALL    --- DOS Exit (JP 5B8C)
1B8F C1      POP     --- Load return addr because we will be     cont-->
1B90 2AA040  LD      --- HL = Start of string data ptr
1B93 2B      DEC     --- HL = Start of string data ptr - 1
1B94 2B      DEC     --- -2
1B95 22E840  LD      --- Stack ptr = start of string data ptr - 2
1B98 23      INC     --- HL = start of string data ptr +1
1B99 23      INC     --- +2
1B9A F9      LD      --- SP = start of string data ptr
1B9B 21B540  LD      --- Initialize literal string poo table as empty
1B9E 22B340  LD      --- Start of LSPT to 40B3
1BA1 CD8B03  CALL    --- Output device = video: Print line printer buffer
1BA4 CD6921  CALL    --- Turn off cassette and set output device = video
1BA7 AF      XOR     --- Zero A then
```

```
1B43 : number < value in DE.  After CCF CARRY is cleared.
1B44 : BC = addr of current line, HL = addr next line

1B46 : BC = addr of current line, HL = addr next line
1B47 : Greater than requested one found
1B49 * ********************************************************
```

```
1B5A : list table as the end of the PST
```

```
1B77 : BREAK, STOP or END.
```

```
1B8F : changing stack pointer
```

```
1BA8 67      LD      --- Clear HL for 'RUN' push
1BA9 6F      LD      --- Zero L
1BAA 32DC40  LD      --- Clear 'FOR' statement flag
1BAD E5      PUSH    --- Signal 'RUN' push
1BAE C5      PUSH    --- Return addr to continue executing code string
1BAF 2ADF40  LD      --- Restore code string addr to HL
1BB2 C9      RET     --- Rtn to caller
1BB3 3E3F    LD      --- A = ASCII ? ***********************************
1BB5 CD2A03  CALL    --- Print ?
1BB8 3E20    LD      --- A = ASCII space
1BBA CD2A03  CALL    --- Print space
1BBD C36103  JP      --- Wait for keyboard input and rtn to caller
1BC0 AF      XOR     --- Zero A ************************************
1BC1 32B040  LD      --- Clear DATA statement flag
1BC4 4F      LD      --- Zero C-reg
1BC5 EB      EX      --- DE = addr of first char after line number
1BC6 2AA740  LD      --- HL = input area ptr = tokenized string addr
1BC9 2B      DEC     --- Backspace
1BCA 2B      DEC     --- twice
1BCB EB      EX      --- DE = input string addr - 2
1BCC 7E      LD      --- HL = current input string addr
1BCD FE20    CP      --- Fetch next char. from input string
1BCF CA5B1C  JP      --- Test for space
1BD2 47      LD      --- Jump if blank
1BD3 FE22    CP      --- Save input character
1BD5 CA771C  JP      --- Test for quote
1BD8 B7      OR      --- If quote, move entire field between quotes to code
1BD9 CA7D1C  JP      --- Set status flags                      :string
1BDC 3AB040  LD      --- Jmp if end of string
1BDF B7      OR      --- A = DATA statement flag
1BE0 7E      LD      --- Set status flags
1BE1 C25B1C  JP      --- Load next char from input string
1BE4 FE3F    CP      --- Jump if DATA stmnt encountered
1BE6 3EB2    LD      --- '?' abbreviation for print
1BE8 CA5B1C  JP      --- Print token replaces question mark
1BEB 7E      LD      --- Jmp if '?' (print token)
1BEC FE30    CP      --- Re-fetch current character
1BEE 3805    JR      --- Test for numeric as alpha-numeric
1BF0 FE3C    CP      --- Char < 30 - that means it's not a letter or digit
1BF2 DA5B1C  JP      --- Char < 3C - that means 0-9,:,;,<        cont-->
1BF5 D5      PUSH    --- Save pointer to buffer orig -2, -1, . .
1BF6 114F16  LD      --- DE addr of syntax tree
1BF9 C5      PUSH    --- Save BC
1BFA 013D1C  LD      --- Rtn add after matching syntax tree
1BFD C5      PUSH    --- W/input string
1BFE 067F    LD      --- B = syntax tree control char count
1C00 7E      LD      --- Current input character
1C01 FE61    CP      --- Test for upper case
1C03 3807    JR      --->: Jump if not lower case
1C05 FE7B    CP      --  : Test for upper case
1C07 3003    JR      --->: Jump if not lower case
1C09 E65F    AND     --  : Make upper case
1C0B 77      LD      --  : Save converted character
1C0C 4E      LD      <--: Reload current character
1C0D EB      EX      --- HL = syntax list, DE = addr of current string
1C0E 23      INC     <--: Bump to next char in syntax list
1C0F B6      OR       . : Set status flags for current char      cont-->
1C10 F20E1C  JP      --->: Scan syntax list till control char found
1C13 04      INC     --- Count of syntax control char passed
1C14 7E      LD      --- Get syntax element
```

1BB3 * ***

1BC0 * ***

1BF2 : Constant or special char. Move it to token area.

1C0F : from syntax list

1C15	E67F	AND	--- Clear sign bit
1C17	C8	RET	--- Zero terminates syntax list, goto 1C3D
1C18	B9	CP	--- Compare input element w/syntax element
1C19	20F3	JR	--- No match, scan till past control element
1C1B	EB	EX	--- HL = start of current symbol in input string
1C1C	E5	PUSH	--- Save starting addr of current symbol
1C1D	13	INC	<------: Bump to next char in syntax list
1C1E	1A	LD	. : Get next syntax list element
1C1F	B7	OR	. : Set status flags for end of name test
1C20	FA391C	JP	-------:->: Jmp if control element, we have a
1C23	4F	LD	. : : Complete match. Save next syntax element
1C24	78	LD	. : : If count of keyword being examined is
1C25	FE8D	CP	. : : 8D then we are testing for a GOTO
1C27	2002	JR	--->: : : Jump if not 'GOTO' token
1C29	D7	RST	. : : Skip following char if its blank
1C2A	2B	DEC	. : : Decrement for following skip
1C2B	23	INC	<----: : : Skip to next char
1C2C	7E	LD	. : : Get next element from input string
1C2D	FE61	CP	. : : Test for upper case
1C2F	3802	JR	--->: : : Jump if not lower case
1C31	E65F	AND	. : : Force upper case
1C33	B9	CP	<--: : : Compare input element & syntax element
1C34	28E7	JR	------>: : Jmp if equal
1C36	E1	POP	--- : Unequal, restart scan from last
1C37	18D3	JR	--- : Point in syntax list
1C39	48	LD	<-------: Syntax list index
1C3A	F1	POP	--- Get rid of HL push at 1C1C
1C3B	EB	EX	--- HL = syntax tree addr for this string, DE =
1C3C	C9	RET	--- current string Goto 1C3D
1C3D	EB	EX	--- HL = current string
1C3E	79	LD	--- A = syntax list index
1C3F	C1	POP	--- Clear rtn addr from stack
1C40	D1	POP	--- DE = input string buffer orgin-2 - cont-->
1C41	EB	EX	--- HL = buffer orgin-2, DE = current string addr
1C42	FE95	CP	--- Test if ELSE token
1C44	363A	LD	--- ':' buffer orgin-2
1C46	2002	JR	--->: Jump if not 'ELSE' token
1C48	0C	INC	-- : Count 1 char in token buffer
1C49	23	INC	-- : Bump to next position in token buffer
1C4A	FEFB	CP	<--: Test for REM token
1C4C	200C	JR	--->: Jump if not ''' (abbreviation for 'REM') token
1C4E	363A	LD	-- : ':' to tokenized buffer
1C50	23	INC	-- : next pos. in token buffer
1C51	0693	LD	-- : 'REM' token
1C53	70	LD	-- : To tokenized buffer
1C54	23	INC	-- : Next pos. in token buffer
1C55	EB	EX	-- : HL = input string addr. DE = token buffer addr.
1C56	0C	INC	-- : Count 2
1C57	0C	INC	-- : More chars to token buffer
1C58	181D	JR	-- : Go move comment to token buffer
1C5A	EB	EX	<--: DE = buffer area-2, HL = current string addr
1C5B	23	INC	--- Bump to next char in input string
1C5C	12	LD	--- Syntax tree index to buffer orgin-2 : or if blank
1C5D	13	INC	--- DE = buffer orgin-1 : move the
1C5E	0C	INC	--- C = index for next syntax element : blank
1C5F	D63A	SUB	--- Test for multi-statement line
1C61	2804	JR	--->: Jmp if multi-statement line
1C63	FE4E	CP	-- : Test for DATA stmnt
1C65	2003	JR	-- : Jump if not 'DATA' token
1C67	32B040	LD	<--: Syntax list index to flag 'data' statement

209

1C40 : loaded at 1CF5

1C6A	D659	SUB	--- Test for REM token
1C6C	C2CC1B	JP	--- Jump if not ´REM´ token. Analyze rest of statement
1C6F	47	LD	--- B = 00
1C70	7E	LD	<---: Get next char from input string
1C71	B7	OR	. : Set status flags so we can test for EOS
1C72	2809	JR	----:>: Jmp if EOS
1C74	B8	CP	. : : Move statement from input buffer to input
1C75	28E4	JR	. : : buffer - 2. Loop till EOS detected. Count
1C77	23	INC	. : : of characters moved in BC. Also entered if
1C78	12	LD	. : : a ´ ´ string is detected.
1C79	0C	INC	. : : Count 1 char added to token buffer
1C7A	13	INC	. : : Bump token buffer addr.
1C7B	18F3	JR	--->: : Loop till EOS or ending quote found
1C7D	210500	LD	<-----: Now, add
1C80	44	LD	--- Five to the length of the
1C81	09	ADD	--- token buffer thus far
1C82	44	LD	--- then leave
1C83	4D	LD	--- New count in BC
1C84	2AA740	LD	--- Get start of input string area
1C87	2B	DEC	--- Backspace once
1C88	2B	DEC	--- Backspace twice
1C89	2B	DEC	--- Three times
1C8A	12	LD	--- Then zero
1C8B	13	INC	--- Last 3 words of tokenized string
1C8C	12	LD	--- Second zero
1C8D	13	INC	--- Bump addr
1C8E	12	LD	--- Third zero
1C8F	C9	RET	--- Rtn to caller
1C90	7C	LD	--- Compute *********** RST 18 sends you here *******
1C91	92	SUB	--- H - D Computes HL-DE
1C92	C0	RET	--- Exit if unequal Z if equal
1C93	7D	LD	--- Compute C if DE>HL
1C94	93	SUB	--- L - E
1C95	C9	RET	--- and rtn to caller
1C96	7E	LD	--- Get value to be compared * RST 08 routine *******
1C97	E3	EX	--- Save rtn addr.
1C98	BE	CP	--- Compare (HL) with value following RST 8
1C99	23	INC	--- Bump rtn addr
1C9A	E3	EX	--- Restore rtn addr to stack, cont-->
1C9B	CA781D	JP	--- CALL RST 10 If expected character found
1C9E	C39719	JP	--- SN error if expected char not found
1CA1	3E64	LD	--- FOR signal value ****************** FOR routine *
1CA3	32DC40	LD	--- Signal FOR statement.
1CA6	CD211F	CALL	--- Evaluates x = y (index)
1CA9	E3	EX	--- Save code string addr. DE=addr of index variable
1CAA	CD3619	CALL	--- Scan stack backwards looking for other cont-->
1CAD	D1	POP	--- DE = current code string addr (addr of TO token)
1CAE	2005	JR	--->: Jmp if nested ´FOR´ not on stack cont -->
1CB0	09	ADD	-- : BC = Offset to end of stack frame cont -->
1CB1	F9	LD	-- : Reset CSP to this addr. Regain the cont -->
1CB2	22E840	LD	-- : NF error next. Save CSP addr in 40E8
1CB5	EB	EX	<---: HL = current code string addr
1CB6	0E08	LD	--- C = 1/2 amt. of space needed
1CB8	CD6319	CALL	--- Make sure there´s 16 bytes of free space
1CBB	E5	PUSH	--- Save code string addr before ´TO´
1CBC	CD051F	CALL	--- Scan till end of statement
1CBF	E3	EX	--- Stack = end of statement, cont-->
1CC0	E5	PUSH	--- Code string addr to stk. should point to TO token
1CC1	2AA240	LD	--- HL = current line no. in binary.
1CC4	E3	EX	--- Stack = end of line addr. FOR line no. cont-->

1C90 * **

1C96 * RST 08 sends you here **************************************

1C9A : HL = current code string pointer

1CA1 * **

1CAA :   FOR/NEXT token with same index (Error if found)

1CAE : If one is found, on exit HL = starting addr of FOR push
1CB0 : After addition we are at end of 1st FOR frame push
1CB1 : stack space and force a NF error

1CBF : HL = current position in statement

1CC4 : in binary for FOR statement

212

1CC5	CF	RST	--- Test for TO token
1CC6	BD	CP	--- DC BD TO token
1CC7	E7	RST	--- Test data type of index variable
1CC8	CAF60A	JP	--- TM error if Z (string)
1CCB	D2F60A	JP	--- TM error if NC (double)
1CCE	F5	PUSH	--- Save type flags
1CCF	CD3723	CALL	--- Evaluate TO side of FOR statement
1CD2	F1	POP	--- Restore index type flags
1CD3	E5	PUSH	--- Save current position in code string after TO
1CD4	F2EC1C	JP	--->: Jmp if index is single precision :token
1CD7	CD7F0A	CALL	. : Current TO value to integer
1CDA	E3	EX	. : Integer value to stack. Reload HL
1CDB	110100	LD	. : DE = increment in case STEP not specified
1CDE	7E	LD	. : Get next element from code string
1CDF	FECC	CP	. : Compare with STEP token
1CE1	CC012B	CALL	. : Call if 'STEP' token - Get step value into DE
1CE4	D5	PUSH	. : Save step value
1CE5	E5	PUSH	. : Save code string position
1CE6	EB	EX	. : STEP value to HL so we test its size
1CE7	CD9E09	CALL	. : Get sign of STEP into A. A=+1 if pos., -1 if neg
1CEA	1822	JR	-----:>: Skip over single precision code for counter
1CEC	CDB10A	CALL	<---: : Convert TO value to single precision :& step
1CEF	CDBF09	CALL	-- : Load counter into BC/DE
1CF2	E1	POP	-- : HL = end of TO expression
1CF3	C5	PUSH	-- : Save TO value (limit)
1CF4	D5	PUSH	-- : All four bytes of it
1CF5	010081	LD	-- : BC = single precision 1 = default STEP value
1CF8	51	LD	-- : 0000 = DE
1CF9	5A	LD	-- : E as well
1CFA	7E	LD	-- : A = next element from code string
1CFB	FECC	CP	-- : Test for STEP token
1CFD	3E01	LD	-- : Default step = 1
1CFF	200E	JR	--->: : Jump if not 'STEP' token
1D01	CD3823	CALL	-- : : Evaluate STEP expression
1D04	E5	PUSH	-- : : Save code string addr
1D05	CDB10A	CALL	-- : : Convert value to single precision
1D08	CDBF09	CALL	-- : : Load STEP expression value into BC/DE
1D0B	CD5509	CALL	-- : : Get sign of STEP value into A. +1=pos,-1=neg
1D0E	E1	POP	<---:-: HL = current code string addr
1D0F	C5	PUSH	<---: Save STEP expression
1D10	D5	PUSH	--- On stack
1D11	4F	LD	--- Sign flag for STEP value to C
1D12	E7	RST	--- Test data type for STEP value
1D13	47	LD	--- B = type for STEP value. cont-->
1D14	C5	PUSH	--- Save type adjusted / sign flag
1D15	E5	PUSH	--- Save current code string addr on stack
1D16	2ADF40	LD	--- HL = addr of index from FOR x = y
1D19	E3	EX	--- HL = code string addr. Stk = addr of x variable
1D1A	0681	LD	--- B = FOR token
1D1C	C5	PUSH	--- Save FOR token / sign of STEP inncrement
1D1D	33	INC	--- Leave a one byte gap on the stack cont-->
1D1E	CD5803	CALL	--- Set status flags for input
1D21	B7	OR	--- If key was hit, check for shift @
1D22	C4A01D	CALL	--- Save address of last byte executed in current line
1D25	22E640	LD	--- Save CSP
1D28	ED73E840	LD	--- Fetch next character from input string
1D2C	7E	LD	--- and test for a compound statement
1D2D	FE3A	CP	--- Jump if ':' - Multiple statement this line
1D2F	2829	JR	--- Else, make sure code string terminates
1D31	B7	OR	--- Set status flags

1D13 : -1 (int), +1 (sing)   C = STEP sign flag

1D1E : Continue execution of code string. Test for keyboard input

1D32	C29719	JP	--- SN error if NC with a byte of zeroes
1D35	23	INC	--- Get LSB of pointer to next statement
1D36	7E	LD	--- Test for non-zero by combining
1D37	23	INC	--- with MSB byte
1D38	B6	OR	--- of pointer to the next statement
1D39	CA7E19	JP	--- Jmp if last executable statement, else
1D3C	23	INC	--- Get line number of next statement
1D3D	5E	LD	--- into DE
1D3E	23	INC	--- Bump to MSB of line number for next statement
1D3F	56	LD	--- DE = binary line number of next statement
1D40	EB	EX	--- HL = Line number for next statement
1D41	22A240	LD	--- Update last executed line to current line nummber
1D44	3A1B41	LD	--- Get TRACE flag
1D47	B7	OR	--- Set status flags
1D48	280F	JR	--->: Jmp if TROFF, fall through if TRON
1D4A	D5	PUSH	-- : Save DE since display routine uses it
1D4B	3E3C	LD	-- : ASCII '<'
1D4D	CD2A03	CALL	-- : Print '<'
1D50	CDAF0F	CALL	-- : Convert line number to binary & print it
1D53	3E3E	LD	-- : ASCII '>'
1D55	CD2A03	CALL	-- : Print '>' (This gives <line number>)
1D58	D1	POP	-- : Restore DE
1D59	EB	EX	<---: HL = code string current line
1D5A	D7	RST	--- Get next token ***** Execution phase starts here **
1D5B	111E1D	LD	--- Rtn addr after executing one verb
1D5E	D5	PUSH	--- Rtn addr onto stack
1D5F	C8	RET	--- Exit if EOS (end of statement) - Go back to 1D1E
1D60	D680	SUB	--- (tokens range from 80 - FB) Compute rel. token
1D62	DA211F	JP	--- Not a token - must be assignment stmt :index
1D65	FE3C	CP	--- Test if token below TAB token
1D67	D2E72A	JP	--- Jmp if token => BC (TAB - MID$,')
1D6A	07	RLCA	--- Double remainder for routine address offset
1D6B	4F	LD	--- BC = routine offset
1D6C	0600	LD	--- BC = 00 / 2 * token
1D6E	EB	EX	--- Save HL (current location in code string)
1D6F	212218	LD	--- Address table of verb action routines
1D72	09	ADD	--- HL = routine table address ptr
1D73	4E	LD	--- C = LSB of verb action routine addr
1D74	23	INC	--- Bump to MSB
1D75	46	LD	--- B = MSB of verb action routine addr
1D76	C5	PUSH	--- Save routine address on stack see note -->
1D77	EB	EX	--- Restore code string address
1D78	23	INC	<---:-: Bump to next character *** RST 10 action rtne *
1D79	7E	LD	. : : Get next character
1D7A	FE3A	CP	. : : Compare it with a colon (:)
1D7C	D0	RET	. : : Rtn if character is :,;,<,.....A - Z
1D7D	FE20	CP	. : : else test for a blank
1D7F	CA781D	JP	--->: : Get next character if this one is a blank
1D82	FE0B	CP	-- : Compare it with a vertical TAB
1D84	3005	JR	--->: : Jump if A >= 0B (not a control code)
1D86	FE09	CP	. : : Test for a horizontal TAB
1D88	D2781D	JP	----:>: Jmp if not horizontal TAB or line feed
1D8B	FE30	CP	<---: Compare with ASCII '0'
1D8D	3F	CCF	--- Set CARRY if numeric (>=30)
1D8E	3C	INC	--- Clear CARRY if not numeric (<30)
1D8F	3D	DEC	--- Set status flags (except CARRY) according to
1D90	C9	RET	--- Rtn to caller : character just loaded
1D91	EB	EX	--- Save HL ********************* RESTORE routine **
1D92	2AA440	LD	--- HL = start of program ptr
1D95	2B	DEC	--- Backspace 1 byte, save HL

1D5A : Find next non-blank character in code string ****************
     : Method:
     : 1. Locate next token in current statement and
     :   branch to verb action routine. Force return to
     :   1D1E after verb routine.
     : 2. After each completed verb action routine test
     :   for BREAK, end of line (bump to next line), end
     :   of program (rtn to INPUT PHASE),or TRON option
     :   goto step 1

     : (It will be popped below)

1D78 * RST 10 routine addr sends you here *************************

1D91 * ***

1D96	22FF40	LD	--- Data ptr = start of program - 1
1D99	EB	EX	--- Restore HL
1D9A	C9	RET	--- Rtn to caller
1D9B	CD5803	CALL	--- Scan keyboard once ******************************
1D9E	B7	OR	--- Set status flags for character strobed
1D9F	C8	RET	--- Return if no key
1DA0	FE60	CP	--- Shift @ ?
1DA2	CC8403	CALL	--- if so, wait until user types a character
1DA5	329940	LD	--- Save character typed
1DA8	3D	DEC	--- A + 1 if break key
1DA9	C0	RET	--- Stop routine ************************************
1DAA	3C	INC	--- Set A = 1, status non-zero
1DAB	C3B41D	JP	--- Use END code
1DAE	C0	RET	--- Syntax error if END XX *********** END routine **
1DAF	F5	PUSH	--- Save zero status (END processing)
1DB0	CCBB41	CALL	--- DOS Exit (JP 60A1)
1DB3	F1	POP	--- Restore END status to A status register
1DB4	22E640	LD	--- Current code string addr for STOP or END
1DB7	21B540	LD	--- HL = start of literal string area
1DBA	22B340	LD	--- Reset pointer to start of literal string area
1DBD	21F6FF	LD	--- 1DBE: OR FF
1DC0	C1	POP	--- Clear stack
1DC1	2AA240	LD	--- Current line no. in binary
1DC4	E5	PUSH	--- Save binary line no. for STOP/END stmt
1DC5	F5	PUSH	--- A = 0 (END), 1 (STOP)
1DC6	7D	LD	--- Combine LSB of current line with
1DC7	A4	AND	--- MSB of current line no.. so we can
1DC8	3C	INC	--- test for uninitialized line no. (FFFF)
1DC9	2809	JR	--->: Jmp if line no. = FFFF pgm execution not started
1DCB	22F540	LD	-- : Else, save line number we ended on
1DCE	2AE640	LD	-- : HL = current line number
1DD1	22F740	LD	-- : Save in 40F7
1DD4	CD8B03	CALL	<---: Initialize output DCB to the video
1DD7	CDF920	CALL	--- Print a CR
1DDA	F1	POP	--- Restore A = 0 (END), 1 (STOP)
1DDB	213019	LD	--- Addr of break message
1DDE	C2061A	JP	--- Jmp if STOP excountered
1DE1	C3181A	JP	--- Jmp if END statement or error in command mode
1DE4	2AF740	LD	--- HL = last stmt byte scanned *** Cont routine ***
1DE7	7C	LD	--- Combine LSB/MSB of addr
1DE8	B5	OR	--- for last statement executed
1DE9	1E20	LD	--- CN error code
1DEB	CAA219	JP	--- Output CN if no continuation addr
1DEE	EB	EX	--- Continuation line number to DE
1DEF	2AF540	LD	--- HL = last line number executed
1DF2	22A240	LD	--- Save line number with error
1DF5	EB	EX	--- then set HL = addr of continuation line no.
1DF6	C9	RET	--- Go begin execution at continuation line
1DF7	3EAF	LD	--- Set A-reg non-zero for TRON *** TRON routine ****
1DF9	321B41	LD	--- 1DF8: XOR A Set A-reg zero for TROFF
1DFC	C9	RET	--- Save TRON/TROFF flag and return to interpreter
1DFD	F1	POP	. These instructions
1DFE	E1	POP	. are not used by
1DFF	C9	RET	. Level II
1E00	1E03	LD	--- E = type for string values ** DEFSTR routine *****
1E02	011E02	LD	--- 1E03 LD E,02 DEFINT routine
1E05	011E04	LD	--- 1E06 LD E,04 DEFSNG routine
1E08	011E08	LD	--- 1E09 LD E,08 DEFDBL routine
1E0B	CD3D1E	CALL	--- Test next element in code string. Make sure its a
1E0E	019719	LD	--- Error addr in case its not :letter

```
1D9B  *  *************************************************************

1DA0  *  *************************************************************

1DA9  *  *************************************************************

1DAE  *  *************************************************************




1DE4  *  *************************************************************




1DF7  *  *************************************************************




1E00  *  *************************************************************
```

218

1E11	C5	PUSH	--- Error addr to stk
1E12	D8	RET	--- Syntax error if no letter follows DEFSTR
1E13	D641	SUB	--- Subtract an ASCII 'A' which gives a value in
1E15	4F	LD	--- range 0-25. Save range value in C
1E16	47	LD	--- and in B
1E17	D7	RST	--- Examine next element in code string
1E18	FECE	CP	--- Test for a dash (-) token
1E1A	2009	JR	--- No range of letters specified
1E1C	D7	RST	--- A range has been specified, get the ending letter
1E1D	CD3D1E	CALL	--- Check for a letter
1E20	D8	RET	--- Syntax error if not a letter
1E21	D641	SUB	--- A = 0 - 26(base 10) corresponding to letters
1E23	47	LD	--- A thru Z
1E24	D7	RST	--- Get next character
1E25	78	LD	--- Now, make sure 2nd letter follows 1st
1E26	91	SUB	--- Subtract 1st letter from 2nd
1E27	D8	RET	--- Syntax error if letter range not in ascending
1E28	3C	INC	--- A=number of type entries to change :order
1E29	E3	EX	--- Clear error addr. Save current code string addr
1E2A	210141	LD	--- HL = type table
1E2D	0600	LD	--- B = 00 / value for 1st letter
1E2F	09	ADD	--- Find next entry in type table
1E30	73	LD	--- Set data type in type table
1E31	23	INC	--- Bump to next entry
1E32	3D	DEC	--- Count of entries changed
1E33	20FB	JR	--- Loop till range of entries changed
1E35	E1	POP	--- Restore code string pointer
1E36	7E	LD	--- and look for more letters
1E37	FE2C	CP	--- Test for comma
1E39	C0	RET	--- Return if not comma
1E3A	D7	RST	--- Fetch next element and
1E3B	18CE	JR	--- go test for a letter
1E3D	7E	LD	--- Get next element from code string ****************
1E3E	FE41	CP	--- Compare to an ASCII A
1E40	D8	RET	--- If not a letter
1E41	FE5B	CP	--- Compare to an ASCII up-arow, gives CARRY
1E43	3F	CCF	--- Set CARRY if not a letter : if a letter
1E44	C9	RET	--- NC if a letter
1E45	D7	RST	--- Fetch next symbol from input. ********** cont--> *
1E46	CD022B	CALL	--- Get value for next expression into cont-->
1E49	F0	RET	--- DE as an integer, set to subscript cont-->
1E4A	1E08	LD	--- FC error if index is negative
1E4C	C3A219	JP	--- Output FC error
1E4F	7E	LD	--- Get next character ********* ASCII to binary ***
1E50	FE2E	CP	--- Check for period abbreviation
1E52	EB	EX	--- DE = current input symbol addr
1E53	2AEC40	LD	--- DE = period address
1E56	EB	EX	--- HL = addr of current symbol
1E57	CA781D	JP	--- Jmp, period
1E5A	2B	DEC	--- Backspace to current character ***** see note--> *
1E5B	110000	LD	--- Initialize accumulation to zero
1E5E	D7	RST	--- Reprocess previous character
1E5F	D0	RET	--- Return if not a digit
1E60	E5	PUSH	--- Save current character pointer (digit)
1E61	F5	PUSH	--- Save digit plus flags from RST 10
1E62	219819	LD	--- HL = 6552
1E65	DF	RST	--- Is accumulated value > 6552
1E66	DA9719	JP	--- SN error if value > 6552
1E69	62	LD	--- No, continue
1E6A	6B	LD	--- Move current value to HL

```
1E3D  *  **********************************************************

1E45  * Called when evaluating A ************************************
      : Subscript for a variable reference
      : evaluation if value positive

1E4F  *  **********************************************************

1E5A  * Start at . pt & work backwards ******** ASCII to binary ****
```

1E6B	19	ADD	--- DE * 2
1E6C	29	ADD	--- DE * 4
1E6D	19	ADD	--- DE * 5
1E6E	29	ADD	--- HE = DE * 10(base 10)
1E6F	F1	POP	--- Get last ASCII digit
1E70	D630	SUB	--- Convert it to binary
1E72	5F	LD	--- and save in E register
1E73	1600	LD	--- DE = 0000 thru 0009 (binary equiv of digit)
1E75	19	ADD	--- Add latest digit to total so far
1E76	EB	EX	--- DE = 10(base 10) * DE + A
1E77	E1	POP	--- Restore ptr to next digit
1E78	18E4	JR	--- Process next digit
1E7A	CA611B	JP	--- Jmp if no byte count *********** CLEAR routine ***
1E7D	CD461E	CALL	--- Get number of bytes into DE
1E80	2B	DEC	--- Backspace code string addr
1E81	D7	RST	--- Examine next char in input stream
1E82	C0	RET	--- Exit if not end of line
1E83	E5	PUSH	--- Save current code string ptr
1E84	2AB140	LD	--- Top of memory ptr into HL
1E87	7D	LD	--- DE = no. of bytes to reserve for string
1E88	93	SUB	--- Subtract LSB of n from top of mem. ptr
1E89	5F	LD	--- Save diff of LSB's
1E8A	7C	LD	--- Get MSB of top of memory ptr
1E8B	9A	SBC	--- Subtract MSB of n from top of mem. ptr
1E8C	57	LD	--- Save diff in D
1E8D	DA7A19	JP	--- OM error if trying to clear more bytes than
1E90	2AF940	LD	--- HL = end of pgm ptr : available
1E93	012800	LD	--- BC = min. amt of variable space needed
1E96	09	ADD	--- Plus end of pgm ptr gives earliest string area
1E97	DF	RST	--- Compare to start of string area addr
1E98	D27A19	JP	--- OM error if string list overlays variable list
1E9B	EB	EX	--- HL = new start of string area addr
1E9C	22A040	LD	--- Load start of string ptr
1E9F	E1	POP	--- Restore code string ptr
1EA0	C3611B	JP	--- Join common code at RUN subroutine
1EA3	CA5D1B	JP	--- Jmp if no line specified ****** RUN routine ****
1EA6	CDC741	CALL	--- DOS Exit (JP 5F78)
1EA9	CD611B	CALL	--- Go initialize RUN time variables
1EAC	011E1D	LD	--- Continuation addr in execution driver :number
1EAF	1810	JR	--- Use GOTO code to begin execution at specified line
1EB1	0E03	LD	--- Make sure there are at least *** GOSUB routine ***
1EB3	CD6319	CALL	--- 6 bytes of available memory
1EB6	C1	POP	--- BC = rtn addr in execution driver
1EB7	E5	PUSH	--- Save code string addr
1EB8	E5	PUSH	--- and create a hole which will be filled later
1EB9	2AA240	LD	--- HL = binary value for current line no.
1EBC	E3	EX	--- Store in hole on stack. Restore code string
1EBD	3E91	LD	--- Save a 145 on stack :pointer
1EBF	F5	PUSH	--- as a GOSUB marker
1EC0	33	INC	--- Backspace stk ptr over status flags
1EC1	C5	PUSH	--- Save rtn addr in execution driver. Use GOTO code
1EC2	CD5A1E	CALL	--- Get line no. to branch to in DE **** GOTO routine*
1EC5	CD071F	CALL	--- Skip to end of this line
1EC8	E5	PUSH	--- Save code string addr, next line
1EC9	2AA240	LD	--- HL = binary equivalent of last line no.
1ECC	DF	RST	--- Compare target line no.
1ECD	E1	POP	--- With current line no.
1ECE	23	INC	--- Restore code string addr
1ECF	DC2F1B	CALL	--- Target line is forward : Locate line # speci-
1ED2	D42C1B	CALL	--- Target line is backwards : fied in DE

1E7A * ***

1EA3 * **

1EB1 * **

1EC2 * ***

1ED5	60	LD	--- On exit BC = addr of requested line no.
1ED6	69	LD	--- Move addr of target line code string to HL
1ED7	2B	DEC	--- Backspace to start of line
1ED8	D8	RET	--- Rtn to execution driver. Start executing new line
1ED9	1E0E	LD	--- UL error. Line number not found
1EDB	C3A219	JP	--- Output UL error message
1EDE	C0	RET	--- Syntax error if RETURN XX *** RETURN routine *****
1EDF	16FF	LD	--- Set DE to dummy addr for search routine cont -->
1EE1	CD3619	CALL	--- Backspace stack ptr 4 bytes. Load value into A
1EE4	F9	LD	--- Set stk ptr to backspaced addr
1EE5	22E840	LD	--- Save backspacd stk addr
1EE8	FE91	CP	--- And look for GOSUB marker
1EEA	1E04	LD	--- RG error if RETURN without GOSUB
1EEC	C2A219	JP	--- Print error message
1EEF	E1	POP	--- HL = binary line no. of GOSUB call
1EF0	22A240	LD	--- Save as current line no.
1EF3	23	INC	--- Bump to next line
1EF4	7C	LD	--- Make sure line no. has not
1EF5	B5	OR	--- overflowed
1EF6	2007	JR	--->: Jmp if no overflow
1EF8	3ADD40	LD	-- : Else we may have a one line pgm
1EFB	B7	OR	-- : Get INPUT PHASE flag and test it
1EFC	C2181A	JP	-- : Jmp if still in INPUT PHASE
1EFF	211E1D	LD	<---: HL = rtn addr in execution driver
1F02	E3	EX	--- Save on stack. HL=code string addr of GOSUB call
1F03	3EE1	LD	--- 1F04: POP HL Now scan to end of GOSUB cont-->
1F05	013A0E	LD	--- ****************************** DATA routine *
1F08	00	NOP	--- 1F07 LD C,00 Set stop scan char to 00
1F09	0600	LD	--- B =00
1F0B	79	LD	<---: Save original stop scan char
1F0C	48	LD	. : Reset stop scan char to 00
1F0D	47	LD	. : B = stop scan value
1F0E	7E	LD	<---:-: Get an element from code string
1F0F	B7	OR	. : : Test for end of line
1F10	C8	RET	. : : Exit if end of line
1F11	B8	CP	. : : Test for stop scan char
1F12	C8	RET	. : : Exit if stop scan encounterred
1F13	23	INC	. : : Bump to next elemennt on code string
1F14	FE22	CP	. : : Test for quote
1F16	28F3	JR	--->: : If quote, reset stop scan value to (00)
1F18	D68F	SUB	. : Not quote, test for IF token
1F1A	20F2	JR	----->: Jump if not ´IF´ token
1F1C	B8	CP	-- : A = 0, if B = 0 then CARRY = 0 and
1F1D	8A	ADC	-- : Add instr does not channge value of D,
1F1E	57	LD	-- : if B <>, then CARRY = 1 and D is
1F1F	18ED	JR	----->: bumped by one loop.
1F21	CD0D26	CALL	--- Get addr of variable into DE *** LET routine *****
1F24	CF	RST	--- Test if var name followed by = , if not error
1F25	D5	PUSH	--- 1F25: DC D5 ´=´
1F26	EB	EX	--- Addr of variable name to HL
1F27	22DF40	LD	--- Save addr of assignment variable
1F2A	EB	EX	--- Restore addr of next input of variable to HL
1F2B	D5	PUSH	--- Save addr of variable
1F2C	E7	RST	--- Determine data type
1F2D	F5	PUSH	--- Save type/flags. see note-->
1F2E	CD3723	CALL	--- Evaluate expression. Save result as current
1F31	F1	POP	--- Restore data to parity A :variable
1F32	E3	EX	--- Push current code sting addr onto stack. cont-->
1F33	C603	ADD	--- Restore data to 2-I, 3-ST, 4-SN, 8-DB
1F35	CD1928	CALL	--- Convert result to proper mode

```
1EDE  *  ***************************************************
1EDF  :  and A - 1 for scan routine




1F03  :  statement & rtn to execution driver
1F05  *  Set stop scan char to :   **********************************
      :                             Search code string until an end
      :                             of line (00) is found or a stop
      :                             scan value of (00) or (:) occurs
      :                             For quotes or 'IF' tokens perform
      :                             the following
      :                             quote - unconditionally reset
      :                                     stop scan char to (00)
      :                              IF token -
      :                                stop scan char = 00 -
      :                                    do nothing
      :                                stop scan char = : -
      :                                    increment D - reg by
      :                                    one




1F21  *  ***************************************************************




1F2D  :  A = -1(integer), 0(string), 1(single), 5(double)


1F32  :  HL = addr of variable
```

1F38 CD030A	CALL	---	Move result to 'current' value area
1F3B E5	PUSH	---	Save addr of variable
1F3C 2028	JR	---	Jmp if result is not string
1F3E 2A2141	LD	---	HL = Pointer to string entry
1F41 E5	PUSH	---	Save it on stack
1F42 23	INC	---	Skip over length
1F43 5E	LD	---	E = LSB of string addr
1F44 23	INC	---	Bump to MSB of addr
1F45 56	LD	---	D = MSB of string addr
1F46 2AA440	LD	---	HL = start of pgm ptr
1F49 DF	RST	---	Compare stack of pgm ptr to addr of string
1F4A 300E	JR	---	Jmp if string precedes program :variable
1F4C 2AA040	LD	---	HL = string data ptr
1F4F DF	RST	---	Compare string addr to lower boundary of string
1F50 D1	POP	---	DE = addr of string pointer : area
1F51 300F	JR	---	Jmp if not in string area
1F53 2AF940	LD	---	HL = end of pgm ptr
1F56 DF	RST	---	Compare string addr to end addr of PST
1F57 3009	JR	---	Jmp if string is a literal in the program
1F59 3ED1	LD	---	1F5A: POP DE DE = pointer to string entry
1F5B CDF529	CALL	---	Backspace to prior literal string pool entry
1F5E EB	EX	---	DE = address of string entry in string list area
1F5F CD4328	CALL	---	Move string to permanent string area
1F62 CDF529	CALL	---	Backspace lit. string pool table one entry
1F65 E3	EX	---	Load ptr to string entry from stack
1F66 CDD309	CALL	---	Move answer to assigned variable location
1F69 D1	POP	---	DE = addr of assigned variable
1F6A E1	POP	---	HL = code string address
1F6B C9	RET	---	Rtn to caller
1F6C FE9E	CP	---	Test token for 'ERROR' **** ON routine ***********
1F6E 2025	JR	---	Jmp if not ON ERROR
1F70 D7	RST	---	Examine next char in input buffer **** ON ERROR **
1F71 CF	RST	---	Test if it is a '8D'
1F72 8D	ADC	---	if it is then GO TO token
1F73 CD5A1E	CALL	---	Convert following constant to binary. Result in DE
1F76 7A	LD	---	Test if ON ERROR GOTO 0000 Clear ON ERROR
1F77 B3	OR	---	Combine LSB & MSB of addr :condition
1F78 2809	JR	---	Jmp if GOTO addr is zero
1F7A CD2A1B	CALL	---	Locate address of line # in basic pgm list
1F7D 50	LD	---	Move addr of basic stmnt to DE
1F7E 59	LD	---	E = LSB of addr
1F7F E1	POP	---	HL = current position in input stream. cont-->
1F80 D2D91E	JP	---	UL error if line number not found
1F83 EB	EX	---	HL = addr of basic line to GOTO. cont-->
1F84 22F040	LD	---	40F0 = addr of statement to resume execution at
1F87 EB	EX	---	Restore code string addr to HL
1F88 D8	RET	---	Rtn to execution driver if not GOTO 0000, else
1F89 3AF240	LD	---	Get error message override all :fall thru
1F8C B7	OR	---	Set status flags
1F8D C8	RET	---	Rtn to execution driver if override flag not set
1F8E 3A9A40	LD	---	else get error code
1F91 5F	LD	---	& move it to E register
1F92 C3AB19	JP	---	Go to error routine
1F95 CD1C2B	CALL	---	Get n value into DE ****************************
1F98 7E	LD	---	A = next token from code string
1F99 47	LD	---	Save token : ON n GOTO
1F9A FE91	CP	---	Test for GOSUB token : ON n GOSUB
1F9C 2803	JR	---	Jump if 'ON n GOSUB'
1F9E CF	RST	---	Test for GOTO token
1F9F 8D	ADC	---	DC '8D' - GOTO token

```
1F6C  *  *********************************************************

1F70  *  *********************************************************




1F7F  :  HL was saved in 1B2A

1F83  :  DE = position in current line




1F95  *  *********************************************************
```

```
1FA0  2B      DEC       --- Backspace code string pointer to GOTO token
1FA1  4B      LD        --- C = n value from ON n
1FA2  0D      DEC       <--: Decrement n
1FA3  78      LD          . : A = GOSUB or GOTO token
1FA4  CA601D  JP          . : We have skipped n lines rtn to execution driver
1FA7  CD5B1E  CALL        . : Get line no. to GOTO into DE as a binary number
1FAA  FE2C    CP          . : Look for comma following line number else it's
1FAC  C0      RET         . : Return if no comma                 : end of stmnt
1FAD  18F3    JR        --->: Loop till n line numbers have been skipped
1FAF  11F240  LD        --- Get addr of error flag ****** RESUME routine ****
1FB2  1A      LD        --- Load error flag (FF if error, zero otherwise)
1FB3  B7      OR        --- Set status flag
1FB4  CAA019  JP        --- Error if resume executed w/o error
1FB7  3C      INC       --- Set error flag to zero
1FB8  329A40  LD        --- Save it
1FBB  12      LD        --- Reset error flag
1FBC  7E      LD        --- Get next element from code string
1FBD  FE87    CP        --- Test for NEXT token
1FBF  280C    JR        --->: Jump if 'RESUME NEXT'
1FC1  CD5A1E  CALL      -- : Get binary equiv. of line no. into DE
1FC4  C0      RET       -- : Rtn to EXECUTION DRIVER if no line number
1FC5  7A      LD        -- : Combine LSB and MSB of
1FC6  B3      OR        -- : line number and test for 0
1FC7  C2C51E  JP        -- : Continue at GOTO if RESUME XXXX
1FCA  3C      INC       -- : Else RESUME 0. Set A = 1 to signal resume 0
1FCB  1802    JR        ----:>: Jmp to RESUME 0 code
1FCD  D7      RST       <--: : RESUME NEXT test for multiple stmnt
1FCE  C0      RET       --    : Rtn to execution driver if :, else fall thru
1FCF  2AEE40  LD        <----: to get addr. of    cont--> **** RESUME 0 *****
1FD2  EB      EX        --- Save in DE
1FD3  2AEA40  LD        --- 40EA = line no. of statement following error
1FD6  22A240  LD        --- Which is where we will resume execution
1FD9  EB      EX        --- Restore addr. of current pos. in line    cont-->
1FDA  C0      RET       --- Go to EXECUTION DRIVER if RESUME 0
1FDB  7E      LD        --- Else, we have a RESUME NEXT
1FDC  B7      OR        --- Test for end of line
1FDD  2004    JR        --->: Jmp if not end of line
1FDF  23      INC       -- : End of line, skip over zero byte terminator
1FE0  23      INC       -- : Skip over
1FE1  23      INC       -- : Pointer to next statement
1FE2  23      INC       -- : Skip over line number in binary for
1FE3  23      INC       <--: line following error
1FE4  7A      LD        --- DE = line no. of stmnt following error
1FE5  A3      AND       --- Test for end of program
1FE6  3C      INC       --- Gives 0 if end of program
1FE7  C2051F  JP        --- Not end of pgm. Skip to end of line w/error &
1FEA  3ADD40  LD        --- Get INPUT PHASE entered flag          :continue
1FED  3D      DEC       --- Test for INPUT PHASE started
1FEE  CABE1D  JP        --- Not started - Go to it
1FF1  C3051F  JP        --- Skip to end of statement before returning
1FF4  CD1C2B  CALL      --- ERROR routine **** Evaluate n if ERROR n *********
1FF7  C0      RET       --- Rtn if not end of statement
1FF8  B7      OR        --- Set status flags for error no.
1FF9  CA4A1E  JP        --- FC error if n is zero
1FFC  3D      DEC       --- n = n - 1
1FFD  87      ADD       --- n = 2 (n - 1)
1FFE  5F      LD        --- Save doubled error no. in E
1FFF  FE2D    CP        --- Compare with 45(base 10)
2001  3802    JR        --- Jmp if error no. in range ( < +45)
2003  1E26    LD        --- UE error code
```

227

```
1FAF * ************************************************************

1FCF * curr pos. in line w/error ********************************

1FD9 : w/error in case we rtn to execution driver

1FF4 * ************************************************************
```

```
2005 C3A219    JP      --- Output error message
2008 110A00    LD      --- AUTO routine ** Default starting line no. is 10 *
200B D5        PUSH    --- Save starting line number
200C 2817      JR      --- No parameters specified, use defaults
200E CD4F1E    CALL    --- Convert 1st parameter from ASCII to binary
2011 EB        EX      --- Save user specified starting line in HL
2012 E3        EX      --- Then exchange it with 10 on the stack
2013 2811      JR      --- Jmp if only one parameter specified
2015 EB        EX      --- DE = 10
2016 CF        RST     --- Test for comma following 1st parameter
2017 2C        INC     --- DC 2C ',' comma
2018 EB        EX      --- DE = current code stmnt addr
2019 2AE440    LD      --- HL = previous auto increment value
201C EB        EX      --- DE = previous value, HL = code string addr
201D 2806      JR      --- Jmp if no 2nd parameter
201F CD5A1E    CALL    --- Convert 2nd parameter - increment value
2022 C29719    JP      --- SN error if NZ
2025 EB        EX      --- HL = auto increment value
2026 7C        LD      --- Test auto increment
2027 B5        OR      --- for zero
2028 CA4A1E    JP      --- FC error if Z
202B 22E440    LD      --- Auto increment
202E 32E140    LD      --- Set auto increment flag for BASIC
2031 E1        POP     --- HL = starting line number
2032 22E240    LD      --- Current input line number
2035 C1        POP     --- Clear stack
2036 C3331A    JP      --- Rtn to INPUT PHASE
2039 CD3723    CALL    --- Evaluate expression *************** IF **********
203C 7E        LD      --- Was element following
203D FE2C      CP      --- Expression a comma
203F CC781D    CALL    --- Yes, get next element
2042 FECA      CP      --- And test for 'THEN token
2044 CC781D    CALL    --- If 'THEN' token skip ahead so backspace below will
2047 2B        DEC     --- leave us positioned at THEN token, else it leaves
2048 E5        PUSH    --- us positioned at element following expression
2049 CD9409    CALL    --- Test for true/false condition
204C E1        POP     --- Restore addr of current position in stmnt
204D 2807      JR      --->: If zero expression was false, look for ELSE or
204F D7        RST     <---:---: end of line. Examine next element in code
2050 DAC21E    JP      --  :     : If numeric must be GOTO address  :stmt string
2053 C35F1D    JP      --  :     : Rtn to execution driver to evaluate rest of
2056 1601      LD      <---:     : Count times to scan to end of line * cont ->
2058 CD051F    CALL    <---:     : Scan to end of line
205B B7        OR       .  :     : A = stop scan value
205C C8        RET      .  :     : Rtn to BASIC if end of line
205D D7        RST      .  :     : Get next element
205E FE95      CP       .  :     : And test for ELSE token
2060 20F6      JR      --->:     : If not ELSE token scan again
2062 15        DEC      .  :     : Match IF's and ELSE's
2063 20F3      JR      --->:     : Loop till all ELSE's passed
2065 18E8      JR      ------->: Execute remainder of statement
2067 3E01      LD      --- A=device code for printer *** LPRINT routine   ****
2069 329C40    LD      --- Save in current device type loc.
206C C39B20    JP      --- Go analyze rest of statement
206F CDCA41    CALL    --- DOS Exit (JP 5A15) ******************** PRINT@ **
2072 FE40      CP      --- Test next element for @ token
2074 2019      JR      --- Jump if not PRINT@
2076 CD012B    CALL    --- Evaluate @ expression.*** PRINT@ routine *********
2079 FE04      CP      --- A = MSB  test for @ value > 1023
207B D24A1E    JP      --- FC error if @ position > 1023
```

```
2008 * **********************************************************

2039 * ************************************************************

2056 * False path of IF statement *********************************

2067 * ************************************************************

206F * ************************************************************

2076 * ************************************************************
```

207E	E5	PUSH	--- Stack = current code string addr
207F	21003C	LD	--- HL = Display area ptr
2082	19	ADD	--- HL = start of display area + @ position
2083	222040	LD	--- Store cursor position in display DCB
2086	7B	LD	--- E = position within line
2087	E63F	AND	--- Not to exceed 63 and save it as
2089	32A640	LD	--- Update cursor offset
208C	E1	POP	--- Restore code string addr (pointer to item list)
208D	CF	RST	--- Make sure a , follows @ expression
208E	2C	INC	--- DC 2C ','
208F	FE23	CP	--- Look for # token
2091	2008	JR	--- Jmp if not PRINT#
2093	CD8402	CALL	--- Analyze rest of string ****** PRINT # ** cont--> *
2096	3E80	LD	--- Set write to cassette flag
2098	329C40	LD	--- Cassette flag (= -1)
209B	2B	DEC	--- Backspace over previous symbol in input stream ***
209C	D7	RST	--- Re-examine next char in input stream
209D	CCFE20	CALL	--- If zero print a CR (end of statement) cont-->
20A0	CA6921	JP	--- Write sync bytes if PRINT, clear output
20A3	FEBF	CP	--- Device flag (409C), and rtn to execution
20A5	CABD2C	JP	--- Jump if print using :driver
20A8	FEBC	CP	--- Test for TAB token
20AA	CA3721	JP	--- Jump if print tab
20AD	E5	PUSH	--- Print item list ************* PRINT # ** cont--> *
20AE	FE2C	CP	--- Test for comma
20B0	CA0821	JP	--- If comma, get next item
20B3	FE3B	CP	--- Test for semi-colon
20B5	CA6421	JP	--- If semicolon
20B8	C1	POP	--- BC = current addr in input stream
20B9	CD3723	CALL	--- Get addr or value of next item to be printed
20BC	E5	PUSH	--- Save addr of terminal symbol
20BD	E7	RST	--- Determine data type
20BE	2832	JR	--- If string
20C0	CDBD0F	CALL	--- Convert binary to ASCII and move to print buffer
20C3	CD6528	CALL	--- Build a literal string pool entry for ASCII number
20C6	CDCD41	CALL	--- DOS Exit (JP 5B9A)
20C9	2A2141	LD	--- HL = addr of current print string
20CC	3A9C40	LD	--- A = output device flag
20CF	B7	OR	--- Test device type flag
20D0	FAE920	JP	--- Jmp if writing to cassette (PRINT#)
20D3	2808	JR	--- Jmp if not LPRINT
20D5	3A9B40	LD	--- A = current line position *** LPRINT continued ***
20D8	86	ADD	--- Add no. chars in new line
20D9	FE84	CP	--- and test for line overflow
20DB	1809	JR	--- Go test results of comparison
20DD	3A9D40	LD	--- Get size of display line *** PRINT ITEM continued '
20E0	47	LD	--- Move it to B so we can compare it
20E1	3AA640	LD	--- Get cursor offset for current line
20E4	86	ADD	--- Add length of new line and
20E5	B8	CP	-- compare to maximum line size :line
20E6	D4FE20	CALL	--- If NC, new line will overflow buffer. Skip to new
20E9	CDAA28	CALL	--- Write line to ****** PRINT# continued ** cont--> *
20EC	3E20	LD	--- A = ASCII space
20EE	CD2A03	CALL	--- Print a space. Rtn w/a non-zero
20F1	B7	OR	--- Set status flags
20F2	CCAA28	CALL	--- If current data type is string, write it output
20F5	E1	POP	--- Restore current code string addr to HL :device
20F6	C39B20	JP	--- and loop till end of statement (E05)
20F9	3AA640	LD	--- A = cursor offset from current line **** cont--> *
20FC	B7	OR	--- Set status flags

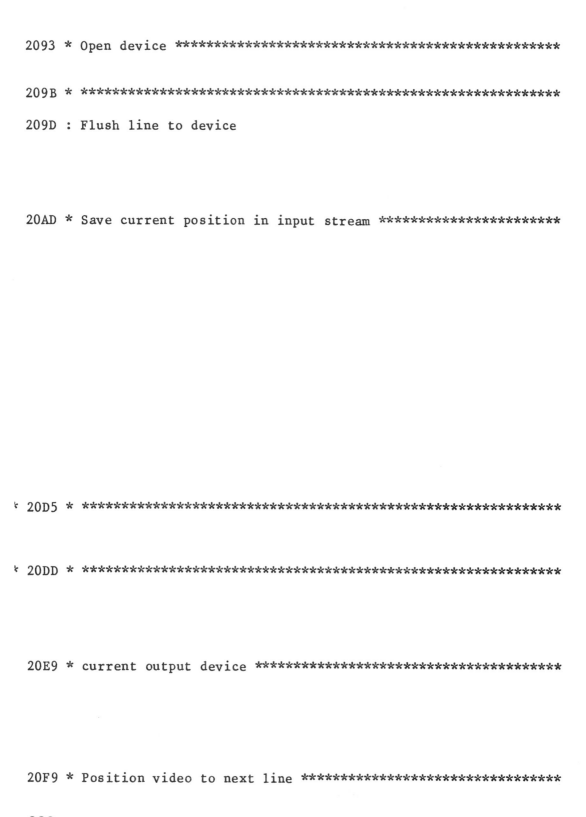

```
2093  * Open device  ***********************************************

209B  * ***********************************************************
209D  : Flush line to device




20AD  * Save current position in input stream ***********************




20D5  * ************************************************************


20DD  * ************************************************************




20E9  * current output device **************************************




20F9  * Position video to next line ********************************
```

20FD	C8	RET	--- Exit if at start of a line
20FE	3E0D	LD	--- Else skip to next line
2100	CD2A03	CALL	--- Call video driver
2103	CDD041	CALL	--- DOS exit (JP 5B99)
2106	AF	XOR	--- Clear A-reg status flags/carry flag
2107	C9	RET	--- Rtn to caller
2108	CDD341	CALL	--- DOS Exit (JP 5B65) ****** PRINT on cassette ******
210B	3A9C40	LD	--- Get current output device
210E	B7	OR	--- and test for type
210F	F21921	JP	--- Jmp if current device not cassette
2112	3E2C	LD	--- A = ASCII comma
2114	CD2A03	CALL	--- Print comma on printer or display
2117	184B	JR	--- Go fetch next char from code string
2119	2808	JR	--- Jmp if current device is video display ***********
211B	3A9B40	LD	--- Device is printer. Get current print pos in A
211E	FE70	CP	--- Compare print pos to 112
2120	C32B21	JP	--- Go test if time for line skip
2123	3A9E40	LD	--- A = line size **********************************
2126	47	LD	--- Save in B
2127	3AA640	LD	--- A = current pos in line
212A	B8	CP	--- Test if room in this line. Subtract cont-->
212B	D4FE20	CALL	--- No, issue a line skip. We are at end of line
212E	3034	JR	--- Jmp if end of line marked
2130	D610	SUB	--- Test for at least 10 print positions left
2132	30FC	JR	--- Loop till positions to within 10 spaces of end of
2134	2F	CPL	--- Gives - number of blanks to print :line
2135	1823	JR	--- Go print blanks
2137	CD1B2B	CALL	--- Get TAB no., * PRINT TAB processing **** cont--> *
213A	E63F	AND	--- Results in A. Do not let it exceed 63
213C	5F	LD	--- Save TAB value in B
213D	CF	RST	--- Look for closing paren
213E	29	ADD	--- DC ´,´
213F	2B	DEC	--- Reposition code string printer to (
2140	E5	PUSH	--- and save addr on stack
2141	CDD341	CALL	--- DOS Exit (JP 5B65)
2144	3A9C40	LD	--- A = output device type code
2147	B7	OR	--- Test device type code
2148	FA4A1E	JP	--- FC error if negative (tape)
214B	CA5321	JP	-->: Jmp if output device video
214E	3A9B40	LD	-- : A = print position in current line
2151	1803	JR	---:->: Skip reload of A register
2153	3AA640	LD	<--: : A = cursor position in current video line
2156	2F	CPL	<-----: A = -current position
2157	83	ADD	--- A = -current position + tab
2158	300A	JR	-->: Jmp if tab less than current position
215A	3C	INC	-- : A = number of blanks to print
215B	47	LD	-- : B = count of blanks to print
215C	3E20	LD	-- : A = ASCII blank
215E	CD2A03	CALL	<-: : Print a blank
2161	05	DEC	. : : Count it
2162	20FA	JR	->: : Loop till B blanks printed
2164	E1	POP	<---: Restore position in input string
2165	D7	RST	--- Examine next character
2166	C3A020	JP	--- Process rest of PRINT TAB statement
2169	3A9C40	LD	--- A = device type code ****************** cont--> *
216C	B7	OR	--- Test for cassette
216D	FCF801	CALL	--- Turn off cassette
2170	AF	XOR	--- Clear A and status flags
2171	329C40	LD	--- and reset current device code to display
2174	CDBE41	CALL	--- DOS Exit (JP 577C)

233

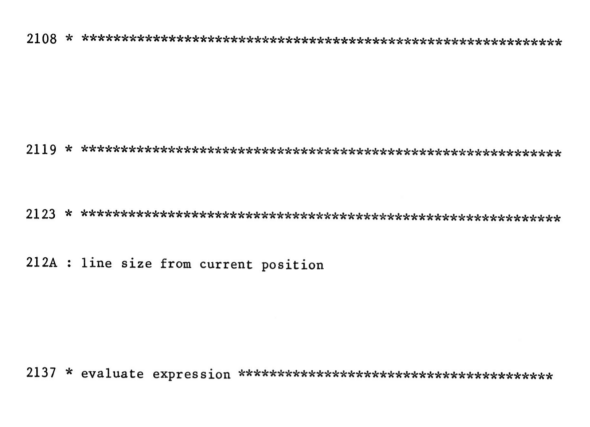

```
2108 * **********************************************************

2119 * **********************************************************

2123 * **********************************************************

212A : line size from current position

2137 * evaluate expression ***************************************

2169 * Turn off cassette annd reset current device to video *******
```

2177 C9	RET	---	Rtn to caller
2178 3F	CCF	---	? ************** REDO error message *************
2179 52	LD	---	R
217A 45	LD	---	E
217B 44	LD	---	D
217C 4F	LD	---	O
217D 0D	DEC	---	Carriage return
217E 00	NOP	---	Message terminator
217F 3ADE40	LD	---	Get read flag *********************** cont--> *
2182 B7	OR	---	Set status flags
2183 C29119	JP	---	SN error in NNN if READ active
2186 3AA940	LD	---	Get type of input flag
2189 B7	OR	---	Test for zero
218A 1E2A	LD	---	FD error code
218C CAA219	JP	---	Output FD error message if cassette input
218F C1	POP	---	Clear the stack
2190 217821	LD	---	Addr of REDO message
2193 CDA728	CALL	---	Output REDO message
2196 2AE640	LD	---	Restore code string addr
2199 C9	RET	---	Rtn to caller
219A CD2828	CALL	---	Check for illegal direct ***** INPUT routine *****
219D 7E	LD	---	(Input without line number)
219E CDD641	CALL	---	DOS Exit (JP 5784)
21A1 D623	SUB	---	Check for unit designation #
21A3 32A940	LD	---	40A9 = 0 if INPUT #
21A6 7E	LD	---	A = next element from code string
21A7 2020	JR	--->:	Jmp if INPUT from console device
21A9 CD9302	CALL	-- :	Find leader and sync bytes
21AC E5	PUSH	-- :	Save code string address
21AD 06FA	LD	-- :	B = max no. of bytes to read (250)
21AF 2AA740	LD	-- :	HL = input area ptr
21B2 CD3502	CALL	<-: :	Read 1 byte from tape
21B5 77	LD	. : :	Save byte just read
21B6 23	INC	. : :	Bump to next location in buffer
21B7 FE0D	CP	. : :	Read into buffer until CR
21B9 2802	JR	. : :	Jmp if CR encountered
21BB 10F5	DJNZ	->: :	Or loop till 250 bytes read
21BD 2B	DEC	-- :	Position to last place in buffer
21BE 3600	LD	-- :	Put a 00H at end and
21C0 CDF801	CALL	-- :	Turn off tape
21C3 2AA740	LD	-- :	Input buffer addr to HL
21C6 2B	DEC	-- :	Backspace one byte
21C7 1822	JR	-- :	And store a comma there so we cont-->
21C9 01DB21	LD	<---:	Continuation addr of 21BD *********** note--> *
21CC C5	PUSH	---	to stack
21CD FE22	CP	---	Look for quote
21CF C0	RET	---	Jump to 21DB if not text in input statement
21D0 CD6628	CALL	---	Quote (text in input statement) cont-->
21D3 CF	RST	---	Look for a trailing semi-colon
21D4 3B	DEC	---	DC = ´,´
21D5 E5	PUSH	---	Save code string addr
21D6 CDAA28	CALL	---	Write prompting message
21D9 E1	POP	---	Restore code string addr
21DA C9	RET	---	Go to 21DB
21DB E5	PUSH	---	Save code string address **********************
21DC CDB31B	CALL	---	Print ´? ´ and accept input on exit cont-->
21DF C1	POP	---	BC = code string addr
21E0 DABE1D	JP	---	Jmp if BREAK key entered
21E3 23	INC	---	Position to first byte of data in buffer
21E4 7E	LD	---	Fetch 1st data byte

2178 * **

217F * Output read/input error messages ***************************

219A * ***

21C7 : can use READ processing
21C9 * INPUT item list ***

21D0 : Build lit. string pool entry for quote.

21DB * ***
21DC : HL = buffer addr −1

21E5	B7	OR	--- Set status flags
21E6	2B	DEC	--- Backspace to buffer orgin -1
21E7	C5	PUSH	--- Save code string addr
21E8	CA041F	JP	--- If 1st data char is binary zeroes, cont-->
21EB	362C	LD	--- Make READ think we are at end of a value in a
21ED	1805	JR	--- DATA statement
21EF	E5	PUSH	--- Save current pos in PST ********* READ routine ***
21F0	2AFF40	LD	--- HL = starting addr of data stmnt
21F3	F6AF	OR	--- 21F4 XOR A - Zero A - Signal INPUT, non-zero
21F5	32DE40	LD	--- Not 00 if read :signal READ
21F8	E3	EX	--- 00 if input HL = rtn addr, stack = DATA addr
21F9	1802	JR	--->:Join common code
21FB	CF	RST	-- : Test for a comma
21FC	2C	INC	-- : 21FC: DC 2C ´,´
21FD	CD0D26	CALL	<--: Get address of current variable into DE
2200	E3	EX	--- Pop pointer to current location in data statement
2201	D5	PUSH	--- Replace it w/ addr of variable
2202	7E	LD	--- Get next char from data statement
2203	FE2C	CP	--- Test for terminal comma
2205	2826	JR	--->: Jump if comma
2207	3ADE40	LD	-- : A = read flag
220A	B7	OR	-- : Test if READ or INPUT processing
220B	C29622	JP	-- : Jmp if READ - go find next DATA statement
220E	3AA940	LD	-- : Test whether or not a unit
2211	B7	OR	-- : Number was specified in INPUT call
2212	1E06	LD	-- : OD error - no unit no. given in call
2214	CAA219	JP	-- : Output OD mesage if no unit specified
2217	3E3F	LD	-- : Print ´?´ sequence error in data cont-->
2219	CD2A03	CALL	-- : Print ´ ´ and accept input
221C	CDB31B	CALL	-- : Accept input from keyboard. Buffer addr -1 in HL
221F	D1	POP	-- : DE = address of next variable
2220	C1	POP	-- : BC = addr of next element in code string
2221	DABE1D	JP	-- : Jmp if BREAK key during input
2224	23	INC	-- : Position to first data byte in buffer
2225	7E	LD	-- : Fetch 1st data byte
2226	B7	OR	-- : Set status flags
2227	2B	DEC	-- : Backspace buffer pointer to buffer orgin -1
2228	C5	PUSH	-- : Save code string address
2229	CA041F	JP	-- : No data in buffer skip to end of cont-->
222C	D5	PUSH	-- : Save addr of variable
222D	CDDC41	CALL	<--: DOS Exit (JP 5E63)
2230	E7	RST	--- Test data type
2231	F5	PUSH	--- Save status from data type test
2232	2019	JR	--- Go convert data to binary, SP, or DP
2234	D7	RST	--- Else we have string data. Examine next char in
2235	57	LD	--- DATA statement
2236	47	LD	--- Save nest char in B, D
2237	FE22	CP	--- Test for quote
2239	2805	JR	--- Jmp if its a quote - string data
223B	163A	LD	--- Else scan DATA statement looking
223D	062C	LD	--- for a : or , and build a literal
223F	2B	DEC	--- string pool entry for it
2240	CD6928	CALL	--- Create a literal string pool entry for DATA string
2243	F1	POP	--- A = flag for destination data type
2244	EB	EX	--- Save HL
2245	215A22	LD	--- Put continuation addr of 225A onto stack
2248	E3	EX	--- and clear stack
2249	D5	PUSH	--- Save addr of variable
224A	C3331F	JP	--- move result to target variable, continue at 225A
224D	D7	RST	--- Examine next character in DATA stream ** cont--> *

21EB : skip to end of line & rtn to BASIC

21EF * ***

2217 : while processing INPUT stmnt

2229 : this line & rtn to BASIC

224D * Convert next value in DATA stmnt from ASCII to binary *******M

238

224E	F1	POP	--- Reload flags from data type test
224F	F5	PUSH	--- and resave. Push rtn addr of 2243 onto stack
2250	014322	LD	--- to be returned to following DATA conversion
2253	C5	PUSH	--- 2243 to stk
2254	DA6C0E	JP	--- Go convert ASCII to binary - not DP
2257	D2650E	JP	--- Go convert ASCII to binary - DP
225A	2B	DEC	--- Backspace one character in DATA stmnt ************
225B	D7	RST	--- Examine terminating character
225C	2805	JR	--->: Jmp if end of line
225E	FE2C	CP	--- : Not end of line, tet for a comma
2260	C27F21	JP	<---: If not a comma go output error message
2263	E3	EX	--- HL = next byte in read stmnt, stack = next in DATA
2264	2B	DEC	--- Backspace over terminal character :stmnt
2265	D7	RST	--- and reexamine it. If non-zero it must be a
2266	C2FB21	JP	--- comma. Go process next variable
2269	D1	POP	--- Clear stack
226A	3AA940	LD	--- Check for FD error
226D	B7	OR	--- Set status flags
226E	C8	RET	--- No error, rtn to BASIC
226F	3ADE40	LD	--- Get READ/INPUT flag
2272	B7	OR	--- Set status flags
2273	EB	EX	--- DE = code string addr
2274	C2961D	JP	--- Jmp if READ error
2277	D5	PUSH	--- Save code string addr. Test for INPUT error
2278	CDDF41	CALL	--- DOS Exit (JP 579C)
227B	B6	OR	--- Test for end of input
227C	218622	LD	--- EXTRA IGNORED message
227F	C4A728	CALL	--- Output message if not end of INPUT
2282	E1	POP	--- Restore code string addr
2283	C36921	JP	--- Turn off cassette, reset output to cont-->
2286	3F	CCF	--- EXTRA IGNORED **********************************
2287	45	LD	--- E
2288	78	LD	--- X
2289	74	LD	--- R
228A	72	LD	--- T
228B	61	LD	--- A
228C	2069	JR	--- Space I
228E	67	LD	--- G
228F	6E	LD	--- N
2290	6F	LD	--- O
2291	72	LD	--- R
2292	65	LD	--- E
2293	64	LD	--- D
2294	0D	DEC	--- CR
2295	00	NOP	--- Message terminator
2296	CD051F	CALL	--- Search for next data statement *** Call DATA *****
2299	B7	OR	--- Scan to end of current DATA line
229A	2012	JR	--- Jmp if : terminated line
229C	23	INC	--- Skip over address of next BASIC statement
229D	7E	LD	--- Get line number for next
229E	23	INC	--- statement. If its zero, then we've reached
229F	B6	OR	--- the end of the program
22A0	1E06	LD	--- OD error if end of program reached before next
22A2	CAA219	JP	--- data statement found
22A5	23	INC	--- Bump to line no. this line
22A6	5E	LD	--- and load it into DE
22A7	23	INC	--- Bump to MSB of line no.
22A8	56	LD	--- DE = binary line no. this statement
22A9	EB	EX	--- HL = code string for DATA statement
22AA	22DA40	LD	--- Save binary line no. of DATA statement

```
225A * ************************************************************
```

```
2283 : video & ret to BASIC
2286 * ************************************************************
```

```
2296 * ************************************************************
```

```
25F2 C5         PUSH  BC         --- Save rtn addr on stack
25F3 FE46       CP    46H        --- Is token an 'OR'
25F5 2006       JR    NZ,25FDH   --->: No, jmp to comparison routine
25F7 7B         LD    A,E        --  : Comp DE with HL. Result in HL
25F8 B5         OR    L          --  : Comp E and L. Result in L
25F9 6F         LD    L,A        --  : Restore L
25FA 7C         LD    A,H        --  : Comp H and D. Result left in A. Will be moved
25FB B2         OR    D          --  : to H at 27FFA
25FC C9         RET              --- : Go to 27FA. Convert result to integer. Rtn to
25FD 7B         LD    A,E        <---: Logical comp DE with HL. Result in HL.    :2346
25FE A5         AND   L          --- And E and L
25FF 6F         LD    L,A        --- Result to L
2600 7C         LD    A,H        --- Load H so we can                    : H at 27FA
2601 A2         AND   D          --- Comp D with H. Result left in A will be moved to
2602 C9         RET              --- Goto 27FA. Make result an integer. Rtn to 2346
2603 2B         DEC   HL         --- Backspace code string pointer ********************
2604 D7         RST   10H        --- Re-evaluate last symbol
2605 C8         RET   Z          --- Exit if end of statement
2606 CF         RST   08H        --- Test next char for single quote
2607 2C         INC   L          --- 2607: DC 2C   single quote
2608 010326     LD    BC,2603H   --- Locate addr of a variable ** Force rtn to 2603 **
260B C5         PUSH  BC         --- 260C : OR AF    Set create mode
260C F6AF       OR    0AFH       --- 260D : XOR A    Zero A, set 40AE = locate
260E 32AE40     LD    (40AEH),A  --- Set 40AE = locate/create mode
2611 46         LD    B,(HL)     --- Save 1st char of variable name
2612 CD3D1E     CALL  1E3DH      --- Check for letter
2615 DA9719     JP    C,1997H    --- SN error if C (not a letter in (HL)      cont-->
2618 AF         XOR   A          --- Clear A and C
2619 4F         LD    C,A        --- Zeros C
261A D7         RST   10H        --- Get next char in input string
261B 3805       JR    C,2622H    ----->: Jump if numeric
261D CD3D1E     CALL  1E3DH      --     : Test for alpha-numeric. Set CARRY if false
2620 3809       JR    C,262BH    --->: : Jump if not a letter. Error if      cont-->
2622 4F         LD    C,A        <---:-: 2nd char of name to C
2623 D7         RST   10H        <-- : Test symbol following 2nd char until a non-
2624 38FD       JR    C,2623H    -->:: numeric symbol is found,               cont-->
2626 CD3D1E     CALL  1E3DH      -- :: Test for letter
2629 30F8       JR    NC,2623H   -->:: Jmp if a letter
262B 115226     LD    DE,2652H   <---: We are now positioned at end of      cont-->
262E D5         PUSH  DE         --- Place 2652H return address on stack
262F 1602       LD    D,02H      --- Test char  following name for %
2631 FE25       CP    25H        --- If so, set D to data type 2
2633 C8         RET   Z          --- Return (jump 2652H) if % (INT) : D = 2
2634 14         INC   D          --- Ret D to 3 in case variable is a string
2635 FE24       CP    24H        --- Test for $ following variable name
2637 C8         RET   Z          --- Return if $ (STR) : D = 3
2638 14         INC   D          --- Ret D to 4 in case variable is SP
2639 FE21       CP    21H        --- Test for ! following variable name
263B C8         RET   Z          --- Return if ! (SNG) : D = 4
263C 1608       LD    D,08H      --- Ret D to 8 in case variable is DP
263E FE23       CP    23H        --- Test for # following variable name
2640 C8         RET   Z          --- Return if # (DBL) : D = 8          cont-->
2641 78         LD    A,B        --- Refetch first char of symbol
2642 D641       SUB   41H        --- Convert from alpha to numeric (0-26)
2644 E67F       AND   7FH        --- Clear possible sign bit
2646 5F         LD    E,A        --- E = 0(A) thru 26(Z)
2647 1600       LD    D,00H      --- DE = 0 (A) thru 26(base 10) (Z)
2649 E5         PUSH  HL         --- Save current position in input stream
264A 210141     LD    HL,4101H   --- Start of data type table
264D 19         ADD   HL,DE      --- Add value of first char of var name (0=A,...26=Z)
```

2603 * ***

2608 * ***

2615 : Variable name does not start with a letter.

2620 : not a letter, or digit, or (

2624 : jmp if char is numeric

262B : variable name. Only 1st two characters are used.

2640 : Variable name was not followed by type suffix. Use 1st char
     : of var name to determine data type.

Address	Opcode	Instr	Comment
264E	56	LD	--- Get data type
264F	E1	POP	--- Restore pointer to current pos in input stream
2650	2B	DEC	--- Backspace 1 position
2651	C9	RET	--- Return with data type in D (Go to 2652)
2652	7A	LD	--- D = data type continuation of locating * cont-->
2653	32AF40	LD	--- Save data type flag
2656	D7	RST	--- Get next char of variable name (call 1D78)
2657	3ADC40	LD	--- Get 'FOR' statement flag
265A	B7	OR	--- Test it
265B	C26426	JP	--->: Jmp if processing 'FOR' statement
265E	7E	LD	-- : Refetch next element from code string
265F	D628	SUB	-- : Compare with a (
2661	CAE926	JP	-- : Jump if '(' (subscripted variable)
2664	AF	XOR	<---: Zero A-reg
2665	32DC40	LD	--- Flag as non-subscripted
2668	E5	PUSH	--- HL = current position in input string
2669	D5	PUSH	--- Save data type flag
266A	2AF940	LD	--- HL = end of pgm ptr = start of simple var list
266D	EB	EX	<-----: DE = addr of a simple variable
266E	2AFB40	LD	. : Start of arrays pointer
2671	DF	RST	. : Compare addr of next simple cont-->
2672	E1	POP	. : HL = data type flag
2673	2819	JR	-----:>: Variable not currently defined
2675	1A	LD	. : : Get type for current variable
2676	6F	LD	. : : Save in L
2677	BC	CP	. : : Compare type
2678	13	INC	. : : Bump to 2nd char of name for this entry
2679	200B	JR	--->: : : Types do not match. Skip to next var in list
267B	1A	LD	. : : : Type matches, compare 2nd char of name from
267C	B9	CP	. : : : VLT w/2nd char of name in BC
267D	2007	JR	. : : : No match, go find next entry in VLT
267F	13	INC	. : : : 2nd char matches, compare 1st char of name
2680	1A	LD	. : : : after bumping to 1st char of name
2681	B8	CP	. : : : Test if first char of names are equal
2682	CACC26	JP	. : : : We have found the addr of a simple var, exit
2685	3E13	LD	<--: : : 2686: INC DE Bump to next entry in simple
2687	13	INC	. : : variable list
2688	E5	PUSH	. : : Save data type flag so it can be reloaded
2689	2600	LD	. : : at 2672
268B	19	ADD	. : : Bump to next entry in list
268C	18DF	JR	----->: : Continue searching for variable name
268E	7C	LD	<-------: Save type
268F	E1	POP	--- Clear stack, HL = current position in input string
2690	E3	EX	--- HL = return addr Stk = current position in input
2691	F5	PUSH	--- A = type :string
2692	D5	PUSH	--- DE = start of arrays ptr
2693	11F124	LD	--- Addr of VARPTR locator
2696	DF	RST	--- Were we called from VARPTR?
2697	2836	JR	--- Yes, jmp to 26CF
2699	114325	LD	--- DE = addr of find addr of variable routine
269C	DF	RST	--- Were we called from find addr of variable?
269D	D1	POP	--- Remove start of arrays ptr from stk
269E	2835	JR	--- Called while evaluating a subscipt cont-->
26A0	F1	POP	--- Clear stack, A = type
26A1	E3	EX	--- HL = current position in input string.
26A2	E5	PUSH	--- Stack = Return addr
26A3	C5	PUSH	--- Place BC (1st char/2nd char of name) on stk
26A4	4F	LD	--- followed by ret addr
26A5	0600	LD	--- Clear B for computations
26A7	C5	PUSH	--- Save 00/type. Now create a new entry in cont-->

2652 * a variable name **

2671 : variable to start of array list

269E : This is the first reference to a simple variable. Define it.

26A7 : free space list for current variable.

260

26A8	03	INC	--- B = 00, C = type
26A9	03	INC	--- Gives type +02
26AA	03	INC	--- Gives type +03 = 3 bytes ovrhd + spare for var
26AB	2AFD40	LD	--- Load start of free memory ptr (fmp)
26AE	E5	PUSH	--- Save free mem ptr
26AF	09	ADD	--- Free mem ptr + type(length) yields new fmp
26B0	C1	POP	--- BC = old free mem ptr
26B1	E5	PUSH	--- Save new free mem ptr
26B2	CD5519	CALL	--- Move array list down. Add value to simple
26B5	E1	POP	--- variable list
26B6	22FD40	LD	--- Save new free mem ptr (it's official)
26B9	60	LD	--- HL = old fmp = 1st byte of new entry
26BA	69	LD	--- L = LSB byte of fmp
26BB	22FB40	LD	--- New start of arrays pointer
26BE	2B	DEC	<---: Zero out new entry. All space between the new
26BF	3600	LD	. : free memory pointer and the start of arrays ptr
26C1	DF	RST	. : have we reached the end of the list
26C2	20FA	JR	--->: No, loop
26C4	D1	POP	--- Get length (type)
26C5	73	LD	--- And store as first word in new entry
26C6	23	INC	--- Bump to next location of entry
26C7	D1	POP	--- Get 2nd char of name and store as 2nd word of
26C8	73	LD	--- entry
26C9	23	INC	--- Bump to 3rd byte of entry
26CA	72	LD	--- And now 1st char of name
26CB	EB	EX	--- DE = addr of start of value in entry
26CC	13	INC	--- Leave addr of variable name in DE
26CD	E1	POP	--- Clear stack before exiting
26CE	C9	RET	--- Return to caller
26CF	57	LD	--- DE = type/type *********************************
26D0	5F	LD	--- E = type
26D1	F1	POP	--- Clear stack
26D2	F1	POP	--- Clear stack
26D3	E3	EX	--- Return addr to stk. Code string addr to HL
26D4	C9	RET	--- Rtn to VARPTR routine
26D5	322441	LD	--- Zero WRA1 ********* Locate subscripted variable **
26D8	C1	POP	--- Clear stack
26D9	67	LD	--- Zero H
26DA	6F	LD	--- and L
26DB	222141	LD	--- Zero string pointer in WRA1
26DE	E7	RST	--- Determine data type
26DF	2006	JR	----> Jmp if not a string
26E1	212819	LD	--- : Addr of READY message
26E4	222141	LD	--- : goes to WRA1
26E7	E1	POP	<---: Restore code string addr
26E8	C9	RET	--- Rtn to caller
26E9	E5	PUSH	--- Current pos in input string ******** see note--> *
26EA	2AAE40	LD	--- HL = 00 locate mode, <> 0 create mode
26ED	E3	EX	--- Stack = (40AE), HL = code string addr.
26EE	57	LD	--- Zero to D
26EF	D5	PUSH	--- D = 0, E = numeric value of 1st char
26F0	C5	PUSH	--- BC = 1st char/2nd char of name in ASCII
26F1	CD451E	CALL	--- Evaluate everything up to the first cont-->
26F4	C1	POP	--- BC = 1st char/2nd char of name in ASCII
26F5	F1	POP	--- A = 0
26F6	EB	EX	--- DE = current pos in input. End of cont-->
26F7	E3	EX	--- Stack = value of subscript, (40AE)
26F8	E5	PUSH	--- Save current pos in input string
26F9	EB	EX	--- HL = current pos in input string, DE = (40AE)
26FA	3C	INC	--- Increment no. of subscripts evaluated

```
26CF  *  *********************************************************


26D5  *  *********************************************************




26E9  * Locate addr of suscripted var ** On entry: D=type, B=1st char
       :                                      C = 2nd char of name,
       :                                      HL = current pos in input
       :                                      string

26F1  : ) or ,.  Result in DE (integer) value

26F6  : subscript exp.  HL = value of subscript
```

26FB	57	LD	--- And save in D
26FC	7E	LD	--- Get terminal symbol
26FD	FE2C	CP	--- Go evaluate next index if terminal symbol was a
26FF	28EE	JR	--- comma, else
2701	CF	RST	--- Test next char in input stream for ´,´
2702	29	ADD	--- 2702: DC 29 ´,´
2703	22F340	LD	--- 40F3 = addr of terminal symbol for subscript exp
2706	E1	POP	--- HL = (40AE) before subscript evaluation. Create
2707	22AE40	LD	--- and save for later use. :locate flag.
270A	D5	PUSH	--- DE = number of subscripts evaluated
270B	2AFB40	LD	--- Start of arrays pointer
270E	3E19	LD	<-------: 270F: ADD HL,DE Compute end cont-->
2710	EB	EX	. : DE = addr of next array :research
2711	2AFD40	LD	. : Load free memory ptr - upper limit for
2714	EB	EX	. : HL = arrays ptr. DE = free memory ptr
2715	DF	RST	. : Compare free mem ptr to array ptr
2716	3AAF40	LD	. : Data type/length flag
2719	2827	JR	----->: : Jmp if name not found & all arrays tested
271B	BE	CP	. : : Compare data type of an arrays entry with
271C	23	INC	. : : the type we´re looking for
271D	2008	JR	--->: : : Types don´t match. Skip to next array
271F	7E	LD	. : : : Data types match. Now look for a match on
2720	B9	CP	. : : : the 2nd character of the name.
2721	23	INC	. : : : 2nd char doesn´t match. Skip to next array
2722	2004	JR	. : : : No match, skip to next entry
2724	7E	LD	. : : : 2nd char matches.
2725	B8	CP	. : : : Test 1st char. Leave Z flag set if a match
2726	3E23	LD	<---: : : 2727:INC HL
2728	23	INC	. : : Bump to next byte in array entry
2729	5E	LD	. : : E = LSB of offset to next array
272A	23	INC	. : : Bump to next byte of array entry
272B	56	LD	. : : DE = offset to next array
272C	23	INC	. : : Bump to number of indexes entry
272D	20E0	JR	-------:>: Named array not found, examine next entry
272F	3AAE40	LD	--- : 1st char matches. We have found the addr of
2732	B7	OR	--- : the variable in the arrays list. Are we in a
2733	1E12	LD	--- : create mode?
2735	C2A219	JP	--- : Yes, then error. Symbol is doubly defined
2738	F1	POP	--- : A = number of subscripts evaluated
2739	96	SUB	--- : Compared to no. specified in DIM statement
273A	CA9527	JP	--- : Jmp if no. of indexes match
273D	1E10	LD	--- : BS error code
273F	C3A219	JP	--- : Output BS error message
2742	77	LD	<-----: Save type. Build a subscripted variable entry
2743	23	INC	--- Bump to 1st char of name (2nd actually, cont-->
2744	5F	LD	--- DE = 00/number of bytes per entry
2745	1600	LD	--- D = 00
2747	F1	POP	--- A = number of indexes
2748	71	LD	--- Save 2nd char of name
2749	23	INC	--- Bump to pos for 2nd char of name
274A	70	LD	--- Save 1st char of name
274B	23	INC	--- Bump to LSB of offset to next entry
274C	4F	LD	--- C = number of indexes
274D	CD6319	CALL	--- Compute amt of space left between HL & free mem.
2750	23	INC	--- Skip over offset entry
2751	23	INC	--- HL = pos for number of indexes in entry
2752	22D840	LD	--- 40D8 = addr of max number of indices
2755	71	LD	--- Save number of indexes for this array (1,2,or 3)
2756	23	INC	--- HL points to first subscript entry in array table
2757	3AAE40	LD	--- A = create/locate flag

270E : of arrays.   Search array for named variable

2743 : because they are stored in last/first order)

275A	17	RLA	--- Set carry flag = 0 - locate, 1 - create
275B	79	LD	--- N = no. of indexes for this array
275C	010B00	LD	<---: Default index = 10+1 if name not cont-->
275F	3002	JR	-->:: Jmp if creating because unable to locate
2761	C1	POP	. :: Else we are in create mode. Get user
2762	03	INC	. :: specified index. Add one
2763	71	LD	<--:: and save
2764	23	INC	. : in the array
2765	70	LD	. : table
2766	23	INC	. : Bump to next set of indices
2767	F5	PUSH	. : Save create/locate flag
2768	CDAA0B	CALL	. : Multiply size of index times bytes per entry.
276B	F1	POP	. : Accumulate product in DE. When done cont-->
276C	3D	DEC	. : Decrement no. of indexes multiplied
276D	20ED	JR	--->: Jmp if more indexes
276F	F5	PUSH	--- Save create/locate flag
2770	42	LD	--- B = MSB of array length
2771	4B	LD	--- BC = length of array in bytes
2772	EB	EX	--- DE = start of array - current addr in array table
2773	19	ADD	--- HL = end of array
2774	38C7	JR	--- Error, overflowed 2**16
2776	CD6C19	CALL	--- Test amt of free space, rtn if enough
2779	22FD40	LD	--- 40FD = LWA of array
277C	2B	DEC	<---: Zero array starting at
277D	3600	LD	. : end and working towards start
277F	DF	RST	. : Are we at start
2780	20FA	JR	--->: No, loop
2782	03	INC	--- BC = no. of bytes in array + 1
2783	57	LD	--- D = 0
2784	2AD840	LD	--- HL = addr of no. of indices
2787	5E	LD	--- DE = max. no. of indexes
2788	EB	EX	--- DE = addr of no. of indices. HL=max no. of indexes
2789	29	ADD	--- HL = 2 * no. of indexes
278A	09	ADD	--- HL = 2 * no. of indexes + size of array
278B	EB	EX	--- HL = no. of indexes addr
278C	2B	DEC	--- Backspace two bytes to offset address
278D	2B	DEC	--- 2nd backspace
278E	73	LD	--- Save offset to next
278F	23	INC	--- entry in arrays
2790	72	LD	--- List
2791	23	INC	--- HL = addr of no. of indexes entry
2792	F1	POP	--- Restore create/locate flag
2793	3830	JR	--- Jmp if in create mode
2795	47	LD	--- BC=0 for first pass thru loop ***** see note--> *
2796	4F	LD	--- C = 0
2797	7E	LD	--- A = no. of indexes in array
2798	23	INC	--- Bump HL to right index (max + 1)
2799	16E1	LD	--- 279A: POP HL Word addr of next index limit
279B	5E	LD	--- E = LSB of index limit
279C	23	INC	--- Bump to pos of MSB
279D	56	LD	--- D = MSB of index limit
279E	23	INC	--- HL = addr of next index limit
279F	E3	EX	--- HL = callers index value. Stk=addr of next index
27A0	F5	PUSH	--- Save number of indexes :limit
27A1	DF	RST	--- Now, compare user subscript against limit for that
27A2	D23D27	JP	--- Jmp if index greater than allowed :index
27A5	CDAA0B	CALL	--- Multiply previous subscript times max allowed
27A8	19	ADD	--- Value for current subscript. Keep sum of products
27A9	F1	POP	--- A = no. of indexes :in HL
27AA	3D	DEC	--- Count index just processed

275C : explicitly dimensioned

276B : DE = size of array in bytes

2795 * Continuation of array processing. Locate address of *******
     * subscripted variable, then load its value. Column major
     * format.

Address	Code	Instr	Comment
27AB	44	LD	--- BC = previous subscript
27AC	4D	LD	--- C = LSB
27AD	20EB	JR	--- Jmp if more indexes to go
27AF	3AAF40	LD	--- A = data type flag
27B2	44	LD	--- Now, prepare to multiply
27B3	4D	LD	--- index by size of each entry
27B4	29	ADD	--- Index * 2
27B5	D604	SUB	--- Test data type
27B7	3804	JR	--- Jump if integer or string
27B9	29	ADD	--- Neither, compute index * 4
27BA	2806	JR	--- Jmp if single precision
27BC	29	ADD	--- Index * 8, must be double precision
27BD	B7	OR	--- Set parity status flags
27BE	E2C227	JP	--- Jump if integer
27C1	09	ADD	--- Index * 3, string
27C2	C1	POP	--- BC = starting addr of array
27C3	09	ADD	--- Add index to base
27C4	EB	EX	--- DE = address of subscripted variable
27C5	2AF340	LD	--- Restore code string position
27C8	C9	RET	--- Rtn to caller
27C9	AF	XOR	--- Clear A, status flags ************ MEM routine ***
27CA	E5	PUSH	--- Save current position in pgm stmnt
27CB	32AF40	LD	--- Set current data not string so FRE will cont-->
27CE	CDD427	CALL	--- Call FRE routine - Rtn amt of free cont-->
27D1	E1	POP	--- Restore current pointer in pgm stmnt
27D2	D7	RST	--- Load next token into A
27D3	C9	RET	--- Rtn to BASIC
27D4	2AFD40	LD	--- HL = start of free memory ******** FRE routine **
27D7	EB	EX	--- DE = start of free mem ptr
27D8	210000	LD	--- clear HL so we can load CSP by adding it to HL
27DB	39	ADD	--- HL = current stack ptr
27DC	E7	RST	--- Test data type
27DD	200D	JR	---> Jump if called from MEM. Variable not a string
27DF	CDDA29	CALL	---: Get addr of string into HL
27E2	CDE628	CALL	---: Go compute amt of space remaining See note -->
27E5	2AA040	LD	---: Load boundry addr for string area
27E8	EB	EX	---: Move limit to DE
27E9	2AD640	LD	---: HL = current string area pointer
27EC	7D	LD	<--: A = LSB of one addr
27ED	93	SUB	--- Minus LSB of other addr
27EE	6F	LD	--- Restore L
27EF	7C	LD	--- H = MSB of one addr
27F0	9A	SBC	--- Minus MSB of other addr
27F1	67	LD	--- Restore H. HL = diff in addr (HL-DE)
27F2	C3660C	JP	--- Convert diff to single precsion & return
27F5	3AA640	LD	--- Load current cursor position ** POS routine **
27F8	6F	LD	--- Sae in L
27F9	AF	XOR	--- Zero A-reg, H-reg
27FA	67	LD	--- HL = cursor position (H = 00, L = Position)
27FB	C39A0A	JP	--- Value in HL to 4121. Flag as integer. Rtn to BASIC
27FE	CDA941	CALL	--- DOS Exit (JP 5679) ***************** USR routine **
2801	D7	RST	--- Get next character from input stream
2802	CD2C25	CALL	--- Evaluate the remainder of the statement. cont-->
2805	E5	PUSH	--- Save addr of next element in code string
2806	219008	LD	--- This continuation addr clears the stack before
2809	E5	PUSH	--- returning to the BASIC caller
280A	3AAF40	LD	--- A = current data type
280D	F5	PUSH	--- Save on stack
280E	FE03	CP	--- Test for string
2810	CCDA29	CALL	--- If a string, get addr into HL

```
27C9  *  *****************************************************************

27CB  :  will do simple compilation
27CE  :  space as current value


27D4  *  *****************************************************************




27E2  *  Remaining space = Current stack addr - start of free mem ptr
      *                         if variable not a string, or
      *                  = next available location in string area -
      *                         start of string area.
      *                         If variable is a string.




27F5  *  *****************************************************************



27FE  *  *****************************************************************

2802  :  Get USR number
```

2813	F1	POP	--- Restore type to A-reg
2814	EB	EX	--- DE = string addr
2815	2A8E40	LD	--- (408E) contains entry pt to USR subr
2818	E9	JP	--- Enter user assembly language subroutine
2819	E5	PUSH	--- Called by LET to convert result of ***** cont--> *
281A	E607	AND	--- A = result type
281C	21A118	LD	--- Address of arithmetic conversion routines
281F	4F	LD	--- Setup BC = 00/type where
2820	0600	LD	--- Type = 0(DP), 1(I), 2(string), 3(SP)
2822	09	ADD	--- Plus offset for result of arithmetic
2823	CD8625	CALL	--- Convert result to proper data type
2826	E1	POP	--- Restore HL
2827	C9	RET	--- Rtn
2828	E5	PUSH	--- Save code string addr * Called from INPUT routine *
2829	2AA240	LD	--- HL = current line no. in binary
282C	23	INC	--- Add 1 so a test for a DIRECT statement
282D	7C	LD	--- can be made. Line no. = FFFF
282E	B5	OR	--- while in INPUT phase
282F	E1	POP	--- Restore code string pointer
2830	C0	RET	--- Exit if line no. not zero (not a DIRECT stmnt)
2831	1E16	LD	--- Else give an ID error
2833	C3A219	JP	--- Print error and rtn to INPUT PHASE
2836	CDBD0F	CALL	--- Current value convert caller's ********* cont--> *
2839	CD6528	CALL	--- Build a literal string, pool entry cont-->
283C	CDDA29	CALL	--- Get addr of current value into HL
283F	012B2A	LD	--- Continuation addr in CHR$ routine to stack
2842	C5	PUSH	--- Put addr on stk
2843	7E	LD	--- A = length of string
2844	23	INC	--- Bump to string address
2845	E5	PUSH	--- HL = address of string pointer
2846	CDBF28	CALL	--- Test remaining string area to make sure new string
2849	E1	POP	--- will fit. Reload HL with string address
284A	4E	LD	--- C = LSB of string addr.
284B	23	INC	--- Bump to MSB :user value
284C	46	LD	--- BC = address of string for ASCII equivalent of
284D	CD5A28	CALL	--- Save length, address of string at 40D3
2850	E5	PUSH	--- HL = 40D3
2851	6F	LD	--- L = length of string
2852	CDCE29	CALL	--- Move string from BC (temp area) to DE (string data
2855	D1	POP	--- DE = 40D3 :area)
2856	C9	RET	--- Rtn to caller
2857	CDBF28	CALL	--- Make sure there's room. Get addr of **** cont--> *
285A	21D340	LD	--- HL = addr of temp storage area
285D	E5	PUSH	--- Save 40D3 on stk so it can be restored
285E	77	LD	--- Save length of string
285F	23	INC	--- Bump to position of LSB of addr
2860	73	LD	--- Save LSB of string addr
2861	23	INC	--- Bump to position of MSB of addr
2862	72	LD	--- Save MSB of string addr
2863	E1	POP	--- Restore starting addr of string control block
2864	C9	RET	--- Rtn to caller
2865	2B	DEC	--- Backspace input pointer to quote * Quote Routine *
2866	0622	LD	--- B = ASCII value for quote (')
2868	50	LD	--- D = terminating search character
2869	E5	PUSH	--- Save addr of starting quote
286A	0EFF	LD	--- Initialize counter to -1
286C	23	INC	--- Skip over quote
286D	7E	LD	--- Get a character
286E	0C	INC	--- Bump count of characters processed
286F	B7	OR	--- Set status flags

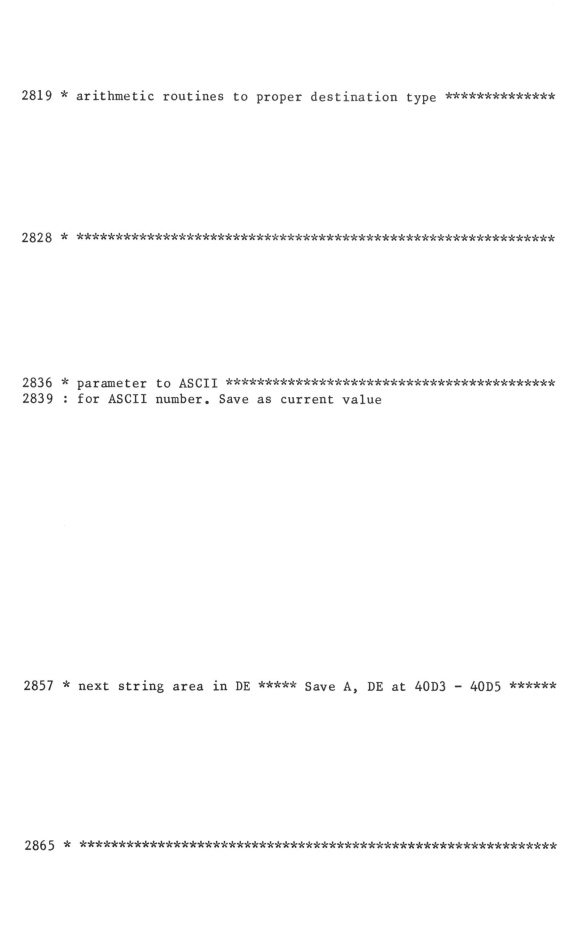

2819 * arithmetic routines to proper destination type **************

2828 * ***

2836 * parameter to ASCII **
2839 : for ASCII number. Save as current value

2857 * next string area in DE ***** Save A, DE at 40D3 - 40D5 ******

2865 * ***

2870	2806	JR	--- Jmp if EOS
2872	BA	CP	--- Test for terminating char (usually quote)
2873	2803	JR	--- Jmp if terminating character
2875	B8	CP	--- Test for second terminating character
2876	20F4	JR	--- Still not terminating character, loop till it is
2878	FE22	CP	--- Was last character a quote ?
287A	CC781D	CALL	--- If yse get following character
287D	E3	EX	--- Address of starting quote see note-->
287E	23	INC	--- Plus one gives address of first char
287F	EB	EX	--- Starting addr of char string to DE
2880	79	LD	--- A = length of string
2881	CD5A28	CALL	--- Move length, addr of string to 40D3
2884	11D340	LD	--- 40D3 = length, addr of the ********* see note-->
2887	3ED5	LD	--- string in the string data area
2889	2AB340	LD	--- HL = addr of next avail literal string entry
288C	222141	LD	--- Addr of current string val = current literal area
288F	3E03	LD	--- Current value type = string :string value
2891	32AF40	LD	--- Save in type flag byte
2894	CDD309	CALL	--- Move length string area addr to current lit.
2897	11D640	LD	--- DE = end of literal are addr to current lit.
289A	DF	RST	--- Make sure we have not overrun lit. string
289B	22B340	LD	--- pool area. Update addr of next aval lit. string
289E	E1	POP	--- Restore code string addr :pool entry
289F	7E	LD	--- A = next element of code string
28A0	C0	RET	--- Ent if temp string area not overrun
28A1	1E1E	LD	--- ST error code
28A3	C3A219	JP	--- Output ST error message
28A6	23	INC	--- Message output routine ***************************
28A7	CD6528	CALL	--- Build literal string pool entry
28AA	CDDA29	CALL	--- Get addr of current variable into HL
28AD	CDC409	CALL	--- Get length of string into D. Starting addr in BC
28B0	14	INC	--- for decrement
28B1	15	DEC	<---: Count 1 character printed
28B2	C8	RET	. : Exit if all characters printed
28B3	0A	LD	. : Character to be printed
28B4	CD2A03	CALL	. : Output char to system output device
28B7	FE0D	CP	. : Then test if it was a carriage return
28B9	CC0321	CALL	. : Exit if char was a carriage return
28BC	03	INC	. : Bump to next character
28BD	18F2	JR	--->: Loop till CR, or D characters printed
28BF	B7	OR	--- Compute amt of space remaining in string area ****
28C0	0EF1	LD	--- 28C1H : POP AF
28C2	F5	PUSH	--- Save length of string
28C3	2AA040	LD	--- Load starting addr of string area into HL
28C6	EB	EX	--- DE = addr of string area
28C7	2AD640	LD	--- Load ptr to next avail string loc into HL
28CA	2F	CPL	--- Compute the negative of the length of the string
28CB	4F	LD	--- and save it in C
28CC	06FF	LD	--- BC = - length of string
28CE	09	ADD	--- HL = new current string pointer
28CF	23	INC	--- plus one
28D0	DF	RST	--- Compare new string pointer against limit
28D1	3807	JR	--->: OS error if CARRY see note-->
28D3	22D640	LD	-- : Save new current string pointer
28D6	23	INC	-- : Bump it by one
28D7	EB	EX	-- : DE = new current string pointer
28D8	F1	POP	-- : A = length of string
28D9	C9	RET	-- : Rtn to caller
28DA	F1	POP	<---: A = length of string, ***************** cont--> *
28DB	1E1A	LD	--- OS error code

287D : Address of 1st non-blank char after quote to stack

2884 * Move length, address from 40D3 to current literal string. ***
     : Pool entry pointed to by 40D3. Set current value to type
     : string and point its addr to the current literal string
     : (40D3)

28A6 * ***

28BF * ***

28D1 : Insufficient room in string area

28DA * get status flags to find out if reorganization has **********
     : been attempted

Address	Bytes	Mnemonic	Comment
28DD	CAA219	JP	--- Error if free space reorganized and still no room
28E0	BF	CP	--- Set status flags to zero and ret
28E1	F5	PUSH	--- Save zero
28E2	01C128	LD	--- Continuation address to retry allocation
28E5	C5	PUSH	--- To stack
28E6	2AB140	LD	--- HL = highest memory pointer
28E9	22D640	LD	--- Reset currentnt string pointer to end of memory
28EC	210000	LD	--- Load a zero
28EF	E5	PUSH	--- And save it on stk
28F0	2AA040	LD	--- HL = boundry of string data area
28F3	E5	PUSH	--- Save it on stack also
28F4	21B540	LD	--- HL = address of first entry in string pointer area
28F7	EB	EX	--- Save HL in DE
28F8	2AB340	LD	--- HL = addr of current entry in LSPT :area
28FB	EB	EX	--- DE = address of currennt entry in string pointer
28FC	DF	RST	--- Is 40B3 pointing to the first entry (40B5)
28FD	01F728	LD	--- Continuation addr in case answer is no
2900	C24A29	JP	--- No, JMP to 294A, RTN to 28F7
2903	2AF940	LD	--- HL = simple variable pointer
2906	EB	EX	<------: Save it in DE
2907	2AFB40	LD	. : HL = arrays pointer
290A	EB	EX	. : HL = variable list pointer. DE = arrays ptr
290B	DF	RST	. : Compare their addresses. Are they equal
290C	2813	JR	->:----: Yes, simple variables have been scanned
290E	7E	LD	: . : Get type for first simple variable
290F	23	INC	: . : Bump to LSB by incrementing HL by 3
2910	23	INC	: . : So that type can be added to give addr of
2911	23	INC	: . : Addr of next variable
2912	FE03	CP	: . : Test if variable is a string
2914	2004	JR	: . : Jmp if not a string
2916	CD4B29	CALL	: . : For a string, get its addr into HL
2919	AF	XOR	: . : Zero A because HL already points to next
291A	5F	LD	: . : Bump to addr of :entry
291B	1600	LD	: . : Next variable
291D	19	ADD	: . : Gives addr of next variable in list
291E	18E6	JR	--:--->: Loop till all simple variables examined
2920	C1	POP	<-:------: Clear HL, push from below
2921	EB	EX	<-: . : DE = points to current array entry
2922	2AFD40	LD	. : HL = addr of next avail mem loc.
2925	EB	EX	. : DE = addr of first avail mem loc.
2926	DF	RST	. : Have we scanned all arrays entries
2927	CA6B29	JP	. : Yes
292A	7E	LD	. : No, get type for this array
292B	23	INC	. : Bump to 2nd char of name
292C	CDC209	CALL	. : Load offset to next array into cont --->
292F	E5	PUSH	. : Save addr of no. of indexes
2930	09	ADD	. : Add offset to get next arrays entry
2931	FE03	CP	. : Is current type a string?
2933	20EB	JR	-------->: No, loop keep looking
2935	22D840	LD	--- Save addr of next array entry
2938	E1	POP	--- HL = addr of no. of indexes
2939	4E	LD	--- C = no. of indexes
293A	0600	LD	--- Set B = 0. Then
293C	09	ADD	--- add 2 times no. of indexes to current
293D	09	ADD	--- addr to get end of index boundries
293E	23	INC	--- HL = addr of end of indexes for this variable
293F	EB	EX	--- Move it to DE
2940	2AD840	LD	--- HL = addr of next variable
2943	EB	EX	--- HL = end of index boundries, DE = addr of next
2944	DF	RST	--- Test for empty list :variable

:BC. Skips over name

2945	28DA	JR	--- Jmp if list empty
2947	013F29	LD	--- Continuation addr for string array processing
294A	C5	PUSH	--- Save continuation addr on stack
294B	AF	XOR	--- Clear all status flags
294C	B6	OR	--- A = length of string
294D	23	INC	--- Bump to next two bytes to
294E	5E	LD	--- get string address
294F	23	INC	--- Bump to MSB of string addr
2950	56	LD	--- DE = string address :addr)
2951	23	INC	--- Bump to next entry in string pointer area (test
2952	C8	RET	--- Exit if string length is zero
2953	44	LD	--- BC = addr of next string pointer
2954	4D	LD	--- Loaded from HL
2955	2AD640	LD	--- HL = current string area pointer
2958	DF	RST	--- Is string in string data area?
2959	60	LD	--- Restore addr of next literal pool entry
295A	69	LD	--- to HL
295B	D8	RET	--- Return if string in string area
295C	E1	POP	--- HL = return address
295D	E3	EX	--- HL = callers test address
295E	DF	RST	--- Compare callers test addr to string addr
295F	E3	EX	--- Restore stack to callers flag, rtn addr
2960	E5	PUSH	--- Restore rtn addr to stack
2961	60	LD	--- HL = addr of next literal string pool entry
2962	69	LD	--- Loaded from BC
2963	D0	RET	--- Exit if string addr below callers addr
2964	C1	POP	--- BC = return address
2965	F1	POP	--- Get rid of callers string addr
2966	F1	POP	--- Callers flag
2967	E5	PUSH	--- Save addr of next string area pointer
2968	D5	PUSH	--- Save addr of current string
2969	C5	PUSH	--- Return addr
296A	C9	RET	--- Rtn to caller
296B	D1	POP	--- DE = addr of last string moved to string area ****
296C	E1	POP	--- HL = addr of next string area pointer
296D	7D	LD	--- If HL = 0 then there were no strings in string
296E	B4	OR	--- area which belonged to the literal cont-->
296F	C8	RET	--- Exit if no temp strings in string area cont-->
2970	2B	DEC	--- Backspace addr to get pointers for literal pool
2971	46	LD	--- B = LSB of addr for string :entry
2972	2B	DEC	--- Skip backwards to next byte of addr
2973	4E	LD	--- C = MSB of addr for string
2974	E5	PUSH	--- Save addr of pointer in lit. string so we update
2975	2B	DEC	--- Bump down to length : it after move
2976	6E	LD	--- L = length of string
2977	2600	LD	--- Zero H so we can do 16 bit arith
2979	09	ADD	--- HL = ending addr of string
297A	50	LD	--- DE = starting addr of string
297B	59	LD	--- Loaded from BC
297C	2B	DEC	--- HL = ending addr -1
297D	44	LD	--- BC = ending addr -1
297E	4D	LD	--- Loaded from HL
297F	2AD640	LD	--- HL = current string data pointer
2982	CD5819	CALL	--- Move string to new area in string area table
2985	E1	POP	--- HL = addr of literal string pointer
2986	71	LD	--- Now, move address of string in string area to
2987	23	INC	--- 2nd and 3rd bytes of literal pool entry
2988	70	LD	--- Save 1st character of name
2989	69	LD	--- Then setup HL so it points to the start of the
298A	60	LD	--- last string moved to the string area

```
296B  *  ******************************************************************

296E  :  string pool (temporary)
296F  :  String area reorganized
```

298B	2B	DEC	--- And loop until no more literal pool entries are
298C	C3E928	JP	--- found which must be moved to the string area.
298F	C5	PUSH	--- String addition. Concatenate two strings * note-->
2990	E5	PUSH	--- Save PV last operand/ last token, and code string
2991	2A2141	LD	--- Stack = addr of string 1, HL = current pos. :addr
2994	E3	EX	--- in input string
2995	CD9F24	CALL	--- Locate next variable
2998	E3	EX	--- HL = 4121, Stack = code string addr
2999	CDF40A	CALL	--- Make sure it's a string
299C	7E	LD	--- A = length of string 1
299D	E5	PUSH	--- Save addr of string 1
299E	2A2141	LD	--- HL = addr of string 2
29A1	E5	PUSH	--- Addr of string 2 to stack
29A2	86	ADD	--- A = length string 1 + string 2
29A3	1E1C	LD	--- Output if carry
29A5	DAA219	JP	--- Jmp if combined string length exceeds 256
29A8	CD5728	CALL	--- Make sure there's enough room for both strings
29AB	D1	POP	--- DE = addr of string 2
29AC	CDDE29	CALL	--- Update string area for string 2 if necessary
29AF	E3	EX	--- HL = addr of string 1
29B0	CDDD29	CALL	--- Update string area for string 1 if necessary
29B3	E5	PUSH	--- Save addr of string 1
29B4	2AD440	LD	--- Get addr of string 2
29B7	EB	EX	--- DE = address of second string
29B8	CDC629	CALL	--- Move strinng 1 from stack to string work area
29BB	CDC629	CALL	--- Move string 2
29BE	214923	LD	--- Continuation addr in expression evaluation
29C1	E3	EX	--- to stack. Code string addr to HL
29C2	E5	PUSH	--- Save code string addr :table
29C3	C38428	JP	--- Save string 1 + string 2 as entry in literal pool
29C6	E1	POP	--- HL = rtn addr, stack = string addr ***** cont--> *
29C7	E3	EX	--- Stack = rtn addr, HL = string addr
29C8	7E	LD	--- A = count of characters to move
29C9	23	INC	--- Bump to LSB of addr
29CA	4E	LD	--- C = LSB of addr
29CB	23	INC	--- Bump to MSB of addr
29CC	46	LD	--- BC = addr
29CD	6F	LD	--- L = no. of bytes to move
29CE	2C	INC	--- Do INC/DEC to set status flags
29CF	2D	DEC	--- Decrement count of characters moved
29D0	C8	RET	--- Exit if all character moved see note-->
29D1	0A	LD	--- Fetch a char
29D2	12	LD	--- Store a char
29D3	03	INC	--- Bump source addr
29D4	13	INC	--- Bump dest. addr
29D5	18F8	JR	--- Loop
29D7	CDF40A	CALL	--- Continuation of VAL, FRE, and PRINT **** cont--> *
29DA	2A2141	LD	--- HL = addr of current string
29DD	EB	EX	--- Move addr to DE
29DE	CDF529	CALL	--- Test : is current variable also
29E1	EB	EX	--- the last lit. string pool entry
29E2	C0	RET	--- No, exit w/DE = current variable addr
29E3	D5	PUSH	--- Yes, current variable was last literal
29E4	50	LD	--- string defined
29E5	59	LD	--- Move string addr to DE
29E6	1B	DEC	--- and save on stack
29E7	4E	LD	--- C = count of characters in current string
29E8	2AD640	LD	--- HL = current string pointer
29EB	DF	RST	--- Is current string=last one defined in string area
29EC	2005	JR	--- No, exit

298F * Called by expression evaluation ******************************

29C6 * Move using stack routine   On entry stack = count/source ****
     : address, DE = destination address.

29D0 : Move L characters from (BC) to (DE)

29D7 * processing. Test current value to make sure it's string. ***
     : Error if number

29EE	47	LD	--- Yes , update current string pointer
29EF	09	ADD	--- HL = addr of string + length = new string ptr addr
29F0	22D640	LD	--- Save new string ptr addr
29F3	E1	POP	--- HL = addr of current string
29F4	C9	RET	--- Rtn to caller
29F5	2AB340	LD	--- HL = addr of next avail string location **********
29F8	2B	DEC	--- Now, backup two words and load
29F9	46	LD	--- addr of previous string into BC.
29FA	2B	DEC	--- Then, compare the address of that entry
29FB	4E	LD	--- against the address of the current
29FC	2B	DEC	--- variable (or whatever's in DE). If unequal
29FD	DF	RST	--- exit, else reset the pointer (40B3) to
29FE	C0	RET	--- point to the current (last) entry
29FF	22B340	LD	--- Update pointer to current entry in LSPT
2A02	C9	RET	--- Rtn to caller
2A03	01F827	LD	--- Continuation addr of POS to stk *** LEN routine **
2A06	C5	PUSH	--- 27F8 to stk
2A07	CDD729	CALL	--- Get addr of current string pointer into HL
2A0A	AF	XOR	--- Clear status, zero A
2A0B	57	LD	--- and D
2A0C	7E	LD	--- A = length of string from string pointer area
2A0D	B7	OR	--- Set status flags for length
2A0E	C9	RET	--- Continue at POS unless entered at 2A07
2A0F	01F827	LD	--- Continuation addr of 27F8 to stk *** ASC routine *
2A12	C5	PUSH	--- Saves value in HL as current value
2A13	CD072A	CALL	--- Get addr of current string pointer into HL. Length
2A16	CA4A1E	JP	--- Error of length of string = 0 :into A
2A19	23	INC	--- Now, load addr of string into DE
2A1A	5E	LD	--- E = LSB of string addr
2A1B	23	INC	--- Bump to MSB
2A1C	56	LD	--- D = MSB of string addr
2A1D	1A	LD	--- A = first character of string
2A1E	C9	RET	--- Rtn to caller
2A1F	3E01	LD	--- A=length of string to be created ** CHR$ routine *
2A21	CD5728	CALL	--- Save length and value of char at 40D3
2A24	CD1F2B	CALL	--- Convert value to integer. Save in DE
2A27	2AD440	LD	--- HL = address of temporary string
2A2A	73	LD	--- Save value in string area
2A2B	C1	POP	--- Clear stack :interpreter
2A2C	C38428	JP	--- Move string from literal pool to string. Rtn to
2A2F	D7	RST	--- STRING$ routine ********************************
2A30	CF	RST	--- Test next char for '('
2A31	28CD	JR	--- 2A31: DC 28 '('
2A33	1C	INC	--- 2A32: CALL 2B1C evaluate expression - get N
2A34	2B	DEC	--- Backspace code string
2A35	D5	PUSH	--- Save integer value for N
2A36	CF	RST	--- Test next char for comma
2A37	2C	INC	--- 2A37: DC 2C comma
2A38	CD3723	CALL	--- Evaluate expression, get value of char
2A3B	CF	RST	--- Test next char for ')'
2A3C	29	ADD	--- 2A3C: DC 29 ')'
2A3D	E3	EX	--- HL = integer value for N/stack = next code string
2A3E	E5	PUSH	--- Followed by N :addr
2A3F	E7	RST	--- Test current value data type
2A40	2805	JR	--->: Jump if string
2A42	CD1F2B	CALL	-- : Convert to integer. Leave in DE, WRA1
2A45	1803	JR	-- : Skip loading of string addr & 1st character
2A47	CD132A	CALL	<---: A = character to be repeated
2A4A	D1	POP	--- DE = value of N from STRING$ (N,'X') call
2A4B	F5	PUSH	--- Save character

```
29F5  *  **********************************************************

2A03  *  ***********************************************************

2A0F  *  ***********************************************************

2A1F  *  ***********************************************************

2A2F  *  ************************************************************
```

2A4C	F5	PUSH	--- Save two copies of the character
2A4D	7B	LD	--- A = number of repetition
2A4E	CD5728	CALL	--- Allocate N bytes in string area. cont-->
2A51	5F	LD	--- E = number of repetition
A52	F1	POP	--- A = character to be repeated
2A53	1C	INC	--- Set status flags
2A54	1D	DEC	--- So we can test for zero
2A55	28D4	JR	--- If zero repetition, exit
2A57	2AD440	LD	--- HL = addr allocated in string area
2A5A	77	LD	<---: Move char
2A5B	23	INC	. : Bump string addr
2A5C	1D	DEC	. : Count repetition
2A5D	20FB	JR	--->: Loop till 'N' copies moved
2A5F	18CA	JR	--- Rtn to caller
2A61	CDDF2A	CALL	--- Test for closing ')' ** LEFT$ routine ** cont--> *
2A64	AF	XOR	--- Clear A, status flags
2A65	E3	EX	--- HL = addr of n. Stack = current code string addr
2A66	4F	LD	--- Zero to C
2A67	3EE5	LD	--- 2A68: LD H,A
2A69	E5	PUSH	--- Save addr of string
2A6A	7E	LD	--- Get length of string
2A6B	B8	CP	--- Compare with number of bytes to return
2A6C	3802	JR	--- Jmp if byte request exceeds size of string
2A6E	78	LD	--- Save no. of bytes to return
2A6F	110E00	LD	--- 2A70: LD C,00
2A72	C5	PUSH	--- Save length of string to return
2A73	CDBF28	CALL	--- Make sure there's room for new string. cont-->
2A76	C1	POP	--- BC = length of string to be returned
2A77	E1	POP	--- HL = string addr
2A78	E5	PUSH	--- Save string addr on stack
2A79	23	INC	--- Skip over character count
2A7A	46	LD	--- B = LSB of string addr
2A7B	23	INC	--- Skip to MSB
2A7C	66	LD	--- H = MSB of string addr
2A7D	68	LD	--- HL = addr of string
2A7E	0600	LD	--- BC = 00/length of string desired
2A80	09	ADD	--- HL = ending addr of last char to be moved
2A81	44	LD	--- Now, move ending
2A82	4D	LD	--- Addr into BC
2A83	CD5A28	CALL	--- Save length (A) and starting addr (DE) cont-->
2A86	6F	LD	--- L = number of chars to move
2A87	CDCE29	CALL	--- Move (L) chars. from (BC) to (DE)
2A8A	D1	POP	--- Clear stack
2A8B	CDDE29	CALL	--- Get addr of literal pool string into 40D3
2A8E	C38428	JP	--- Go move string to string area. Ret to interpreter
2A91	CDDF2A	CALL	--- Setup registers *************** RIGHT$ routine **
2A94	D1	POP	--- Load string address
2A95	D5	PUSH	--- And restore it to stack
2A96	1A	LD	--- A = number of characters in string
2A97	90	SUB	--- Subtract no. of bytes to isolate
2A98	18CB	JR	--- Use LEFT$ code
2A9A	EB	EX	--- HL = code string addr *********** MID$ routine **
2A9B	7E	LD	--- A = terminal character
2A9C	CDE22A	CALL	--- BC = position, DE = string address
2A9F	04	INC	--- Set status flags to
2AA0	05	DEC	--- correspond to position value
2AA1	CA4A1E	JP	--- Error if starting position is zero
2AA4	C5	PUSH	--- Save starting position
2AA5	1EFF	LD	--- E = 256 in case number of bytes not given
2AA7	FE29	CP	--- Test for right paren following P

2A4E : Save addt of allocated area at 40D4 - 40D5

2A61 * Setup registers ***** On entry   HL = address of LEFT$ *****
     :   stack = string address
     :   stack + 1 = n
     :   DE = code string addr

2A73 : Get addr of next string area in DE

2A83 : next avail loc in lit pool

2A91 * ***

2A9A * ***

2AA9 2805	JR	---->: Jmp if no byte count given, else
2AAB CF	RST	-- : Test next input value for comma
2AAC 2C	INC	-- : 2AAC: DC 2C comma
2AAD CD1C2B	CALL	-- : Evaluate expression. Get byte count as integer
2AB0 CF	RST	<---: Test next char for ')' :into DE
2AB1 29	ADD	--- 2AB1: DC 28 ')'
2AB2 F1	POP	--- A = starting position
2AB3 E3	EX	--- HL = string addr. Stack = current code string addr
2AB4 01692A	LD	--- Continuation of MID$ processing in LEFT$
2AB7 C5	PUSH	--- Address to stack
2AB8 3D	DEC	--- Starting position minus one
2AB9 BE	CP	--- Compare starting position with length of string
2ABA 0600	LD	--- B = 00
2ABC D0	RET	--- Continue at 2A69 if starting position-1 > length of
2ABD 4F	LD	--- C = starting position -1 :string
2ABE 7E	LD	--- A = length of string
2ABF 91	SUB	--- C = no. of chars between P and end of string
2AC0 BB	CP	--- Compare with number of characters to return
2AC1 47	LD	--- B = no. of characters to return
2AC2 D8	RET	--- Continue at 2A69 if more characters cont-->
2AC3 43	LD	--- Else, return number of characters requested
2AC4 C9	RET	--- Continue at 2A69
2AC5 CD072A	CALL	--- Get length into A-reg ************** VAL routine *
2AC8 CAF827	JP	--- Address of string pointer block in HL
2ACB 5F	LD	--- Exit if length = 0. Move length to E, D = 0
2ACC 23	INC	--- Skip over length
2ACD 7E	LD	--- A = LSB of string addr
2ACE 23	INC	--- Bump to MSB of addr
2ACF 66	LD	--- H = MSB of string addr
2AD0 6F	LD	--- Now, HL = string addr
2AD1 E5	PUSH	--- Save string addr then add length which
2AD2 19	ADD	--- gives HL = ending addr
2AD3 46	LD	--- Save last char of string
2AD4 72	LD	--- Replace it with a zero
2AD5 E3	EX	--- Stack=ending addr of string. HL=starting addr of
2AD6 C5	PUSH	--- Save replaced char of string :string
2AD7 7E	LD	--- A = 1st char of string
2AD8 CD650E	CALL	--- Convert numerics at start of string from ASCII to
2ADB C1	POP	--- B = replaced character :binary
2ADC E1	POP	--- HL = ending addr of string
2ADD 70	LD	--- Restore replaced char
2ADE C9	RET	--- Rtn to BASIC
2ADF EB	EX	--- DE = addr of calling routine *********** cont--> *
2AE0 CF	RST	--- Look for right paren following parameters
2AE1 29	ADD	--- DC 28 ')'
2AE2 C1	POP	--- Return address
2AE3 D1	POP	--- DE = count of bytes to isolate
2AE4 C5	PUSH	--- Restore return addr
2AE5 43	LD	--- B = byte count
2AE6 C9	RET	--- HL = code string addr
2AE7 FE7A	CP	--- Test if token in range *****************************
2AE9 C29719	JP	--- SN error if NZ. Error if token => FA
2AEC C3D941	JP	--- Disk BASIC Exit. Let Disk BASIC handle TAB-MID$
2AEF CD1F2B	CALL	--- Get port no. into A-reg ********* INP routine ****
2AF2 329440	LD	--- Save port number
2AF5 CD9340	CALL	--- Go execute IN XX instr. Rtn to execution driver
2AF8 C3F827	JP	--- Evaluate expression . ** OUT routine ** cont--> *
2AFB CD0E2B	CALL	--- Value to A-reg.
2AFE C39640	JP	--- Go execute OUT XX instr. Rtn to execution driver
2B01 D7	RST	--- Position to next char in input stream ** cont--> *

2AC2 : requested than string has in it

*   2AC5 **

2AE7 * HL = code string addr **** Called by LEFT$, MID$, & RIGHT$ **
     :   to test for ending ')'.
     :   Entry   Exit
     :   Stk=string addr   string addr
     :   byte count   DE=byte count
     :   ret addr   B=byte count

2AEF * **

2AEF : **

2AFB * Port no. to 4094, 4097 ***********************************

2B01 * Evaluate an expression . Leave result as integer in DE ******

2B02	CD3723	CALL	--- Evaluate expression. Result to WRA1
2B05	E5	PUSH	--- Next code string addr
2B06	CD7F0A	CALL	--- Convert result to integer. Put it in HL
2B09	EB	EX	--- DE = result (in integer form)
2B0A	E1	POP	--- Restore position in input stream
2B0B	7A	LD	--- MSB of result to A
2B0C	B7	OR	--- Rtn to caller
2B0D	C9	RET	--- Ret sign/zero flags for result
2B0E	CD1C2B	CALL	--- Evaluate expression. Get port no. ****** cont--> *
2B11	329440	LD	--- Save port no. in DOS addresses
2B14	329740	LD	--- 4094 and 4097
2B17	CF	RST	--- Test following char for single quote
2B18	2C	INC	--- 2B18: DC 2C single quote
2B19	1801	JR	--->: Skip over PRINT TAB entry point
2B1B	D7	RST	--- : Examine next char (called by PRINT TAB)
2B1C	CD3723	CALL	<---: Evaluate expression. Get value
2B1F	CD052B	CALL	--- Convert result of exp to intger, load cont-->
2B22	C24A1E	JP	--- FC error value > 255
2B25	2B	DEC	--- Backspace input string
2B26	D7	RST	--- Get next char from input string (bump HL & ret
2B27	7B	LD	--- LSB of result to A :flags)
2B28	C9	RET	--- Rtn to caller
2B29	3E01	LD	--- Device type for printer ********* LLIST routine **
2B2B	329C40	LD	--- Set current output device to printer
2B2E	C1	POP	--- Remove rtn addr from stk ********* LIST routine **
2B2F	CD101B	CALL	--- Get range of line nos. list on exit cont-->
2B32	C5	PUSH	--- Save start line ptr
2B33	21FFFF	LD	--- Set current line number to -1
2B36	22A240	LD	--- Save in current line number location
2B39	E1	POP	--- HL = addr of first line to be listed
2B3A	D1	POP	--- DE = addr of last line to be listed
2B3B	4E	LD	--- Now, get the pointer the next line
2B3C	23	INC	--- C holds LSB of pointer to next line
2B3D	46	LD	--- B = MSB of pointer to next line
2B3E	23	INC	--- HL=addr of first byte for current line (line no.)
2B3F	78	LD	--- If the pointer to the next line cont-->
2B40	B1	OR	--- Check for end of pgm
2B41	CA191A	JP	--- Return to READY routine if end
2B44	CDDF41	CALL	--- DOS Exit (JP 579C)
2B47	CD9B1D	CALL	--- Test keyboard input. Pause if cont-->
2B4A	C5	PUSH	--- Save addr of next line to be printed
2B4B	4E	LD	--- Get LSB of line number for current line
2B4C	23	INC	--- Bump to next byte of line number
2B4D	46	LD	--- Load MSB of current line number
2B4E	23	INC	--- HL = first byte of pgm statement for current line
2B4F	C5	PUSH	--- Save line no.(in binary) for current line on stack
2B50	E3	EX	--- Rearrange : stk=addr of 1st byte of pgm cont-->
2B51	EB	EX	--- DE = addr of current line, HL = addr of last line
2B52	DF	RST	--- Test to see if all lines listed :to list
2B53	C1	POP	--- BC = addr of 1st byte of current line
2B54	DA181A	JP	--- Rtn to Input Phase if all lines listed
2B57	E3	EX	--- HL = addr of last line to be printed cont-->
2B58	E5	PUSH	--- Save addr of current line
2B59	C5	PUSH	--- Save line no. (binary) for current line
2B5A	EB	EX	--- HL = addr of current line
2B5B	22EC40	LD	--- Save in loc. for line number with error
2B5E	CDAF0F	CALL	--- Output a line # in ASCII
2B61	3E20	LD	--- A = ASCII blank
2B63	E1	POP	--- HL = addr of current line
2B64	CD2A03	CALL	--- And a blank

2B0E * Continuation of OUT routine ********************************

2B1F : it into DE. Set A = MSB

2B29 * ***
****
2B2F : BC = addr of first line. Stk = addr of last line

2B3F : is zero, then the end of the pgm has been found

2B47 : shift @ hit, rtn when any release key hit

2B50 : HL = binary line no.

2B57 : Stk = line no. of current line

2B67	CD7E2B	CALL	--- Move current line to work area(40A7) and expand it
2B6A	2AA740	LD	--- HL = addr of expanded line
2B6D	CD752B	CALL	--- Buffer to screen (print current line)
2B70	CDFE20	CALL	--- Terminate line w/carrige ret line feed
B73	18BE	JR	--- Loop till all lines printed
2B75	7E	LD	--- Output area pointed to by HL ********************
2B76	B7	OR	--- Fetch next character to print
2B77	C8	RET	--- Exit if end of message
2B78	CD2A03	CALL	--- Print (HL)
2B7B	23	INC	--- Bump to next char
2B7C	18F7	JR	--- Keep printing till (HL) = 0
2B7E	E5	PUSH	--- Save addr of line to be moved ***** see note--> *
2B7F	2AA740	LD	--- HL = addr of input buffer. Move it
2B82	44	LD	--- to BC where it will be used as
2B83	4D	LD	--- an output buffer for expanded line
2B84	E1	POP	--- Restore addr of line to be moved/expanded
2B85	16FF	LD	--- D = max. no. chars in a line
2B87	1803	JR	--- Jmp into middle of move/expand code
2B89	03	INC	<---: Bump to next loc. in print/work buffer
2B8A	15	DEC	. : Count of chars moved
2B8B	C8	RET	. : Exit if 256 chars moved
2B8C	7E	LD	<---:-: Get a char from program table (PST)
2B8D	B7	OR	. : : Set status flags so we can test for EOS or
2B8E	23	INC	. : : Bump to next char in code string :token
2B8F	02	LD	. : : Save last char in print/work buffer area
2B90	C8	RET	. : : Exit if EOS (end of statement)
2B91	F2892B	JP	--->: : Jmp if char is not a token cont-->
2B94	FEFB	CP	. : Test for quote token
2B96	2008	JR	--->: : Not a quote token, go search RW list for
2B98	0B	DEC	. : : full syntax for this token
2B99	0B	DEC	. : : We have a quote token
2B9A	0B	DEC	. : : Backspace expanded buffer ptr
2B9B	0B	DEC	. : : by 4
2B9C	14	INC	. : : Then adjust
2B9D	14	INC	. : : count of characters
2B9E	14	INC	. : : in buffer
2B9F	14	INC	. : : by four
2BA0	FE95	CP	<---: : Test for ELSE token
2BA2	CC240B	CALL	. : Backspace expanded buffer ptr if ELSE
2BA5	D67F	SUB	. : A = the number of the entry cont-->
2BA7	E5	PUSH	. : Save current code string addr
2BA8	5F	LD	. : B = number of entries to skip
2BA9	215016	LD	. : HL = reserved word table ptr
2BAC	7E	LD	<---: : Get a byte from reserved word (RW) table
2BAD	B7	OR	. : : Set status to test for start of entry
2BAE	23	INC	. : : Bump to next word in RW table
2BAF	F2AC2B	JP	--->: : Jmp if not start of entry
2BB2	1D	DEC	. : : Count one entry skipped see note-->
2BB3	20F7	JR	--->: : Jmp if we have not skipped enough entries
2BB5	E67F	AND	. : Clear sign bit in first word of entry
2BB7	02	LD	. : Move a byte of RW (in ASCII) to print/work
2BB8	03	INC	. : buffer. Bump to next work buffer addr
2BB9	15	DEC	. : Count total chars moved to print buffer
2BBA	CAD828	JP	. : Jmp if 256 moved (Rtn to caller cont-->
2BBD	7E	LD	. : Get next word from RW list
2BBE	23	INC	. : Bump to next entry in RW list
2BBF	B7	OR	. : Set status flags so we can test cont-->
2BC0	F2B72B	JP	. : Jmp if not end - Move rest of chars cont-->
2BC3	E1	POP	. : Restore code string addr
2BC4	18C6	JR	----->: Continue scannning/moving code string

2B75 * **

2B7E * Called by LIST and EDIT. Move line pointer to by HL to *****
      : input buffer area. Expand each token into its key word

2B91 : (does not need expansion) go get next char

2BA5 : we are looking for in the reserved word list (RW)

      : Scan the reserved word list looking for the nth (E-reg)
      : entry. Each entry in variable length and starts with a
      : byte where the sign bit is on, the entry itself will
      : be reserved word in ASCII that we are searching for

2BBA : after clearing push at 2BA7)

2BBF : for end of this word
2BC0 : to print/work buffer

```
2BC6  CD101B  CALL     --- Get range of line nos. to del **  DELETE routine *
2BC9  D1      POP      --- DE = ending line no. in binary
2BCA  C5      PUSH     --- BC = addr of starting line in pgm table area
2BCB  C5      PUSH     --- Save it twice
2BCC  CD2C1B  CALL     --- Get addr of ending line to delete          cont-->
2BCF  3005    JR       --- Jmp if ending line no. not found
2BD1  54      LD       --- Move addr of next line(one following the last one
2BD2  5D      LD       --- to be deleted) from HL to DE
2BD3  E3      EX       --- Save addr of last line +1 on stack          cont-->
2BD4  E5      PUSH     --- Save addr of first line to be deleted
2BD5  DF      RST      --- Make sure first line addr <= last line addr
2BD6  D24A1E  JP       --- FC error if NC
2BD9  212919  LD       --- HL = address of 'READY' message
2BDC  CDA728  CALL     --- Send message to system output device
2BDF  C1      POP      --- BC = addr of first line to be deleted
2BE0  21E81A  LD       --- HL = continuation addr after moving         cont-->
2BE3  E3      EX       --- Save rtn addr onn stk so we can exit via RET
2BE4  EB      EX       --- DE = addr of next line
2BE5  2AF940  LD       --- HL = addr of next line              see note-->
2BE8  1A      LD       --- Fetch a byte from line n
2BE9  02      LD       --- Move it to line n-1. BC = addr of current line
2BEA  03      INC      --- Bump store addr
2BEB  13      INC      --- and fetch addr
2BEC  DF      RST      --- then compare fetch addr with end of pgm area
2BED  20F9    JR       --- Jmp if all lines not moved down
2BEF  60      LD       --- Move addr of end of last line
2BF0  69      LD       --- of program to end of program
2BF1  22F940  LD       --- addr. (Start of simple variable area)
2BF4  C9      RET      --- Rtn to caller
2BF5  CD8402  CALL     --- Write sync bytes and ** CSAVE routine ** cont--> *
2BF8  CD3723  CALL     --- Evaluate rest of CSAVE expression
2BFB  E5      PUSH     --- Save current code string addr
2BFC  CD132A  CALL     --- Get addr of file name into DE
2BFF  3ED3    LD       --- A = byte to write on cassette
2C01  CD6402  CALL     --- Write a 'S' with sign bit on
2C04  CD6102  CALL     --- Write 2 more 'S's
2C07  1A      LD       --- Get name of file to save
2C08  CD6402  CALL     --- Write file name onto cassette (one byte)9
2C0B  2AA440  LD       --- HL = starting addr in DE
2C0E  EB      EX       --- Save starting addr in DE
2C0F  2AF940  LD       --- HL = ending addr of pgm table area
2C12  1A      LD       --- Get a byte of resident program
2C13  13      INC      --- Bump to next byte of pgm
2C14  CD6402  CALL     --- Write current byte to cassette
2C17  DF      RST      --- Have we written entrie pgm
2C18  20F8    JR       --- No, loop
2C1A  CDF801  CALL     --- Yes, turn off drive
2C1D  E1      POP      --- Restore code string addr
2C1E  C9      RET      --- Rtn to input phase
2C1F  CD9302  CALL     --- Turn on motor. Find ************ CLOAD routine **
2C22  7E      LD       --- sync pattern.  Get token following
2C23  D6B2    SUB      --- CLOAD. Test for CLOAD?
2C25  2802    JR       --- Jmp if CLOAD?
2C27  AF      XOR      --- Clear A, status flags
2C28  012F23  LD       --- 2C29: CPL      A = -1 if CLOAD? , 0000 if CLOAD
2C2B  F5      PUSH     --- 2C2A: INC HL   Position to file name
2C2C  2B      DEC      --- Backspace code string pointer since        cont-->
2C2D  D7      RST      --- Examine next element of code string
2C2E  3E00    LD       --- Initialize A-reg for no name
2C30  2807    JR       --- Jmp if no file name specified
```

2BC6 * ***

2BCF : DE = ending line no. to locate

2BD4 : HL = addr of first line to be deleted

2BE0 : all following lines down

         : Move all lines down starting with line whose addr is in DE
         : Move all lines down to line whose addr is in BC

2BF5 * trailing AS ***

2C1F * ***

2C2C : RST10 will skip forward

2C32	CD3723	CALL	--- Evaluate expression. Get file name
2C35	CD132A	CALL	--- Get addr of file name string into HL
2C38	1A	LD	--- Get file name to search for
2C39	6F	LD	--- Save file name
2C3A	F1	POP	--- Restore CLOAD, CLOAD? flag
2C3B	B7	OR	--- Set status for type of CLOAD
2C3C	67	LD	--- Save CLOAD type flag
2C3D	222141	LD	--- as current value in WRA1
2C40	CC4D1B	CALL	--- If CLOAD, call NEW routine to initialize system
2C43	2A2141	LD	--- Restore CLOAD type flags :variables
2C46	EB	EX	--- and save in D-reg
2C47	0603	LD	<--: B = no. of bytes to try and match against
2C49	CD3502	CALL	<--:-: Read a byte
2C4C	D6D3	SUB	. : : Compare with 'S' with sign bit on
2C4E	20F7	JR	-->: : No match, keep scanning till 3 'S's are found
2C50	10F7	DJNZ	---->: Loop for 3 in a row
2C52	CD3502	CALL	--- 3 'S's have been found read file name
2C55	1C	INC	--- Did user specify a file name
2C56	1D	DEC	--- Set status according to file name
2C57	2803	JR	--->: Jmp if no file name given. Load first program
2C59	BB	CP	-- : Comp. callers file name with that found on tape
2C5A	2037	JR	-- : They so not match so skip to end of current file
2C5C	2AA440	LD	<---: HL = start of pgm table area
2C5F	0603	LD	<---: B = no. of consecutive zeros to cont-->
2C61	CD3502	CALL	. : Read a byte of program
2C64	5F	LD	. : Save for possible storage
2C65	96	SUB	. : Compare with corresponding byte of current pgm
2C66	A2	AND	. : D = FFFF if CLOAD?, 0000 if CLOAD
2C67	2021	JR	----:>: If CLOAD? and mis-match, we have an error
2C69	73	LD	. : : They compare, or else it's a CLOAD. Anyway
2C6A	CD6C19	CALL	. : : save byte just read
2C6D	7E	LD	. : : Fetch byte just read
2C6E	B7	OR	. : : and test for zero
2C6F	23	INC	. : : Bump to next word in pgm table area
2C70	20ED	JR	--->: : Loop if not end of pgm or end of stmnt (EOS)
2C72	CD2C02	CALL	-- : Blink an '*'
2C75	10EA	DJNZ	-- : Look for 3 zeros in a row for cont-->
2C77	22F940	LD	-- : Save addr of end of pgm. Gives starting addr
2C7A	212919	LD	-- : HL = addr of 'READY' message :of variable
2C7D	CDA728	CALL	-- : Write 'READY' HEMMOXE TA LNDEA
2C80	CDF801	CALL	22 " Turn off cassette
2C83	2AA440	LD	-- : HL = starting addr of pgm
2C86	E5	PUSH	-- : Save on stack
2C87	C3E81A	JP	-- : Begin execution at end of new line input
2C8A	21A52C	LD	<-----: HL = address of 'BAD' message
2C8D	CDA728	CALL	--- Send message to system output device
2C90	C3181A	JP	--- Re-initialize BASIC interpreter and cont-->
2C93	323E3C	LD	--- Save name of file to search for **** see note--> *
2C96	0603	LD	--- B = no. of machine zeros to look for
2C98	CD3502	CALL	--- Read a byte
2C9B	B7	OR	--- Set status and test for zero
2C9C	20F8	JR	--- Not zero, get next byte
2C9E	10F8	DJNZ	--- Zero, look for three in a row which terminate file
2CA0	CD9602	CALL	--- found end of one file look synch and leader of
2CA3	18A2	JR	--- file then test for leading 'S'. Match on file name
2CA5	42	LD	--- B *********************** BAD message *******
2CA6	41	LD	--- A
2CA7	44	LD	--- D
2CA8	0D	DEC	--- Carriage return
2CA9	00	NOP	--- Message terminator *******************************

2C5F : look for as file terminator

2C75 : end of pgm, else we have EOS

2C90 : continue execution
2C93 * Search for end of file - 3-bytes of machine zeros *********

2CA5 * ***

2CA9 * ***

2CAA	CD7F0A	CALL	--- Get addr of loc to examine into HL ****** PEEK routine **
2CAD	7E	LD	--- Get value of 'PEEKED' addr
2CAE	C3F827	JP	--- Save as current value and rtn to input phase
2CB1	CD022B	CALL	--- Evaluate expression ** POKE routine **** cont--> *
CB4	D5	PUSH	--- Save addr of byte to change
2CB5	CF	RST	--- Test following char for comma
2CB6	2C	INC	--- 2CB6: DC 2C comma
2CB7	CD1C2B	CALL	--- Evaluate expression. Get value to be stored into
2CBA	D1	POP	--- DE = addr of byte to change :A-reg
2CBB	12	LD	--- Store new byte
2CBC	C9	RET	--- Rtn to input phase
2CBD	CD3823	CALL	--- Evaluate test expression ***---PRINT USING routine
2CC0	CDF40A	CALL	--- Insure current data type in string
2CC3	CF	RST	--- Test for ; as next char!
2CC4	3B	DEC	--- DC 3B semi-colon
2CC5	EB	EX	--- DE = address of next input symbol
2CC6	2A2141	LD	--- HL = addr of USING string
2CC9	1808	JR	--->: Go evaluate USING string
2CCB	3ADE40	LD	-- : Load READ flag ********************************
2CCE	B7	OR	-- : Set status according to flag
2CCF	280C	JR	----:>: Jmp if INPUT statement as opposed to READ
2CD1	D1	POP	-- : : Restore code string address
2CD2	EB	EX	-- : : and move it to HL. D= length of string
2CD3	E5	PUSH	<---: : Save starting addr of description string
2CD4	AF	XOR	-- : Zero A and flags
2CD5	32DE40	LD	-- : Clear READ/INPUT flag see note-->
2CD8	BA	CP	-- : compare length of string to zero
2CD9	F5	PUSH	-- : Save difference
2CDA	D5	PUSH	-- : Save addr of next input symbol from code
2CDB	46	LD	-- : Get length of string into B :string
2CDC	B0	OR	-- : Set flags and make sure it's not zero
2CDD	CA4A1E	JP	<-----: FC error code if Z
2CE0	23	INC	--- Bump to address of string
2CE1	4E	LD	--- LSB of string addr to C
2CE2	23	INC	--- Bump to addr of MSB of string addr
2CE3	66	LD	--- H = MSB of string addr
2CE4	69	LD	--- HL = starting addr of string
2CE5	181C	JR	--- Go analyze field description cont-->
2CE7	58	LD	--- E = count of ****** % for PRINT USING ** cont--> *
2CE8	E5	PUSH	--- Save current position in string
2CE9	0E02	LD	--- C = count for starting & ending %
2CEB	7E	LD	--- Now, scan rest of string looking
2CEC	23	INC	<--: for closing %. Count all blanks
2CED	FE25	CP	. : in C. Exit when % or non-blank char found.
2CEF	CA172E	JP	. : Jump if %
2CF2	FE20	CP	. : test for blank
2CF4	2003	JR	. : Jump if not blank
2CF6	0C	INC	---->: Count a blank
2CF7	10F2	DJNZ	-->: : and loop till end of string or % or non-blank.
2CF9	E1	POP	<----: We have exhausted the input, or found a non-blank
2CFA	43	LD	--- char. In either case restore HL to first symbol
2CFB	3E25	LD	--- beyond the starting % and B to no. cont-->
2CFD	CD492E	CALL	--- Print '+' after printing a single %
2D00	CD2A03	CALL	--- Print contents of A-reg
2D03	AF	XOR	--- Clear flags and
2D04	5F	LD	--- Zero E and D
2D05	57	LD	--- (count of #'s before dec pt)
2D06	CD492E	CALL	--- Print leading + if required
2D09	57	LD	--- Zero D
2D0A	7E	LD	--- A = a field description from string

2CB1 * Get addr of byte to change ********************************

**** **

2CCB * **

: Continue PRING USING

2CE5 : B = no. of chars to analyze. Rtn to 2D99
2CE7 : chars remaining *****************************

2CFB : of symbols left & continue

```
2D0B 23      INC    --- Position to next character
2D0C FE21    CP     --- Test for !
2D0E CA142E  JP     --- Jump if !
2D11 FE23    CP     --- Test for # sign
D13 2837     JR     --- Jump if #
2D15 05      DEC    --- Count of characters processed
2D16 CAFE2D  JP     --- Jmp if string exhausted
2D19 FE2B    CP     --- Test for + sign
2D1B 3E08    LD     --- Set flag to force leading +
2D1D 28E7    JR     --- Jump if +
2D1F 2B      DEC    --- Backspace so we can refetch current char
2D20 7E      LD     --- Fetch current char and
2D21 23      INC    --- Bump to next one
2D22 FE2E    CP     --- Test for decimal point
2D24 2840    JR     --- Jump if .
2D26 FE25    CP     --- Test for %
2D28 28BD    JR     --- Jump if %
2D2A BE      CP     --- Now, test if current char equals following char
2D2B 20D0    JR     --- If not, then skip test for $$
2D2D FE24    CP     --- Two sucessive char the same, test for $$
2D2F 2814    JR     --- Jump if current & following char are $
2D31 FE2A    CP     --- Not $$, test for **
2D33 20C8    JR     --- Jump if not * continue scan until string exhausted
2D35 78      LD     --- A = count of chars left in string    see note-->
2D36 FE02    CP     --- There must be at least two left, and
2D38 23      INC    --- they should be an *$.  Bump to next char
2D39 3803    JR     --- should put us at a $.
2D3B 7E      LD     --- Jmp if not 2 char left
2D3C FE24    CP     --- Fetch next char and test for $
2D3E 3E20    LD     --- A = flag for **. Turn on bit 2**5 in EDIT flag
2D40 2007    JR     --- Jump if not $
2D42 05      DEC    --- Decrement count of char left in string
2D43 1C      INC    --- Bump count of descriptors before dec point
2D44 FEAF    CP     --- 2D45: XOR A ********************* see note--> *
2D46 C610    ADD    --- Add flag for $. Set bit 2**4 in EDIT flag
2D48 23      INC    --- Bump to next char in input string
2D49 1C      INC    --- Bump count of descriptors before dec point
2D4A 82      ADD    --- Combine EDIT flags
2D4B 57      LD     <--: D = Save updated EDIT flags
2D4C 1C      INC     . : E = count of #'s before          see note-->
2D4D 0E00    LD      . : Initialize count of #'s after . or $$
2D4F 05      DEC     . : Count of string chars examined
2D50 2847    JR      . : Jmp if string exhausted!
2D52 7E      LD      . : Fetch next character in string
2D53 23      INC     . : And position to following one
2D54 FE2E    CP      . : Test for dec point
2D56 2818    JR      . : Jump if dec point. Go look for trailing #'s
2D58 FE23    CP      . : Test for # sign
2D5A 28F0    JR      . : Jump if #. Keep count of them in E-reg.
2D5C FE2C    CP      . : Test for a comma
2D5E 201A    JR      . : Jump if not a comma
2D60 7A      LD      . : Load EDIT flags
2D61 F640    OR      . : Turn on commas flag
2D63 57      LD      . : Save updated EDIT flag
2D64 18E6    JR     -->: Loop till string exhausted or          cont-->
2D66 7E      LD     --- Fetch description after dec point ** see note--> *
2D67 FE23    CP     --- Test for a #
2D69 3E2E    LD     --- A = ASCII value for decimal point
2D6B 2090    JR     --- Jump if not #
2D6D 0E01    LD     --- C = Count of #'s after decimal point
```

2D35 : * processing for PRINT USING

2D44 * $ processing for PRINT USING ********************************

2D4C : # processing for PRINT USING and processing following $$

2D64 : dec pt, #, or comma found
2D66 : . processing for PRINT USING ********************************

```
2D6F 23      INC  HL          --- Bump to next symbol in input string
2D70 0C      INC  C           --- C = count of #'S following
2D71 05      DEC  B           --- Decrement count of string chars examined
2D72 2825    JR   Z,2D99H     --- Jmp if string exhausted
2D74 7E      LD   A,(HL)      --- Get next symbol from string
2D75 23      INC  HL          --- Bump to next addr in string
2D76 FE23    CP   23H         --- Test for #
2D78 28F6    JR   Z,2D70H     --- If #, count & loop until string exhausted
2D7A D5      PUSH DE          --- Save counts
2D7B 11972D  LD   DE,2D97H    --- Transfer address following tests for    cont-->
2D7E D5      PUSH DE          --- DE = addr of next symbol in string
2D7F 54      LD   D,H         --- Save current string address
2D80 5D      LD   E,L         --- in DE
2D81 FE5B    CP   5BH         --- Test for exponential notation
2D83 C0      RET  NZ          --- Return if not [ (up arrow)
2D84 BE      CP   (HL)        --- Test for [[
2D85 C0      RET  NZ          --- Goto 2D97 if not [[ format
2D86 23      INC  HL          --- Bump to next element in input string
2D87 BE      CP   (HL)        --- Test for 3rd up arrow
2D88 C0      RET  NZ          --- Goto 2D97 if not [[[
2D89 23      INC  HL          --- Bump to next character in input string
2D8A BE      CP   (HL)        --- Test for 4th up arrow
2D8B C0      RET  NZ          --- Goto 2D97 if not [[[[
2D8C 23      INC  HL          --- We have a #.##[[[[ type format
2D8D 78      LD   A,B         --- Get count of chars left in string specification
2D8E D604    SUB  04H         --- Are there at least 4 left
2D90 D8      RET  C           --- No, go to 2D97
2D91 D1      POP  DE          --- Yes, clear 2D97 from stack
2D92 D1      POP  DE          --- Restore counts and flags to DE
2D93 47      LD   B,A         --- B = count of descriptors remaining
2D94 14      INC  D           --- 2D97: EX  DE,HL    Save current position in input
2D95 23      INC  HL          ---                    string
2D96 CAEBD1  JP   Z,0D1EBH    --- 2D98: POP DE       Restore counts & flags
2D99 7A      LD   A,D         --- Get flag word for +, - into A ********************
2D9A 2B      DEC  HL          --- Backspace one descriptor        : Descriptor string
2D9B 1C      INC  E           --- Count 1 descriptor processed    : analysis complete
2D9C E608    AND  08H         --- Test if + previously encountered
2D9E 2015    JR   NZ,2DB5H    ---->: Yes, skip test for +,-
2DA0 1D      DEC  E           --   : No, then test
2DA1 78      LD   A,B         --   : if any descriptors remain
2DA2 B7      OR   A           --   : Set status flag
2DA3 2810    JR   Z,2DB5H     ---->: Jmp if no descriptors left
2DA5 7E      LD   A,(HL)      --   : Get next descriptor
2DA6 D62D    SUB  2DH         --   : Test for -
2DA8 2806    JR   Z,2DB0H     -->: : If - go turn on - flag bit
2DAA FEFE    CP   0FEH        -- : : Not a -, test for +
2DAC 2007    JR   NZ,2DB5H    ---->: Jump if not +
2DAE 3E08    LD   A,08H       -- : : Set bit 2**3 (+ encountered)
2DB0 C604    ADD  04H         <--: : Set bit 2**2 (- encountered)
2DB2 82      ADD  A,D         --   : Combine flags for + and -
2DB3 57      LD   D,A         --   : Restore flags to D register
2DB4 05      DEC  B           --   : Count descriptors just processed
2DB5 E1      POP  HL          <----: HL = Current code string address
2DB6 F1      POP  AF          --- Restore last char examined and its status
2DB7 2850    JR   Z,2E09H     --- Jmp if end of string
2DB9 C5      PUSH BC          --- Save count of #'s after dec point (C)
2DBA D5      PUSH DE          --- Save count of #'s before dec point (E)
2DBB CD3723  CALL 2337H       --- Evaluate expression (get value to be printed)
2DBE D1      POP  DE          --- Restore count of #'s before . (E)
2DBF C1      POP  BC          --- and after dec point (C)
```

2D7B : exponential format [[[

2D99 : **

2DC0	C5	PUSH	--- Save count of #'s following
2DC1	E5	PUSH	--- Save current code string addr
2DC2	43	LD	--- B = count of #'s before
2DC3	78	LD	--- Add count of #'s before and after the dec. pt.
2DC4	81	ADD	--- Add count of #'s after
2DC5	FE19	CP	--- Compare total #'s against 25
2DC7	D24A1E	JP	--- FC Error - more than 24 #'s
2DCA	7A	LD	--- D = $$, +, -, comma flag
2DCB	F680	OR	--- Set called from PRINT USING flag
2DCD	CDBE0F	CALL	--- Convert current value to ASCII
2DD0	CDA728	CALL	--- And it according to the string specifications
2DD3	E1	POP	--- Print current value
2DD4	2B	DEC	--- Restore HL to tokenized input string
2DD5	D7	RST	--- Examine next element from code string
2DD6	37	SCF	--- Turn on CARRY for subroutine at 2E04, in case
2DD7	280D	JR	--->: Jmp if end of string : at end of string
2DD9	32DE40	LD	-- : Save next element
2DDC	FE3B	CP	-- : Test for a semicolon
2DDE	2805	JR	--->:: Jmp if ; go get item list
2DE0	FE2C	CP	-- :: Test for a comma
2DE2	C29719	JP	-- :: SN error if no comma
2DE5	D7	RST	<---:: Get element following ; in code string
2DE6	C1	POP	<----: B = number of characters to print
2DE7	EB	EX	--- DE = current code string addr
2DE8	E1	POP	--- HL = address of string
2DE9	E5	PUSH	--- Save on stack
2DEA	F5	PUSH	--- Save element following ;
2DEB	D5	PUSH	--- Save current code string address
2DEC	7E	LD	--- A = length of string
2DED	90	SUB	--- Compare with number of to print
2DEE	23	INC	--- Bump to LSB of string addr
2DEF	4E	LD	--- C = LSB of string addr
2DF0	23	INC	--- Bump to MSB of string addr
2DF1	66	LD	--- H = MSB of string addr
2DF2	69	LD	--- HL = string address
2DF3	1600	LD	--- DE = length of string
2DF5	5F	LD	--- D = 0, E = Length
2DF6	19	ADD	--- HL = address of end of string
2DF7	78	LD	--- Now, test count of characters
2DF8	B7	OR	--- to be used from string
2DF9	C2032D	JP	--- If non-zero, go examine string for print
2DFC	1806	JR	--- If zero, go back to code string :description
2DFE	CD492E	CALL	--- Print A + if D non-zero ***************************
2E01	CD2A03	CALL	--- Print contents of A-register
2E04	E1	POP	--- HL = current code string addr
2E05	F1	POP	--- A = last element examined. CARRY on if cont --> :
2E06	C2CB2C	JP	--- Jmp if not end of code string
2E09	DCFE20	CALL	--- If end of string, skip a line
2E0C	E3	EX	--- Code string addr to stack string addr to HL
2E0D	CDDD29	CALL	--- Get address of string into De
2E10	E1	POP	--- HL = code string address
2E11	C36921	JP	--- Rtn to execution driver
2E14	0E01	LD	--- C = count of characters to print ******* cont--> *
2E16	3EF1	LD	--- from following string. 2E17: POP AF Clear stack
2E18	05	DEC	--- Decrement count of char remaining in string
2E19	CD492E	CALL	--- Print + if D-reg non-zero
2E1C	E1	POP	--- HL = addr of next token in input string
2E1D	F1	POP	--- Pop start of push marker
2E1E	28E9	JR	--- Exit if end of ! pushes
2E20	C5	PUSH	--- Save length of '!' string/ no. of bytes to print

```
2DFE * ****************************************************************

2E05 : end of string CARRY off otherwise



2E14 * ! processing for PRINT USING string ***********************
```

2E21	CD3723	CALL	--- Evaluate next expression. Get addr cont-->
2E24	CDF40A	CALL	--- Make sure it's a string, else error
2E27	C1	POP	--- Restore count of chars to print
2E28	C5	PUSH	--- Save count
2E29	E5	PUSH	--- Save code string address
2E2A	2A2141	LD	--- Get string address to print from
2E2D	41	LD	--- B = number of characters to print
2E2E	0E00	LD	--- C = 0
2E30	C5	PUSH	--- Save count on stack
2E31	CD682A	CALL	--- Use LEFT$ processing to build another sub string
2E34	CDAA28	CALL	--- of chars to print. Get addr of sub string and
2E37	2A2141	LD	--- HL = address of major string :print it
2E3A	F1	POP	--- A = count of chars printed from major string
2E3B	96	SUB	--- A = number of unprinted characters = no. of blanks
2E3C	47	LD	--- Save in B
2E3D	3E20	LD	--- A = ASCII blank
2E3F	04	INC	--- Test count of blanks
2E40	05	DEC	--- to print
2E41	CAD32D	JP	--- Go examine rest of stmnt if all blanks printed
2E44	CD2A03	CALL	--- Prints blanks
2E47	18F7	JR	--- Loop till all blanks printed
2E49	F5	PUSH	--- Save status flags A-reg *************************
2E4A	7A	LD	--- Get D-reg
2E4B	B7	OR	--- And test if non-zero
2E4C	3E2B	LD	--- '+' is printed if D <> 0
2E4E	C42A03	CALL	--- Print + if called with D-reg non-zero
2E51	F1	POP	--- Restore callers A-reg flags
2E52	C9	RET	--- Rtn to caller
2E53	329A40	LD	--- Clear error number call *************************
2E56	2AEA40	LD	--- Get line number where error occurred
2E59	B4	OR	--- If FFFF execution has
2E5A	A5	AND	--- not begun
2E5B	3C	INC	--- Test for line no. FFFF
2E5C	EB	EX	--- DE = line no. with error
2E5D	C8	RET	--- Rtn to input phase if line no. was FFFF
2E5E	1804	JR	--- Else go print line no. and enter EDIT routine
2E60	CD4F1E	CALL	--- Get 1st line number ************* EDIT routine **
2E63	C0	RET	--- Syntax error if anything follows 1st line number
2E64	E1	POP	--- Get code string address
2E65	EB	EX	--- Move it to DE. Line number to HL
2E66	22EC40	LD	--- Move edit line number to communications area
2E69	EB	EX	--- Restore line # to DE so we can search for it
2E6A	CD2C1B	CALL	--- Search for addr of current line in pgm table
2E6D	D2D91E	JP	--- UL error if NC
2E70	60	LD	--- Move addr of current
2E71	69	LD	--- line from BC to HL
2E72	23	INC	--- Skip over pointer to
2E73	23	INC	--- next line
2E74	4E	LD	--- and load current line no.
2E75	23	INC	--- (in binary)
2E76	46	LD	--- into BC
2E77	23	INC	--- Bump the first position in edit line
2E78	C5	PUSH	--- Save line no.
2E79	CD7E2B	CALL	--- Move current line to print/work area
2E7C	E1	POP	--- Get current line into HL
2E7D	E5	PUSH	--- and save it on stack
2E7E	CDAF0F	CALL	--- Convert line no. to ASCII and write it out
2E81	3E20	LD	--- followed by a space
2E83	CD2A03	CALL	--- Writes space
2E86	2AA740	LD	--- HL = addr of expanded current line

2E21 : of string from which to print

2E49 * **

2E53 * **

2E60 * **

2E89	3E0E	LD	--- Display cursor command
2E8B	CD2A03	CALL	--- Send to video
2E8E	E5	PUSH	--- Save addr of expanded line
2E8F	0EFF	LD	--- C = count of chars to examine. cont-->
2E91	0C	INC	--- Count 1 char tested
2E92	7E	LD	--- Fetch a char from expanded buffer
2E93	B7	OR	--- Set status so we can test for end of line
2E94	23	INC	--- Bump to next char in expanded buffer
2E95	20FA	JR	--- Jmp if not end of line
2E97	E1	POP	--- HL = starting addr of expanded buffer cont-->
2E98	47	LD	--- Zero B. Will contain count of char inserted
2E99	1600	LD	--- Clear D
2E9B	CD8403	CALL	--- User types a character (DOS Exit 41C4H) note-->
2E9E	D630	SUB	--- Test char for alphaetic or alphanumeric
2EA0	380E	JR	--- Neither, go test for EDIT command
2EA2	FE0A	CP	--- Test for alpha numeric
2EA4	300A	JR	--- Not numeric, go test for EDIT command
2EA6	5F	LD	--- Save binary value of alpha numeric digit
2EA7	7A	LD	--- Convert to decimal. Set value thus far
2EA8	07	RLCA	--- Times 2
2EA9	07	RLCA	--- Times 4
2EAA	82	ADD	--- Plus value, thus far gives times 5
2EAB	07	RLCA	--- Gives times 10
2EAC	83	ADD	--- Plus new digit
2EAD	57	LD	--- Save as value thus far
2EAE	18EB	JR	--- Loop till command found
2EB0	E5	PUSH	--- Save current addr for expanded buffer ** note -->
2EB1	21992E	LD	--- Save 2E99 on stack as continuation addr
2EB4	E3	EX	--- HL = expanded buffer addr (current pos.)
2EB5	15	DEC	--- Test if sub-command preceeded by a numeric value
2EB6	14	INC	--- Set status flags
2EB7	C2BB2E	JP	--- Jmp if numeric value preceeded sub-command
2EBA	14	INC	--- D = 1
2EBB	FED8	CP	--- Test for a user typed backspace
2EBD	CAD22F	JP	--- Jmp if backspace entered
2EC0	FEDD	CP	--- Test for CR
2EC2	CAE02F	JP	--- Jmp if user typed CR
2EC5	FEF0	CP	--- Test for space
2EC7	2841	JR	--- Jmp if space entered
2EC9	FE31	CP	--- Test for lower case letter
2ECB	3802	JR	--- Jmp if not lower case
2ECD	D620	SUB	--- Convert lower case to uppercase
2ECF	FE21	CP	--- Test for Q
2ED1	CAF62F	JP	--- QUIT command
2ED4	FE1C	CP	--- Test for L
2ED6	CA402F	JP	--- LIST command
2ED9	FE23	CP	--- Test for S
2EDB	283F	JR	--- SEARCH command
2EDD	FE19	CP	--- Test for I
2EDF	CA7D2F	JP	--- INSERT command
2EE2	FE14	CP	--- Test for D
2EE4	CA4A2F	JP	--- DELETE command
2EE7	FE13	CP	--- Test for C
2EE9	CA652F	JP	--- CHANGE command
2EEC	FE15	CP	--- Test for E
2EEE	CAE32F	JP	--- END command
2EF1	FE28	CP	--- Test for X
2EF3	CA782F	JP	--- X command
2EF6	FE1B	CP	--- Test for K
2EF8	281C	JR	--- KILL command

2E8F : Count no. of char in expanded buffer

2E97 : C = no. of chars in buffer

2E9B : --- Adjust value entered

2EB0 * Look for EDIT sub-command **********************************

2EFA FE18	CP	---	Test for H
2EFC CA752F	JP	---	Jmp if HACK
2EFF FE11	CP	---	Test for A
2F01 C0	RET	---	Exit EDIT if not A
2F02 C1	POP	---	Clear the stack ************** Cancel & RESTORE **
2F03 D1	POP	---	Load current line number in binary
2F04 CDFE20	CALL	---	Skip to next line on video display
2F07 C3652E	JP	---	Re-enter EDIT routine
2F0A 7E	LD	---	Fetch current byte from work area ****************
2F0B B7	OR	---	Set status flags, so we can test for end of line
2F0C C8	RET	---	Exit if end of line
2F0D 04	INC	---	Bump index into work buffer
2F0E CD2A03	CALL	---	Print current character see note-->
2F11 23	INC	---	Bump to next char in work buffer
2F12 15	DEC	---	Decrement count of chars to print
2F13 20F5	JR	---	Jmp if required no. of chars not printed
2F15 C9	RET	---	Exit. HL = end of line. B = index
2F16 E5	PUSH	---	Save current position in work buffer ***** KILL **
2F17 215F2F	LD	---	Put continuation addr of 2F5F (prints final !)
2F1A E3	EX	---	onto stack. Restore buffer addr to HL
2F1B 37	SCF	---	CARRY flag signals KILL versus SEARCH
2F1C F5	PUSH	---	Save KILL/SEARCH flag
2F1D CD8403	CALL	---	Get character to search for
2F20 5F	LD	---	Save search character
2F21 F1	POP	---	Load KILL/SEARCH flag
2F22 F5	PUSH	---	Restore KILL/SEARCH flag
2F23 DC5F2F	CALL	---	Jmp if leading '!' needs to be printed cont-->
2F26 7E	LD	---	Fetch current character
2F27 B7	OR	---	Set status flags
2F28 CA3E2F	JP	---	Exit if end of line found
2F2B CD2A03	CALL	---	Print character to be deleted/examined
2F2E F1	POP	---	Load KILL/SEARCH flag
2F2F F5	PUSH	---	Save flag word
2F30 DCA12F	CALL	---	Move remainder of work buffer down one character
2F33 3802	JR	---	Jmp if KILL sub-command if KILL
2F35 23	INC	---	For SEARCH - bump to next char
2F36 04	INC	---	For SEARCH - count char just printed
2F37 7E	LD	---	For KILL /SEARCH fetch next character
2F38 BB	CP	---	Test for match with SEARCH character
2F39 20EB	JR	---	No match, loop
2F3B 15	DEC	---	Have we found all requested occurrences of SEARCH
2F3C 20E8	JR	---	No, loop :character
2F3E F1	POP	---	Yes, clear KILL/SEARCH flag
2F3F C9	RET	---	Exit edit sub-command
2F40 CD752B	CALL	---	Print current line (expanded by EDIT) **** LIST **
2F43 CDFE20	CALL	---	Skip to next line. PRINT or CR
2F46 C1	POP	---	Restore current line number
2F47 C37C2E	JP	---	Print current line no. and await next EDIT command
2F4A 7E	LD	---	Get current char from working buffer *** DELETE **
2F4B B7	OR	---	Set status flags so we can test for end of line
2F4C C8	RET	---	Exit if end of line
2F4D 3E21	LD	---	A = ASCII '!'
2F4F CD2A03	CALL	---	Print '!' to mark start of deleted area
2F52 7E	LD	---	Fetch current character
2F53 B7	OR	---	Test for end of line
2F54 2809	JR	---	Jmp if end of line encountered before D exhausted
2F56 CD2A03	CALL	---	Print character to be deleted
2F59 CDA12F	CALL	---	Delete character from work buffer
2F5C 15	DEC	---	Count 1 character deleted
2F5D 20F3	JR	---	Loop if 'D' characters not deleted

```
2F02  *  *************************************************************


2F0A  *  *************************************************************


      : Print (D) characters from current line (expanded version)
      : or until end of line is encountered.  Bump index into work
      : area (B-reg) for each char printed


2F16  *  *************************************************************
```

2F23 : (KILL sub command)

```
2F40  *  *************************************************************


2F4A  *  *************************************************************
```

```
2F5F  3E21    LD    A,21H        --- Done print '!' & mark end of deleted area
2F61  CD2A03  CALL  032AH        --- Print '!'
2F64  C9      RET                --- Exit delete sub-command
2F65  7E      LD    A,(HL)       --- Get char to be changed ***************** CHANGE **
2F66  B7      OR    A            --- Test for end of line
2F67  C8      RET   Z            --- Exit chage sub-command if end of line
2F68  CD8403  CALL  0384H        --- Get next char from keyboard char to      cont-->
2F6B  77      LD    (HL),A       --- Replace current char in work buffer
2F6C  CD2A03  CALL  032AH        --- Display new character
2F6F  23      INC   HL           --- Bump to next position in work buffer
2F70  04      INC   B            --- Count 1 character changed
2F71  15      DEC   D            --- Decrement count of chars changed
2F72  20F1    JR    NZ,2F65H     --- Loop more chars to change
2F74  C9      RET                --- Exit sub-command
2F75  3600    LD    (HL),00H     --- Terminate current line ***** HACK/INSERT and X ***
2F77  48      LD    C,B          --- Set line size in C
2F78  16FF    LD    D,0FFH       --- Set no. of bytes to print at 255
2F7A  CD0A2F  CALL  2F0AH        --- Print 255 bytes or until end of line.    cont-->
2F7D  CD8403  CALL  0384H        --- Call keyboard scan. Rtn when a key pressed *INSERT
2F80  B7      OR    A            --- Test for a non-zero character
2F81  CA7D2F  JP    Z,2F7DH      --- This test is unnecessary because 384 makes same
2F84  FE08    CP    08H          --- Test for a backspace                      :test
2F86  280A    JR    Z,2F92H      --- Jmp if a backspace entered. Go backspace cursor
2F88  FE0D    CP    0DH          --- Test for carriage return               :one char
2F8A  CAE02F  JP    Z,2FE0H      --- CR entered. Go print line and add line to current
2F8D  FE1B    CP    1BH          --- Test for escape                          :pgm
2F8F  C8      RET   Z            --- Exit from EDIT mode if ESC
2F90  201E    JR    NZ,2FB0H     --- Unconditional jmp. Add new char to current line
2F92  3E08    LD    A,08H        --- A = code for backspace ****** BACKSPACE CURSOR ***
2F94  05      DEC   B            --- Before backspacing, test count of
2F95  04      INC   B            --- characters in current line
2F96  281F    JR    Z,2FB7H      --- If zero we are at start of line. Go to INSERT code
2F98  CD2A03  CALL  032AH        --- Send backspace cursor command to video
2F9B  2B      DEC   HL           --- Backspace pointer into work buffer
2F9C  05      DEC   B            --- Decrement count of characters in current line
2F9D  117D2F  LD    DE,2F7DH     --- Put continuation address of 2F7D (INSERT)
2FA0  D5      PUSH  DE           --- onto stack                       see note-->
2FA1  E5      PUSH  HL           --- Save current address in work buffer
2FA2  0D      DEC   C            --- Decrement count of characters in buffer
2FA3  7E      LD    A,(HL)       --- Fetch next char to be overlaid
2FA4  B7      OR    A            --- Set status flags for end of line test
2FA5  37      SCF                --- Carry flag signals char deleted
2FA6  CA9008  JP    Z,0890H      --- Exit if all characters moved down one
2FA9  23      INC   HL           --- Else fetch character n
2FAA  7E      LD    A,(HL)       --- into A-reg
2FAB  2B      DEC   HL           --- Backspace pointer to character n-1
2FAC  77      LD    (HL),A       --- Store char (n-1) = char (n)
2FAD  23      INC   HL           --- Reposition buffer addr to char n
2FAE  18F3    JR    2FA3H        --- Loop till all of work buffer shifted down one byte
2FB0  F5      PUSH  AF           --- Save char to be added ***************** cont--> *
2FB1  79      LD    A,C          --- Get count of characters in current line
2FB2  FEFF    CP    0FFH         --- Test to see if max. line size reached
2FB4  3803    JR    C,2FB9H      --- Jmp if line not 255 bytes long
2FB6  F1      POP   AF           --- Else, restore last char typed - it will be ignored
2FB7  18C4    JR    2F7DH        --- And return to insert. Loop till          cont-->
2FB9  90      SUB   B            --- Gives current byte position in buffer ************
2FBA  0C      INC   C            --- Add 1 to count of characters in current line
2FBB  04      INC   B            --- Bump count of characters added
2FBC  C5      PUSH  BC           --- Save added char count/no. of chars in current line
2FBD  EB      EX    DE,HL        --- DE = starting addr of current line
```

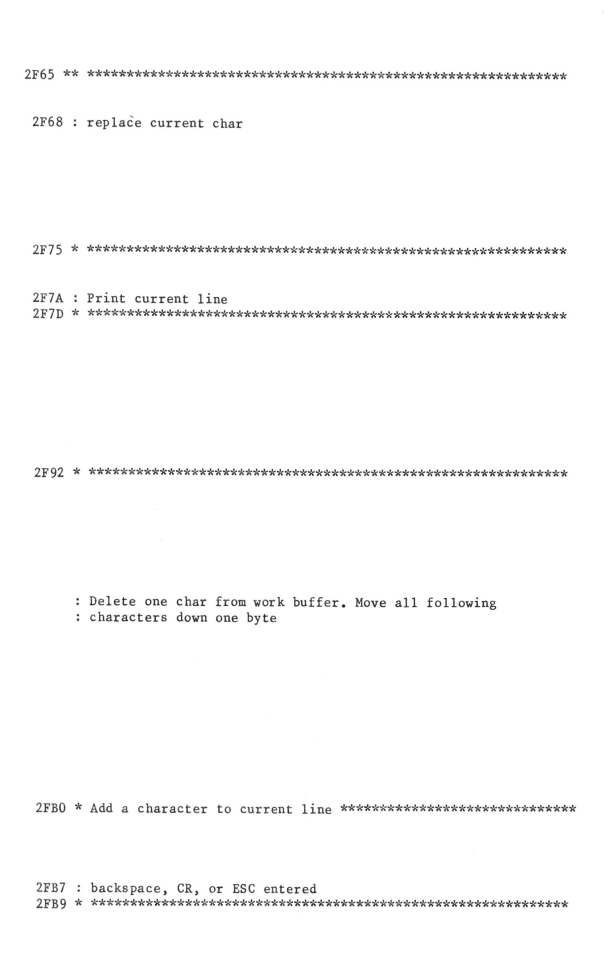

```
2F65 ** ****************************************************************

2F68 : replace current char




2F75 * *****************************************************************

2F7A : Print current line
2F7D * *****************************************************************




2F92 * *****************************************************************




     : Delete one char from work buffer. Move all following
     : characters down one byte




2FB0 * Add a character to current line ****************************




2FB7 : backspace, CR, or ESC entered
2FB9 * *****************************************************************
```

```
2FBE  6F        LD       --- Move current char index to HL
2FBF  2600      LD       --- Zero upper 8-bits so we can use 16-bit arith
2FC1  19        ADD      --- Add index to starting buffer addr to get current
2FC2  44        LD       --- Save addr of                          :char addr
2FC3  4D        LD       --- current char in BC
2FC4  23        INC      --- HL = addr of next avail char position       :buffer
2FC5  CD5819    CALL     --- Move new line with space for inserted char to work
2FC8  C1        POP      --- Restore count of chars added/count of chars in line
2FC9  F1        POP      --- Restore char to add to current line
2FCA  77        LD       --- Insert new char into line
2FCB  CD2A03    CALL     --- Print char added
2FCE  23        INC      --- Bump to next position in work buffer
2FCF  C37D2F    JP       --- Go wait for next char or CR, ESC, or backspace
2FD2  78        LD       --- B = no. of characters to backspace ***************
2FD3  B7        OR       --- Test for zero
2FD4  C8        RET      --- Rtn to 2E99 if done backspacing
2FD5  05        DEC      --- Count 1 char backspaced
2FD6  2B        DEC      --- Backspace pointer into EDIT buffer
2FD7  3E08      LD       --- Backspace command
2FD9  CD2A03    CALL     --- Backspace video
2FDC  15        DEC      --- Count of chars backspaced
2FDD  20F3      JR       --- Loop till D characters backspaced
2FDF  C9        RET      --- Rtn to 2E99
2FE0  CD752B    CALL     --- Print rest of current line ************ cont--> *
2FE3  CDFE20    CALL     --- Skip to next line on video
2FE6  C1        POP      --- Clear stack
2FE7  D1        POP      --- Load line no. in binary for current line
2FE8  7A        LD       --- Combine LSB and MSB
2FE9  A3        AND      --- of line number
FEA   3C        INC      --- Bump to next line no.
2FEB  2AA740    LD       --- HL = starting addr of work buffer
2FEE  2B        DEC      --- Work buffer starting addr minus 1
2FEF  C8        RET      --- Exit if BASIC execution has not started
2FF0  37        SCF      --- Set CARRY flag to signal a BASIC pgm stmnt. Test at
2FF1  23        INC      --- Bump to start of work buffer addr            :1AA4
2FF2  F5        PUSH     --- Save stmnt vs. command input flag
2FF3  C3981A    JP       --- Add new line to pgm
2FF6  C1        POP      --- Clear stack *********************** QUIT ****
2FF7  D1        POP      --- DE = current line no.
2FF8  C3191A    JP       --- Return to BASIC 'READY' routine
2FFB  00        NOP
2FFC  00        NOP
2FFD  00        NOP
2FFE  00        NOP
2FFF  00        NOP
3000  C34232    JP
3003  C3DA32    JP
3006  C35C33    JP
3009  C36D33    JP
300C  C38233    JP
300F  C37F34    JP
3012  C38734    JP
3015  2AE640    LD
3018  C31E1D    JP
301B  C36534    JP
301E  C32A33    JP
3021  C36E33    JP
3024  C35F32    JP
3027  C36433    JP
302A  C39A34    JP
```

0000 = PROGRAM ENTRY POINT

```
2FD2  *  ***************************************************************

2F88  *  END and CR during insert and command input mode *************

2FF6  *  ***************************************************************
```

310

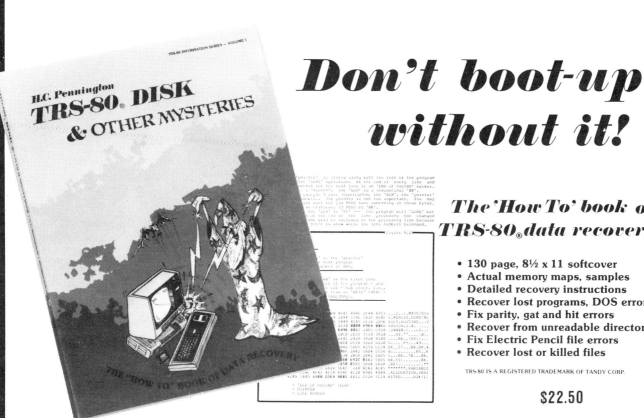
TRS-80 DISK & OTHER MYSTERIES TABLE OF CONTENTS

INTRODUCTION
HEXADECIMAL - BINARY - DECIMAL

READING & USING SUPERZAP 2.0
"SUPERZAP" FUNCTIONS
"SUPERZAP" COMMANDS
SPECIAL COMMANDS
SPECIAL SYMBOLS
"SUPERZAP" DISPLAY FORMAT
EXAMPLES
SUPERZAP 3.0
NEW FUNCTIONS ● NEW COMMANDS ● USING 3.0

OTHER UTILITIES
RSM-2D
MONITOR 3
DEBUG
DIRCHECK
READING & USING DIRCHECK ● BAD 'HIT' SECTOR BYTE ●
GRANULE FREE BUT ASSIGNED ● GRANULE ALLOCATED,
ASSIGNED TO MULTIPLE FILES ● GRANULE ASSIGNED, NOT
ASSIGNED TO ANY FILE ● GRANULE LOCKED OUT BUT FREE
LMOFFSET

THE DOS
TRSDOS 2.1
TRSDOS 2.2
VTOS 3.0
NEWDOS 2.1
FUTURE DEVELOPMENTS

DISK ORGANIZATION
GENERAL
FORMATTED DISKS
'SYSTEM' DISKS

THE DIRECTORY
INTRODUCTION
THE 'GAT' SECTOR
THE 'HIT' SECTOR
THE 'FPDE/FXDE' SECTORS
DECODING DIRECTORY ENTRIES ● DECODING EXTENTS

PASSWORDS & OTHER TRIVIA
GENERAL
MASTER DISK PASSWORD
REMOVING ACCESS & UPDATE PASSWORDS
REMOVING 'PROTECT' STATUS
MORE TRIVIA

DATA RECOVERY PROCEDURES & TECHNIQUES
PROCEDURES
METHODS
THE SHELL GAME WITH DISKS
TRICKS

9.0   DATA RECOVERY
9.1   RECOVERING 'HASH' CODES
9.2   RECOVERING A 'KILLED' FILE
9.3   RECOVER 'DISK WON'T READ OR BOOT' ● CLOBBERED OR
        UNREADABLE DIRECTORIES ● SECTOR ZERO ● PHYSICAL
        OR ELECTRICALLY DAMAGED DISKS
9.4   RECOVERING A 'BAD PARRITY' ERROR
9.5   RECOVERING A 'DIRECT STATEMENT IN FILE' ERROR ●
        ASCII 'BASIC' & BINARY 'BASIC' FILES
9.6   RECOVER 'HIT' SECTOR ERRORS
9.7   RECOVER 'GAT' SECTOR ERRORS
9.8   RECOVERING 'ELECTRIC PENCIL' ERRORS: ● DOS ERROR
        22 ● LOST PENCIL FILES IN MEMORY ● LOST PENCIL
        FILES ON THE DISK ● OVERWRITTEN PENCIL FILES ●
9.9   RECOVERING DATA FILES ● ASCII AND RANDOM FILES ●

10.0   CORRECTING THE GAT AND HIT SECTORS
10.1   THE 'HIT FIX
10.2   THE 'GAT' FIX

11.0   FILES - STRUCTURE
11.1   BINARY 'BASIC' PROGRAM FILES
11.2   ASCII 'BASIC' PROGRAM FILES
11.3   ASCII DATA FILES
11.4   RANDOM DATA FILES
11.5   ELECTRIC PENCIL FILES
11.6   SYSTEM FILES
11.7   MACHINE LANGUAGE LOAD MODULES & LOADER CODES

12.0   SOME THINGS YOU CAN DO
12.1   CONSTRUCTING ELECTRIC PENCIL FILES IN 'BASIC'
12.2   MAKING DATA FILES INTO ELECTRIC PENCIL FILES
12.3   CONVERTING 'DATA TYPES' IN RANDOM FILES
12.4   CONVERTING DATA IN ASCII FILES
12.5   READING 'BASIC' FILES INTO ELECTRIC PENCIL
12.6   READING 'PENCIL' FILES INTO 'BASIC'
12.7   MAKE 'BASIC' PROGRAMS 'UNLISTABLE'
12.8   'FIXING' OTHER SOFTWARE

GLOSSARY ● LEVEL II 'BASIC' TOKENS ● DIRECTORY HEX DUMPS FOR
TRSDOS 2.2, VTOS 3.0 & NEWDOS 2.1 ● HEX CONVERSIONS

MURPHY'S LAW AND OTHER COROLLARIES
ORDERING NEWDOS AND SUPERZAP
"SEARCH" PROGRAM LISTING & DOCUMENTATION

DISK MAP (TRSDOS 2.2) ● DIRECTORY MAP ● GAT SECTOR MAP
GRANULE ALLOCATION MAP ● HIT SECTOR MAP
FPDE/FXDE SECTOR MAP ● DIRECTORY ENTRY MAP

ACTUAL TYPE SIZE

```
 4D45 4                  2E30
9 4659  2052  4E32  2032  300D
52 5349  4F4E  3430  243A  2049  462
54 4F20  3130  4559  3530  3A2
49 4E4B  454E  2031  2841  24
220 5448  3D41  5343  2049  46
520 4258  0D32 3030  4420  4258
5455  524E  414E  4420  582D
3D34 3820  4E20  4258  3D42  2049
4845  4E20  0D32 3530         583C
5455  524E  2042  2042  2D35
3635  2041  583D  4258  4258
454E  2042  3330 3020  4258
5552  4E0D  3A52  4554  5552
204C  5345  3A52  4554  5552
```

(SIMULATE ERROR
(Also see figure

|||||||= 'END OF RECORD'
         LINE NUMBER

BINARY BASIC PROGRAM FILES

one is a little tougher
essed binary format and
The BASIC st

Keep Ahead of Microcomputer Developments
With the Professional's Choice

Interface Age is the most up-to-date source of microcomputer hardware and software advances. Whether you need to be informed for future purchases or to make comparisons, Interface Age should be #1 on your list.

- It has **more new product information** than any other small systems publication

- Graphics

- Indepth hardware and software reviews

- Software and hardware applications

- Programming

- Latest technologies

- Book reviews

- Business applications

- Educational applications

Fill out and mail this card today. Save $12 off the newsstand price.

Subscribers Write About Interface Age

Mail the card today.
You'll get INTERFACE AGE
entirely at our risk.

BUSINESS REPLY MAIL

First Class   Permit No. 11   Cerritos, CA 90701

Postage will be paid by

INTERFACE AGE Magazine

P.O. Box 1234

Cerritos, CA 90701